THE SECRET CITY

A HISTORY OF RACE RELATIONS

IN THE NATION'S CAPITAL

THE SECRET CITY

A HISTORY OF RACE RELATIONS

IN THE NATION'S CAPITAL

BY CONSTANCE MC LAUGHLIN GREEN

PRINCETON, NEW JERSEY

PRINCETON UNIVERSITY PRESS

1967

FOR ROSS AND MARY

FOREWORD

Much of this book may be a twice-told tale to many Negro Americans. Some of it may be only less familiar to white readers. Parts of the text offer merely a fuller discussion of topics treated in *Washington, Village and Capital* and *Washington, Capital City*. But in this study the omission of material that has no bearing on the life and attitudes of the Negro community should provide a continuity missing in those earlier volumes. And because the sweep of 175 years permits a perspective hard to arrive at in viewing shorter periods of time, I dare hope that *The Secret City* will throw new light on the whys and wherefores of race relations in the national capital today and, in the process, widen understanding of what went on in the rest of the country.

My title doubtless needs justification. It is only partly applicable to Washington and Georgetown before 1820, when both cities were too small to have any element of either wholly secret from the rest, and as slaves greatly outnumbered free Negroes in those years, to suggest that a close-knit distinctive colored community had already come into being is perhaps to claim too much. Nevertheless, virtually from the beginning, white citizens of the District of Columbia manifestly were acquainted with only the most obvious facts about how free Negroes lived and knew almost nothing about what they thought. Certainly the paucity of comment on Negro life in the District cities points to an unawareness on the part of the "superior race" that a separate entity was taking form within the municipalities. Indeed at every period before mid-twentieth century, except possibly for a brief span of time in the early 1870's, colored Washington was psychologically a secret city all but unknown to the white world round about. Invisible walls built by whites did not rise until after World War I, when fears mounted lest an overflow into white Washington

vii

occur. The name, first assigned to the Negro city in an anonymous article in *Crisis* in 1932, never came into popular use. The walls crumbled after World War II, but the long years of isolation left a *terra incognita* that people of both races were only learning to cross fifteen years later. Even today the measure of separateness still remaining keeps white Washington from fully understanding the Negro community.

I have used *Negro* and *colored person* interchangeably because I have discovered that the dark-skinned American over sixty years of age considers *Negro* a less acceptable term than *colored person,* whereas the younger thinks *Negro* the more dignified. Hence without intentionally assigning any value judgment to one or the other, I use both. Certainly in 1910 the NAACP chose the name *colored people.* All Washingtonians down to 1954 spoke of the colored school system, not the Negro school system. I have not attempted to draw a sharp date line.

For a white person to attempt to describe the past of any Negro community smacks of presumptuousness. Because I believed that an outsider could not fully recapture the feelings and responses of insiders, I set myself to a different and more possible task: to analyze the interplay between the races, rather than seek to set forth in its entirety the mode of life of some eight generations of Negro Washingtonians. And because the historian must depend upon the written record or the evidence of paint brush and photographer's film, the analysis is thin in its coverage of the inarticulate groups of both races. Even in my discussion of the last thirty years, when sociological data begin to multiply, I have necessarily given more attention to Negroes at the upper socio-economic levels than to those of the lower classes. Part of the Secret City indeed still remains secret to me. And my last three chapters are more nearly a summary of the civil rights movement in Washington than a history of day-by-day life on either side of the fence.

Long passages of my text, especially in the chapters on pre-World-War-II Washington, are distressing to read. The temptation was often strong to avoid dreary repetitiveness by dismissing particulars with the truthful generalization that for sixty years discrimination and intolerance worsened. But the bill of particulars is essential. For if the story is worth telling at all, it has to carry the conviction that only specifics can furnish. Even so, the facts that I have put on paper here constitute little more than a sampling of the available evidence. If the picture I have painted is singularly unrelieved by bright spots, the lack of vindictiveness the Negro record displays throughout fills me with wonder and humility.

Had I carried my narrative through the 1963 March on Washington I could have concluded on a note of more positive optimism than the situation of 1960 warranted. The rapid pace of change between 1961 and today has produced an exciting ferment of ideas and activities that merit careful exploration. But lack of perspective, enlarging or diminishing the dimensions of recent events, strips the historian of sound judgment about their ultimate significance. My text as it is brings the story of the Secret City virtually to an end, closing a somber and painful chapter in American history. A new chapter begins in 1961. Mindful, however, of the inscription at the National Archives, "What Is Past Is Prologue," I have inserted at the beginning of this study of the past a thumbnail sketch of Washington in 1965. The attempt is much like trying to pin currant jelly to the wall, for the fluidity of race relations in Washington at this moment blurs every outline. Yet the appraisal, for all its listing of appalling unresolved problems, may encourage hope for the future in readers who pursue the narrative of what preceded the 1960's.

My indebtedness to the scores of people who have helped me locate material and who have encouraged me to persist in my self-chosen but often agonizing task is overwhelming. The staffs of the Library of Congress, the National Archives, the Washingtoniana Room of the District of Columbia Public Library, and, above all, Mrs. Dorothy Porter, head of the Moorland Collection of the Howard University Li-

brary, have been unfailingly helpful. Mrs. H. S. Butcher
and Miss Charlotte Atwood, longtime Washingtonians and
teachers in the public school system for a number of years,
have let me use their family papers and, by their reminiscences and appraisals of events and people, have broadened my understanding of many problems of the pre-
New-Deal era. Miss Ida Fox did me a similar service
for the years from 1943 to 1948 by putting at my disposal
the records she had collected as a member of the Minorities
Workshop and executive secretary of the Committee for
Racial Democracy. The complicated story of civil rights
battles after the Second World War I could never have
pieced together without the voluminous files lent me by
Phineas Indritz, National Counsel for the American Veterans Committee, and without his patient explanations of
the legal issues involved and the interlocking or conflicting
interests of participants in the fight. In addition, I owe a
great deal to a long list of people who have discussed with
me special aspects of that many faceted struggle. My profound thanks go to Charles and Kelly Wiltse, who scruti-
nized every line of my first nine chapters and gave me the
benefit of their historical insights and literary skills. I am
particularly grateful to G. Franklin Edwards, Professor of
Sociology at Howard University, for reading critically the
most controversial chapters of this book; his wisdom and
his intimate knowledge of Negro Washington vis-à-vis white
have saved me from making a number of faulty judgments.

The interpretations presented in this study are nevertheless my own. Implicit in them are my choices of topics to
explore carefully and those to dismiss quickly or omit altogether. At no point have I attempted to present an all-
inclusive, definitive history. If, after reading my pages,
scholars are impelled to challenge my conclusions, I shall
feel rewarded at having inspired a more intensive examination of Negroes' past and their relationships with white
America.

CONSTANCE McLAUGHLIN GREEN

Washington, D.C.
January 1966

CONTENTS

ILLUSTRATIONS

Illustrations 1 through 20 follow page 112

The noticeable gap in pictures from the 1880's to the mid-1930's is in great part an indication of the lack of white America's interest in Negro life.

Illustrations 21 through 38 follow page 240

THE SECRET CITY

A HISTORY OF RACE RELATIONS

IN THE NATION'S CAPITAL

CHAPTER I

WASHINGTON IN 1965

The United States capital of 1965 was a different city from the Washington of 1950 or indeed of 1960. Outwardly the changes were minor, or at least no more noticeable than those of other American cities that had been undergoing urban renewal, with new highway construction, the accompanying demolition of old neighborhoods, the erection of glass, aluminum, steel, and stone-faced office buildings, the multiplication of many-storied apartment houses, and the steady, inexorable eradication of any remnant of a simpler semirural past. Yet whatever the alterations in Washington's physical appearance, the basic change lay in the prevailing spirit of the community. For the first time in history, 1965 saw Negro residents of a major American city outnumber white by more than 10 percent. That it was the national capital that contained six Negroes to every four whites shocked a good many Americans. Among Washingtonians, ultraconservative whites resented their new minority status, but most white citizens accepted it equably: it mattered less than they had thought possible a few years before.

To the provincial visitor one of the most striking aspects of the Washington of 1965 was the number of well-dressed, self-possessed Negroes to be seen almost everywhere, on the streets, in downtown restaurants, as customers in the department stores and chic specialty shops, and everywhere receiving the same services as white patrons. Fifteen years earlier many a Negro confined his shopping to stores in his own neighborhood rather than expose himself to the rudeness he could expect in the central business district. Other newcomers to the city might be more impressed at finding Negroes occupying positions of some importance in

3

executive departments of the federal government. Nine offices out of ten had some Negroes on their staffs, more often, it is true, in clerical than in administrative capacities, but nonetheless recognized as an integral part of the organization; in agencies handling housing, civil rights, poverty, and military programs, Negroes often held supervisory jobs with a dozen to a hundred whites working under them. To a much lesser extent the same situation obtained within the District government.

Guest lists for official receptions and dinners not infrequently included not only African dignitaries but native American Negroes also, for as one witty Washingtonian observed, "We add color to the parties." More significant, white people without compelling official obligations were beginning to invite Negroes of similar interests to their homes. Close friendships between Negroes and whites were still a rarity, but as personal contacts multiplied between thoughtful Negroes and intelligent whites, both groups found the association enriching. Instead of attempting to ignore race, conversations usually revolved around the deep-seated nature of the enduring American dilemma. The cultivated Negro did not jump at the chance to mingle with whites. His reticence and innate dignity made him wary of being lionized in a new form of exploitation. He still found his own people congenial. Pointing out that the most eminent colored families in Washington had "no money or power to speak of," a distinguished Negro explained that "in the Negro community it's the educated people who make up society."[1] Members of that society generally exhibited extraordinary patience and generosity in dealing with whites. When white people anxious to prove themselves part of the Avant Garde unwittingly betrayed astonishment at the attainments of Negro acquaintances, the latter usually concealed their irritation or amusement at white obtuseness and ignorance.

[1] New York *Times*, 28 Dec 1965.

Some of the ostentatious display attributed to rich Negroes in other American cities still existed in colored Washington, but in rather muted form. Although *Jet* published a list of thirty to forty families who had incomes over $50,000 a year and lived on an extravagant scale,[2] the black bourgeoisie fitting E. Franklin Frazier's earlier description cut a lesser swathe than formerly. The Negroes who commanded attention and deference from their fellows now were not the show-offs who attempted to conceal their limitations by the trappings of wealth and who preferred poker and football to books and ideas; in 1965 it was the alert, competent men and women whom the Kennedy and Johnson administrations had drawn to the capital to share in directing the fight for a new America. Expensive sports cars, elaborate household furnishings, and costly debuts for daughters might still evoke envy but no longer ensured prestige; certainly a chauffeur-driven government limousine transporting a Negro official intent on serious public business awakened a deeper respect in the Negro community. While the center for Negro writers and artists still lay elsewhere, Washington contained a larger proportion of outstanding colored intellectuals and doers than any other place in the country. Their presence reduced the tasteless conspicuous consumer to a minor role.

Complacency among second-string colored officialdom was proving a greater impediment to the Great Society than did the naïveté of the Negro who relied on a show of material wealth. Since the number of Negroes in policy-making positions could be counted on the fingers of two hands, scores who occupied plush-looking offices knew without admitting it that they were largely window dressing. Determination to conceal that fact from themselves produced an acceptance of a scheme of things which had put them in comfortable circumstance but denied them substantive power. While frustration gnawed at them secretly,

[2] *Jet*, 27 Jan 1966.

most of them settled for the outer signs of a nonexistent authority without troubling unduly about the Negroes they had left far behind. Many a white person caught up in the bureaucracy of government service felt a similar frustration, but unlike his Negro counterpart, he could take it or leave it at minimal cost to himself.

Along upper 16th Street bordering the eastern fringes of Rock Creek Park lay the newly emerging Negro "Gold Coast," where well-to-do colored families occupied some of the mansions of the 1925 vintage, town and ranch houses built in the 1950's, or suites in some of the roomy new apartment buildings looking out over the park. In this area, as in sections of redeveloped Southwest Washington, Negro families and white lived side by side. If neighborly intercourse was distinctly formal, it was seldom marred by overt mutual hostility. Manifestly Washington Negroes in the upper socio-economic brackets were well established.

The Cosmos Club, having elected four distinguished Negroes to membership, was willing to accept other colored men whose literary, scientific, or scholarly qualifications were unmistakable. No color bars remained at the University Club or, more extraordinary, at the Army-Navy Club. But Negro patrons were extremely few. Negro attendance at the National Theatre was also slim, only less so at the Arena and smaller theatres and at the concerts and opera performances open to the public. Nor did more than a handful of colored parents take their children to the Smithsonian museums, the exhibits at the National Geographic Society, and the art galleries, all of which were flooded year in and year out with white Washingtonians and white tourists. What Negro children could see there were still the artifacts and art of an alien world of an earlier day in which colored people had had no recognized place. Whether Negroes' failure to make use of the cultural opportunities now available to them sprang from a reluctance to expose themselves to another reminder of how little their existence had counted in the white man's

6

civilization, or from a preference for rubbing elbows with people of their own race, or was a carry-over from the recent past when their presence in customarily white preserves would have caused acute discomfort at best and, at worst, outright rebuffs—whatever the reason, by 1965 the luxury of free choice had become theirs.

Below the top levels of society, however, understanding between whites and Negroes and a reciprocal give-and-take had not progressed far. Through PTAs in mixed neighborhoods some rapport was beginning to develop, but it was tenuous and uncertain; with Negro children forming 90 percent of public school enrollments, the prospects for an early flowering of mutual parental appreciation were dim. The pupils themselves adapted well enough, but the differences between white and colored children's backgrounds tended to limit shared extracurricular activities, particularly in the junior and senior high schools. Negroes at every social level, moreover, resented the *de facto* segregation in the schools. Largely a product of housing patterns and the geographical distribution of the two races in Greater Washington, it was more pronounced within the District of Columbia in 1965 than it had been in the mid-1950's.

That fact, coupled with the even more alarming failure of Washington's schools to keep pace with educational improvements in other cities, troubled a number of white and all Negro citizens, but the latter had come to believe that white Washington was no longer much concerned about the state of public education. For the Negro it was the key to the future; for the white it might be a matter of vital interest but more generally was a bothersome problem too difficult and, in view of availability of good private schools, not pressing enough to agitate about. With rare exceptions, neither the Negro nor the white members of the Board of Education took a vigorous stand. The superintendent of schools insisted that the meager budgets allowed by the Southern-dominated House Subcommittee on District Appropriations made rapid progress impossible.

7

But his critics observed that he had not appointed well-qualified colored candidates to policy-making positions and that his own unshakable confidence in old-fashioned teaching methods blinded him to the virtues of less antiquated techniques and the teaching aids in use in first-rate city school systems. In short, the schools which enlightened Washingtonians in 1955 had expected to set an example of social adjustment to the rest of the country were now lagging badly. And to no small degree the lag was due to the apathy of white people over whom traditional racial attitudes still had a strong enough hold to paralyze their will to fight for better public education.

Equally discouraging was the continuing existence, in fact the growth, of what civic-minded people came to call "the Other Washington"—the city of slums and broken homes, of unemployed fathers, of wretched living conditions, and of drab streets where vice, disease, and hopelessness were ever-present. A glance at the illustrations in "O, Say Can You See?" A Bifocal Tour of Washington, published in late 1965, must convince even the most insensitive person that the District of Columbia was neither the "colored man's paradise," as unobservant whites had once labeled it, nor was it in its entirety the "Magnificent Capital" portrayed not long ago in a best-selling picture book. The black ghettoes were as much part of Washington as were the stretches of greensward and the gleaming white marble façades of public buildings.

Unemployment and underemployment accounted for much of the poverty, preposterously low wages for most of the rest, at a time when agencies were scrambling for qualified people. A report released in 1965 told of "Negro families striving to live on a budget that provided . . . a maximum of 40¢ per person per day for food, clothing, medicine, transportation, entertainment, and sales tax." In an area near the Capitol 41 percent of the families earned less than $3,000 a year, 9 percent less than $1,000. The area, needless to say, had high crime and delinquency rates.[3] Throughout the city, despite increased police patrols, street crimes and housebreaking threatened persons and property, while wolfpacks of teenagers terrorized Negro neighborhoods. For although "whitey" was the arch enemy, black hoodlums were not discriminating. Here, as in Los Angeles' Watts, Harlem, and elsewhere, antisocial behavior was the inevitable consequence of long-accumulating cause. But the sobering facts furnished no clues to quick-working correctives. Earnest citizens of both races striving to wipe out the Other Washington were only beginning to comprehend the frightening proportions of the problem. Whites who not very long ago had believed that, because they were now ready to act, they could quickly bring a new order into being were awakening to a realization that they did not speak the same language as the people they wanted to help. To break through a century of noncommunication demanded more than good will.

In the late 1950's and the early 1960's white Washingtonians had prided themselves on having adjusted to far-reaching but peaceable change. "What we have been witnessing," said the director of the Washington Urban League in September 1965, "is not a social revolution. It is merely a rebellion and not yet a large-scale rebellion." Many of his listeners were startled. Composed of thoughtful, well-to-do people drawn together for a symposium on "The Church and the City" sponsored by St. John's Church, Lafayette Square, his predominantly white audience digested the import of that disconcerting diagnosis: the changes of the preceding decade were only a beginning. Yet the very fact that St. John's parishioners and others were gathering to examine church obligations to the community and how to meet them was a hopeful indication that influential citizens were no longer thinking of past achievements but were dedicating themselves in a spirit of humility to learning

[3] Community Advisers on Equal Employment, *Equal Employment in the Nation's Capital,* p. 33.

9

how to travel over the long road ahead. The cheery Dr. Pangloss philosophy of everything's being for the best in the best of all possible worlds had vanished from white Washington before 1941; the exaggerated optimism of 1954 had evaporated by 1957; by early 1965 the sullen suspiciousness that had long lain over the bottom tiers of the social pyramid was lessening somewhat. Before the end of the year people were becoming determined to let neither ignorance, nor sentimentality, nor apathy, nor profound discouragement halt the hard march toward the goal of racial equity.

Yet each of those obstacles was present. The ignorance of thousands of colored Washingtonians about how to help themselves repeatedly baffled inexperienced well-wishers; and the constant inflow of newcomers unfamiliar with the demands of urban life meant that organizations undertaking to provide assistance had, like the White Queen, to run faster, faster to stay where they were. Sentimentalists' inclination to think black people always the innocent victims, whites always the beasts of prey, tended to nurse Negroes' grievances rather than elicit colored cooperation. Indifference to the well-being of the anonymous masses, an age-old characteristic of one segment of urban society, hampered every antipoverty campaign, and because Washington's campaign was directed largely at Negro indigents, racial prejudice created a nearly insurmountable block to citywide collaboration. Discouragement at the slow progress was perhaps the greatest hazard of all, for it syphoned off talent and energy at critical moments and threatened periodically to hamstring the recruitment of new personnel.

Eagerness to place Negroes in responsible posts in public and privately supported agencies occasionally put a colored man in a position outside his experience and hence outside his competence to handle effectively. Critics often forgot that few white men could have done better. The error meanwhile tended to undermine white faith in all Negroes' capabilities. If, on top of that, rumors gained credence that the

10

colored administrator was toadying to influential whites or, conversely, showing favoritism to incompetent Negroes, confidence sagged further. During 1965 endeavors to widen Negro opportunities for employment ran into new difficulties: multiplying complaints from would-be employers declared that well-paid jobs were going begging for want of qualified Negro applicants. A number of Southern congressmen's derogations of the entire interracial program further dampened the spirits of faint-hearted Washingtonians. While the President asserted his belief in the Great Society, money for the District's participation had to come from the Hill. How was the city to weather the only half-foreseen reverses, to overcome incipient disillusionment, and to prevent far-flung plans from bogging down in a slough of despond? As the younger generation, not yet burdened with the responsibility of translating ideals into workable reality, clamored for faster action, older heads concluded that patience and more patience would alone serve the cause.

Washington was not the only American city to be reappraising the tasks of the future. In grappling with them, however, it had—and has—peculiar handicaps, notably the lack of a locally elected government that could respond to local wishes, and, a corollary, the insistence of Americans elsewhere on keeping the national capital as a showplace for visitors regardless of what went on in the Other Washington. The appointment in 1961 and reappointment in 1964 of a Negro as one of the three District commissioners was, it is true, an epoch-making departure from the past, but John Duncan and his two white associates proved unable to do more than pick at the edges of the massive problems confronting them. Whether pleased or disappointed at what they succeeded in accomplishing, the bulk of citizens, white and colored alike, believed that as long as committees of Congress acted as the city council, the District of Columbia would suffer from neglect and from biased or uninformed ideas of the community's needs. Congressmen, after all, were

11

prone to lend a closer ear to their constituents' demands than to the pleas of nonvoting residents of the capital.

On the other hand, because in the eyes of the rest of the world the District of Columbia represented the United States, local citizens knew that their deeds would always attract wide attention. The attention at times might have been unwelcome, as in the case of the publicity given the city's deplorable crime rate, but, when directed at such matters as the historic March on Washington in the summer of 1963, it fostered civic pride: the congratulatory comment in the national press on the orderliness and cordiality that had prevailed inspired District citizens to fresh effort. If they could create a truly interracial community in which dark-skinned and white people could live amicably alongside each other and work together constructively, they would be serving their country as well as themselves. Few Washingtonians today are indifferent to that challenge.

12

CHAPTER II

THE EMERGENCE OF A

SELF-RELIANT NEGRO COM-

MUNITY, 1791-1831

In 1791, when President George Washington selected a site for a national capital on the Potomac River below the small port of Georgetown, some Negroes were already living in the ten-mile square newly ceded to the United States by Maryland and Virginia. Most of the colored people were slaves owned by the proprietors of the tobacco plantations, farms, and woodlands that occupied the countryside. A few free Negroes may have lived in Georgetown or in the tiny hamlet of Hamburg across Rock Creek or in Carrollsburg on the shores of the Potomac's Eastern Branch, where Daniel Carroll hoped to develop a trading center. On the far side of the Potomac, Virginia law forbade freedmen to remain in the state more than six months after manumission on pain of being sold back into slavery; hence any free Negroes who lived in or near the city of Alexandria must either have been there on sufferance or have been born free, for, until Congress was ready to make laws for the new federal territory, Virginia law was to govern the trans-Potomac part of the District of Columbia and Maryland law was to rule in the rest. That arrangement left colored people subject to the racial restrictions imposed by slave-holding agricultural states. Certainly no Negro in 1791 owned a patch of ground or a dwelling within the area where the new city was to rise. By agreement with the President, each of the

13

proprietors of that land received sixty-seven dollars an acre for the property he sold to the United States.[1]

Inasmuch as the commissioners whom the President put in charge of laying out the city and erecting the government buildings expected to meet the costs by the sale of lots to private individuals, the task of surveying the ground and platting the streets and lots was a matter of some urgency; potential purchasers would have to have a detailed map of the city-to-be in order to see what they were bidding for. Washington had entrusted the planning of the city to Major Pierre Charles L'Enfant, a French engineer who had served under him during the Revolution. As L'Enfant needed help in surveying the terrain before he could submit a complete plan, Andrew Ellicott of Baltimore, one of the commissioners, recommended a colored man of his acquaintance who had taught himself enough mathematics and astronomy to prepare a remarkably accurate almanac and who thus easily qualified for the post. So from March to August 1791 the dark-skinned Benjamin Banneker accompanied the French planner on his rounds. To the slaves still working in the fields over which the two men trod, the sight must have seemed extraordinary. The servants at the Georgetown inn where the two men stayed must have been equally astonished at the learned Negro's dining at a table next to that of white patrons. L'Enfant unfortunately never finished the map. A perfectionist, he revised and rearranged, seemingly heedless of President Washington's warning that if construction of the public buildings did not start in the near future, Congress might decide to keep the seat of government in Philadelphia. In February 1792 Washington, deeply troubled by the months of delay, dismissed the Frenchman and requested Andrew Ellicott to finish the job. Ellicott had his predecessor's sketch map, but as it

[1] *Annals of the Congress of the United States*, First Congress, Second Session, pp. 2234-35 (hereafter cited as *Annals*, —C, —S). For a fuller account of the founding of the city, see Constance McLaughlin Green, *Washington, Village and Capital, 1800-1878*, pp. 12-20.

14

lacked many details, the commissioner may have turned to Banneker for information about what L'Enfant had intended. Nothing suggests that the "Afric-American astronomer," as white dignitaries called him, originated any feature of the design for the capital. Indeed he had left while L'Enfant was still making changes. Banneker's fame rested on other achievements.

Shortly after his return to his small farm outside Baltimore to resume work on his almanacs, Banneker sent a copy of his ephemeris for 1792 to Thomas Jefferson with an explanation that its compiler was of a "race of beings who have long labored under the abuse and censure of the world and . . . been considered rather brutish, than as human, and scarcely capable of mental endowments." Jefferson replied that he had sent the almanac on to the secretary of the Academy of Sciences at Paris, "because I considered it as a document to which your whole color had a right, for their justification against the doubts which have been entertained of them." [2] By revealing to competent judges the intellectual powers which "a sable descendant of Africa" might possess, Banneker was a first exponent of rational race relations.

After auctions of lots in the federal city permitted work to begin on the government buildings and private dwellings, stone masons and carpenters were in demand. While craftsmen from Baltimore and other Northern cities undertook some of the work, hired slaves formed the core of the labor force building the Capitol. Skilled freedmen also may have shared in putting up the first dwellings in the federal city. By 1800, when government clerks moved from Philadelphia into offices in Washington, 123 of the federal city's 3,200

[2] Henry E. Baker, "Benjamin Banneker, The Negro Mathematician and Astronomer," *Journal of Negro History*, III, 99-118; Moncure D. Conway, "Benjamin Banneker, the Negro Astronomer," *Atlantic Monthly*, XI, 79-84; *Banneker, the Afro-American Astronomer from Data collected by Will W. Allen assisted by Daniel Murray*, pp. 12-14, and, for Banneker's letter of 19 Aug 1791 and Jefferson's reply of 30 Aug 1791, pp. 21-29.

inhabitants were free Negroes. Doubtless most of the men earned their living as day laborers or carters, the women as laundresses, seamstresses, and cooks for householders who neither owned nor wanted to hire slaves. In Washington slaves outnumbered freedmen by five to one. In the older, more settled community of Georgetown and in the farming countryside of the county beyond the cities' limits, the disparity was still greater, 1,449 slaves to 277 free Negroes. No later decade showed so low a proportion of freedmen.[3] (See Table I.)

Freedom was the first aim of every slave, even though life as a freedman might be harder than as a chattel bondsman. Manumission was not uncommon in Washington and Georgetown, but a more usual path to the slave's goal was by "hiring his own time," an arrangement whereby his master allowed him to find work for himself and keep his earnings above a fixed sum; the industrious thus gradually accumulated enough money to buy his freedom and later that of his family. For enterprise and selflessness Aletha Tanner set a record in Washington. Early in the century she started a small market garden near the "President's Square," built up an appreciative clientele headed by Thomas Jefferson, by 1810 was able to complete payment of $1,400 for her freedom, and over the next quarter century bought that of 22 relatives and friends. The process, repeated on a lesser scale by her neighbors, steadily reduced the proportion of slave to free. That "the peculiar institution," primarily useful as an agricultural labor system, was ill-adapted to city life hastened the change. After 1810 Washington and Georgetown masters seldom owned more than a few household servants each and perhaps three or four slaves for hire.

Because, next to freedom, an education was the most

[3] Letters sent by the Board of Commissioners for the District of Columbia, 22 Nov 1798, v, 177-78, Record Group 42, National Archives (hereafter cited as R.G.—, N.A.); enumerator's return for the District of Columbia, Second Census of the U.S., 1800, ms, N.A.

valuable legacy with which a colored man could endow his children, as early as 1807 three illiterate Negroes, two of them Navy Yard employees, set about providing a school for colored children. They built a small frame schoolhouse in northwest Washington and engaged a white man as teacher. Three other schools for colored children opened within the next four years, one started by an Englishman, another by British-born Mary Billings in Georgetown, and the third by a colored woman on Capitol Hill. The children enrolled learned little beyond the three R's, and lack of money forced all but Mrs. Billings' school to close before 1813, but the first white public schools in Washington had little more to offer and suffered much the same fate. Although white men had raised funds by subscription and in 1806 the city council voted tax money to help support the Permanent Institution for the Education of Youth, one of its two schools shut down in 1812 and the other limped along with a single teacher and a mere handful of pupils.[4]

Disappointingly little information has survived about the daily lives of colored families during the federal city's early years. Until the first city *Directory* appeared in 1822 with its listing of residents' occupations as well as their addresses, an occasional brief item in the *National Intelligencer* and fleeting allusions in travelers' descriptions of the capital supply a skimpy assortment of fact and impression. Michael Shiner, a Negro workman employed at the Navy Yard, kept a diary in 1813 and added a few entries over the next fifty years, but interesting as those ink-scrawled pages are as testimony to Negro literacy, they tell little or nothing about Shiner's neighbors or himself. White Washingtonians' letters rarely mentioned colored people, and visitors, if talking

[4] Papers relating to Aletha Tanner, Jane Eleanor Datcher Mss (Howard University); Special Report of the Commissioner of Education on the Condition and Improvement of Public Schools in the District of Columbia, House Executive Document 315, 41C, 2S, pp. 50-52, 195-97, Serial 1427 (hereafter cited as *Spec Rpt Comr Ed*). For a discussion of the system of slaves' "hiring their own time," see Richard C. Wade, *Slavery in the Cities, The South, 1820-1860*, pp. 38-54.

about Negroes at all, generally confined their comments to the slave trade. After the Civil War a white man eager to extol Negro accomplishments prepared an account of Negro education and Negro churches in the antebellum cities, obviously drawing much of his data from old colored residents' word-of-mouth reminiscences. His report rescued some significant facts from oblivion, but his narrative failed to depict Negro modes of life and Negro attitudes of mind.[5] The law books unhappily only provide a frame for the blanks in the story.

Although Washington's mayor and council had not interjected any legal obstacle in the path of Negro education, in 1808 the six-year-old municipality enacted a law imposing a five dollar fine on any Negro or any "loose, idle, disorderly person" found on the streets or at a meeting "at a tippling or other house" after ten o'clock at night; a slave whose master refused to pay his fine was to be whipped. The implied equating of all Negroes with "loose, idle, disorderly persons" doubtless hurt Negro pride, but respectable colored people were otherwise little affected during the next four years. In 1812, however, an amended city charter empowered the corporation to prescribe the conditions upon which freedmen "without visible means of support" might reside in the city. Mayor and council thereupon rewrote the municipal regulations. They quadrupled the five dollar fine and, if unpaid, authorized six months' jail sentences for free Negroes and mulattoes and forty lashes for slaves caught at "nightly and disorderly meetings," placed a ten dollar penalty upon a black found playing cards, dice, or "any other game of immoral tendency," and required every free Negro to register and carry with him a certificate of freedom. In addition to expecting thus to forestall possible disorders, the city fathers probably counted on the new restrictions to

[5] *Spec Rpt Comr Ed*, pp. 195-280; Diary of Michael Shiner, 1813-1865, Ms (Library of Congress. Unless otherwise noted, all manuscript materials cited throughout my study are to be found in the Library of Congress).

18

check the influx of free Negroes, an unwelcome element in most southern cities, if only because the mere presence of freedmen seemed likely to stir up discontent among slaves. Washington officials evidently were persuaded that if freedmen enjoyed privileges here denied them in the rest of the South, irresponsible blacks would swarm into the city from every corner of Dixie. The black codes in most of the slave states were far more severe than Washington's; they forbade schooling for slaves and discouraged it among free Negroes, put heavier penalties upon them for disregarding the curfew, and sometimes established restrictions on manumission or required manumitted slaves to leave the state within six months. But the new black code here dealt a blow to free Negroes' hopes of achieving an honorable place in the city's life such as Benjamin Banneker had earned before the municipal government had come into being.

The required certificate of freedom, it is true, gave the freedman, particularly the newcomer to Washington, a modicum of protection from kidnaping. Without proof of his freedom he might be arrested as a runaway slave, and, by the terms of one of the eighteenth century Maryland laws that Congress kept in force in Washington and Georgetown, unless some white person supplied evidence that the Negro was indeed free and paid for his keep while in prison, the authorities might sell the colored man to recoup the jail fees. As kidnaping had become a real danger by 1812, free Negroes may have considered the certificates a greater safeguard than humiliation.[6]

The domestic slave trade in the District of Columbia

[6] *Acts of the Corporation of the City of Washington*, 6 Dec 1808, 16 Dec 1812 (hereafter cited as *Wshg Acts*); *Annals*, 8C, 1S, pp. 2284-91; 2 *U.S. Statutes at Large*, 721-27 (hereafter cited as — Stat. —); Walter C. Clephane, "The Local Aspects of Slavery in the District of Columbia," Columbia Historical Society, *Records*, III, 225 (hereafter cited as CHS *Rec*). On comparative restrictions in Charleston and other cities of the Deep South, see John Lofton, *Insurrection in South Carolina, The Turbulent World of Denmark Vesey*, pp. 80-84, and Carter Woodson, *The Education of the Negro before 1861*.

had not reached large proportions until 1808, after the constitutional provision prohibiting the importation of slaves from Africa had gone into effect. Before then an occasional sale of one or two slaves in Washington and Georgetown and perhaps twice a year an auction in Alexandria of as many as sixty had constituted the entire traffic. A good many residents and visitors objected to it from the beginning. From Alexandrians had come a petition in 1802 vainly begging Congress to forbid "the practise of persons coming from distant parts of the United States into this district for the purpose of purchasing slaves." Washingtonians were equally repelled by scenes of "wretchedness and human degradation disgraceful to our characters as citizens of a free government." In 1809 Edward Coles, President Madison's young secretary, spoke to the President of the effect upon foreign ministers of witnessing "such a revolting sight" on the streets of the American capital as the "gangs of Negroes, some in chains, on their way to a southern market." But the President was powerless to stop the trade as long as Congress refused to act, and for Virginia and Maryland plantation owners the sale of their surplus slaves to planters in the expanding Cotton Kingdom was as important as it was to influential constituents of congressmen from the Deep South. By 1812 Washington and Alexandria had become major centers whence slave dealers shipped their human merchandise to the Carolinas and Georgia.

Citizens of the capital, on the other hand, however much they disliked the trade carried on under their noses, rarely spoke out against the existence of the peculiar institution itself in the federal district. Only thirteen years before Congress convened for the first time in the new federal city, delegates to the Constitutional Convention had rejected the proposal of George Mason of Virginia for the gradual abolition of slavery throughout the Union. In 1805 a resolution submitted in Congress called for emancipation of all slaves in the District of Columbia when they reached

20

the age of twenty-five, but the defeat of that plan killed hope of making the federal ten-mile square free territory in the near future. Both Thomas Jefferson and James Madison, slaveowners though they were, disapproved of slavery. Jefferson called it "a mortal reproach" to the republic, a source of "moral and political reprobation." Yet the Presidents and like-minded District citizens obviously did not feel strongly enough to campaign for abolition.[7] Any local slaveowner whose conscience hurt him could manumit his slaves without subjecting them to the necessity of leaving Washington or Georgetown. He might postpone action but specify in his will that upon his death they were to be free and were to receive from his estate a piece of land or a sum of money for a nest egg. During his lifetime, he might give the slave children of his household a smattering of education by letting them sit in at lessons with his own white children. Thus many a colored family acquired a solid economic footing along with freedom. But in the new capital neither Northerners nor Southerners wanted to discuss the slavery question. The Union must not be imperiled by untimely attempts to amend the hard-won Constitution.

As long as the proportion of free colored to white people in Washington and Georgetown ran no higher than about 15 percent, Negroes could enjoy a number of simple pleasures—some of which would later be denied them; fishing and bathing in the river; marveling at the huge grizzly bears brought from the Rocky Mountains and kept in a cage on the President's lawn; hunting squirrel in the woodlands and the wild duck, snipe, and geese in the tidal swamps along the creeks; watching the races and placing small bets on the trotters at the Jockey Club meets held

[7] *National Intelligencer*, 22 Jan 1802 (hereafter cited as *N.I.*) ; *Annals*, 8C, 2S, pp. 995-96; David B. Warden, *Chorographical and Statistical Description of the District of Columbia*, pp. 45-46, 64; *Alexandria Advertiser* and *N.I.*, advertisements of sales, 1801-1812; Ralph L. Ketcham, "The Dictates of Conscience: Edward Coles and Slavery," *Virginia Quarterly Review*, XXXII (Winter 1960), pp. 46-62, especially ltr, Jefferson to Coles, p. 53.

every autumn at the track laid out in a field north of the city. More often than anywhere else in the United States colored people here, like white, could see strange and wonderful sights, ranging from a view of the silk-clad, bejeweled Tunisian envoy and his exotic entourage to a close look at the Osage and Sac Indian braves and chiefs with gaudily painted faces and bodies who stalked up Pennsylvania Avenue in 1806 to negotiate a treaty with the white man's government. Negroes, furthermore, were still allowed to walk into the Capitol to admire the splendors of its spacious corridors and the already famous carved "corn stalk" columns in the Senate wing. A colored man might in fact penetrate into the House or Senate chambers to listen to a congressional debate.[8]

When war with Great Britain broke out in 1812 and British marines began to harry the countryside along Chesapeake Bay and the Potomac, fear of a slave uprising worried white people in the vicinity almost as much as did prospective attacks from Redcoats. While some slaves in eastern Maryland offered their services to the British admiral with the mistaken expectation of thereby winning their freedom, "our enemy at home," as one frightened woman called the slaves in and about Washington, remained quiescent. Free Negroes, in fact, responded to the mayor's plea for help in the summer of 1814 when British troops were closing in upon the capital; colored men worked alongside white in digging earthworks at Bladensburg at the District line. That line of defense proved useless. The British captured the city and burned every public building except the Post Office. White Washingtonians, however, had the grace to acknowledge their debt to their colored neighbors: "The free people of color of this city acted as become patriots: there is scarcely an exception of any

---

[8] Margaret Bayard Smith, *The First Forty Years of Washington Society,* ed. Gaillard Hunt, pp. 393-403 (hereafter cited as M. B. Smith, *First Forty Years*); [Charles Jared Ingersoll,] *Inchiquin, the Jesuit's Letters,* p. 43.

failing to be on the spot . . . manifesting by their exertions all the zeal of freemen. At the same time, highly to their credit, conducting themselves with the utmost order and propriety." [9]

If the subjects of that encomium hoped for more than words of thanks, they met with disappointment. With the coming of peace in 1815, the rebuilding of the half-destroyed city opened up jobs to some of them, but in 1816, to the consternation of free Negroes, well-intentioned white people began to promote a scheme of sending them back to Africa. To men who had not only behaved as "became patriots" but who considered themselves truly native Americans, the plan of the American Colonization Society to establish a settlement on the African coast to be called Liberia and to transplant them to that alien land came as a shock. Appalled as they were, they saw that they would have to depend upon themselves if they were to be part of a stable community in the familiar western world. They organized the Resolute Beneficial Society in 1818, a mutual-aid group formed initially to provide health and burial benefits for members but which used most of its funds to open a school for colored children.

In Charleston, South Carolina, mulattoes had founded the Brown Fellows Society in 1790, which admitted no full-blooded Negroes; free blacks had later started their own benefit societies. In Washington all free colored people were eligible for membership in the new organization. If memory of Benjamin Banneker of "pure African descent" encouraged the more generous attitude, the lesser financial resources of Negroes in the younger city left little choice. The Resolute Beneficial Society indeed soon found itself unable to carry the costs of a school, but, shortly after it had to close, Henry Smothers furnished a classroom and taught his neighbors' children free of charge. From that time onward, Negroes always maintained at least one school

[9] M. B. Smith, *First Forty Years*, pp. 89-91, 105-15; *N.I.*, 20, 23, 24 Aug 1814.

in Washington. Smothers built a schoolhouse near the present site of the New York Avenue Presbyterian Church and there taught as many as a hundred pupils. When Smothers could no longer carry the expense, John Prout took over, charging each child 12½ cents a month for tuition. Here Aletha Tanner sent her young nephew, John Cook, after she had bought his freedom, and it was at Prout's "Columbia Institute" that Cook acquired the training he later put to use in teaching a younger generation.

Despite the city council's fears of giving Negroes any encouragement to settle in Washington, some white people lent them constructive help. Mrs. Mary Billings moved her school from Georgetown to Washington and upon her death two Englishmen carried it on. From time to time a Maryland philanthropist taught Negro children in sessions held outdoors under a tree when he could find no suitable place indoors. Two churches organized Sunday evening classes where adult Negroes might learn to read, and every denomination in the city enrolled colored children in Sunday school, first in classes with white children, later, as the colored population multiplied, in separate units. In 1827 the priest of the Holy Trinity Church in Georgetown founded the first seminary for colored girls and himself taught classes of Negro boys. And contrary to the assumptions of later generations, during the 1820's colored children in Washington and Georgetown sometimes attended white private schools.[10]

Negroes also began to organize their own churches. As early as 1814 colored Methodists in Georgetown, with financial help from a devout white man, built the Mt. Zion Negro Church. While it came under the supervision of the parent white congregation for some years, members of Mt. Zion worshiped without white patronage. In Washington an independent colored congregation came into being in 1820 when Negro parishioners of the Ebenezer Methodist

[10] *N.I.*, 7 Jan 1817; Lofton, *Insurrection*, p. 84; *Spec Rpt Ccmr Ed*, pp. 197-200, Ser 1427.

Episcopal Church, irked at being subject to the spiritual guidance of a slaveowning pastor and at being always relegated to benches in the gallery, formed the Israel Bethel Church. Several years later they purchased from a white Presbyterian congregation a building on South Capitol Street. In thus cutting themselves off from the white church they sacrificed some material assistance, but the loss was minor compared to the gratification of listening to colored preachers and managing their own religious lives. Whether or not white people recognized the significance of the separation, the colored churches marked an important step in creating a self-reliant Negro community.[11]

Free Negroes early realized that the city ordinances subjecting them to special restraints constituted a serious obstacle to the colored community's progress. Until a new charter of 1820 had broadened the corporation's control over colored people, the city had largely confined its surveillance to unruly slaves and freedmen "without visible means of support." Now all Negroes faced sharply cramping limitations. In the spring of 1821 a new ordinance imposed further burdens and indignities: free people of color had to appear in person before the mayor, show him their papers of freedom and certificates each signed by three white residents vouching for the good character of each colored family; each then had to furnish a "peace bond" of twenty dollars with a respected white man as surety for continued good behavior. Although Southern states refused to allow Negroes to bear witness against white men, in the federal ten-mile square, where all judges and justices of the peace were federal officials, the remote possibility existed that the courts might rule the free colored man entitled to the enjoyment of the rights guaranteed to other free men. Six months after the passage of the city council's new act, William Costin decided to put its legality to test.

[11] Richard Jackson, *Chronicles of Georgetown*, p. 214; Washington *Sun*, 12, 26 Feb, 9 Apr 1915; Henry S. Robinson, "Some Aspects of the Free Colored Population of Washington, D.C., 1800-1862," pp. 17-19.

If any person with some Negro blood could succeed in that undertaking, that man was Costin. Believed to be the son of a distinguished Virginian by the granddaughter of a Cherokee Indian chief, he was born free; his mother, rumor had it, was a half-sister of Martha Dandridge Custis Washington. He had purchased his wife's freedom from Eliza Custis Law to whom Mrs. Washington had given the slave woman as a wedding present. For years Costin had been a trusted messenger for the Bank of Washington and was probably the most respected colored man in the capital. He refused to obtain the surety bond and, when fined by a justice of the peace, carried an appeal to the Circuit Court. His case challenged the authority of the corporation of Washington "to prescribe the terms and conditions upon which free Negroes and mulattoes may reside in the City," since Congress could not delegate powers to the city which were unconstitutional, and, his argument ran, "the constitution knows no distinction of color. That all who are not slaves are equally free; that they are . . . equally citizens of the United States." The fact that Judge William Cranch, New England born and bred, heard the case gave it added interest.

Judge Cranch ruled that "the power, given by the Congress to the Corporation" to regulate such matters, "is not repugnant to the Constitution"; but he reversed the decision of the justice of the peace in fining Costin, on the grounds that the wording of the new act was "prospective" and could not apply to a person of color who had resided in Washington before the city charter and the "bye law" had come into being.[12] Cranch based his primary interpretation upon the then generally accepted premise that a state or a municipal corporation by delegated authority could legally, in the interest of protecting society, place binding restrictions upon any group which, irrespective of proved

[12] Samuel Burch, *A Digest of the Laws of the Corporation of the City of Washington to June 1, 1823*, pp. 126-35; 6 *Federal Cases*, 612-14, Case 3266, Oct 1821.

misconduct by individual members or the group as a whole, appeared likely to disturb the peace. By that line of reasoning he might have decreed that a city could limit the freedom of all red-haired women because traditionally they were prone to ill-tempered outbursts. But Costin's counsel was unable effectively to controvert the learned judge. Thus the main verdict ran against the principle for which Costin was fighting. That long residence in Washington exempted him and, inferentially, some of his fellows from the workings of the ordinance in question was scant consolation to him, still less to the city's newer-come Negroes. Costin's action nevertheless heightened the self-respect of all members of the emerging colored community.

The economic status of colored people meanwhile improved very slowly. As Washington had no manufacturing establishments other than a sash and door factory, a small foundry, a few rope walks, and a sailmaking shop, the principal source of industrial employment was the government Navy Yard and the Army Arsenal on Greenleaf's Point on the Eastern Branch, but there, as in privately owned shops, Negroes seldom if ever got as high wages as whites for the same work. After the Columbia Typographical Union formed in 1815, its refusal to accept Negro apprentices or admit Negro printers to membership cut literate colored men out of jobs in the city's most rapidly expanding business. Probably skilled freedmen occasionally had chances to build houses for white patrons, but in rebuilding the Capitol, the White house, and other public structures destroyed by the British in 1814, gangs of hired slaves did the bulk of the work. The first city *Directory* showed in 1822 as many free colored women as freedmen employed. The former were practically all domestic servants. The latter, except for two or three government or banking-house messengers, were bricklayers, carpenters, oystermen, carters, livery-stable hands, hackmen, blacksmiths, shoemakers, waiters, barbers and hairdressers, tailors, cooks, and common laborers. Even before the 1820's, moreover, Irish immigrants were beginning to compete with Negroes for unskilled jobs. In 1815 Irishmen dug the Washington Canal, which, by cutting across the foot of Capitol Hill to Tiber Creek, linked the Eastern Branch with the Potomac beyond the White House. When the newly incorporated Chesapeake and Ohio Canal Company hired men in 1829 to start digging the waterway above Georgetown, Negroes got some of the jobs, but the next year the company replaced them with European laborers imported under contract.[13]

If white Washingtonians were unconcerned about the plight of the free Negro, a good many nevertheless were raising their voices against the barbarities of the domestic slave trade. Jesse Torrey's *Portraiture of Domestic Slavery in the United States* spared no details in describing the miseries he had witnessed when he visited the capital in 1815. The county jail, he explained, had become a "store house" for slave merchants; "several hundred people, including not legal slaves only but many kidnapped freemen, . . . are annually collected at Washington (as if it were an emporium of slavery) for transportation to the slave regions." Shocked by his account of watching from the door of the Capitol a coffle of slaves shuffle by, "a procession of men, women and children, resembling that of a funeral . . . bound together in pairs, some with ropes, and some with *iron chains,*" Americans in the postwar "era of good feeling" could no longer tell themselves that the Union would fall apart if they reopened the question of the slave trade and slavery.

As nonresidents handled most of that trade in Washington, its profits did not benefit the city. The two or three

[13] *N.I.*, 10 Jun, 20 May, 23 Nov 1815, 14 Jan, 23 Sep 1829; Warden, *Chorographical Description,* pp. 63-64; *Documentary History of the Construction and Development of the U.S. Capitol Building and Grounds,* House Report 646, 58C, 2S, pp. 232-33, Ser 4585; *Washington Directory,* 1822, compiled by Judah Delano.

local dealers, unlike the "gentlemen" who conducted the business in Alexandria, were unsavory characters despised by their fellow citizens. The principal slave pens lay in the heart of the city, across the road from the place where the Smithsonian Institution would rise in the 1840's. Disturbed by the ill name the community acquired among Northerners as a result of traders' activities, slaveowners on the city council in 1819 joined with other citizens in begging Congress to empower the corporation to forbid Maryland dealers and other outsiders from transporting slaves through the city or depositing them here preparatory to shipment south. Congress ignored the petition. Some years later when the mayor and council attempted to achieve their ends by levying a heavy tax on owners of bondsmen in transit, the courts declared the act invalid; the corporation had exceeded its lawful authority and had interfered with legitimate interstate commerce.[14]

Although an increasingly powerful proslavery bloc in Congress tried to shelve any discussion of the peculiar institution, several congressmen questioned the legality of the interstate trade in the federal city. A Maryland statute of 1796, one of several laws forming the legal basis of the trade in Washington, sanctioned the passage of slaves through the county but forbade importing them for sale. Hence most of the big auctions held in the city were patently illegal. A law of 1719, on the other hand, expressly authorized the jailing of any Negro unable to prove himself free and who was therefore presumed to be a runaway slave. Northerners were especially horrified to discover that it was the presidentially appointed marshal of the District or his deputy who sold the Negro into slavery if, though he established his free status, he could not pay for his

[14] Jesse Torrey, *A Portraiture of Domestic Slavery in the United States,* pp. 33-34, 41; petition, H 16A–G5.5, 13 Dec 1819, R.G. 233, N.A. (since all petitions to the House are in R.G. 233 and all to the Senate in R.G. 46, that locational detail will hereafter be omitted); *Wshg Acts,* 28 Jul 1831, p. 7.

keep while in prison. The first angry protest in Congress over this procedure arose in 1826 when a free Negro from New York, come to see the sights of the capital, was arrested and jailed as a runaway; only the intervention of the state governor saved him from being sold. A New York congressman demanded to know what law authorized such action, and the House investigated. The remedy proposed was not the repeal of the statute but a scheme requiring the corporations of Washington or Georgetown to pay the jail fees for a free Negro arrested as a fugitive slave. But an indignant outcry rose from Georgetowners, and Congress dropped the plan.[15]

Two years later Congressman Charles Miner of Pennsylvania told the House that thirty years of neglect of the local slave laws had allowed "numerous and gross corruptions" to creep in; dealers exploiting their general "impunity" had made the District their headquarters; they used the federal jails freely to house their chattels in transit. He objected to allowing officers of the federal government to receive "emoluments" from the trade. If, he asked, a free Negro was sold for $300 in order to recover $50 in jail fees, what happened to the remaining $250? It did not go into the public treasury but into the marshal's pocket. Investigation showed, Miner asserted, that in five years' time the District jails had lodged 452 slaves and 290 Negroes taken as runaways; fifteen had later proved to be free men but five of them had been sold into life slavery. A hundred years later a study in the *Journal of Negro History* presented the thesis that kidnaping in the District of Columbia was relatively rare, that most of the Negroes taken into custody and sold had in fact been fugitive slaves. Late in 1828 the House called for a report but took no other action.[16]

---

[15] *N.I.*, 11 Apr 1816; *Register of Debates in the Congress of the United States*, 19C, 2S, pp. 555-56 (hereafter cited as *Reg Deb*); House Document 71, 19C, 2S, Ser 151 (hereafter cited as H Doc).

[16] *Reg Deb*, 20C, 2S, pp. 167, 176-77, 191-92; H Doc 215, 20C, 1S,

For nearly seven years after Congress had denied the city government any control over the trade, few Washingtonians had seen any use in hammering away with fresh petitions touching upon any aspect of slavery. Inasmuch as influential Northern congressmen had been unable to prevent the admission of Missouri to the Union as a slave state, how could unrepresented local citizens counter the power of Southern planters? Indeed white men sensitive to slavery's evils hesitated at seeking to make the District of Columbia an island of freedom surrounded by slave territory. But the Missouri Compromise debates of 1819 and 1820 had lifted the thirty-year tabu on discussion of emancipation in the states. The antislavery movement was gaining ground in Virginia. When the Old Dominion enacted emancipation, then would be the moment to launch a vigorous compaign in the ten-mile square. Meanwhile many people undertook to abet the work of the American Colonization Society, which had helped a first group of Negroes to settle in Liberia in 1822. No one suggested that local slaveowners abused their bondsmen, but in 1827 the recently organized Washington Abolition Society believed the time ripe to issue a summary of slavery's "deleterious influence upon the welfare and prosperity of our city."

Captain Basil Hall, an English visitor in Washington, publicized this statement. Disclaiming any "squeamish sensibility" and passing over "the detrimental effects of slavery upon the morals of the community [as] too obvious to need illustration," the society declared that "the first evil consequence . . . is the prostration of industry; an effect especially visible in the labouring classes of the community, but felt in its remote ramifications in every class of society." Although the city levied a large tax on the slaves of nonresidents, the use of hired slaves on public works

Ser 173; H. Doc 60, 20C, 2S, Ser 190; William T. Laprade, "The Domestic Slave Trade in the District of Columbia," *Journal of Negro History,* XI, No. 1, 19-34.

continued, leaving free laborers unemployed. As masters usually allowed their hired slaves only a pittance to live on, and that frequently went for intoxicants, "the burden of the support of many of these labourers falls upon society at large, while the proceeds of their labour go to fill the coffers of a distant master." Consequently Washington failed to attract "industrious and enterprising men, from various parts of our country." Because immediate whole-sale emancipation might endanger the "tranquillity" of the South, the memorialists urged a system of gradual emancipation in the District and, a far more radical idea, "enfranchisement of all that shall be born after such period as the wisdom of Congress may determine upon." [17]

If abolitionist societies elsewhere vaguely assumed that Negroes, when free, would become full-fledged voting citizens once they had met property or other special qualifications, in Washington the idea was revolutionary. Not improbably it was alarm at that proposal and fear of its drawing a stream of Negroes to Washington that led the municipality in 1827 to place larger restrictions upon colored people—heavier fines for disturbing the peace, a stricter curfew, and for every free Negro family a peace bond increased from the former $20 to $500 and signed by two white men. The actor-manager Joseph Jefferson complained at one point that the new curfew cost his company $10 a night, since colored people, forced to leave early, no longer formed part of his audience. In 1828 Congress instructed the commissioner of public buildings to bar Negroes from the Capitol grounds except when there on "business," presumably to carry out some menial task. Still the new rulings, laxly enforced as they were, failed to check Negro migration into the city or to weaken the abolitionist drive. Eleven hundred memorialists appeared to be merely the

[17] *Annals,* 15C, 2S, p. 273; Basil Hall, *Travels in North America in the Years 1827 and 1828,* 3rd ed., III, 39, 41-47; *Wshg Acts,* 5 Apr 1823, pp. 46-47; *N.I.,* 18 May, 2 Aug 1827.

TABLE I

POPULATION OF THE DISTRICT OF COLUMBIA[a]

	1800	1810	1820	1830	1840	1850	1860	1870
D.C. TOTAL	14,093	24,023	33,039	39,834	43,712	51,687	75,080	131,700
White	10,266	16,088	23,164	27,563	29,655	37,941	60,764	88,298
Free Negro	783	2,549	4,048	6,152	8,461	10,059	11,131	43,422
Slave	3,244	5,505	6,277	6,119	4,694	3,687	3,185	
WASHINGTON								
TOTAL	3,210	8,208	13,117	18,826	23,364	40,001	61,122	109,199
White	2,464	5,904	9,376	13,367	16,843	29,730	50,139	73,731
Free Negro	123	867	1,796	3,129	4,808	8,158	9,209	35,455
Black							5,831	
Mulatto							3,378	
Slave	623	1,437	1,945	2,330	1,713	2,113	1,774	
GEORGETOWN								
TOTAL	2,993	4,948	7,360	8,441	7,312	8,366	8,733	11,384
White	3,394[b]	3,235	5,099	6,122	5,124	6,080	6,798	8,113
Free Negro	277[b]	551	894	1,204	1,403	1,561	1,358	3,271
Black							562	
Mulatto							796	
Slave	1,449[b]	1,162	1,521	1,115	785	725	577	
WASHINGTON								
COUNTY[c] TOTAL	1,941	2,135	2,729	2,994	3,069	3,320	5,225	11,117
White			1,514	1,828	1,929	2,131	3,827	6,434
Free Negro			168	167	288	340	564	4,678
Black							238	
Mulatto							326	
Slave			1,047	999	812	849	834	
ALEXANDRIA								
CITY TOTAL	4,971	7,227	8,345	8,241	8,459			
White	3,727	4,903	5,742	5,609	5,758			
Free Negro	369	836	1,168	1,371	1,627			
Slave	875	1,488	1,435	1,261	1,064			

[a] Compiled from *U.S. Census*, Second through Ninth, 1800-1870
[b] Georgetown and Washington County together
[c] Washington County encompassed all the area beyond the Eastern Branch, and all above Washington's present-day Florida Avenue and Georgetown's present-day R Street.

vanguard of a growing local army determined to rid the District of slavery.[18] Although the decade of the 1820's saw new arrivals, manumission, and purchases of slaves' freedom increase the number of Washington's free colored inhabitants by 74 percent, a rising spirit of toleration toward

[18] *Wshg Acts*, 31 May 1827, pp. 68-72; *Spec Rpt Comr Ed*, p. 215, Ser 1427; Jeannie Tree Rives, "Old Families and Houses, Greenleaf's Point," CHS *Rec*, V, 57, 59.

those misfits in American urban society of the day was beginning subtly to make itself felt.

Like all his predecessors except John and John Quincy Adams, President Andrew Jackson was a slaveowner, but at his inaugural reception in 1829 colored people joined the throng that inundated the White House to celebrate. While a newly organized white-sponsored African Education Society undertook to provide "persons of color destined to Africa" with schooling "in letters, Agriculture and Mechanic Arts," early in 1831 Benjamin Lundy began publication in Washington of his newspaper *Genius of Universal Emancipation.* That summer a single vote in the Virginia Assembly defeated a bill for gradual emancipation in the Old Dominion; assemblymen agreed to reconsider the proposal at the next session. Confidence in the Liberia colonization plan undoubtedly heightened whites' interest in the antislavery movement; the scheme simultaneously salved tender consciences and allayed apprehensions about whether any American city, the capital above all, could assimilate a large free Negro population. Washington Negroes, on the other hand, still passionately opposed colonization. In the spring of 1831 a "large and very respectable" gathering of colored people at the African Methodist Episcopal Church formally declared that "the soil that gave us birth is our only true and veritable home." [19] Defiance of white men's plans for them might create a certain amount of ill will toward them, but colored leaders manifestly believed that they could overcome latent hostility by proving their people useful, law-abiding members of a biracial community.

[19] M. B. Smith, *First Forty Years,* 294-97; *N.I.,* 6 Mar 1829, 4 May 1831; Leonidas Polk to Colonel D. Polk, 21 Jan 1829, Leonidas Polk Mss (Southern Historical Collections, University of North Carolina Library, hereafter cited as SHC); *Report of the Proceedings at the Formation of the African Education Society Instituted at Washington, December 28, 1829,* in *Miscellaneous Pamphlets,* 411:20 (L.C.); *The Life, Travels and Opinions of Benjamin Lundy,* pp. 236, 238.

CHAPTER III

THE CHALLENGE OF NEW

ADVERSITY, 1831–1860

In August 1831 a slave insurrection in southern Virginia shattered colored men's dream for the future and terrified white people from Maryland to the Gulf of Mexico. Nat Turner's rebellion caused a revulsion of feeling among whites that not only killed the Virginia emancipation bill when it again came before the Assembly, but led otherwise sensible citizens of the District of Columbia to speak of abolitionists as dangerous agitators and slaves as creatures "unfit for freedom; ignorant, servile, and depraved." Although Georgetowners admitted that free Negroes had behaved better than whites in 1832 when a serious fire broke out in the town, the city fathers for the first time enacted a black code. In general it duplicated Washington's, but among the punishable Negro offenses the new code listed the possession or circulation of literature "calculated to excite insurrection or insubordination among the slaves or colored people . . . and particularly a newspaper called the *Liberator.*" Eight months after the Turner insurrection Benjamin Lundy observed that in Washington "opposition to everything like emancipation runs high." The District's abolition society ceased to meet, and fear of inflammatory abolitionist literature gradually rose to hysteria. It was heightened by an avalanche of petitions from Northerners begging Congress to outlaw slavery in the District.[1]

[1] *Columbian Gazette*, 8 Nov 1831, 30 Aug 1832; *Benjamin Lundy*, p. 277; Samuel Flagg Bemis, *John Quincy Adams and the Union*, p. 340; Kenneth Stampp, *The Peculiar Institution: Slavery in the Antebellum South*, pp. 132-37.

35

Tension reached the bursting point in 1835 when a slave attempted to murder Mrs. William Thornton, widow of the architect who had designed the United States Capitol; hearsay had it that the man had been "inflamed" by abolitionist teachings. As a new arrival from the North, a botany teacher who had come to study and lecture in Washington, had brought with him specimens wrapped in abolitionist newspapers, a visitor to his lodgings, seeing the wrappings, denounced him as an agent sent to stir up local Negroes. His arrest started a week's witch hunt carried on, like many another race riot in America, chiefly by gangs of boys and irresponsible young men out of work. The mob's main objective was the intimidation of free Negroes and "the punishment of such as have circulated the incendiary pamphlets." The mayor, knowing that the half-dozen ward constables could not restrain several hundred angry men, called for military protection. Soldiers and clerks guarded government buildings while citizens enrolled as patrols under the command of the mayor and the head of the District militia. No Negro was injured bodily, but the mob demolished a Negro school and several Negro tenements, broke the windows of a colored church, burned a house of ill fame, and smashed the furnishings of a fashionable restaurant owned by a mulatto, Beverly Snow, who reportedly had made derogatory remarks about the wives of white mechanics.

At the height of the riot a clerk in the Patent Office wrote: "The principal messenger of our office (who is a cold. man) decamped today; it seems there was some danger of the mob getting hold of him. He had been a great patron of the abolition journals, and used to get leave of absence every summer to attend the negro congress at Philadelphia as the Washington delegate." Most Negroes simply laid low, keeping their feelings to themselves. Upper-class whites later attempted to explain that riots in Baltimore coupled with some weeks of layoffs at the Navy Yard had inspired the demonstrations. "Mechanics" deprecated the lawlessness and denied responsibility for it. Nevertheless the "Snow storm" severely damaged the spirit of the community.

White men's shame over the violence intensified rather than lessened their resentment at the mere presence of free blacks in Washington. "We have already too many free negroes and mulattoes in this city, and the policy of our corporate authorities should tend to the diminution of this insolent class," declared an anonymous letter writer. "A motion is now before the Common Council for prohibiting shop-licenses henceforth to this class of people. If they wish to live here, let them become subordinates and laborers, as nature has designed." The city council passed the new ordinance. Thenceforward Negroes could drive carts and hackneys but could not run taverns or eating houses. Urged on by complaints that the black code had "resumed its old character of a dead letter," the municipality also increased the bond required of every Negro family to $1,000 with five white freeholders as surety. The plain intent was to reduce every colored person in Washington to a completely servile status.[2]

Further evidence of change in the prevailing temper of the white community lay in the cessation of local petitions for prohibition of the slave trade. But the flood of appeals from the North reached such a volume and debates in Congress became so bitter that in 1836 the House voted to receive no petitions relating to slavery or the trade in the District. The "gag rule" which John Quincy Adams, "Old Man Eloquent," fought against for the next eight years was a denial of freedom of speech and petition. Yet even newspapermen who disapproved of slavery but believed that local citizens should be allowed to settle their own domestic problems tacitly approved of the gag. The labor

[2] *N.I.*, 6, 11-15, 20, 28 Aug, 15 Sep 1835; [Josephine Seaton,] *William Winston Seaton of the National Intelligencer*, pp. 217-19; William P. Hoyt, "Washington's Living History; The Post Office Fire and Other Matters, 1834-1839," CHS *Rec*, XLVI-XLVII, 63-65; James W. Sheahan, *Corporation Laws of the City of Washington*, pp. 248-50.

paper, the *Washingtonian,* advocated hanging Northerners who invaded the South to stir up slaves. Members of the Grand Jury of Washington County protested in 1837 at what they labeled outside interference; they had maintained silence till then in hope "that time and due reflection" would cause critics of District institutions to stop "their iniquitous proceedings," but now Congress should intervene. Georgetown, long the most liberal of the three District cities in race matters, added her objections to being "the political football of the nation." Leading Washingtonians presented a formal memorial to Congress in 1839: "It is not that your memorialists are slaveholders . . . many of them do not own slaves, and some of them might be forbidden by conscience to hold any, but these, nevertheless, unite with others in this prayer . . . not only from the just respect due to the legal rights of those of their neighbors who do possess slaves, but from a deep conviction that the continual agitation of the subject by those who can have no right to interfere with it is calculated to have an injurious influence on the peace and tranquility of the community." [3] The petitioners, however, had no plan beyond a vague notion of discouraging free people of color from making their homes in the capital.

The attempt to limit the colored population was futile. By 1840 Washington contained, in addition to 1,700 slaves, 4,800 free Negroes. Whatever the difficulties they faced in the District of Columbia, they knew that unless they were willing to move to the alien-seeming North, they could not hope for less unfriendly treatment elsewhere. Northerners in Congress represented to them safeguards against excesses. The "Snow storm" had occurred when Congress was not in session. Here, once any given crisis passed, relaxation of the black code tended to follow. Washington,

---

[3] Bemis, *John Quincy Adams,* pp. 326-83; H Doc 140, 23C, 2S, Ser 274; *Washingtonian,* 10 Dec 1836; *William Winston Seaton,* pp. 265-66; ptns, S24A-G3, 17 Jan 1837, S25A-G4, 7 Feb 1839.

if no longer a sure haven for Negroes, was as safe a place as any below the Mason-Dixon Line.

While a large proportion of the 16,800 white residents of the city would doubtless have welcomed laws forbidding the ingress of more colored people, upper-class white families differentiated between the undesirables and those with admirable qualities. Not every free Negro was law-abiding, but official statistics showing that half the inmates of the penitentiary and jail were Negroes charged with acts of violence or, more frequently, drunkenness and thieving may have reflected the prejudices of the police and the courts quite as clearly as Negro amorality. Colored men who had had the tenacity and ambition to spend years in purchasing their freedom and that of their relatives were unquestionably people of character capable of showing true civic spirit. Although a seemingly dispassionate outlander described Washington's freedmen as "ignorant, poor and vicious," Judge Cranch remarked of the Methodists among them: "They are seldom or never brought before the criminal Courts for misconduct." That was a weighty statement from a jurist with thirty-five years on the bench in a city where local justices of the peace inclined to attribute criminal tendencies to all colored people. Judge Cranch reiterated the judgment given in the Costin case by again ruling that the municipality could enforce a curfew for free Negroes as well as for slaves, but he upheld the right of a colored peddler to sell perfume from door to door in Washington. Some other whites also admitted that their free colored neighbors "constituted a very superior class of their race." [4]

This superiority was most evident among Negroes who had lived for some years in Washington. From them new arrivals learned how to conduct themselves as responsible

[4] H Ex Doc 49, 22C, 2S, Ser 234; H Ex Doc 81, 24C, 1S, Ser 288; H Ex Doc 140, 25C, 2S, Ser 326; Ethan Allen Andrews, *Slavery and the Domestic Slave Trade in the United States*, pp. 119, 121-22, 127-28; *Columbian Gazette*, 20 Aug 1832; 5 *Federal Cases*, No. 2404, Nov 1836.

free men and city-dwellers; those who failed to do so had no recognized place in the distinctive colored community taking form in the 1830's. The struggle for education and the new Negro churches knit that group closely together. John Prout continued to teach at his famous Columbia Institute until his former pupil John F. Cook succeeded him in 1834 and renamed the school the Union Seminary. As head of the largest Negro school in Washington and thus a leader among his fellows, Cook had to flee for his life during the "Snow storm," but he returned a year later, reopened the seminary, and taught even after he was ordained in 1843 by the regional synod as Washington's first colored Presbyterian minister. Of the five or six other schools in the city Louisa Parke Costin's on Capitol Hill was perhaps the best known. Her father provided the schoolhouse. As William Costin had imbued his daughters with a passion for service to their race, upon Louisa's death her younger sister carried on her school until 1839. All told, several hundred colored children yearly obtained some schooling during the thirties. In the interval Negroes organized a Baptist church, two additional Methodist churches, and in 1841 the Colored Presbyterian Church.

The Negro churches were the center of Negro social as well as religious life. While some families still worshiped with white congregations, colored people without any church affiliation had little standing in the Negro community. Class distinctions within it developed early; they still marked it in mid-twentieth century. Lower-class Negroes looked up to superior colored persons as fully as the upper class looked down upon the inferior. Not improbably, well before 1840 all Negroes in Washington were employing the prefix Mr. or Mrs. in speaking of their most respected fellows, the ministers and teachers above all; the rest remained Tom and Sam or Mary and Sally. The appellation "Brother" or "Sis" was reserved for members of the same church as a mark of Christian fellowship. Determination

40

to prove their right to be acknowledged as Americans contributed to the stress upper-class Negroes placed upon exemplary behavior.[5]

Little by little free Negroes overcame the worst of the hostility under which they suffered between 1831 and 1836. When John F. Cook preached his ordination sermon at Washington's Fourth Presbyterian Church, despite the disapproval of part of the congregation at letting a black man occupy a white pulpit for a Sunday, most of his white listeners were as impressed with his dignity as were the colored people who came for the occasion. Negroes ordinarily mingled with the crowds at public outdoor celebrations, although the congressional ruling of 1828 barred them from the terrace of the Capitol where the Marine band played on summer afternoons. They would not again attend an inaugural reception as they had in 1829, but like everybody else they enjoyed the sunshine of March 4, 1837, which made Martin Van Buren's inauguration festive, the more so because bitter weather and President Jackson's feeble health had prevented a parade four years before. Washingtonians, white and black together, cheered as the President-elect, accompanied by a resplendent military escort, rode to the Capitol in a phaeton built of wood from the frigate *Constitution*. Later that year when the famous and still fearsome Black Hawk, Chief Keokuk, and some thirty Sac and Fox braves got off the steam cars at the B & O railroad depot, a fascinated many-complexioned throng gathered and followed them up Pennsylvania Avenue to the beat of Indian drums and the wail of Sac musical instruments.[6]

Living conditions for most Negro families were un-

[5] *Spec Rpt Comr Ed*, pp. 198-204; George W. Williams, *History of the Negro Race in America*, II, 182-85; Lucille W. Wilkinson, "Early Baptists in Washington," CHS *Rec*, xxx, 246, 254-55; William I. Lee, *Nineteenth Street Baptist Church, One Hundredth Anniversary, 1839-1939;* John F. Cook, Diary, Howard Univ Lib.

[6] J. T. Kelly, "The Reverend John C. Smith, D.D.," CHS *Rec*, xxiv, 130-31; *N.I.,* 6 Mar, 2 Oct 1837; William J. Simmons, *Men of Mark, Eminent, Progressive and Rising*, p. 302.

comfortable at best, wretched at worst. Slaves ordinarily occupied quarters at the rear of their masters' house lots, but Washington was probably no stranger to an arrangement not uncommon in other Southern cities whereby bondsmen hiring their own time found places to live with free Negroes. In all likelihood, accommodations were no worse for colored householders than for European immigrants. Sanitation was primitive throughout the city before mid-century. Owners of houses along a two-block stretch of Pennsylvania Avenue had piped water from a nearby spring into their dwellings early in the century, and government office buildings and the White House were similarly supplied from 1832 onward, but most residents had to rely on cisterns or the wells and pumps in the public squares. People generally dumped their slops into the streets, with the result that seepage into the public wells spread dysentery and cholera from time to time. When an epidemic of Asiatic cholera broke out in 1832, the city board of health attributed its ravages to the "large number of foreign emigrants [sic] . . . employed on the public works. Most of these were from Germany and Ireland, men who neither understood our language, nor were accustomed to our climate, habits and mode of living." Physicians noted that the disease was also "extremely fatal to our colored population, and more especially to the free blacks," a comment that pointed to the better care slaves generally received than free Negroes could provide for themselves. Vital statistics were so casually kept that the death toll was a matter of guesswork, but Negro mortality in the antebellum city was presumably as high as that of later years, at least twice that for whites.[7]

Yet some colored families were able to live in modest comfort, and a few acquired enough property to live well. William Costin, for one, owned a number of building lots

[7] M. B. Smith, *First Forty Years*, 335-38; *N.I.*, 8, 29 Aug, 29 Sep 1832, 7, 8 Jan, 10 Apr 1833.

and several houses and carried $300 of insurance on his household furnishings. The prohibition on Negro-run businesses collapsed early; like other provisions of the black code it was a weapon put to use only when white people became frightened and vindictive. Two or three years after the race riot of 1835, Absolom W. Shadd reopened Beverly Snow's restaurant at 6th Street and Pennsylvania Avenue; he sold it twenty years later for $25,000 and moved his family to Canada. Alfred Jones ran a feed store valued by 1860 at some $16,000. While such sums were unusual, industriousness and frugality enabled a score of other men in the 1840's and 1850's to accumulate pieces of real estate and personal property. By pursuing occupations that white men regarded as menial, colored men could earn a competence and sometimes enviable economic security. Cooks were an example, for slave boys, sent by their masters to serve apprenticeships under French chefs in foreign diplomats' households, learned the secrets of French cuisine; the ambitious, if then allowed to hire their own time, could purchase their freedom and eventually set up as caterers with a large clientele ready to pay well for their services. In that fashion James Wormley came to be a man of means: a number of white businessmen who had observed his skills asked him to serve as the steward of a private club on G Street, and, after experience there before the Civil War, he opened his own hotel, which fastidious and wealthy visitors found the most agreeable in the city. For the exceptionally well-educated Negro, moreover, the extremely remote but nonetheless challenging possibility existed of obtaining a salaried government job. Just as a colored man had held the post of chief messenger at the Patent Office in 1835, Solomon G. Brown, thanks to the recommendation of a white mentor, got a departmental appointment in 1844. All told, opportunities in the city were varied enough to draw ambitious Negroes to the District from the nearby states. While the Negro rank and file, and especially newcomers, seldom earned more than a bare subsistence, the success of some of their race inspired many of the rest to emulating effort.[8]

The late 1840's and 1850's nevertheless were a period of growing anxiety for colored people. In 1846 Congress, yielding to pleas of Virginia planters, Alexandria slave traders, and other merchants of the port, retroceded the trans-Potomac third of the ten-mile square to the Old Dominion. The change of jurisdiction held out no benefits to free Negroes in Alexandria. No one kept a tally of the number who left after the retrocession, but some colored families must have preferred to move to the capital, where Northerners might temper the winds of anti-Negro sentiment. Certainly after 1844, when the House of Representatives canceled the gag rule, petitions from Northerners begging Congress to ban the slave trade and abolish slavery in the District of Columbia again began appearing. Yet a good many Yankee residents of Washington had ambivalent feelings about the city's swelling Negro population. A young woman born and bred in New York state wrote soon after her arrival in 1846: "No sane-minded man acquainted with the black population South could wish them liberated and allowed to remain in the States. If the black population could be expelled from the south the greatest advantage would accrue to the white population. Slave labor is the bane of all industry and enterprises, labour is looked upon as so degrading. I think that is the most despicable trait in the southern character . . . and that feeling is engendered by an inferior race of people performing all manual labour."[9] Mary Bowen later changed her mind about eman-

<hr />

[8] Jessie Benton Fremont, *Souvenir of My Time,* pp. 97-98; Robinson, "Some Aspects of the Free Negro Population," pp. 8-13; enumerators' returns, Free Inhabitants, D.C., for 7th and 8th U.S. Census, 1850 and 1860, N.A.; Andrew F. Hilyer, *The Twentieth Century Union League Directory,* pp. 8-10, 44.

[9] Mary Barker Bowen to Harriet Barker Underhill, 14 Nov 1846, Bowen Mss (in possession of Prof. C. A. Barker of The Johns Hopkins University).

cipation as her husband became one of Washington's leading Free-Soilers, but even people who accepted the morality of slavery were beginning to doubt the utility of the peculiar institution in the city; white men spoke of the worthlessness of slaves constantly exposed to the corrupting influence of free blacks.

The shift in white public opinion was by no means universal. In 1848, shortly after Dr. Gamaliel Bailey of Boston began publication in Washington of an antislavery newspaper, the *National Era,* an episode threatened to end the life of the paper before it was well started. On a Sunday morning in April a number of Washington and Georgetown householders awakened to find no breakfast in preparation and the family slaves absconded. Immediate pursuit of the schooner *Pearl,* which had sailed before dawn, discovered the seventy-six slaves aboard bound for the North under the protection of Captain Daniel Drayton. Drayton and his mate were immediately jailed, while an angry mob, sure that Dr. Bailey had abetted the abduction, gathered at his shop to demand that he leave the city. The courage of the captain of police and several private citizens prevented violence, the *National Era* continued publication, and eventually public wrath subsided. The owners of the runaways sold them to dealers who shipped them South, and Drayton and his mate after a prolonged and fiercely fought trial were finally sentenced to long prison terms as kidnapers. But slaveholders' indignation over the Drayton affair did not blind them to the economic disadvantages of slaveowning in the District cities. In December 1848 a conservative Georgetown paper, remarking upon local eagerness to be rid of the slave trade, concluded: "Or, if the public would make provision to purchase out the slaves now held in the District, compensating the owners of them therefore, we do not suppose that the slaveholders of the District would have any serious objection thereto. . . . From the increasing insecurity, and unsatisfactoriness of

45

this kind of property, the pecuniary advantage of slave owners would probably be promoted by such a course." His command evoked no protest.[10]

At the end of the war with Mexico the addition to the United States of a large piece of the continent confronted Congress with the problem of whether to permit the extension of slavery into the new territory. The sectional controversy that ensued quickly became so bitter that it threatened to burst the bonds of the Union. In January 1849 the debate on the Hill widened when an obscure Illinois congressman named Abraham Lincoln introduced a bill for the abolition of slavery in the District of Columbia, a measure which, he contended, a majority of residents would endorse. Fearful of precipitating disaster, Washingtonians kept very quiet about local slaveowning. A memorial signed by about seventy District men, two thirds of them county farmers, merely requested Congress not to change the laws without first obtaining local approval by formal referendum. Prohibition of the slave trade was quite another matter. The Washington city council pronounced it "alike prejudicial to the interests of our city and offensive to public sentiment." Southerners in Congress, on the contrary, believed that to outlaw the trade here would be a first step on a path that would end in enforced emancipation throughout the South. But determination to preserve the Union effected a compromise in 1850. Although disappointing to Washingtonians who had hoped for total abolition, and wholly unsatisfactory to the five or six local dealers and their hangers-on who had been profiting handsomely from the slave trade, the outlawing of the traffic within the federal area met with approval from most District citizens. They subscribed to Henry Clay's view that the new act would "give peace and security to the maintenance of

[10] *National Era,* 4 Feb 1848, 4 Jan 1849; *News,* 22, 29 Apr, 1 Jul, 5, 26 Aug, 7 Oct 1848; *N.I.,* 29 Dec 1848; *Ggtn Advocate,* 30 Dec 1848.

46

slavery within this District, until it exhausts itself by the process of time, as it would seem to be most rapidly doing." [11]

The steady decline in the number of locally owned slaves during the 1850's indicated that Senator Clay and Representative Lincoln had correctly gauged local sentiment. But in District citizens' minds the old quandary remained: how was it possible to prevent their cities from becoming the catch-all for the restless freedmen of Maryland and Virginia? The 70 percent increase in Washington's free colored population during the 1840's perhaps accounted for white men's outward acquiescence in the harsh new Fugitive Slave Act which was a part of the 1850 compromise; for runaways in the District, if unapprehended, would usually be absorbed into the city's free Negro community and expand it further. A good many whites were ready to try any workable legal method of keeping the proportion of blacks to whites in Washington to its then 26 percent. The Colonization Society held out no prospect of a mass migration of Negroes to Liberia. Baltimore, protected by Maryland laws forbidding the ingress of freedmen from other states, was only 20 percent colored, St. Louis, in slaveowning Missouri, 5.4 percent, and Cincinnati, adjacent to slaveholding Kentucky, 2.8 percent. An enforceable black code, unlike those of the past, seemed to be the one measure that might serve in Washington. The city council accordingly tried modifications. They reduced the peace bond to $50 for every free Negro over twelve years of age and required the surety of only one white freeholder, but every colored person applying for residence had to report within five days of his arrival or pay the penalty of a fine or a term in the workhouse, followed in either case at the magistrate's discretion by expulsion from the city. The mayor's express permission

[11] *Congressional Globe,* 30C, 2S, pp. 212, 31C, 1S, 944-48, 1743-44, 1794-95, 1810, 1837, 1954 and appendix, p. 1647; ptns, H30A-G5.1, 7 Feb 1849.

47

was required for any public gathering of Negroes, and secret meetings were forbidden.[12]

Local magistrates now and again meted out excessively harsh punishments to Negroes for trivial offenses. Frederick Law Olmsted, a New York newspaperman on a fact-finding journey through the seaboard slave states in 1853, wrote of twenty-four "genteel colored men," as the police record described them, arrested in Washington for meeting privately to devise plans "to relieve the sick and bury the dead" and to purchase the freedom of a young slave woman; four of the men were sent to the workhouse and the others fined $111. In proportion to the size of the colored population, Negro arrests throughout the decade were three times as frequent as white. But the results of strict law enforcement during a three-year period satisfied the local authorities. By 1854 only 8 of the 603 persons sent to the workhouse were committed for being "out after set hours" and only two for being "resident without bonds." Gradually white fears of a black inundation waned, for, contrary to alarmists' predictions, the 1850's saw an increase of only 1,050 free Negroes in Washington compared to 3,350 in the 1840's. While the white population rose in ten years by nearly 69 percent, the increase for slave and free Negro together was less than 7 percent. The colored population of Georgetown dropped at the same time from 27 to 22 percent of the whole; by 1860 the town had about four hundred fewer free Negroes and slaves than a decade before.[13]

If the federal Fugitive Slave Act of 1850 was partly responsible for preventing an illegal expansion of the District's free colored population, the workings of the law in

[12] *News*, 2, 23, 30 Nov, 7 Dec 1850; *Seventh U.S. Census*, 1850, pp. 221, 235-36, 662, 830; Sheehan, *Corporation Laws*, pp. 250-54.

[13] *News*, 22 Apr 1854, 23 Jan 1858; *Evening Star*, 22 Aug 1859, 5 Apr 1860 (hereafter cited as *Star*); *Washington Laws*, 15 Dec 1853, 3 Apr 1854, 14 Nov 1856; Frederick Law Olmsted, *A Journey in the Seaboard Slave States in the Years 1853-1854*, 1904 ed., I, 16-17. See Tables I and II.

other respects distressed more than a few conscientious white residents. The sizable rewards offered in the frequent advertisements in the local press for the capture of Maryland and Virginia runaways corrupted unscrupulous men into acting as slave chasers, and, while outright kidnapings apparently were seldom successful—and certainly less often than tales told in the North suggested—free Negroes were subject to more harassment than humane whites could readily stomach. It gave Washington a bad name outside the South and left decent white citizens of the capital with a mounting sense of guilt and impotence. Although the Free Soil Party steadily gained adherents in the District after 1855, slowly shifting political sentiment was of little immediate help to the colored community.[14]

Yet in spite of spasmodically rigid surveillance, considerable police brutality toward Negroes suspected of minor transgressions, and all too frequent attacks by white bullies, hard-working Negro families who observed the law meticulously made astonishing progress and won new respect from upper-class whites. The mayors, waiving the city ordinances, repeatedly granted shop- and restaurant-keepers' licenses to colored men. White workingmen, to be sure, particularly Irish immigrants who depended upon common laborers' jobs, seized every opportunity to proclaim their own superiority. Irishmen's resentment of blacks deepened when voters elected a Know-Nothing mayor in 1854, for, as the Know Nothing Party was intensely hostile to foreigners and Roman Catholics, immigrants tended to vent their anger on the only people lower than themselves in the city's social hierarchy. Their antagonism, however, failed to halt the Negroes' upward climb. Although circumspect behavior was no guarantee of freedom from persecution, hundreds of free colored people lived peacefully in the District of Columbia

[14] William Goodell, *Slavery and Anti-Slavery in the United States,* pp. 226, 243-46; Laprade, "Domestic Slave Trade," *Journal of Negro History,* XI, 19-34; B. B. French to H. F. French, 30 Jun, 9 Dec 1855, 29 May, 15 Jul 1856, B. B. French Mss (L.C.).

during these years when white men were endeavoring to drive them altogether out of the Deep South.[15]

Hope that the compromise of 1850 had ended sectional controversy fell apart in 1854 as soon as debates opened in Congress over the territorial organization of Kansas and Nebraska. While the protracted fight over keeping "bleeding Kansas" free territory did not directly affect the position of Negroes in the capital, the worsening political climate induced by the struggle throughout the country was ominous. Utter catastrophe struck colored people in 1857 when the Supreme Court rendered its decision in the Dred Scott case: the decree announced that persons of African descent were not and could never be American citizens. At a stroke of Chief Justice Taney's pen, the future for Washington's colored community crumbled. The decades of effort Negroes had invested in proving themselves worthy of acceptance seemed wasted. Even the abolition of slavery throughout the nation would not assure Afro-Americans a dignified place in American society. Still, because no other course seemed possible, colored men in the District cities quietly continued the struggle for self betterment. And a growing number of whites encouraged them.

Although the proposal of a mayoral candidate to open colored public schools died with his defeat, at the end of the fifties over 42 percent of the free colored population was literate, and some 1,100 Negro children were attending private schools. On the "Island," the section of Washington cut off from the rest of the city by the canal that linked the Eastern Branch near Arsenal Point with the Potomac below the White House, Arabella Jones, one-time servant in John Quincy Adams' household, conducted an unusually fine school for girls. Under the aegis of the priest at St. Matthews, white teachers instructed pupils at the St. Vin-

[15] *News,* 6 Sep 1851, 14, 17 Sep 1853, 9 Jan 1854; *Ntl Era,* 19 Apr 1855; *Washington and Georgetown Directory,* 1855, 1858 and 1860; enumerator's return, Free Inhabitants, D.C., for the eighth U.S. Census, 1860.

50

cent de Paul Free Catholic Colored School. At the Union Seminary John Cook's pupils, divided into a male and a female department, studied composition, the scriptures, reading, "recitation," a manual of morals, and physiology, including the teeth, the respiratory organs, and—perhaps a matter of special interest to his students—the skin. Probably here as in most of the other schools, whether taught by colored teachers or white, children got at most a sound elementary education. Miss Myrtilla Miner's "high school" went much further. The colored girls enrolled there received a better education than that available to most white children. Miss Miner, a frail middle-aged white woman from New York state, opened her school in 1851 with the backing of Friends and such ardent abolitionists as Harriet Beecher Stowe. The quality of the teaching, the range of subjects, and the pervasive atmosphere of mutual affection and mannerliness between white staff and Negro pupils combined to make Miss Miner's such a model institution that envious white people objected. Ex-Mayor Walter Lenox accused her of educating colored children beyond their station in life and warned the city that her activities might turn Washington into a Negro educational center. Unhappily, ill health and the outbreak of war forced her to close the school in 1861.[16]

Religious faith helped many a colored family to withstand the mounting pressures of the late 1850's. The congregations at the 19th Street Baptist Church and the Asbury Methodist Church now worshiped in buildings of their own, although white pastors assisted by colored docents conducted the services for Asbury parishioners. Members of the 15th Street Colored Presbyterian Church carpeted the church floor, installed handsome chandeliers, and took pride in having the

[16] *Spec Rpt Comr Ed*, pp. 313-22, Ser 1427; illiteracy figures computed from *Seventh U.S. Census*, 1850, pp. 235-37, and *Eighth Census*, 1860, *Misc Statistics*, p. 508; John Cook's Diary, 1850-1851, ms (Howard Univ); *News*, 9 May 1857; *Ntl Era*, 14 May 1857; Ellen M. O'Connor, *Myrtilla Miner, A Memoir*, pp. 59-79.

51

most famous choir in the city. On Sundays devout Negroes could forget the tribulations of week days. In most of the white churches, on the other hand, dissension over the slavery issue divided congregations. Even among Quakers and Unitarians who disapproved of the peculiar institution, opinion split over whether or not Christian duty demanded political action. A young Unitarian clergyman was dismissed for speaking out against the do-nothing course. A few white men must have secretly helped the Washington station of the underground railway smuggle slaves north to free soil, but such deeds were too dangerous to talk about; no record of who participated ever appeared. While the Roman Catholic parishes permitted no racial discrimination, segregated seating and segregated ministration of communion generally obtained in the Protestant churches. Yet Dr. Bailey of the *National Era,* the publisher of *Uncle Tom's Cabin,* believed that although white Washingtonians usually failed to recognize "the thrift and industry of the great mass" of their colored neighbors and the "dignity, decorum and good taste they display," racial toleration was wider spread here than in most Northern cities.[17]

When John Brown's raid at Harpers Ferry in October 1859 threw the United States into turmoil, rumors ran through the capital that "hostile demonstrations from outside the city" were about to take place. For twenty-four hours crowds waiting for news gathered about the hotels and the telegraph offices, while vague talk of an attack on the *National Era* office went the rounds. But no disorders occurred. For a year thereafter permanent residents trod warily, realizing that any incident could set off an explosion in the city with no one knew what disastrous consequences. In the summer of 1860 the nomination of Abraham Lincoln as presidential candidate of the new Republican Party troubled Washington's arch conservatives, but by then the city contained a good many Free-Soilers, and the newly

[17] *Ntl Era,* 9 Nov 1854, 27 Mar, 11 Dec 1856, 30 Jun 1859; *Star,* 19 Dec 1857, 22 Jun, 12 Aug, 5 Dec 1859, 27 Jul 1860.

elected city council included several avowed Republicans. A week before the presidential election, when a parade of five hundred Republican "Wide-Awakes" followed by a few Negroes marched up Pennsylvania Avenue, some of the on-lookers shouted: "Damn niggers! They oughtn't to be allowed on the streets." The outburst was brief; an Indiana congressman calmed the crowd by reminding the vociferous that Republicans wanted only to stop the expansion of slavery into the territories.[18] Still everyone knew that the next occupant of the White House might determine not only the fate of slavery in the United States but the future of the nation itself. No District citizen could vote in the election. The white community, like the colored, could only wait.

With the possible exception of New Orleans, no other American city in which the proportion of colored people was high offered them wider opportunities than they had in antebellum Washington and Georgetown. In sixty years slavery had lost ground as a locally acceptable institution; it endured but largely on sufferance and with the tacit as-sumption that in time it would disappear. A great many whites still looked upon abolitionists as anarchists, but property owners were determined never again to let fear of "outside interference" in local affairs create race riots. Men long resident in the District of Columbia saw what had not been clear earlier, that the two races would have to live side by side in amity. Some whites unquestionably still believed dangerous any move that might encourage Negroes to reach beyond the lowly position to which the Creator speaking through the white man's Holy Writ had assigned them, but a majority of upper-class whites were adjusting themselves to the idea of having colored people of growing self-sufficiency living alongside. While economic insecurity nursed the racial antagonisms of lower-class whites, the attitude of their social superiors weakened their

[18] *Star*, 18-20 Oct 1859, 4 May, 5 Jun, 10 Jul, 29 Oct 1860.

belligerence. Whether more than a handful of white citizens could contemplate a society in which Negroes had political and legal equality is highly doubtful, but Washington and Georgetown as a whole had nevertheless evolved over the years a scheme of racial coexistence far less biased than that of most of the South.

The bright hope that life in the federal city had once held for free Negroes had dimmed early in the century. Black code succeeding black code had narrowed their scope. But adversity, so far from crushing them, had drawn them into a tight-knit, self-respecting community. In spite of the geographic dispersion of Negroes common within antebellum cities below the Mason-Dixon Line, colored people in Washington, scattered as they were from the Navy Yard area to Rock Creek, had developed a cohesiveness rarely equaled among other Negro city-dwellers. Here far-sighted selfless leaders intent upon educating their fellows had not only provided schooling for their children but taught newcomers how to behave as responsible members of the group. And their numbers, though more than nine times as large in 1860 as half a century before, had multiplied slowly enough to make possible the assimilation of families come to the city from rural surroundings. Compared to most colored people elsewhere in America, Negroes in the capital had prospered. They had weathered the "Snow storm" of the 1830's with an eventual slight gain in status. Twenty years later even the deadly blow of the Dred Scott decision had not completely broken their spirit, and white responses to the decree little by little had restored to them a modicum of confidence. By 1860 educated Negroes looked to a day when no municipal restrictions would bar them from occupations and professions for which their individual talents qualified them. Assuming they could maintain their influence over new arrivals, established Negro families in the District cities faced the future with faith in their capacity ultimately to win a dignified place for their people in the white world around them.

54

CHAPTER IV

CIVIL WAR AND SOCIAL

REVOLUTION, 1861-1865

 "Abraham Lincoln, the Black Republican, is elected President of the United States, the greatest calamity that has ever befallen the United States," a North Carolinian wrote from Washington on November 8, 1860. "The sun that rose on Tuesday morning cast its bright rays on a powerful & noble Republic, in the evening it went down on a ruined and tattered Union, for such I believe will be the result." [1] Perhaps colored men in Washington half hoped for a break-up of the Union and the end of the "slavocracy's" power in Northern counsels, but, like white men, they could envisage the immediate disastrous consequences. If war came, everybody would suffer. If the Union were to split peacefully, the Northern states would almost certainly insist on moving the capital to a new site, and Washington and Georgetown would then revert to being small river ports without a future. The two cities' 11,000 free Negroes could not influence the course of events, but the well informed among them watched and again waited anxiously.

In December, South Carolina members of Congress, announcing that their state had seceded from the Union, stuck Palmetto cockades in their hats and left Washington for home. In January, Georgia, North Carolina, and the Gulf states followed that example, and while delegates met in Montgomery, Alabama, to draft a constitution for the Confederate States of America, Northern congressmen listened

[1] Andrew Harllee to John Harllee, 8 Nov 1860, William Curry Harllee Mss (SHC).

55

to tales of a conspiracy that would deliver the capital on the Potomac into the hands of the Confederacy. Thirty-odd "well-known and esteemed gentlemen of the District" thereupon undertook to enlist and train companies of volunteers to protect the federal District from invaders. In February delegates from Maryland, Virginia, and the other border states met with Northern representatives at the Willard Hotel on Pennsylvania Avenue in an earnest endeavor to reach a compromise that would reestablish and preserve the Union. At the end of the month, as the conference broke up without finding any acceptable remedy, a gaunt, uncouthlooking six-footer unobtrusively moved into the lodgings reserved for the President-elect. Five days later under a lowering sky Abraham Lincoln, accompanied by a cavalry guard, drove down Pennsylvania Avenue to the Capitol, took the oath of office, and delivered his inaugural address to an attentive, undemonstrative crowd gathered about the steps of the East Portico.[2] In defiance of the thirty-year-old order forbidding Negroes to enter the Capitol grounds, a few colored people doubtless formed part of that audience. They had quite as much at stake as other Americans, indeed rather more.

During the months that followed, swift-moving events succeeded by intervals of paralyzing uncertainty confused white and colored Washington alike. In mid-April when South Carolinians fired on the American flag flying over Fort Sumter in Charleston harbor and forced the evacuation of the United States garrison, an uneasy peace turned into war. Virginia seceded from the Union a few days later. Companies of volunteers and regiments of militia from Northern states soon began to pour into the capital. Billeted in tents on the public squares and in the Capitol until the government opened camps outside the city limits, soldiers

---

[2] *Star*, 11, 13, 18, 22, 26 Dec 1860, 22, 23 Feb, 4 Mar 1861; H Rpt 79, 36C, 2S, Ser 1105; Charles P. Stone, "Washington on the Eve of War," *Century Magazine*, IV (Jul 1883), pp. 458-64; *N.I.*, 27 Feb 1861.

were everywhere. Some of them had never seen a colored person before and probably enjoyed occasionally tossing a small "darky" a penny for running an errand. But all Negroes had to be on their guard. Fugitive slaves from the Maryland countryside were taking cover in the District, and federal marshals, in attempting to return the property of citizens of a state still loyal to the Union, were prone to make mistakes. Furthermore, despite the nearly 50,000 raw troops stationed in and about the capital spending money freely while awaiting orders to march across the Potomac to crush the rebels in a single battle, times were hard that spring in Washington and Georgetown. Colored men with carts got some work hauling army supplies from the wharves and railroad depot, but the disorganization of the War Department delayed payment for services, and the price of foodstuffs rose at a dizzying rate. As pickpockets and gamblers swarmed into the city, Negroes had to take special precautions to avoid arrest for white men's thieving.[3]

Toward the end of July a confident light-hearted army crossed the Long Bridge into Virginia to teach the rebels a lesson. The Union defeat in the first Battle of Bull Run, fought scarcely thirty miles south of Washington, stripped the capital of optimism about an early victory over the South. Of necessity citizens settled down grimly to the tasks ahead. By late fall newcomers arriving to fill the multiplying government posts or to meet the personal needs of the swelling temporary population had restored a measure of prosperity to the District cities, and by the next spring the demand for food, lodging, household wares, and clothing set off a business boom. But although operations at the Navy Yard expanded and Washington became the chief hospital and supply center for the Army of the Potomac, the upward spiral of living costs tended to outrun wage increases for

[3] *Star*, 11-12, 15-20, 22-23 Apr, 14 May, 25 Jun, 2 Jul 1861; *N.I.*, 13, 18 Jun 1861; Alexander Howard Meneely, *The War Department, 1861*, pp. 111-18, 149-53, 182-83; Rpt, Secretary of the Interior, 1861, pp. 911-13, Ser 1117, 1862, p. 649, Ser 1157.

workingmen. As most Negroes fell into the category of laborer, the colored community was particularly hard hit, and because government salaries were fixed at rates set in 1853, colored men on the federal payroll also felt the pinch.[4]

Meanwhile, another problem, social as well as economic, was confronting the city. Weeks before the first Battle of Bull Run, fugitive slaves from Virginia in larger numbers than for years past had been finding their way into the capital. The most legalistically minded magistrate in the District of Columbia could see the impropriety of returning the property of rebels, but who was to be responsible for slaves without masters? In June 1861 General Ben Butler, in command at Fortress Monroe, produced the formula for justifying the army's custody of runaways; they were "contraband."[5] Relieved at so simple a legal evasion, the entire North adopted the term. But as the stream of black field hands, old men, women, and children trickled over the Long Bridge day after day and month after month, worries beset Washington. Most of the newcomers, unfamiliar with city life and accustomed to constant supervision, were unprepared to fend for themselves. Someone had to attempt to find them employment, to house, feed, and clothe them until they could support themselves, to watch over their health lest they suffer needlessly or spread epidemics, and to prevent them from turning lawless.

Contrabands, termed by Secretary of State Seward "the property of the United States," were not free people during the first fifteen months of the war. Protégés of the government though they were—"government pets" a Southern sympathizer called them—until Congress passed a law in July 1862 expressly freeing them, they were not safe from arrest as runaways. If jailed on any pretext, a contraband was likely to be at the mercy of the new warden of the Dis-

[4] Rpt Sec/Int, 1862, p. 649, Ser 1157, 1863, pp. 719-24, Ser 1182; *Star*, 6 Feb, 2 Mar 1862, 4 Apr, 14 Sep 1863.

[5] *N.I.*, 1 Jun 1861; S Misc Doc 2, 37C, 2S, Ser 1124; *Star*, 7 Apr, 19 May 1862.

trict jail, a notorious Negro-hater who reportedly sold more than one free colored man into slavery.[6] A Negro refugee from Virginia might have difficulty in proving that he was not a Maryland fugitive salable for jail fees when no master claimed him. Most Marylanders early in the war abandoned attempts to recapture their runaways in the District of Columbia, where mobs or Union soldiers undertook now and again to abduct slaves before the federal marshal could get them back to their lawful owners. Although that kind of disturbance largely ceased before the repeal of the Fugitive Slave Act in July 1864 and Maryland's adoption of a new state constitution outlawing slavery,[7] passions aroused over the place of colored people in the scheme of things contributed to the turmoil in Washington.

If anyone dared believe contrabands merely a temporary phenomenon, certainly no Washingtonian questioned the permanence of the social change effected by a congressional act of April 1862 emancipating the 3,100 slaves owned by District citizens. The act ensured owners compensation and included a provision for colonizing freedmen outside the United States; nobody put faith in the colonization plan. While the bill was under debate, white householders, fearful of the timing, fought the main proposal with petitions and memorials, published letters, and newspaper editorials. Mayor Wallach and the majority of Washington's councilmen besought Congress to delay legislation which at this "critical juncture in our national affairs" would convert the city, "located as it is between two slaveholding states, into an asylum for free negroes, a population undesirable in

[6] *Star,* 5 Dec 1861, quoting ltr, Secretary of State Seward to General McClellan; *Star,* 4 Dec 1861, 16 Jan, 13 Feb, 22 May 1862; *Cong Globe,* 37C, 2S, pp. 412-13; H Rpt 11, 37C, 2S, Ser 1144; S Rpt 60, 37C, 2S, pp. 1-5, Ser 1125; Diary of William Owner, 5 Apr 1862; *National Republican,* 14 Aug 1862; *Daily Chronicle,* 15 Apr, 31 Jul, 1 Aug, 2 Sep 1863; 12 *United States Statutes at Large,* 589-92 (hereafter cited as —Stat—).

[7] *Republican,* 24, 28 Feb 1862; *Star,* 17, 22, 23 May 1862; *Chronicle,* 15 Apr, 13 May 1863.

every American community, and which it has been deemed necessary to exclude altogether from some even of the non-slaveholding states." [8] The strongly proadministration *National Republican* supported the bill on the grounds that Washington would benefit from "the free principles and free industry which have built up the great cities of the North," but the *Star* and the *Intelligencer,* although favoring gradual emancipation, insisted it should be in conjunction with the border states, and both papers deplored the burden to be put upon local taxpayers to care for infirm and helpless ex-slaves. The *Star,* moreover, considered the compensation offered, $300 at most for each slave, wholly inadequate. Probably the *Intelligencer* summed up fairly the prevailing white point of view: no one would regret the end of slavery in the District were the act not plainly a first move toward congressional "regulation of society of the slave states." That reason heightened the gratification of colored people.

Emancipation in the District of Columbia marked the first break in sixty years in the protective wall about slavery. To the joy of the colored community, the repeal of the municipal black codes followed within a matter of weeks, thereby opening up new opportunities to enterprising Negroes. Colored men could now engage in any kind of business and several who had patrons on the Hill obtained custodial posts in the government. Negroes, no longer impeded by a curfew, could occupy the "nigger heaven" at Grover's Theatre.[9] Intelligent colored people, nevertheless, almost certainly foresaw that an inundation of black field hands from the South would create acute difficulties for all Washington residents. In the past, Negro newcomers had arrived a few at a time, in a fashion that had permitted local Negro leaders to indoctrinate them in the obligations

[8] *Cong Globe,* 37C, 2S, App., pp. 347-48; *Star,* 19, 21, 25 Mar 1862; *Republican,* 20 Aug, 24 Sep 1862; ptn, S37A-J4, 2 Apr 1862.

[9] *Republican,* 15 Feb 1862; *Star,* 8, 17, 29 Mar, 4 Apr 1862; *N.I.,* 4, 12, 17 Apr 1862.

incumbent upon all members of the city's self-respecting and self-protecting Negro group. A mass migration would make that kind of tutelage impossible.

Yet the pessimists of both races were not immediately proved right in anticipating serious trouble. Household slaves who had long lived in Washington and Georgetown in frequent association with free Negroes had learned something about the responsibilities of freedom; a few went North, some took service with army officers, and others apparently stayed on as paid servants to their former masters. The contrabands, on the other hand, were generally trained only to the hoe. Loath as they were to leave the District, where they felt sure of government protection, contrary to every expectation they were not at first a heavy financial burden upon the community. During 1862 about four hundred lived in Duff Green's Row on East Capitol Street where seventy years later the Folger Shakespeare Library would stand. As the early comers moved out to live with other Negro families in Washington or found quarters of their own, new arrivals moved into the Row. Others huddled into improvised shacks about the forts on the District perimeter. Ignorant, penniless, ragged, dirty, and hungry on arrival, some of them never adjusted to the new mode of life, but until the number of contrabands ran into thousands, a good many of those ex-field hands, aided by the government and private philanthropy, got on astonishingly well.[10]

In March 1862 humane people in Washington and the North organized first a local and then a national Freedmen's Relief Association to furnish contrabands "clothing, temporary homes, and employment, and, as far as possible, to teach them to read and write, and bring them under moral influences." [11] Federal officials, moreover, saw that the gov-

[10] H Ex Doc 42, 37C, 3S, p. 8, Ser 1189; *Republican,* 31 Oct 1862; *Star,* 30 May 1862.

[11] National Freedmen's Relief Association, *First Annual Report,* 1863 (hereafter cited as NFR Assn); *Star,* 22 Mar, 10 Apr 1862.

ernment must undertake a systematic program for handling the multiplying throng. In June the governor of the Military District of Washington appointed the former head of the Chicago Reform School to be superintendent of a "contraband department" with headquarters at an army barracks on the outskirts of the city at north 12th and O streets. There contrabands registered and received passes to ensure them military protection. The government furnished them rations and employed the able-bodied men at forty cents a day at the army corrals, at menial tasks in and about the military hospitals, and in repairing the avenues used for army transport. The Freedmen's Relief Association provided clothing and food for the ill. When the military converted Duff Green's Row into a prison, the contraband department moved its charges to tents at "Camp Barker" adjacent to its own headquarters. Till the end of 1862 these arrangements sufficed, although the number of refugees grew from about 400 in April to some 4,200 in October. The superintendent, defending the work of his department, declared that all of his charges except a very few old and infirm had found work. Employers in the Northern and Western states were eager to hire these Negroes, but "not *one* in a *hundred* can in anywise be persuaded to go North." [12] He later added that they seldom saved their earnings, a few enjoyed idleness, and drunkenness was increasing, but they were generally "a docile people," [13] a term usually meaning to the abolitionist "teachable."

By the spring of 1863, in addition to the 3,000 in Alexandria, 10,000 contrabands had gathered in Washington. And they continued to pour in: by 1865 some estimates put the four-year total of black newcomers at 40,000. In April 1863 a few colored families moved across the Eastern Branch

[12] *Star*, 30 May, 24 Oct 1862; *Republican*, 21 Jul, 11 Aug, 31 Oct 1862; *Chronicle*, 3, 11 Nov, 1 Dec 1862.

[13] "Reports and Addresses," *Documents Relating to Freedmen*, 16 Dec 1862, pp. 9-11 (Howard Univ Library).

TABLE II
POPULATION OF THE CITY OF WASHINGTON[a]

	1800	1810	1820	1830	1840	1850	1860	1870
TOTAL	3,210	8,208	13,247	18,827	23,364	40,001	61,122	109,199
TOTAL WHITE	2,464	5,904	9,606	13,365	16,843	29,730	50,139	73,731
Native						24,817[b]	48,299[b]	59,974
Foreign-born						4,913[b]	12,465[b]	13,757
Germany and Austria							3,254[b]	4,159
United Kingdom							1,306[b]	1,557
Ireland							7,258[b]	6,948
TOTAL NEGRO	746	2,304	3,641	5,448	6,521	10,271	10,983	35,392
Free	123	867	1,696	3,129	4,808	8,158	9,209	
Slave	623	1,437	1,945	2,319	1,713	2,113	1,774	
% Negro of total pop.	23.24	28.07	27.48	28.93	27.92	25.68	17.97	32.38
% Free Negro of total pop.	3.83	10.56	12.80	16.61	20.58	20.39	15.06	
% Free Negro of color pop.	16.48	37.63	46.88	57.43	73.50	79.42	83.83	
% Foreign-born of total pop.						12.28	17.61	12.59
% Foreign-born of white pop.						16.19	21.49	22.93
% Increase in white pop. in ten years		139.65	62.70	28.86	25.89	76.14	68.98	40.60
% Increase in Negro pop. in ten years		208.84	58.02	49.61	19.69	57.51	6.93	222.24
% Increase in Free Negro pop. in ten years		604.87	95.61	84.49	52.75	69.67	12.88	

[a] Compiled from U.S. *Census*, Second through Ninth

[b] Figures for entire District, but since the growth of the white population between 1810 and 1850 was only 2,545 in Georgetown and 925 in the county, and during the next decade 718 and 1,696, respectively, the assumption seems reasonable that the bulk of European immigration was into Washington. The rapid increase in the white population of the county between 1850 and 1860, however, may have been the result of immigrants' choosing to live in the cheap quarters available across the Eastern Branch in and about Uniontown.

into "a vast wilderness," as one man described the area today known as Hillsdale, and in May the government opened a contraband village across the Potomac in the bottomlands of Arlington on Confederate General Robert E. Lee's confiscated estate; there a thousand Negroes raised hay and vegetables for the army. A year later the contraband department persuaded about 3,000 more to move to the village from the northern sections of Washington. But most freedmen refused to budge from the District. Their ignorance of elementary hygiene coupled with the overcrowding in the government quarters or the housing they found for themselves rapidly converted whole areas of Washington into breeding spots for small pox and other diseases.[14]

Living conditions deteriorated steadily. Shanties sprang up in the alleyways, and, on the swampy land along the lower stretches of the Washington Canal, the clusters of huts pieced together from scrap lumber, tar paper, and odd bits of junk composed a slum that won the name "Murder Bay." "I have visited the freedmen in their cabins," wrote one man in the last year of the war, "their sufferings are most heart rending. The weather is cold; they have little or no wood. Snow covers the ground; and they have a scanty supply of rags called clothes. The hospital is crowded with the sick. . . . Government gives them a very, *Very* small allowance of soup. Ninety gallons was given yesterday; but what is that to feed thousands of families. . . . The feeling against them, among many in this place, is bitter, malignant, devilish. . . . Many will die."[15] Many did die, exactly how many no record told.

[14] NFR Assn, *1st Anl Rpt*, pp. 1-6; S Ex Doc 53, 38C, 1S, Ser 1176; *Chronicle*, 6, 7 Nov, 5, 9, 15 Dec 1862, 7 Jan, 19 Feb, 9 Apr, 14 Aug 1863, 31 May 1864, 2 Mar 1865; *Republican*, 3 Jul 1862; S Rpt 17, 38C, 1S, Ser 1178; Medical Society of D.C., *Report*, 1864; *Star*, 22 May, 31 Aug, 4 Dec 1863, 14 Jul 1864; Wade H. Carter, ed., "Anacostia," typescript notes compiled 26 Sep 1921 after meetings of the survivors of the first settlers on the Barry Farm (hereafter cited as Barry Farm notes).

[15] *The National Freedman*, I, 1 Mar 1865, p. 60.

While more than a few white Washingtonians were generous in their help, the kindness well-established colored families showed the newcomers was more remarkable, for the contraband invasion threatened the complete disruption of the well-ordered colored community. Throughout the South, a sociologist of mixed blood later wrote, "generations of distrust had built up a wall of enmity between the darker-skinned field hands and the favored mulatto house servants." That enmity had not appeared in antebellum Washington and Georgetown, since virtually all slaves had been household servants except for the temporary gangs that "masters in distant places" hired out on construction jobs; and nearly half the free colored people of both cities had some white blood. Now alien blacks seemed about to engulf them all, as whites appeared increasingly prone to make no distinction between educated, responsible colored people and the mass of ignorant, often shiftless freedmen flooding in from the South. When Negro delegates from Northern cities met in Washington to celebrate the eighteenth anniversary of the founding of the Grand United Order of Colored Odd Fellows, a military guard had to accompany the parade to "quell any outbreak."

The upper stratum of the Negro community struggled to preserve its position as best it could. In 1863 a group of colored men, some of them government clerks, organized the Lotus Club, to which only leading Negroes might belong. White people and contrabands knew nothing about it, and yet its founding was a significant event in a city where only twelve months before a curfew had interfered with all Negro social life. Insofar as the club's originators intended it to set a standard of civilized behavior, they fell short of their aim, for the very exclusiveness of the organization soon encouraged a form of unwholesome snobbery. The Freedmen's Relief Association congratulated colored Washingtonians for "contributing largely to [freedmen's] comfort from their slender stores," but the praise contained

65

a note of condescension and failed to recognize the rapidly widening rift between upper- and lower-class Negroes.[16]

The predominant white attitude toward all colored people became increasingly hostile from mid-1862 onward. As the proportion of Negroes in the population rose, apprehensions grew about what Congress would next force upon Washington and Georgetown. Joseph Henry, secretary of the Smithsonian Institution, was so troubled over the mounting tension in the city that he refused to let abolitionists lecture at the Smithsonian. The history of the preceding fifteen years and the report of the commissioners appointed by the President to handle the compensation of local slaveowners indicate clearly that citizens reluctant to have emancipation go into effect in wartime had nevertheless generally recognized the ultimate, if not the immediate, rightness of the law. But emancipation was only a beginning. After the repeal of the municipal black codes white people felt they had lost control of irresponsible blacks. Not infrequently the misdeeds of contrabands who used their new freedom to turn to thieving or worse were attributed to their law-abiding fellows; complaints against all Negroes multiplied. As early as July 1862 a congressional committee reported that with the disappearance of the legal barriers established by slavery, "the prejudice of caste becomes stronger and public opinion more intolerant to the negro." White supremacy, a phrase not as yet coined, had been a basic social premise too long to be discarded quickly and painlessly. Government protection could not guarantee black people toleration. Hoodlums attacked Negroes on the least provocation or none. The Washington and Georgetown Street Railroad Company refused to permit them to ride inside its cars until Congress threatened to revoke its charter and later expressly forbade discriminatory seating on all street rail-

[16] Pauli Murray, *Proud Shoes, The Story of an American Family*, p. 53; *Star*, 5 Jun 1862, 9 Oct 1863; *Chronicle*, 6 Jun 1864; NFR Assn, *1st Anl Rpt*; enumerator's return, Free Inhabitants, D.C., 8th U.S. Census, 1860, NA.

ways and railroads in the District.[17] Meanwhile new colored school laws and the enlistment of colored troops crystallized the resentment of white people.

The law enacted in May 1862 requiring Washington, Georgetown, and the county to open public schools for Negro children met with only brief opposition from whites. As the 58 percent illiteracy among free colored adults before the war climbed to an undetermined figure after the freeing of slaves and the influx of contrabands, white people could admit the wisdom of helping Negro education, if only because an ignorant colored population, no longer restrained by the black code, might be a danger to society. By the terms of the law, 10 percent of the taxes on Negro property was to be set aside to finance colored schools under the supervision of a board of trustees to be appointed by the Secretary of the Interior. The colored schools were thus legally under federal control, although the money was to come from local taxes. Congress, persuaded that Negro property in Washington and Georgetown was extensive, expected the arrangement to produce some $3,600 yearly, enough to start a primary school system. Neither city, however, kept separate records of white and colored taxes; officials merely allotted what they thought just to the trustees of the colored schools—Washington $265 in 1862 and $410 in 1863, Georgetown nothing in 1862, $70 the next year. No white taxpayer had to feel alarmed over those sums.[18]

The American Tract Society of New York had started a free school for contrabands in the spring of 1862. Soon afterward the National Freedmen's Relief Association had opened two evening schools and eighteen months later a day school on the Island, that section of the city enclosed

[17] Thomas Coulson, *Joseph Henry: His Life and Work*, pp. 237-38; *Star*, 22 May 1862; H Rpt 148, 37C, 2S, Ser 1145; Rpt Sec/Int, 1863, p. 726, Ser 1182; 12 Stat 88; 13 Stat 329, 537; 15 Stat 88.

[18] *Star*, 20 May, 9 Jun 1862; *Cong Globe*, 37C, 2S, p. 1854 and App., pp. 356-57; H Misc Doc 48, 38C, 1S, Ser 1200.

by the Washington Canal, the Eastern Branch, and the Potomac. By early 1864 association volunteers were teaching five Negro classes in church basements and halls, while Josephine Griffing, the association's District agent, organized sewing classes for contraband women. That March the trustees of the colored schools, having accumulated money enough to engage a teacher at $400 a year, opened the first colored public school in the Ebenezer Church, southeast of the Capitol. A hundred adults and children immediately tried to enroll, but one teacher and an inexperienced assistant, unable to handle so many, had to turn some away. Philanthropic groups then redoubled their efforts. Government employees offered to teach evening classes, and in the course of a few weeks nearly eight hundred colored adults and children were learning to read. By summer the newly formed Association of Volunteer Teachers of Colored Schools reported 32 persons sharing the teaching of 12 classes.[19] Privately sponsored schools, however, did not build the tax-supported system Congress had instructed the city corporations and the levy court of the county to establish.

The second colored school law, enacted in June 1864, put teeth into the first: each city was to pay over to the colored schools the same proportion of the total school fund as the number of Negro children between the ages of six and seventeen bore to the number of white children; to ease the financial strain, the federal courts of the District were to pay into the school fund all money accruing from fines and forfeitures, a quarter of it to the colored schools of the county, a quarter to the cities' colored schools, and a quarter each to Washington's and Georgetown's white schools.[20] If some enlightened residents admitted the necessity of prodding the corporations into action, many more

[19] H Misc Doc 48, 38C, 1S, Ser 1200; NFR Assn, *2nd Anl Rpt*, 1864, p. 4; *Star*, 24 Dec 1863; *Chronicle*, 7 Jan, 6 Feb, 8 Jul 1864; *Spec Rpt Comr Ed*, pp. 223-29, Ser 1427; James M. McPherson, *The Struggle for Equality*, p. 391.
[20] *Cong Globe*, 38C, 1S, App., pp. 196-98.

taxpayers indignantly dubbed the act unwarranted coercion, an interference foreshadowing other forms of arbitrary social regulation of loyal Union supporters.

Their anger was not entirely groundless. From the Ordinance of 1787 onward, federal land grants had helped support public schools in the territories and states, but Congress had never contributed a penny to common schools in the District of Columbia. The trustees of the colored schools themselves observed in 1864 that the propertyless new freedmen increased educational needs without adding to the cities' revenues.[21] Colored people's taxes in Washington, according to judicious local estimates, amounted to 2 percent of whites', the colored school population to perhaps 50 percent of the white. Washington spent yearly a fifth of her revenues for public education, and still the 36 classrooms of 1862 could accommodate only a fraction of the city's children. Among those who attended, furthermore, were children of federal employees who paid no local taxes. The sums henceforward obtainable from fines promised to be a drop in the bucket that Washington and Georgetown taxpayers must fill. Citizens felt, and with reason, that senators and representatives were enacting legislation for an unrepresented area that they would not dare propose for their home states and leaving the local community to pay the costs of educating contrabands who were properly a federal charge.[22]

The city council consequently continued mere token payments to the Negro schools—in 1864-1865 only $628 out of a total school fund of $25,000. At the end of the war colored schools in the county still existed only on paper. Everywhere in the District white taxpayers' indignation flared out at Congress and at hypercritical temporary residents without stakes in the community. And indeed,

[21] H Misc Doc 48, 38C, 1S, Ser 1200.

[22] *Star*, 9 Jun 1862; *Chronicle*, 23 Jul 1863; *Journal of the 63rd Council of the City of Washington*, p. 188 (hereafter cited as *Journal—Council*); *Spec Rpt Comr Ed*, pp. 268-69.

many a Northerner who would later return home tended to display a self-righteousness coupled with a sentimentality about the virtuousness of all Negroes that infuriated Washingtonians who knew that it would eventually fall to them to construct a stable social order. Anger burned hottest of all at the intended beneficiaries of the congressional acts, for white property owners believed that but for the contraband invasion the District would have escaped many problems that peace would not solve. Long-time Negro residents naturally viewed the situation differently, but they too could see that the enormous increase in the numbers of Negro indigents was adding to municipal burdens.[23]

The decision in the spring of 1863 to recruit Negro troops was a second, though short-lived, irritant in race relations. The plan grew out of the difficulties of meeting the local quota of volunteers in 1862. Washington's council had voted $50,000 for bounties, $50 for each man enlisting, but bounty jumping and "a stampede among the foreign element" had run the costs up; the price of substitutes rose to $1,000 a man. As the 1863 draft became imminent, official disapproval of enlisting Negroes yielded to expediency. A good many whites expected colored troops to inspire "uppityness" in all colored people. Although recruiting agents reported encountering "serious and sometimes violent opposition," before mid-1863 two companies of colored troops were mustered in and encamped on Analostan Island, the present-day Roosevelt Island, once the home of James Mason, a former slaveowning United States senator from Virginia and later Confederate emissary to Great Britain.[24] The island location protected the recruits from white hostility, but demonstrations against colored civilians occurred more than once. Hatred of colored people,

[23] *Star,* 25 Jan, 22, 27, 28 May, 3 Jun 1862; *Journal 62nd Council,* 27 Mar 1865, p. 2.

[24] *Star,* 29 Jul, 7, 9 Aug 1862, 22 May 1863; *Journal 63rd Council,* p. 189; *Chronicle,* 5 Nov 1862, 8, 16 May 1863; Baltimore *Sun,* 16 May 1863; H Rpt 80, 38C, 1S, Ser 1206.

the *Star* observed that summer, was growing. Only the lag in recruitment of the District's draft quota, 3,863 men to be drawn from 19,327 males between the ages of 20 and 45, wore down the objections of whites. By 1864 "substitute brokers" offering a bounty first of $30 and later of $150 a man were advertising for colored recruits and, according to later accounts, with official connivance were taking Negro prisoners from the county jail to fill the quotas.[25] All told, in the course of the war the District furnished to the Union forces 3,269 colored and 13,265 white men. The pride colored men took in wearing the United States uniform and fighting for their country would sustain them in the trying years to come and inspired in their descendants of the next four generations a sense of special distinction.[26]

The number of colored soldiers recruited supplied a powerful argument for Negro enfranchisement. In January 1864, at the invitation of a hundred Republican congressmen, eloquent twenty-one-year-old abolitionist Anna Dickinson of Philadelphia addressed the House in a moving plea for Negro suffrage; she received an ovation. In March a colored delegation from New Orleans arrived to beg for Negro voting in Louisiana. In April a petition signed by 2,500 Washington Negroes asked Congress for local voting rights. The memorial quoted from the Declaration of Independence, pointed to colored men's military service, and stated that "a large portion of the colored citizens of the District are property holders," unfortunately, as the colored school trustees' comment indicated, a palpable exaggeration if contrabands rated as District citizens. "The experience of

[25] *Star*, 16, 18 May, 10 Jun, 18 Jul 1863; Baltimore *Sun*, 23 May, 4, 5 Jun 1863; *Chronicle*, 30 Jul, 2 Oct, 12 Dec 1863, 25 Apr, 1, 9, 20 Sep, 14 Oct, 15 Nov 1864, 1, 3 Mar 1865; H Rpt 23, 38C, 2S, Ser 1235.

[26] Rpt Sec/War, 1863, pp. 55, 134-36, Ser 1184; Rpt Board of Colored Troops, in Rpt Sec/War, 1865, p. 58, Ser 1249; Frederick H. Dyer, *A Compendium of the War of Rebellion*, p. 11; Final Rpt Provost Marshal Gen, in Rpt Sec/War, 1865, pp. 69, 78, Ser 1251; Christian A. Fleetwood, ltrs and newspaper clippings, 1863-1912, Fleetwood Mss.

the Past," the petition concluded, "teaches that all reforms have their opponents, but . . . apprehensions of evils rising from reforms founded, in justice are scarcely, if ever, realized." [27] Congress tabled the petition. Again the colored community had to wait.

While pain and grief, ever-present in wartime Washington, were no respecters of color, Negroes, like white people, enjoyed gay interludes in the humdrum routine of hard work amidst deprivation and constant anxiety. Colored people watched the stirring military parades through the streets in the early months of the war, ogled at thirty-two-inch high Tom Thumb and his thirty-inch wife as they drove to a ball at the Willard Hotel, and very occasionally attended a play or a burlesque show at one of the theatres. In December 1863 some of them witnessed the raising of the bronze Freedom to the top of the cupola crowning the newly finished dome of the Capitol while cannon boomed from every fort in the area. They could repeat the current tales of spies' adventures and find amusement in the never-ending gossip about the private lives of men and women in the public eye. Mrs. Elizabeth Keckley, the colored seamstress Mrs. Lincoln employed at the White House, doubtless supplied her friends with some choice bits. When her book *Behind the Scenes* appeared in 1868, frantic officials would attempt to suppress it lest its revelations of the former First Lady's idiosyncrasies damage the Grand Old Party. All colored people were gratified at the President's receiving Sojourner Truth, that strange, compelling elderly Negro who had set her heart on talking to the author of the Emancipation Proclamation. He showed her the Bible Baltimore Negroes had presented to him, but as Sojourner could neither read nor write, the public was left to guess at what passed between the compassionate, troubled statesman in the White House and the dignified Negro peasant in her severely plain white muslin bonnet. Perhaps

[27] Ptn, S38A-J6, 15 Apr 1864; *Journal 63rd Council,* p. 380; Mc-Pherson, *The Struggle for Equality,* pp. 128-29, 131, 244.

Sojourner spoke of the plan she would later press upon Congress, to abandon all notions of colonizing freedmen in Liberia and instead allot them public lands in the West for a Negro state within America.[28]

As the war dragged into its fourth winter, left-wing Republicans assembled enough votes in Congress to pass the 13th constitutional amendment, which when ratified would end chattel slavery throughout the country. To mark the momentous event, at the suggestion of the chaplain of the House, members invited the Reverend Henry Highland Garnet to preach before them on a Sunday in February. Ten months earlier, when Garnet had begun his pastorate at the 15th Street Colored Presbyterian Church, the rule imposed in 1827 still forbad any Negro to set foot in either legislative chamber at the Capitol. On February 12, 1865, every seat in the House was filled when the Negro minister, accompanied by the beautifully trained choir from his church, entered the hall. From the speaker's rostrum Garnet addressed the solemnly silent gathering. His discourse concluded with a ringing plea to the legislators: "Emancipate, Enfranchise, Educate, and give the blessings of the Gospel to every American citizen." Grateful members of Garnet's church published the sermon in its entirety. Many a white Washingtonian in reading the appeal for Negro suffrage undoubtedly had misgivings, but most of the city at least breathed easier in March 1865 when the act establishing a federal Freedman's Bureau became law; it meant that local taxpayers would not have to assume unaided the care of contrabands after the army ceased to serve as custodian and Northern aid societies withdrew their help.[29] And the fall of Petersburg, the

[28] *Star*, 5 Sep 1861, 6, 22 Feb, 11 Jul 1862, 13 Nov, 2 Dec 1863; *Chronicle*, 29 Oct 1863; Elizabeth Keckley, *Behind the Scenes, Life of a Colored Woman Thirty Years a Slave, Four Years at the White House;* Hertha E. Pauli, *Her Name Was Sojourner Truth.*

[29] 13 Stat 507; *A Memorial Discourse; by Rev. Henry Highland Garnet, delivered in the hall of the House of Representatives, Washington city, D.C., on Sabbath, February 12, 1865.*

capture of Richmond, and on April 9th Lee's surrender at Appomattox foretold the end of the war.

Rejoicing over the virtual collapse of the rebellion gave way to grief and new anxiety on April 15th when Washington learned with horror that an assassin's bullet had killed Abraham Lincoln. White men were shocked; colored men were profoundly distressed, whatever their personal feelings about the martyred President. In 1861 Lincoln had seemed to abolitionists to be an appeaser of the slave interests, but in 1863 he had issued the Emancipation Proclamation and had steadfastly resisted pressure to withdraw it. Thereafter most Negroes had admired and trusted him. Now, with Andrew Johnson of Tennessee in the White House, uncertainties about the new President's racial attitudes made colored people's immediate future look precarious despite the sizable pro-Negro bloc of radical Republicans in Congress.[30] The war had brought farreaching changes to colored Washington. Whether the peace would bring larger opportunities was the question. For the moment, Negroes mourning Lincoln could only ease their sorrow by laying plans for a memorial: eleven years later, Thomas Ball's statue of the Great Emancipator, a freed slave at his feet, would be unveiled in Lincoln Park, a tribute of gratitude from colored Americans.

[30] See discussion in McPherson, *Struggle for Equality*, pp. 72-124, 336-40.

CHAPTER V

REACHING TOWARD

CITIZENSHIP AND ITS

RESPONSIBILITIES, 1865–1867

 During the late spring and summer of 1865, soldiers mustered out of the army headed for home, government offices reduced staff, and the Navy Yard and Quartermaster repair shops cut their payrolls drastically. By autumn all but two of the military hospitals in and about the capital had closed down. While men returning to civilian life were hunting for jobs and the Freedmen's Bureau was trying to find work for its protégés, forlorn-looking, idle blacks thronged the streets. The simultaneous curtailment of public and private business accompanied by a 21 percent shrinkage of population from the estimated 140,000 souls of 1864 indeed left scores of unemployed white men bitterly resentful of Negro competition in the labor market. How to halt and reverse the business decline concerned every intelligent citizen.[1]

At the same time Washingtonians realized that the District of Columbia, where state laws and constituents' preferences could not interfere, was likely to serve the Republican party as a proving ground for legislation in-

[1] Rpt Sec/Navy, 1865, pp. x, xxv-xxvii, Ser 1253; Rpt Sec/War, 1865, pp. 19, 88-89, 252-53, 622-27, Ser 1249; *Chronicle*, 13, 25, 27 Oct 1865; Rpt Asst Comr Freedmen's Bureau, S Ex Doc 27, 39C, 1S, pp. 151-55, Ser 1238; S. M. Clark to Brig Gen C. H. Howard, 31 Mar 1866, D.C. file, Bureau of Refugees, Freedmen and Abandoned Lands, RG 105, N.A. (All Freedmen's Bureau reports and correspondence hereafter cited as F.B., and as all are, unless otherwise noted, in D.C. file, R.G. 105, N.A., the location is hereafter omitted.)

tended later to be applied to the country at large. Just as a federal act had wiped out slavery here nearly nine months before the Emancipation Proclamation, so postwar congressional acts might introduce into the District further social and political innovations which, when put into the form of constitutional amendments, the states might not ratify. Distasteful to many a white Washingtonian as was the prospect in 1865 of having to accept the Negro as a fellow citizen, the strong possibility of having federal law force racial equality upon the District of Columbia, but nowhere else, was far harder to swallow. Aware that thousands of contrabands were determined to stay permanently within the federal area, Washington's city council prepared to fight a Negro suffrage bill that would certainly come before Congress when it convened in December. A committee drafted a statement of the city's official view:

> The white man, being the superior race, must . . . rule the black. . . . Why he is black and we white, or why we the superior and he the inferior race are matters past our comprehension. It, then, becomes a civil as well as a Christian duty to weigh his capacity for advancement in civil rights, and the only test by which his claim to the right of suffrage can best be ascertained will be by a comparison with the white race under like circumstances. . . .
>
> If it took the ancient Briton a thousand years to emerge from his only half-civilized condition . . . to reach the point to qualify him for the exercise of this right, how long would it reasonably take the black man, who but about two hundred years ago was brought from Africa. . . .

Observing that some colored men had increased in intelligence and might qualify for suffrage, the councilmen nevertheless declared "that not one grown-up Negro in a hundred can read or write" and that "more forcible means exist why ladies of a given age should be entitled to the privilege."

The United States was a white man's country; let the dissatisfied colored man go elsewhere. "Already does there exist among the laboring men in our midst, a deep-seated hostility because employment is made more scarce by their [Negroes'] great influx into this city since the rebellion began, and a trivial circumstance will be made a pretext for collision."

The council discarded an alternative statement: "That we are not opposed to granting the right of suffrage to colored men *simply because they are colored men,* but that we believe the safety of our free institutions demands that the elective franchise should only be granted to men who can read or write" or to those who, *"without regard to color,"* possess mental and moral qualifications acceptable to an enlightened public.[2]

A month later Benjamin Wade, a determined defender of the Negro, presented his franchise bill in the Senate. Some 2,500 Negroes headed by John F. Cook, son of the distinguished educator and Presbyterian minister, petitioned Congress to enact the bill; Mayor Wallach immediately checked the names and reported only 573 taxpayers among the signers. The president of the board of aldermen, in answer to the frequently heard Negro argument that colored men who had served in the army had every right to vote, insisted that the District's first colored regiment had not been recruited by voluntary enlistment but by kidnaping carried on by Negro agents. "Of the Negroes residing here in 1861 and 1862, . . . not one hundred entered the service of the United States, but those who did go were refugees and contrabands who came here to seek bread and who were taken possession of by men of their own color, and sold into the service of the United States." In mid-December Washington and Georgetown each conducted a referendum. In Washington the outcome was 6,591 against, 35 for, Negro suffrage; in Georgetown 465 against, no one in favor. The vote was small, and some citizens labeled it unrepre-

[2] *Journal 63rd Council,* pp. 313-16, 318.

sentative. Sayles J. Bowen, postmaster of Washington and later mayor, believed the assessors had registered only men they wished to see vote, and the *Star* fulminated: "The ballot box at the special election doubtless received many ballots from fingers that pulled rebel triggers." [3]

The House debate on the bill began in January 1866. While a minority protested at the proposal as a tyrannical imposition upon unwilling white people, a Maryland representative, pointing out that he himself had worked and voted for emancipation at home, argued that congressmen from Northern states where the proportion of Negroes was small should not pass upon a problem with which they had no first-hand experience. But the abolitionist wing of the 39th Congress and Republican opportunists held the floor. A speech of George Julian of Indiana, an idealist, a proponent of woman suffrage, a land reformer, and usually a man of sound judgment, revealed the temper of the radicals who professed to believe that a majority of the city's whites had been and still were "rebels at heart." After asserting that District Negroes owned property worth "at least $1,225,000," supported twenty-one churches, twenty Sabbath schools, and thirty benevolent and civic organizations, had furnished three full regiments to the Union Army, and supplied 60 to 70 percent of the men for the drafts, Julian concluded:

> I have argued that the ballot should be given to the negroes as a matter of justice to them. It should likewise be done as a matter of retributive justice to the slaveholders and rebels. . . . Congress in this District has the power to punish by ballot, and there will be a beautiful, poetic justice in the exercise of this power. . . . The rebels here will recoil from it with horror. . . . To be voted down by Yankee and negro ballots will seem to them an intolerable grievance, and this is among the

[3] *Ibid.*, p. 380, and *65th Council*, p. 9; *N.I.*, 18 Dec 1865; *Star*, 23 Dec 1865; *Chronicle*, 16 Dec 1865.

excellent reasons why I am in favor of it. . . . Nor shall I stop to inquire very critically whether the negroes are *fit* to vote. As between themselves and white rebels, who deserve to be hung, they are eminently fit.[4]

Shortly after Julian's impassioned speech, George Downing of Rhode Island, one of the wealthiest Negroes in the country, and Frederick Douglass, one-time slave, for the past twenty-five years a noted abolitionist lecturer and, as the most famous Negro in America, spokesman for his race, journeyed to Washington to join with several locally prominent colored men in begging the President to endorse Negro suffrage. President Johnson received the delegation, listened to brief introductory speeches from Douglass and Downing, and then held forth himself about his experience in handling slaves and his knowledge of how to treat Negroes. The only solution to the race problem, he asserted, was Negro emigration. That said, he dismissed his eminent callers. When they had left in stunned silence, according to a later story, Johnson growled to his secretary: "Those d—d sons of b—s thought they had me in a trap." Douglass, "just like any nigger, . . . would sooner cut a white man's throat than not." On April 16 Negro Washington celebrated District Emancipation Day with anxious restraint. Two regiments of Negro veterans and a brass band led a parade of ten thousand colored people to the White House where the President greeted them with unexpected cordiality. After cannon fired a salute and the band had played several martial airs, the marchers gathered in Franklin Square for an hour of speeches and prayers.[5]

When the Senate took up the suffrage bill in June, a counterproposal, fights over modifications, and the excessive heat of the Washington summer combined to delay action.

[4] *Cong Globe*, 39C, 1S, pp. 256-59, 261-63; H Rpt 2, 39C, 1S, Ser 1272.

[5] McPherson, *Struggle for Equality*, pp. 343-46; Lewanda Cox and John H. Cox, *Politics, Principle, and Prejudice, 1865-1866; Dilemma of Reconstruction America*, p. 163; *Harper's Weekly*, 12 May 1866.

Lot Morrill of Maine wished precedence for a bill revoking the two cities' charters, returning their powers to Congress, and thus eliminating all local suffrage. When that plan was dropped, he and several supporters urged a literacy qualification for every male except taxpayers and returned soldiers; 19 nays to 15 yeas defeated the amendment. In order to prevent a pocket veto of the original bill, the Senate chose to let the final vote wait till the next session. In December 1866, nineteen months before ratification of the Fourteenth Amendment, the bill for unrestricted manhood suffrage in the District went through quickly. President Johnson's veto message pronounced the measure premature and, in view of local sentiment, unjust. Many of the men who voted for Negro enfranchisement here, he observed truthfully, would not have advocated it at home. Connecticut, Minnesota, and Wisconsin had already rejected it in their own states, and Kansas, Ohio, and Michigan would soon forbid it. But the House and Senate overrode the veto the day after it reached Capitol Hill.

Omission of a literacy qualification from the suffrage act meant that the District cities would have several thousand new voters who, though elated at the prospect of sharing white men's political privileges, still were unfamiliar with the obligations voting entailed. At least two thirds of the colored men in the District had been slaves only three or four years before and, as slaves, had been denied education. Now as freedmen they were little better qualified for political responsibility than as slaves. Small wonder that ardent woman suffragists at times marveled at the vagaries of a Congress which enfranchised ignorant male contrabands and refused educated white women votes. Forebodings rose in the white community during the spring of 1867 when some 9,800 white and 8,200 colored men registered to vote in Washington's municipal election.[6]

---

[6] *Cong Globe*, 39C, 1S, pp. 3191, 3432, 39C, 2S, pp. 303-14, and App., p. 9; Wilhelmus Bryan, *History of the National Capital*, II, 563, n. 3.

Yet contrary to gloomy expectations, colored voters under the guidance of Negro leaders displayed discretion; they made no attempt to put inexperienced Negroes into office. For the time being, they were content to have achieved the major badge of American citizenship: the elective franchise.

But the battle for a decent life for colored people had scarcely begun. Neither congressional law, nor the Freedmen's Bureau, nor public-spirited educated Negroes could greatly lighten the immediate miseries of freedmen. Ill-prepared to earn a living in a competitive world, contrabands who had had jobs of sorts during the war were stranded when the army demobilized, the corrals shut down, and the military hospitals closed. The Freedmen's Bureau during 1865 turned army barracks into tenements for about 350 families, issued weekly rations of food and fuel, and now and again found jobs for some of the able-bodied, but need constantly outran what the bureau could supply. Relief societies and individuals contributed food, clothing, medicines, and even rudimentary lessons in house-keeping. The Association for the Relief of Destitute Colored Women and Children found homes in the North for a few contraband orphans and, after the official pardon of the rebel whose Georgetown house had served as the orphanage during the war, moved its charges to a farm in the country above the present-day Florida Avenue. The Freedmen's Hospital, newly converted from military to civilian control, in its first eleven months treated 22,798 Negroes and reduced the death rate among patients to less than four per hundred. Nevertheless, according to a Washington councilman, official records showed that "of these people who have migrated to this District between the first of January 1862 and the first of January 1866, more than a third are already in their graves." And in early 1867 an observant Englishman wrote of the countrywide situation: "Mortality has been so great that some [white men] have

81

predicted a solution of the difficulty in the disappearance of the whole colored race in the next fifty years." [7]

In Washington thousands of freedmen lived in utmost squalor. Some occupied hovels near the river below L Street on the Island; others crowded into "Adams shanties" east of the Capitol; in 1866 in "Fredericksburg" on Rhode Island Avenue 213 persons lived in a space 200 feet square. "Murder Bay," located on land where the buildings of the Departments of Commerce and Labor would later stand, was still more notorious. "Here," reported the superintendent of the Metropolitan Police, "crime, filth and poverty seem to vie with each other in a career of degradation and death. Whole families . . . are crowded into mere apologies for shanties. . . . During storms of rain or snow their roofs afford but slight protection, while from beneath a few rough boards used for floors, the miasmatic effluvia from the most disgustingly filthy and stagnant water . . . renders the atmosphere within these hovels stifling and sickening in the extreme. . . . In a space about fifty yards square I found about one hundred families, composed of from three to ten persons each, . . . living in shanties one story high . . . and from five to eight dollars per month are paid for the rent of these shanties except . . . where a ground rent of three dollars per month is paid for a few square feet—there some of the more enterprising have erected cabins of their own. There are no proper privy accommodations. . . . Nor can the sanitary laws be properly enforced against delinquents, for they have no means wherewith to pay fines and a commitment to the workhouse is no punishment." An officer of the Freedmen's Bureau spent four months and used a thousand barrels of lime in whitewashing freedmen's quarters, but disinfectant, though fore-

[7] Rpt F.B., H Ex Doc 11, 39C, 1S, pp. 16, 24, 36-39, Ser 1255; Rpt Asst Comr F.B., S Ex Doc 6, 39C, 2S, pp. 35-42, Ser 1276; S Misc Doc 14, 39C, 2S, Ser 1278; *Journal 65th Council,* pp. 711-27; Henry Latham, *Black and White, a Journal of a Three Months' Tour in the United States,* p. 270.

stalling citywide epidemics of typhoid and dysentery, ended neither overcrowding nor unsanitary living conditions. The once half-empty, sprawling city had suddenly acquired slums as horrifying as those of New York.[8]

Frederick Douglass, for one, was critical of the paternalism of the aid societies and the Freedmen's Bureau. If colored people were to become an integral part of the American nation, he believed that they must make their own way, find their own level. Shortly after the war, when whites asked "What shall we do with the Negroes?" he had replied, do nothing with them. "They have been undone by your doings and all they now ask and really have need of at your hands is just to let them alone. . . . Let the American people who have thus far only kept the colored race staggering between partial philanthropy and cruel force, be induced to try what virtue there is in justice."[9] But Douglass was not then a District resident and had seen little of the wretchedness prevailing in postwar Washington. Leaving freedmen here to their own devices would not resolve the difficulty that all ill-educated or illiterate persons faced, regardless of their race, in finding work in a predominantly white-collar city.

Men in charge of the Freedmen's Bureau employment office tried in vain to persuade former field hands to take the jobs that farm labor shortages in other parts of the country opened to them; even a threat to strike from the relief rolls those who balked at settling on farmland across the Eastern Branch failed to move most of them out of the capital. The families who accepted the Bureau's offer of land on the Barry Farm were able to build small houses there, raise corn and chickens, and over the years buy their house lots on easy terms. But ex-contrabands generally felt safer in the city. Josephine Griffing of the Freedmen's Bureau, it is true, reported that between 1865 and 1867

[8] *Cong Globe,* 39C, 1S, pp. 1307-09; see n. 7, Ser 1278.
[9] Quoted in McPherson, *Struggle for Equality,* pp. 187-88.

she had found homes and jobs in the North for some 7,000 Washington Negroes. Still, penniless newcomers always outnumbered the departing. A widely traveled Quaker declared "the suffering and the poverty of the poor of this city in excess of anything she had seen anywhere else on the face of the globe." Congress chartered the Freedmen's Savings and Trust Company to encourage thrift among colored people who might be able to get their heads above water, but the plight of the utterly helpless continued to receive greater attention on Capitol Hill.

Authority vested in the Freedmen's Bureau to convert additional government-owned buildings into low-rental tenements for freedmen of "good character" meant to bureau officials authority to rent to people who would pay their rent promptly, keep their homes clean, and live by the moral code of whites. "No persons professing to be husband and wife," read one regulation, "will be permitted to occupy a tenement until they give satisfactory proof of lawful marriage." Freedmen without jobs could not pay their rent, families living in overcrowded quarters and ignorant of the elementary principles of hygiene soon turned their tenements into filthy shambles, and former slaves who understood cohabitation rarely understood the legal formalities of marriage. Patient teaching and opportunities to earn a living manifestly offered the only way out of the wilderness through which, Henry Ward Beecher declared, all must pass "who travel from the Egypt of ignorance to the promised land of civilization." [10]

An adequate colored school system would hasten that journey. At the end of the war Mayor Wallach had announced Washington's readiness to remit to the trustees

[10] *Ibid.*, pp. 389-91; H Ex Doc 142, 41C, 2S, pp. 29-30, Ser 1417; J. W. Bushong to F.B., 10 Oct 1865, S. N. Clark to Rev. Roberts, 27 Mar 1866, circular ltr, 1 Oct 1866, J. N. Vandenburgh to F. B., 20 Oct 1866, W. W. Rogers to Lt Col S. M. Beebe, 1 Apr 1867, C. H. Howard to Miss Lowell, 4 Apr 1867, and to Sayles J. Bowen, 14 Jul 1868, F. B. to Supt O. S. B. Wall, 24 Jul 1868, F.B. files; Barry Farm notes; *Journal 66th Council*, pp. 711-27.

of the colored schools the entire amount Negroes paid yearly in taxes, but he stated flatly that the city could not do more and still support "the thousands of colored forced upon the city by the General Government." When he presented the case for federal aid for indigent whites and for the white as well as the colored schools, the Secretary of the Interior supported his plea. In the summer of 1866 Congress authorized the use of empty army barracks for Negro schoolrooms, appropriated $10,000 for building schoolhouses for colored children in the county, gave three lots for a similar purpose in Washington, and, without extending any help to the white schools, empowered the trustees of the colored schools to sue the cities for the principal and 10 percent interest on the money long overdue by the terms of the colored school law of 1864. City officials, incensed at what they considered discrimination against whites, thereupon chose to defy the order to increase the Negro school fund. Anger warped their judgment. George Julian's speech on Negro enfranchisement in the District pointed to the punitive character of recent congressional laws seemingly inspired by belief in the wickedness of local people whose anti-Negro sentiment, rooted in the doctrine of white supremacy, proved them all rebels. At city council meetings consequently the pleas for moderation urged by men who believed in Negro rights and in the wisdom of cooperating with Congress fell on deaf ears; indignation got the upper hand.

Unwise and ungenerous as this defiance was, the die-hards marshaled statistics to defend their position. Freedmen's Bureau records, a councilman averred, showed nearly a third of all District children to be colored, whereas the value of Negro property, but a seventieth of white, brought in "very little in excess of a sum sufficient to meet the burdens their presence imposes upon society here." Another councilman characterized the authors of the local school laws as wealthy self-advertisers seeking national prominence but indifferent to the welfare of the ignorant impoverished children in their own states. Mayor Wallach, throwing conciliation to the winds, observed sarcastically that Congress, "in its zeal for education," had given "to states and other territories, 78,130,000 acres of public land, which . . . would yield the enormous sum of $97,662,500, [but] to the District of Columbia, . . . whose people it now inordinately taxes to educate the thousands of contrabands allured to this 'paradise of freedmen' by the temptation to indolence offered by the gratuities of the Freedmen's Bureau, it has never given a foot of land or a dollar of money." As the school board reported that 34 percent of the pupils attending the white public schools were the children of government employees, 10,050 taxpayers in a city of 20,073 families had to bear the cost of educating the children of nontaxpaying residents. By mid-1867, however, expanding government activity and a spate of private building in Washington had revived business sufficiently to make the mayor's jeremiad of municipal poverty sound rather silly.[11]

The unequal fight with Congress could not last forever. Indeed Washington could not afford obduracy, for petitions from Midwestern state legislatures were urging the federal government to move the capital to a locality "free from the taint" of secessionist treason, and Congress appeared to be ready to listen to them. City officials had to yield. Since the 1860 census data were clearly inapplicable to the postwar District and since reliable figures on the relative numbers of white and colored children would be more useful than name-calling in determining a just division of school funds, in the fall of 1867 Mayor Wallach, Mayor Addison of Georgetown, the newly appointed federal commissioner of education, and the president of the county

---

[11] Rpt Sec/Int, 1865, pp. xxii, 855-69, Ser 1248; *Journal 63rd Council,* pp. 146, 182-89, 412-17, App., pp. 3-15, *64th Council,* pp. 376-78, 395, 432-33, 442-43, and *65th Council,* pp. 14, 23-30, 34-35, 663-69; *Spec Rpt Comr Ed.,* pp. 259-60; *Twenty-second Annual Report of the Trustees of Public Schools of Washington,* 1867, p. 28 (hereafter cited as *Rpt School Trustees*).

levy court jointly requested a special census calculated to show "the wants of the local government." Congress approved, though it made no appropriation to cover the expenses.

Directed with scrupulous care by a skilled statistician, the District census of 1867 turned into far more than an enumeration of school children. The final report, running to more than nine hundred closely printed pages, included comparative data on public schools in Europe and in other American cities, a history of education in the District since its beginning, and a wealth of detailed information ranging from analyses of occupations to tables showing where residents voted—altogether a more elaborate compilation of facts and figures on social conditions than any decennial census had ever assembled. If the historical essay on Negro education in Washington and Georgetown presented a somewhat uncritical eulogy of Negro achievements and the figures on Negro illiteracy in 1867 were too low, the findings nevertheless were sufficiently illuminating to serve the primary purpose of the survey. Georgetown immediately paid over the sums due the colored schools, and Washington agreed to remit $34,000 of the $51,000 the trustees claimed.[12]

Of the facts the special census brought to light perhaps none was more surprising than the evidence that a larger percentage of colored children than of white were attending the public schools. The federal figures collected three years later would show 75 percent of Negro adults unable to write, instead of the 52 percent claimed in 1867, but even allowing for exaggeration in the local census, the record was astonishing, inasmuch as over three fifths of the colored population had come from Southern states after 1861. For the extraordinary progress of Negro schooling in the District of Columbia the Freedmen's Aid societies and the federal

[12] *Journal 66th Council,* pp. 543, 558-60, 629; S Ex Doc 20, 41C, 3S, pp. 4-5, Ser 1440; *4th Rpt F.B.,* 10 Oct 1868, p. 10, in *Documents Relating to Freedmen* (Howard Univ).

TABLE III

SPECIAL CENSUS OF 1867[a]

	Washington	Georgetown	County	Total
Total population	106,052	11,793	9,145	126,990
White population	74,115	8,509	5,703	88,327
Negro population	31,937	3,284	3,442	38,663
White children ages 6 to 18	17,801	2,152	1,494	21,447
Negro children ages 6 to 18	8,401	894	951	10,246
% Negro children of all children	32.1	29.3	37.4	32.3
Av. attendance in white public schools	4,631	362	356	5,349
Av. attendance in Negro public schools	2,415	333	323	3,071
Av. attendance white private schools	4,717	635	—	5,352
Av. attendance Negro private schools	232	—	—	232
% white children in public school of total white children	26.	16.8	23.8	24.9
% Negro children in public school of total Negro children	28.7	37.24	33.9	29.9
Teachers, white pub. schools	89	8	8	105
Teachers, Negro pub. schools	49	8	7	64
% illiteracy among whites over 20 years				2.66
% illiteracy among Negroes over 20 yrs: unable to read unable to write				45.7 51.9

[a] *Spec Rpt Comr Ed*, pp. 5-9, 15-79, Ser 1427. The figures on illiteracy are computed from the tables listing the number of inhabitants of every age between one and twenty-one, and from the total illiteracy figures given on pp. 30, 42, 76.

Freedmen's Bureau could claim most of the credit; they had supplied most of the teachers and kept interest in the school crusade alive in the North. In January 1866 some 100 men and women were teaching about 5,600 colored children in 54 day schools; 25 Sabbath schools had enrolled over 2,300 pupils; and another 500 children were attending the "eight or ten self-supporting schools taught by colored teachers." Six months later the Freedmen's Bureau reported 10,000 Negroes receiving some instruction. By 1868 Northern philanthropists concluded the Negro education program

88

so well established that it no longer needed their help; all but one group withdrew their aid.[13]

Congress, moreover, acting upon the request of General O. O. Howard of the Freedmen's Bureau and fellow members of the Congregational Church, chartered Howard University in 1867. General Howard, the first president, borrowed money to buy land for a large campus near the Soldiers' Home on the city's outskirts. Private gifts and student tuition fees of three dollars a term supplied funds to open a preparatory unit, a normal school class, courses in theology, and in 1868 medical and law schools. Although Baptist money had started Wayland Seminary in 1865 to train Negroes for the ministry, Howard University, the first university south of the Mason-Dixon Line to be expressly dedicated to biracial education, seemed to its founders to mark the path to racial peace. Several of their sons and daughters enrolled in the first classes along with young Negroes.[14]

At the end of 1867 a backward look at the changes of the past six years was an exhilarating experience for the District's colored people and their well-wishers. Every Negro was now free; the legal restraints of the black code were gone; blacks could sit where they pleased when they rode the horse cars; a few colored men were filling government clerkships and others were starting businesses; a number of families were buying their own homes; tax-supported colored schools would soon be multiplying; a university education, including medical or legal training, was now within reach of ambitious students; and manhood suffrage in local elections gave the adult Negro community

[13] S Ex Doc 56, 40C, 3S, Ser 1360; Williston Lofton, "The Development of Public Education for Negroes in Washington, D.C., a Study of Separate but Equal Accommodations," pp. 143-44 (Dissertation, American Univ., 1943, hereafter cited as Lofton, "Separate but Equal").

[14] Abstract of Circular Relative to Howard University, 1867, #20, Appendix F, F.B. files; *Cong Globe*, 39C, 2S, App., p. 1992; Dwight O. W. Holmes, "Fifty Years of Howard University," *Journ Neg Hist*, III, 128-38

a voice in municipal affairs which promised to ensure further social and economic progress. If Congressman Julian had overestimated the number of solvent Negro mutual benefit societies and the extent of Negro property-holding, hard work unimpeded by white obstructionism might quickly turn inflated figures into sober fact. Educated colored people still encountered rudeness and, irrespective of their skills and intellectual attainments, suffered from various forms of racial discrimination; of the thousands of field hands who had moved into Washington and Georgetown during and since the war, a great many were still desperately poor and seemingly without the capacity to help themselves. Yet in view of the extraordinary record of the recent past, the future looked bright.

CHAPTER VI

THE STRUGGLE FOR FULL CIVIL

RIGHTS, 1868–1878

The municipal election of June 1868 put colored men into office for the first time: John F. Cook, now a clerk in the city tax collector's office and one of the best-known Negroes in Washington, won a seat on the fourteen-man board of aldermen and Stewart Carter, a barber, a place on the twenty-one-man common council. Georgetown's council was still solidly white, but the three-thousand-odd Negroes in the smaller community were apparently not keenly disappointed. The county beyond the cities' limits had never had elected officials; members of the levy court were all presidential appointees. It was the victory in the capital that mattered to all District Negroes. Washington's new mayor, Sayles J. Bowen, was a staunch advocate of colored men's rights. While his enemies accused him of having imported Negroes from Virginia and Maryland to swing the election, his success rested chiefly on his campaign promise to modernize the city and thereby to end talk on the Hill of moving the capital to the Midwest. That commitment reconciled a great many white voters to seeing two of his colored supporters seated in the City Hall.[1]

City officials faced two extremely difficult problems that summer: first, how to inaugurate and pay for street paving and lighting, the construction of new sewer lines, and a large-scale expansion of the public school system; second, and equally urgent, how to reduce unemployment among former

[1] *Star*, 3 Jun 1868; *National Republican*, 16, 26 May 1868; *Evening Express*, 3 Jun 1868; *Georgetown Courier*, 6 Jun 1868.

contrabands and devise some workable method of providing relief for unemployables—young orphans, widows with small children, the aged, and the physically disabled. During the war heavily laden wagons carrying army supplies had cut the graveled and cobble-stoned streets to ribbons, leaving the main thoroughfares all but impassable with mud in wet weather and choked with dust in dry. Lack of proper sewage facilities exposed the city to epidemics of dysentery and typhoid fever. Visitors to the capital and congressmen apparently shared the views of Horace Greeley, editor of the New York *Tribune:* "The rents are high, the food is bad, the dust is disgusting, the mud is deep and the morals are deplorable." [2] The sheer discomfort of living in so shabby, ill-equipped a city was discouraging well-to-do people from settling in Washington, just as it strengthened the argument for moving the seat of the national government. Both the white and the colored public schools needed additional buildings and a much larger teaching staff. With hundreds of colored and some white people out of work, the burden of poor relief was growing more onerous month by month. Yet to increase the tax rate sharply might defeat any plan of drawing new enterprise to the city.

After fruitless attempts to persuade Congress to accept some financial responsibility for Washington's welfare, Mayor Bowen decided that the city must create jobs for the unemployed by putting them to work on the streets. During the next two years the municipal payroll lengthened as men graded and graveled highways, laid fifteen miles of sidewalks and four miles of sewers, and, along a fashionable four-block stretch of K Street, set off the carriageway from the sidewalks by tree belts planted with elms and grass. Several hundred colored men thus got work, and the looks of the city improved. But the municipal debt rose to $2,400,000, nearly half again as much as when Bowen took

[2] Quoted in *Star*, 14 Dec 1867.

office, and his make-work program rescued only a fraction of the needy from want.[3]

Belatedly admitting that local taxpayers should not have to carry the burden alone, Congress spent months discussing possible relief measures. The only permanent solution, one senator insisted, was "to send freedmen out of this sink of poverty, wretchedness and vice, . . . colonize them all over the country, and enable them to get suitable labor." The plan was neither novel nor feasible in view of the limited skills of ex-field hands and the determination of most of them to stay in Washington under the sheltering wing of Congress. Ratification of the Fourteenth Amendment in July 1868, forbidding the states to deny equal protection of the law to anyone because of race, failed to dispel Negroes' reluctance to leave the city. During late 1868 and 1869 about 150 colored families joined the Barry Farm colony in Anacostia, but living conditions in the primitive little village were hard and were made harder by the sprinkling of Irish newcomers who disliked having Negro neighbors. When in early 1870 Congress appropriated $30,000 for emergency relief and, in order to guarantee that indigent freedmen got the bulk of the benefits, vested in the Secretary of War responsibility for distributing the fund, the army lieutenant put in charge reported that in a single month he had issued coal and rations to about 16,600 people. As charity societies had recommended 23,221 colored adults and 25,348 colored children for relief, the figures, even allowing for duplication, indicated that well over half the District's colored population was in desperate want.[4]

Educated Negroes attuned to city life, on the other hand, made out well. Some of them obtained government clerkships or teaching posts in the public schools; a few were

[3] *Ibid.*, 15 Dec 1869; *Journal 66th Council,* pp. 151, 165-67, and *68th Council,* p. 28.

[4] S. Misc Doc 153, 41C, 2S, Ser 1408; *Cong Globe,* 40C, 3S, p. 776, 41C, 2S, pp. 841-48; Barry Farm notes; H Ex Doc 57, 41C, 3S, Ser 1453.

doctors, lawyers, or ministers, others had businesses with two or three colored employees and some white customers, and, as in the antebellum period, a good many were hack drivers, barbers, or dressmakers. At the Freedmen's Savings Bank in a handsome building across from the Treasury elegantly dressed colored tellers and an affable Negro cashier conducted the bank's routine affairs, while a board of white trustees passed upon loans. Although the House of Representatives refused to honor the credentials of John Menard, elected from a Louisiana district in 1868 by a large majority, the pronouncement attributed to James Garfield that it was "too early to admit a Negro to Congress" soon ceased to count. As colored professors joined the Howard University faculty and in 1870 Negro congressmen took seats in the House, Washington's upper-class Negroes attained a stature that would have been unthinkable half a decade before. The founding in January 1870 of a well-edited, readable Negro newspaper, the *New Era,* increased that stature.

The years 1869 and 1870 were notable in local colored annals. Twelve months before ratification of the Fifteenth Amendment, Congress erased the word *white* wherever it appeared in Washington's and Georgetown's charters and laws and specified that colored men were to be eligible for jury duty. A duplicate of a bill passed twice before in earlier sessions and twice vetoed by President Johnson, the act had met strong opposition in the Senate, but now signed by President Grant it promised at last to guarantee equality before the law to all men. It was the last congressional measure for ninety-five years to deal with race relations in the District of Columbia. The compiler of the Washington and Georgetown *Directory* promptly dropped the asterisk or the (c) after the names of colored residents. More astonishing, in May 1869 the city council carried civil rights very much further: it passed a bill forbidding racial discrimination in places of public entertainment on pain of a $20 fine. The mayor signed the law ten days later.

Nobody expostulated. A single violation was reported that autumn.[5]

How a city whose leaders had fought Negro suffrage in 1865 and 1866 could accept so revolutionary a measure in 1869 without vociferous protest is hard to explain. Obviously the law could not have passed without the endorsement of white council members. The school census of 1867 indicated that 40 percent of the white population had come during or since the war; in short, most new white residents were Northerners. Yet that fact offers at best only a partial answer, for racial prejudice existed in the North as well as the South; despite the ratification of the Fourteenth Amendment in July 1868, Northern states and municipalities were moving very slowly to extend civil rights to Negro citizens. Ratification of the amendment, however, almost unquestionably influenced Washington's attitudes. For sixty years the white community had dreaded becoming a catch-all for Negroes driven out of neighboring states by harsher legislation than Congress sanctioned in the capital city or than local authorities could enforce. Now important equal rights were written into the law of the land, and the District of Columbia need no longer represent a unique haven for colored Americans.

While positive evidence to account for Washington's about-face is skimpy, a reasonable possibility remains that a majority of white voters, after two years of unrestricted manhood suffrage, had come to see Negro potentialities in a new light and was therefore willing to lower the color bars further. The warm friendships springing up among members of the racially mixed faculties at the Howard University medical and law schools were natural developments probably not lost on the rest of the city.[6] The new

[5] *New Era*, 20 Jan, 24 Mar, 14 Apr 1870; *Star*, 29 May 1867, 15 Oct 1869; Baltimore *Sun*, 30 Sep, 16 Oct 1869; Washington and Georgetown *Directory*, 1868; *Cong Globe*, 40C, 2S, p. 720, 40C, 1S, App., p. 35; *Journal 66th Council*, p. 873, and *67th Council*, p. 25.

[6] *Spec Rpt Comr Ed*, pp. 28-29, 37. An oral description of relation-

act would not force white householders to open the doors of their homes to colored people, but, by establishing a standard of public behavior, it should gradually ease day-by-day encounters between the races. With federal officials from President Grant on down displaying a certain amount of cordiality toward Negroes, the ordinance, moveover, was likely to conciliate powerful radicals in Congress and thus be a means of restoring friendly relations between the city and the Hill. That was an argument the most conservative citizen could appreciate.

In January 1870 a Negro councilman proposed a second, more comprehensive antidiscrimination law, widening the application of the first to include restaurants, bars, and hotels, and raising the fine for noncompliance to $50. While one white Democrat indulged in a venomous attack on the bill, the principal dissent came from two Negro members of the council who argued that racial prejudice was rapidly disappearing and a second ordinance was therefore needless. Both men withdrew their objections, perhaps because of reminders that the powerful Typographical Union, the Bar Association, and the Medical Society of the District of Columbia still refused to admit Negroes to membership. Curiously enough, the second law, like the first, occasioned little stir. Washington's three leading dailies printed the text before the act passed but withheld comment. Only the reactionary Georgetown *Courier* disdainfully dismissed the new legislation as ridiculous. Yet the civil rights acts were not empty gestures; a test case the next winter won a court verdict for the complainant which was affirmed on appeal.[7] As if taking all this for granted, *The New Era* did not mention the new act or local responses to it.

---

ships at the medical school was given me by the daughter of one of the first colored graduates.

[7] *Journal 67th Council,* pp. 978, 1176-77, 1208; *Star,* 4 Jan, 1 Mar 1870; *Chronicle,* 4 Jan 1870; *Republican,* 1 Mar 1870; District Court of Appeals, Dockets, 23 May 1871, Case 9000, p. 190, N.A.; *New Era,* 12 Jul 1871.

The quality of the *New Era* astonished a good many white people, even those who recognized the distinction of its editors, Frederick Douglass and the Reverend J. Sella Martin, pastor of the Fifteenth Street Colored Presbyterian Church and a man highly regarded in Boston and England. The paper veered between pride in the progress the race had made in a scant half-dozen years and anger at white people's imperceptiveness or deliberate snubs. An article discussing the growth of Negro self-reliance since Negro enfranchisement in Washington and Georgetown concluded: "Each feels that he is a part, and has an interest in, the welfare of the city, the District, and the nation." A particularly elegant Negro party might receive brief coverage, but when John Forney of the *Chronicle* invited several Negroes to a "gentlemen's" party which President Grant and Cabinet officers also attended, the *Era* called it a "noticeable matter; but we doubt not, that, in the newer and better life upon which we have now entered, the color of the skin will cease to be a bar to recognition of gentlemanly qualifications here in the United States." Not long afterward the paper remarked: "No man need be afraid now, since the Chief Magistrate of the nation receives all alike at his levees—since, in fact, the chief men of Washington society invite colored men to their receptions." At the same time editorials blasted the "skin aristocrats" in the District who, displaying "the inherent prejudices of slaveholders, violate the whole spirit of our institutions and put us to shame before the world." The discriminatory attitudes of white workingmen received still sharper censure. Very occasionally the editors' criticisms extended also to colored merchants, physicians, and lawyers who catered more to white than to Negro patrons: "The worst form of infidelity in regard to negro capacity is to be found among negroes themselves." [8]

Leadership in colored Washington fell to notables like

[8] *New Era*, 20, 27 Jan, 24 Feb, 24 Mar, 14 Apr 1870, 2 Feb 1871.

Douglass and Martin, Dr. Alexander T. Augusta, a surgeon who rose to the rank of lieutenant colonel in the Union army during the war, Dr. Charles B. Purvis, professor at the Howard Medical School and chief surgeon at Freedmen's Hospital, and a dozen other men rather recently settled in the capital, but members of the old, established families who had grown up in freedom formed a scarcely less influential element in the Negro community. They had little in common with contrabands and, in spite of the *Era*'s optimistic statements about the progress of all Negroes, realists could not blink at the fact that the great mass of freedmen, concerned primarily with sheer survival, was still a fearful drag upon men who had fought their way up the social and economic ladder. As many white people tended to lump all Negroes together, self-interest put pressure upon Negro aristocrats to do what they could to raise the level of intelligence of their inferiors and to inspire in them a sense of responsibility as citizens. Some upper-class Negroes, overwhelmed by the magnitude of the task, evaded it; others accepted the challenge. But the class distinctions that had developed in the 1830's or earlier sharpened during the Reconstruction period.

Old families occupied a higher social position than newcomers except for the handful of nationally known figures. Education, professional status, and money were also important and, according to critics of the class structure of the next generation, sheer character—selflessness, honesty, and industriousness—still counted in 1870. Degree of color evidently affected a person's place in the Negro social hierarchy less directly than it would in later decades. But while a black skin manifestly did not constitute an insurmountable barrier to social recognition, light color, a sign of the admixture of white blood, was undoubtedly an asset. It was a carry-over from the days when household slaves, many of whom were mulattoes, felt themselves, and indeed often were, several cuts above the lowly black field hand. In the 1940's a Negro student of the post-Civil-War era in

Washington meticulously noted the complexion of every Negro office holder in the city government. Alderman John F. Cook and Councilman Carter Stewart were both "light." Of the seven Negro councilmen elected in 1869, three, a caterer, a preacher, and a brickmaker, were "black," four were "light," a government messenger, a cloakroom attendant at the Capitol, and two laborers. The common council chosen in June 1870 included a black preacher, a black government clerk, and four light men, two of them government messengers, one a teacher, and one a day laborer.[9] The prestige attaching to a minister, a government clerk, or a businessman apparently offset the handicap of blackness, while the light skin of a common laborer counterbalanced the humbleness of his occupation.

If color lines in local Negro society were already checking its fluidity and creating a rigidity that had no counterpart in white society, at the end of the sixties the most enterprising and adaptable freedmen were still able to narrow the gulf between themselves and upper-class Negroes. Ambitious ex-contrabands made use of their chances for education, moved out of the Negro slums as soon as they could afford anything better, and, by the exercise of utmost frugality, often succeeded in following the example of provident upper-class Negroes in salting away savings in the Freedmen's Savings and Trust Company.[10]

The schools were the chief source of worry to Negro leaders. In 1868 the Secretary of the Interior appointed two Negroes to the board of trustees of the colored schools, and

[9] *Ibid.*, 13 Nov 1873; Ada Piper, "Activities of Negroes in the Territorial Government of the District of Columbia, 1871-1874," p. 61 (M.A. thesis, Howard Univ). My interpretation of the class structure of the Negro community cannot be documented from contemporaneous materials. I base my presentation upon nuances in Negro newspaper articles of the later 1870's and the 1880's, upon some of the sketches in William J. Simmons, *Men of Mark, Eminent, Progressive and Rising*, published in 1887, and upon the educated guesses of colored Washingtonians of the 1950's.

[10] *Journal 68th Council*, pp. 16-19; Investigation into the Freedmen's Bank, H Rpt 502, 44C, 1S, pp. 92-93, Ser 1710.

the trustees engaged a superintendent, but after the withdrawal of help from Northern aid societies the progress of Negro education slowed. Classes for adults stopped. In the public schools the trustees reported tardiness nearly universal; most colored families had no way of telling time. Although by law three months' schooling a year was compulsory for every child, by 1870 few more than a third of the Negro children of school age in the District of Columbia were attending any school; Washington, Georgetown, and the county together had only sixty-six classes for Negro children. Superintendent and trustees had to contend with restricted budgets, inadequate equipment, the opposition of white people to having Negro schoolhouses built in their neighborhoods, and, still more discouraging, numbers of uncooperative Negro parents, badly trained Negro teachers, and bored, undisciplined children. The colored private schools taught little beyond the ABC's. Only at Howard University's "model school" conducted by a dedicated woman from Maine, Miss Sallie Grant, could a colored boy obtain a secondary school education at small cost.

Early in 1869 Congress sought to better matters by merging the white and colored school boards; Negroes, fearful lest their own schools suffer, persuaded President Johnson to veto it. Seven months later, to the astonishment of many people, a group of white and Negro residents of Washington's fourth ward requested a mixed school in their neighborhood. Living east of North Capitol Street in a thinly built-up, poor section where the streets were unusually muddy in winter, the 57 white and 28 Negro petitioners stressed the economy and other benefits of having one school for the 120 to 130 children of both races. Mayor Bowen, several aldermen, the superintendent of the white schools as a private citizen, and the colored school trustees approved. Negro voting, they reasoned, had caused no disturbance, colored men sat alongside white on the city council, and liberals saw no occasion now to forbid educating white and colored children together. The recent congressional act

100

that had stricken the word *white* from the District cities' charters and laws might well apply to all local tax-supported institutions. While a formal decision remained pending, the Reverend J. Sella Martin chose to test public opinion and clarify the situation by sending his fair-skinned nine-year-old daughter to a white school. The principal accepted the child, and everything went smoothly until several other parents, discovering the little girl's racial background, angrily withdrew their children. When a committee of aldermen asked the corporation attorney for an opinion on the legality of the token integration, the counsel hedged: he recommended waiting for Congress to authorize a unitary system. Whereupon the superintendent of the white schools ordered the principals serving under him to admit no colored children, however light-skinned, until Congress had enacted new legislation. Yet in early 1870 three more Negro children attended white public schools.[11]

As anticipated, at the next congressional session Senator Sumner of Massachusetts introduced a bill for desegregated schools in both Washington and Georgetown. By a vote of eleven to eight, the Washington common council begged Congress to pass the measure quickly, but national affairs and growing interest on the Hill in establishing an entirely new form of government for the District of Columbia sidetracked Sumner's proposal. In the interim dissension within City Hall over Mayor Bowen's costly make-work program and political integrity largely submerged the school issue.

In the end the hopeful campaign failed because only a timid, ill-organized minority endorsed it. To citizens who looked upon all Negroes as intrinsically inferior, the mere existence of even one racially mixed school was vaguely alarming; the idea might prove contagious, a possibility

[11] S Ex Doc 20, 41C, 3S, pp. 1-18, Ser 1440; Daniel Lamb, *Howard University Medical Department, A Historical, Biographical and Statistical Survey; Cong Globe,* 40C, 2S, p. 3928, 40C, 3S, pp. 935, 1164; *Journal 67th Council,* pp. 88-89, 463-69, 1300-02; *Star,* 27, 30 Nov 1869, 5 Jan, 8 Mar 1870; *Chronicle,* 5 Jan 1870.

peculiarly unwelcome to many white workingmen. Although the question again cropped up at intervals during the next dozen years, it did not receive the serious consideration it had commanded in 1869 and 1870. The archconservative *Daily Patriot* asserted that the trial of integration had all but wrecked the school system. White people deploring racial segregation on principle or because of the extravagance of maintaining two separate systems were as impotent to win over the community at large as were the Negroes who protested segregation's "depressing effect on the minds of colored children." Educated Negroes themselves were not solidly behind integration. A good many felt it would subject Negro children to competitive stresses they were not yet able to endure and would deny professional opportunities to qualified colored teachers; first let the race prove its ability to handle an independent educational system. Supporters of that position were elated in the autumn of 1870 when the Miner Fund, established by philanthropists in Myrtilla Miner's memory, provided money to start a Negro high school class in the basement of the Fifteenth Street Colored Presbyterian Church. Although the undertaking anticipated by some nine years the opening of a white public high school, the Negro triumph seemed hollow to the far-sighted Negro minority. The trustees of the colored schools replaced the white superintendent with George F. T. Cook, brother of the first colored alderman, but like the Negro city councilmen, they posed the unanswerable question: "If the fathers are fit to associate, why are not the children equally so?" [12]

The strivings of the colored community, however, after the early weeks of 1870 received less and less attention from white Washingtonians anxious about the city's future. Congressional lack of confidence in local officials and local

[12] S bill, 361, 41C, 2S; *Journal 68th Council,* pp. 828-29, 1474-75; S Misc Doc 130, 41C, 2S, Ser 1408; *Patriot,* 6, 9 Feb, 3 Apr 1871; *New National Era,* 5 Jun 1872, 31 Jul 1873, 6 Nov 1873; S Ex Doc 20, 41C, 3S, Ser 1440.

competence was matched by the electorate's loss of faith in Mayor Bowen. Whites generally blamed him and the Negro councilmen for the large increase in the municipal debt and for the meager results of his spending program. Negroes believed their vastly strengthened position in the city due solely to their own and congressional action, not to the mayor's. As they saw no reason to suppose a new mayor would try to obstruct the further advance of the social revolution of the last five years, they joined with white voters in repudiating Bowen. But his successor was no better able than he to solve the city's financial and administrative problems. Georgetown's troubles, though less acute, paralleled Washington's.[13]

Inasmuch as frequent battles with Congress seemed likely to paralyze both cities, residents increasingly wondered whether the wisest solution might not lie in abandoning local self-government and letting congressional committees run the federal district. When Senator Lot Morrill of Maine had urged that plan in 1866, House and Senate had rejected it chiefly because wiping out all local voting would prevent the politically important experiment of Negro suffrage. In 1870, when the Senate again considered the scheme, Henry Davis of Kentucky chilled white citizens' enthusiasm for it; never, he said, in all his years in Congress had any member of the two District committees shown himself a true friend of the District. "These committees," he declared, "have been organized on the principle of elevating the negro and, when there was a conflict, of subordinating the rights and interest and feelings of the white man to those of the negro." Rather than risk that kind of regime, 150 influential white citizens begged Congress to establish a territorial government for the entire District with a popularly elected governor, legislature, and delegate to the House of Representatives.[14]

---

[13] *New Era*, 27 Jan, 19 May, 16 Jun 1870.
[14] S Misc Doc 24, 41C, 1S, Ser 1399; *Star*, 5, 12 Oct 1869, 4 Jan 1870; *Cong Globe*, 41C, 2S, pp. 3912-14.

While the *New Era,* now renamed the *New National Era,* labeled the plan a step backward, in January 1871 the House District Committee presented a bill offering far less local autonomy than the petitioners had asked for. Instead of a territorial government like that established for areas destined to become states, the House bill specified a presidentially appointed governor and eleven-man upper house, leaving only a lower chamber and a nonvoting delegate to Congress to be elected by popular vote. An appointed board of health was to supervise the abatement of nuisances, and an appointed five-man board of public works was to take charge of public improvements and fix the assessments or issue bonds to meet the cost. Enacted on February 21, 1871, the new law went into effect in mid-May. Although some of the local public was dismayed at seeing so much authority vested in nonelective officials, no Washingtonian objected openly; and no one foresaw that the board of public works, responsible neither to the local electorate nor to Congress, would exercise despotic power.

If colored voters suspected that the new scheme was designed to curtail their role in the cities' administration, their apprehensions subsided when President Grant announced his nominees for the governor's council. Besides eight undistinguished white men, he named Frederick Douglass, John Gray, a caterer who occupied a secure place among colored Washington's aristocrats, and Adolphus Hall, a miller deeply respected in the Negro community. Neither Gray nor Hall were well known to white people, but the Negro appointees were obviously better qualified than most of their white associates, three of whom were new arrivals in the District. Equally gratifying to colored people was the President's selection for legal counsel of the board of health—the handsome, light-skinned, Ohio-born John Mercer Langston, who had served with the Freedmen's Bureau and recently come to Washington to head Howard University Law School. Their one serious disappointment arose when the election returns of mid-April showed only two of the twenty-two seats in the territorial House of Delegates filled by Negroes.[15]

As Frederick Douglass and Sella Martin had predicted, the short-lived territorial government gave far less scope to colored men than they had enjoyed during the last two and a half years of the municipalities. At the peak, in 1872, five Negroes sat in the House of Delegates, three in the upper chamber, never a large enough proportion of either body to carry much weight. Unemployment among day laborers, it is true, declined sharply during 1871 as the board of public works embarked on its "comprehensive plan of improvements," grading, paving, and lighting the streets, laying sewer mains, planting shade trees, and ripping up the railroad tracks laid in the 1850's across the Mall at the foot of Capitol Hill. But the benefits of the sudden rush of activity quickly diminished. According to a colored minister, workingmen were subjected to coercion to vote for large public bond issues, and the high wage scale announced by the board of public works soon proved to be window dressing, for as soon as New York and Philadelphia firms landed contracts they imported labor gangs at cheaper rates, and local contractors seeking to compete adopted the lower pay scale. Furthermore, the special assessments levied on private property by the board of public works early forced many homeowners to sell. By September 1872 sixteen eight-column pages of fine print in the *Evening Star* listed the official notices of houses, shops, and land to be sold at auction for nonpayment of taxes. White families as well as colored suffered, but fewer Negroes than whites could withstand the financial strain.[16]

[15] *New Era,* 27 Jan, 10 Mar 1870; *Cong Globe,* 41C, 3S, pp. 639-47, 685-88; *Star,* 21 Apr 1871; *Patriot,* 12, 14 Apr 1871, 20 Aug 1872.

[16] Investigation into the Affairs of the District of Columbia, H Rpt 72, 42C, 2S, pp. 9, 89, 170, 190, 442, 614, 698, Ser 1542 (hereafter cited as Investigation, 1872); Baltimore *Sun,* 7 Aug, 18 Nov 1871; *Patriot,* 29 Oct, 25 Nov 1871; H Misc Doc 58, 42C, 2S, Ser 1525; *Star,* 30 Sep 1872. For fuller discussion, see Green, *Washington, Village and Capital,* pp. 341-60.

The demise of the Freedmen's Bureau in 1872, moreover, left the District's indigent colored population without any federal agency to turn to for help. And the extravagant display and elaborate entertaining staged by high-ranking District and federal officials and by the *nouveaux riche* of the Gilded Age who flocked to the capital for the social "season" emphasized the miseries of the working classes. "There was never a time in Washington," wrote one observant resident, "when the wants of the laboring man and the poor were so little understood and so much neglected." The House of Delegates, composed though it was of rather humble men, appeared to be as irresponsible as the oblivious and affluent members of high society.

In testifying about the mismanagement of District affairs, one witness at a congressional hearing estimated that the expenses of the territorial government were 300 to 400 percent higher than the city's had been, a difference by no means explainable by the addition of services for Georgetown and the county to those for Washington. "Boss" Shepherd, head of the board of public works and a protégé of President Grant, successfully evaded specifics about how he spent the millions of tax dollars and borrowings allotted to the board for its "comprehensive plan of improvements." Suspicions that the District treasurer, a colored man who had been a cloakroom attendant at the Capitol, kept the accounts carelessly evaporated when he explained that the board of public works never submitted vouchers to him and never permitted him to see its books. By the early summer of 1873 the District of Columbia was bankrupt. Schoolteachers, clerks in District government offices, police, firemen, and day laborers in the street department went for months without pay. And in September a countrywide panic set off a five-year depression that within a few months destroyed every hope of restoring the Territory to solvency.[17]

[17] Investigation, 1872, pp. ii-xix and *passim;* F. C. Adams, *Our Little Monarchy, Who Runs It and What It Costs*, p. 15; Investigation into

Yet in the realm of public health, the territorial government served the District cities well, especially the poorest segments of colored Washington. Though unpopular with white people who preferred to disregard the exacting new sanitary regulations, the board of health introduced several salutary innovations. Its officials conducted house-to-house sanitary inspections, particularly in slum areas, took landlords to task for not providing tenants with adequate facilities, compiled careful vital statistics, and, by means of informing reports, carried on a campaign of education to teach a reluctant public facts about local health problems and how to lessen them. The board doubled the number of garbage and rubbish collections per week and contracted with the Odorless Excavating Apparatus Company to remove night soil from privies by suction pumps emptying into air-tight containers, a vast improvement over the old method of letting scavengers use buckets and open carts to haul loads to the wharf near the White House preparatory to dumping the refuse into the Potomac. Board members called attention to the shocking conditions in the alleyways, where the neediest Negro families lived in a squalor as appalling as that described by the chief of police in 1865 when he inspected Murder Bay. Although unable more often than not to force landlords and tenants to clean up their premises, health officials condemned the worst tenements, and fright over a smallpox epidemic raging in nearby cities in 1872 induced citizens to acquiesce in the demolition of about 350 irredeemably unsanitary dwellings. Some of the former occupants, unhappily, had to move into quarters very little better than the old, but at least civic-minded people learned how closely allied public health and decent housing were in a rapidly growing city.

The presence of John Mercer Langston on the board of health, moreover, stirred pride in other colored people. If

the Affairs of the District of Columbia, S Rpt 453, 43C, 1S, 1, 462-69, II, 12, 428, Sers 1590 and 1591 (hereafter cited as Investigation, 1874); *Patriot*, 1 Jul, 1 Oct 1872; *Star*, 3, 8, 25 Jul 1873.

his friendship with his white colleagues found expression chiefly in professional relationships, the doctors' appreciation of his warm human qualities and his legal competence encouraged less eminent Negroes to hope for similar acceptance. Langston's polished manners and his very light complexion eased matters for him. His inclination to brag rarely offended whites. When he accompanied Dr. Bliss, Washington's leading white physician, to a conference in Boston, a New Englander, remarking that he had heard that one of the Washington representatives was a Negro, turned inquiringly to them; silently Langston pointed to the darker-skinned Dr. Bliss, whereupon, to the confusion of their hosts, both men burst into laughter.[18] Few colored men possessed Langston's prestige, but other gifted, if less personable, Negroes learned to cast off inhibiting self-consciousness. Although professors at Georgetown University generally remained somewhat aloof from local affairs, Washingtonians took note that a Negro priest, Father Patrick Healy, became the university's acting president in 1873 and president in 1874. And the ability and the social graces of the Negroes teaching in the Howard University professional schools won them standing in what appeared to be a world in which race was rapidly ceasing to count.

That world was not all-encompassing. In fact, it did not wholly embrace doctors, lawyers, and other learned men. After repeatedly talking of abrogating the charter of the District Medical Society unless Negroes were admitted to membership, Congress dropped the matter. Nor could the best-mannered colored people frequent many public places without risking rebuffs; the Negro rank and file, no matter how decorously behaved, were never welcome in white establishments except as servants. In June 1872 the territorial

18 *Star*, 18 Oct 1872, 15 Feb, 9, 13 May, 26 Jul 1873; Rpt Board of Health in Report of the Commissioners of the District of Columbia, 1874, pp. 279, 281-95 (hereafter cited as Comrs Rpt); John Mercer Langston, *From Virginia Plantation to the National Capitol*, pp. 298, 318-34.

legislature took steps to end discrimination as far as law could check it in places that had to have licences to operate. The act was much like the Washington ordinance of 1870 except for including the entire District, adding bathing houses, barber shops, bars, and ice cream parlors to the list of establishments, requiring the posting of prices, and raising the penalty for noncompliance to a $100 fine and loss of the proprietor's licence for a year.[19]

Perhaps because the loss of a licence was a severe punishment, the new law provoked more overt and covert resistance than had the earlier municipal acts; observing the Negro's steady recent progress, segregationists concluded perhaps they were approaching a last-ditch fight. That summer and fall attempted evasions took the form of long delays in serving colored customers and the posting of exorbitant prices, such as "Steak $2, ham and eggs $3," or "Haircut $30, Shampoo $40," with a notice in small print announcing "a liberal reduction . . . to our regular patrons." In the four or five cases taken to court, the complainants won verdicts, only to have the Court of Appeals reverse three on legal technicalities. Yet Judge Snell's rebuke to one defendant rang loud in many ears: "Rights that have cost a Revolution will not stand aside for a pretext." To block off openings for pretexts—offering, for example, to serve colored patrons in a restaurant's pantry—a supplementary law enacted in 1873 stipulated that accommodations for all respectable customers must be identical. The White House set an example of fitting behavior; at President Grant's second inaugural ball in March 1873 colored congressmen's wives danced alongside West Point cadets. When financial disasters later in the year first overtook the District, reports of local civil rights cases ceased to appear in the press. Either economic troubles left no space for other issues, or no suits arose to discuss. People pinched for money could not afford to frequent bars and restaurants, and proprietors

[19] See n. 6; *Laws of the District of Columbia*, 20 Jun 1872, ch 51, pp. 65-66; *New Ntl Era*, 13, 20, 27 Jun, 25 Jul, 7 Nov, 19 Dec 1872.

needing patrons were presumably disinclined to offend any customer, white or black. On the whole the probabilities were that people who disliked the laws ceased to defy them.[20]

"Our only drawback today," wrote the *New National Era* in the autumn of 1873, "is in the matter of schools." Except for the small high school now headed by the scholarly Richard Greener of Howard University, all the colored schools were undeniably inferior to the white. Repeated complaints about the division of school monies gradually had some effect, but when the territorial legislature authorized funds for a normal school and the House of Delegates voted to open it to colored as well as white students, the governor's council, at the instigation of the Negro member who had replaced Frederick Douglass, overruled the lower chamber. "The recreancy of our representatives in the Council," a group of colored citizens observed bitterly, defeated the best possibility of terminating the "separate but equal" arrangement. Nearly ten years of separate systems, however, had strengthened the vested interest of Negro teachers in keeping the Negro schools independent. When the Miner Fund supplied the means of organizing a separate Negro teacher training unit, colored candidates for teaching posts apparently thought the classes a satisfactory substitute for a racially mixed normal school. In the opinion of the Negro majority, civil rights did not enter into school questions, provided the distribution of funds were equitable. Meanwhile, the never-ending stream of illiterate colored people pouring in from the South diluted the effectiveness of the colored schools and indeed made all racial adjustments more difficult.[21]

In-migration of rural Negroes bothered conservative whites more than any other one phase of the racial situation.

---

[20] *Laws of D.C.*, 26 Jun 1873, ch 46, pp. 116-19; *Star*, 13, 27, 30 Aug, 3 Sep, 2 Nov, 5 Dec 1872; *The Nation*, XVI, 173.

[21] *New Ntl Era*, 22 Feb 1872, 5 Jun, 3, 10, 31 Jul, 9 Oct 1873, 22 Jan 1874; *Star*, 30 Jun 1873; *Journal of the Council of the District of Columbia*, IV, 158, 184-85, V, 222-23.

An estimate in the *Patriot* at the end of 1872 put the number of newcomers in the preceding two years at some 5,000, bringing the total Negro population to about 48,000. "The native and natural colored population of this District," wrote the editor, "is excellent in character, intelligent, and has always been respected," but the "shiftless" new arrivals were "eating us out of house and home." The *New National Era,* on the contrary, put much of the blame for racial friction upon the younger generation of colored Washingtonians: "How many sons have inherited the undoubtedly good traits of their fathers?" asked the editor. Was it not plain that "a systematic depreciation of young colored men by each other has stripped them of whatever consideration their talents or their standing might entitle them to among the whites"? The older generation had exhibited a humility, public spirit, and independence that had "helped to create the possibilities of the present day, and nothing but these traits of character in young colored men will save them from the failures begot by egotism, the guilt of selfishness, the disgrace of sycophancy, and the disgust which ever waits on bad manners." [22] This analysis was one of the last pieces to appear in the *Era.* Financial difficulties ended publication in 1874.

District affairs by then had reached such a chaotic state that Congress conducted a long investigation. Discovery that Boss Shepherd had exceeded by more than $8 million the $10 million debt limit authorized for public works and that the deficit for routine operating expenses was running to over $1 million a year sealed the fate of the territorial government. Congress appropriated $75,000 to pay the arrears in schoolteachers' salaries, but while United States Treasury auditors set to work to unsnarl the tangle of board of public works financial commitments, a congressional act put three presidentially appointed commissioners in charge of other local administrative matters. All elective offices

[22] *Patriot,* 26 Sep 1872; *New Ntl Era,* 13 Nov 1873.

disappeared; only the school boards, the board of health, the fire department, and the Metropolitan Police force survived the demolition of the Territory. Inasmuch as Congress authorized a bond issue backed by the credit of the United States to pay off over a period of fifty years the District's $20 million debt, most local taxpayers felt relieved. Wanton spending would now cease, injured property owners could expect to collect damages, and Washingtonians assumed that Congress would eventually return control of their own affairs to District citizens if by then they wanted it.

While the new arrangement disposed of what the Georgetown *Courier* labeled the "curse" of Negro suffrage, a preposterous incident silenced men who regretted the change. Several members of the House of Delegates, upon hearing of the Territory's demise, rushed to the legislature's hall and pocketed inkwells and other small objects; one pilferer, caught walking out with a red feather duster protruding from his trouser leg, fastened the label "Feather Duster legislature" upon the entire assembly. Ridicule killed the Territory more thoroughly than congressional law. Thereafter whites opposed to the return of any local suffrage that included colored voters spoke of "the Feather Dusters" and "the Murder Bay politicians"; by implication, the ten or twelve Negroes among the scores of officials of the territorial regime were alone responsible for its every disaster. Racists shut their eyes to a fact fair-minded citizens acknowledged, namely that the Territory's collapse was due to the financial irresponsibility of the five white men the President had appointed to the board of public works.[23]

Colored men naturally resented the anti-Negro insinuations, but on the death of the *New National Era* the best gauge of Negro public opinion vanished, and with it the

[23] Investigation, 1874, I, x-xx and *passim; Congressional Record*, 43C, 1S, pp. 5116-24, 5154-56 (hereafter cited as *Cong Rec*) ; 18 Stat. 116-21; *Courier*, 20 Jun 1874; *Chronicle*, 21 Jun 1874; *Star*, 18 Jun 1874, 28 Jan, 25 Feb 1878; *Republican*, 22 Mar 1878.

1. Sunday prayer service at Freedman's Village on the former Arlington estate of General Robert E. Lee, ca. 1864.

3. The first colored public schoolhouse, at Second and C Streets, Southeast, 1865.

2. Abraham Lincoln showing Sojourner Truth the Bible presented to him by Baltimore freedmen, ca. 1864. A composite picture pieced together later.

4. "Scene in the House [of Representatives] on the Passage of
the Proposition to Amend the Constitution, January 31, 1865."
Wood engraving in *Harper's Weekly*.

5. "Celebration of the Abolition of Slavery in the District of Columbia by the Colored People, in Washington, April 19, 1866." Wood engraving from sketch by F. Dielman in *Frank Leslie's Illustrated Newspaper.*

6. "The Georgetown Election—The Negro at the Ballot-Box," February 1867. Thomas Nast cartoon in *Harper's Weekly.* The figure at the left is a caricature of President Andrew Johnson.

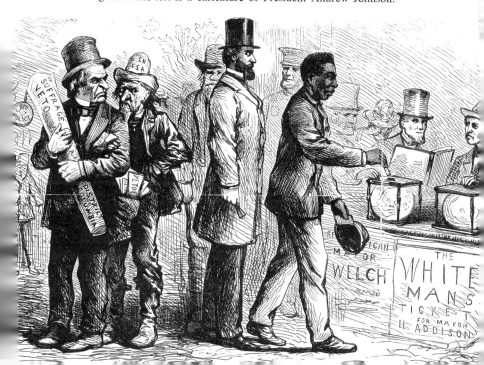

7. Howard University, ca. 1870.

8. Faculty of the Howard University Medical Department, 1869-1870. From left to right: A. T. Augusta, S. L. Loomis, G. S. Palmer, O. O. Howard, R. Reyburn, J. T. Johnson, C. B. Purvis, P. H. Strong. Photograph from Daniel Lamb's *The Howard University Medical Department.*

9. "The African Race in Congress—Hon. John Willis Menard Addressing the House of Representatives, Washington, D.C., February 27, 1869." Wood engraving from a sketch by **James F. Taylor** in *Frank Leslie's Illustrated Newspaper.*

10. "The First Colored Senator and Representatives." From left to right: H. R. Revels, Benjamin S. Turner, Robert C. de Large, Josiah T. Walls, Jefferson H. Long, Joseph H. Rainy, R. Brown Elliot. Currier & Ives print.

11

12

NEGRO NOTABLES. 11. Frederick Douglass. 12. Blanche K. Bruce, senator from Mississippi and later register of the Treasury. 13. Henry Highland Garnet, pastor of the Fifteenth Street Presbyterian Church and later minister to Liberia. 14. Richard T. Greener, principal of the Negro High School and later dean of Howard University. 15. Alexander Crummell, pastor of St. Mary's Chapel and later rector of St. Luke's Episcopal Church. 16. John Mercer Langston, legal counsel for the board of health.

13

14

15

16

17. "Field Trip: School Children at the Library of Congress."
Photograph by Frances Johnston, 1898.

Metropolitan A.M.E. Church,
Parent of the Bethel Literary
and Historical Association.

19. Bridal party of high colored society, 1882. Marian Parke and her cousins.

Reception Dr Shadd
cor 9th and R St NW Dec 26th '95

Menu

Oyster Rice Candy and Macaroons)
Side " " Fancy Charlotte de Russe
" " " Fruit in Pyramid

Chicken Croquette with Mushrooms
Scalloped Oysters
Chicken Salad
Lobster Salad
Spermacetic Rolls
Chow Chow
Assorted Fancy Creams and Water Ice
" " Cake
" Salad Punch at 11 Pm
4 Men Waiters

I will furnish the above menu for 200 persons
with all necessary China, Glass and Silver
ware, table linen, every thing to be first-
class for $165 —
yr friend
Calvin

20. Menu for a Negro housewarming reception, 1895. Freund was the best caterer in Washington.

Negro community's most effective organ of protest at injustice. The loss of suffrage at the same time cut off colored men from the contacts with whites that local politics had automatically created. Probably few former voters recognized the long-term consequences of that stoppage of day-by-day interracial communication, but to Negroes, who had first exercised the elective franchise in 1867, the new denial must have caused an uneasiness only partly offset by belief that the Republican Stalwarts on the Hill would always stand by them. That faith seemed justified when Congress passed the Civil Rights Act of 1875, which promised Negroes in every state of the Union the kind of protection that the municipal and territorial acts had given to colored Washington.

Hard times meanwhile were pushing political uncertainties into the background. Howard University, burdened with heavy debts, managed to avoid closing altogether only by dropping courses and cutting faculty salaries in half. The failure of the Freedmen's Bank in June 1874 wiped out the savings of hundreds of families, and, if anything could have added to that tragedy, it was white people's inclination to attribute the disaster to Negro incompetence, not to the folly and shady transactions of the white trustees who had controlled the bank's investments. As the depression deepened, unemployment rose to new peaks. The Navy Yard dismissed 400 employees and the Bureau of Engraving 700, while the commissioners, forbidden by law to increase the public debt by borrowing and hampered by shrinking tax revenues, sharply reduced the number of persons on the District payroll and cut the wages of common laborers from $1.50 a day to $1. At the same time the resources of charitable organizations dwindled as their principal supporters faced severe financial losses. In asking Congress to vote $20,000 for local relief, Representative Adlai Stevenson of Illinois spoke in 1876 of the "absolute starvation in this city." The appropriation was only a stop-gap. Since unemployment was countrywide, nothing came of a

113

plan proposed by one of the District commissioners to open a labor exchange to send jobless men to sections of the country that needed workmen. By 1877 laborers jumped at a chance to work a ten-hour day for fifty cents.[24]

Fortunately, permission to draw on the United States Treasury against future local taxes eventually enabled the commissioners to hire men to redo the faulty work and complete the unfinished jobs of the territorial board of public works. Congressional appropriations of $15,000 to fill the swampy land southwest of the Capitol, $5,000 for medical care of the poor, and $1,500 for a "Penny Lunch House" also helped lift the gloom enveloping Washington. It lifted further when a number of landlords decided to make repairs on rundown tenements while prices were low. Thus the capital weathered through the long depression.[25]

Every public service had suffered in the interim. Cuts in the budget of the board of health reduced its efficiency at a time when Negro mortality stood at 48.95 per thousand, a figure considerably higher than the Negro birth rate and nearly two and a half times the death rate among whites. As sheer want increased the incidence of petty crime, particularly among destitute Negroes, the police resorted to arbitrary arrests. All the public schools were overcrowded, and there were no accommodations at all for about 4,200 of the District's nearly 10,000 colored children. Not more than a handful of teachers in either the colored or the white schools had had more than a grammar school education. The commissioners' consolidation of the school boards in the autumn of 1874 brought together into a single body the colored and white trustees for the two cities and the

---

[24] Holmes, "Fifty Years of Howard University," *Journ Neg History,* III, 368-75; Walter Fleming, *The Freedmen's Savings Bank,* pp. 53-84; *Star,* 7 May, 7 Jun, 10, 21 Jul, 1 Nov, 6 Dec 1875, 26 Feb, 20 Sep 1876, 3, 7, 15 Sep, 3 Oct 1877; *Chronicle,* 3 Jan 1875, 1 Jul, 23 Dec 1877; 19 Stat. 211; Comrs Rpts, 1876, pp. 21, 510-24, and 1877, pp. 54, 203-43, Sers 1751 and 1802; *Cong Rec,* 44C, 2S, pp. 1059, 1088-92, 1186.

[25] *Cong Rec,* 45C, 2S, pp. 1840, 2135, 3590, 3786, 4490; *Star,* 5 Mar 1877, 15 Feb, 2 Apr 1878.

county, but the administrative simplification failed to solve financial problems. Although radicals on the District's Central Republican Committee in 1876 drafted a platform condemning racially segregated schools, nobody in power listened.[26]

As Congress postponed from session to session a decision about a permanent form of government for the District and what share, if any, of the costs should fall upon the federal Treasury, the newspapers discussed the pros and cons of continued congressional and commissioner rule over against popular elections, while articulate citizens of every shade of opinion submitted their ideas to House and Senate. Well-informed residents early perceived that Congress would insist upon keeping control of the purse strings if federal money were to pay any sizable proportion of the District's expenses. Hence large taxpayers tended to think disenfranchisement a small price to pay for the financial security that would be ensured by congressional appropriations and freedom from the extravagances of a local electorate dominated by propertyless voters and heavily weighted with irresponsible Negroes. But when the *Star,* Washington's most widely read newspaper, contended that "the peaceable, law-abiding portion of our citizens" was tired of "the disgraceful scenes attending elections regulated by 'Murder Bay,'" John Forney of the *Chronicle* retorted: "Whatever corruption the 'Feather Dusters' and 'Murder Bay' slums perpetrated . . . was not as much of their origination as the Executive-appointed power behind," meaning of course the board of public works and the territorial governor. The danger to the community of having no voice whatsoever in its own government, Forney added, should be obvious to every

[26] Rpts Bd of Health, 1875-1877, Sers 1682, 1751, 1802; Comrs Rpts, 1874, pp. 19, 105-11, 1875, pp. 18, 22, 317, 427, 442-45; School Trustees Rpt, 1876-1877, pp. 119, 143, 261, and 1877-1878, pp. 217-22; Rpts Sec/Int, 1875, p. xiv, 482, Ser 1681, 1876, pp. xxvii, xli, 439-40, Ser 1750, 1877, p. xxi, Ser 1801; enclosure to ltr, A. M. Green, Republican Central Executive Committee, D.C., to S. J. Bowen, 19 Jan 1876, Bowen Mss.

person who had observed the commissioners' high-handed procedures.

A great many white workingmen and some Negroes supported Forney's view, but a number of colored people preferred to rely upon Congress rather than entrust their future to a two-thirds white local electorate. On the Hill, old-line Republicans' advocacy of Negro voting strengthened the home rule cause before 1877, but their influence waned after the new President, Rutherford B. Hayes, began his program of conciliating Southern whites. From 1878 onward, colored people ceased to be a major concern of the Grand Old Party.[27]

The act of June 1878 that at long last settled the question of who was to run the District of Columbia for the next ninety years was tantamount to a bargain struck: Congress would govern the federal area with three presidentially appointed commissioners serving as executives, and, in return for the denial of any local say about taxes and every other local problem, the federal government would share expenses equally with District taxpayers. Elaborate fiscal restrictions written into the new law would protect the public purse. The President of the United States was to name the justices of the District Supreme Court, and the chief justice was to appoint all lesser court officials. Two of the three commissioners must be civilians with at least three years of local residence; the third was to be an officer of the Army Engineer Corps. The commissioners were to appoint the police, members of the school board, and a single health officer who, with sharply lessened authority and a curtailed budget, was to assume the duties formerly assigned to a five-man board. The new organic act thus promised to provide efficient and economical government, but it placed autocratic power

[27] Draft petition, Committee of 100, 9 Oct 1877, enclosure to Addison Dent to Bowen, 19 Mar 1877, Bowen to George Holmes, 20 Mar 1877, Bowen Mss; *Star,* 13 Apr 1876; *Chronicle,* 3 Feb 1878; ptns, S44A-J3, 2 Oct and 13 Nov 1876, H44A-D1, B-12, 13 Nov 1876, and H45A-D1, B14, n.d.; *Cong Rec,* 45C, 1S, p. 165.

in the hands of three men who would be in no way responsible to the local public.[28]

Most of that public was satisfied. If colored men foresaw that they were unlikely to receive appointive offices comparable in number and importance to the positions they had won and might win in popular elections, few Negroes anticipated the loss of other significant gains of the postwar years. Colored men held seats in Congress, and Congress would control District legislation. The educated colored men holding clerkships in the federal executive departments appeared to be safe enough. Three Negroes sat on the District's nine-man school board, the number of teachers in the colored school system was expanding, a colored Ohioan occupied the post of Recorder of Deeds, and Frederick Douglass was serving as United States Marshal for the District, albeit shorn of the ceremonial functions which the position had entailed when white men held it. In 1877 the first Negro to receive an appointment to the United States Naval Academy had returned to Washington, without graduating to be sure, but with sufficient experience to put him in a responsible, well-paid position in the Patent Office. The local civil rights laws were still in force, and the federal Civil Rights Act of 1875, while not as yet bringing in verdicts for complainants in most of the states, was an additional safeguard in the District of Columbia. The well-being of colored Washington need not depend on the restoration of local balloting.

Although some 15,000 colored newcomers since 1870 imposed a burden upon the established Negro community, the rate of increase was a fraction of that of the preceding decade. Furthermore, while the lowest social stratum expanded faster than any other, some colored families who had seemed utterly improvident a few years before were now slowly moving up into the ranks of colored Washington's middle class. John Forney had counseled his colored

[28] 20 Stat 102-108.

friends against starting a new Negro newspaper, as he thought it likely to impede Negro assimilation into the larger community, but from the beginning the flat dimension of color had set Negro Washington apart; deeper understanding alone would bridge the gap. When *The People's Advocate* began publication in the city in 1878, its readers could follow the course of race relations more fully than had been possible since the demise of the *New National Era*. Overtures from the White House and Northern capitalists to Southerners who were anxious to develop industry pointed, it is true, to an opening of the doors to a new racism in the Southern states, but Washington's colored intelligentsia clung to faith in Judge Snell's pronouncement: "Rights that have cost a Revolution will not stand aside for a pretext." [29]

[29] See advertisements in *People's Advocate*, 1878; Andrew F. Hilyer, *The Twentieth Century Union League Directory, A Historical, Biographical and Statistical Study of Colored Washington.*

CHAPTER VII

THE WITHERING OF

HOPE, 1879-1901

 "We live," wrote the famous army surgeon Dr. John Shaw Billings, "in a fortunate time and place—in the early manhood of a mighty nation, and in its capital city, which every year makes more beautiful and richer in the treasure of science, literature and art." White Washington in the 1880's enjoyed a material prosperity and amenities richer than any the city had ever known before. For Negroes the satisfactions of life diminished steadily after 1878. Between white and colored people such tolerant friendliness as survived the seventies slowly disappeared. The change was gradual enough to permit colored people for a time to persuade themselves that a year or two would suffice to reestablish them on the footing they had attained earlier. Not until the autumn of 1883 did they clearly sense how much the atmosphere had chilled in a decade, and not until the 1890's did they realize that no effort of theirs was likely to restore warmth to the city's race relations.

In 1888 the Washington *Elite List,* a forerunner of the *Social Register,* carried the names of five or six Negroes; by 1892 they had been dropped. After John Forney of the *Chronicle* retired, the white press, increasingly critical of Negroes' "shiftlessness" and the high rate of crime among them, gradually reduced other news about them to an occasional facetious comment on a colored social gathering. Exasperation or disgust blotted out compassion for the great mass of blacks, while white people's interest in the careers of gifted Negroes became so condescending as to

119

be insulting, the more so as the condescension was unconscious. By the mid-nineties a reader of the white newspapers might have supposed that Washington had no colored community, let alone three virtually separate Negro communities. White people, in short, in the course of the twenty-odd years resolved the problem of race relations by tacitly denying its existence.

How to explain so drastic a shift in attitude? The two decades under scrutiny encompassed a period of far greater national change than was apparent to Americans experiencing it. It was marked by an inundation of foreign immigrants, by a concentration of wealth in the hands of a half-hundred daring and often ruthless industrialists and railroad executives, by an accompanying decline in the influence of a somewhat bewildered middle class, by violent conflicts between labor and capital, by the "rise of the city" in a formerly agricultural nation, and finally by the emergence of the United States as a world power. Of those factors several had less direct bearing on life in the national capital than in other cities. Relatively few foreign-born came to Washington. Being nonindustrial, the city escaped the full force of labor battles and kept some aspects of its bucolic past. To outsiders the District seemed singularly placid, untouched by the intensely competitive spirit of the rest of the country. Nevertheless, as the capital Washington was highly sensitive to new political winds, of which a wooing of the newly industrializing South was one of the strongest. Ostensibly in a position to mould American public opinion and guide public policies, in actuality the city was a follower, "yr obdt servant," accepting the standards of behavior of communities whose votes in national elections counted heavily. Along with the "bloody shirt" Washington rapidly discarded concern for racial justice. Colored men were economically too insecure to affect the climate of opinion in a nation increasingly dedicated to material progress and all too ready to embrace the thesis of Social Darwinism about the "survival of the fittest."

120

In Washington, where Negroes had made greater strides than anywhere else in the United States, local disenfranchisement abruptly ended political associations between Negroes and whites. Social intercourse, only beginning to develop in 1870, consequently died out for want of nourishment from natural, day-by-day encounters of fellow citizens with obvious common interests. As time went on, the failure of the bulk of the city's black population to evince a sense of responsibility disillusioned formerly well-disposed whites who professed to think they had more than discharged their obligations to colored people. That disillusionment fed racial hostility as surely as racial discrimination undermined Negroes' determination to help themselves. The result was a vicious spiral. Whites concluded that most Negroes would never make good citizens, and Negroes, feeling themselves steadily shoved further into a corner by prejudice, ceased to stand up for one another and let the fight degenerate into that of each for himself. The exceptions were too few to alter the large picture. Well-educated aristocrats of predominantly white blood drew further away from the darker-skinned middle-class families, while the gulf separating both groups from inarticulate blacks widened. Except as seen in all Negroes' search for "*whiteness*—the ability to pass unnoticed in the crowd, the power to avoid humiliation and abuse," a community in the sense of people united by common aspirations and cultural identity fell apart before it had outgrown infancy. The biological accident of pigmentation created growing resentments which colored people directed at each other more bitterly than at whites. By the 1890's most Negroes in the District were adhering to the social pattern common in the deep South: conflict within the caste and compliance with or carefully concealed hostility toward the white group outside.[1]

[1] A. Hunter Dupree, *Science in the Federal Government*, p. 230; Pauli Murray, *Proud Shoes, The Story of an American Family*, p. 53; see

For upper-class Negroes civil rights were still the key to progress. During the Hayes administration violations of the antidiscrimination laws apparently multiplied but were either too trivial or too skillfully cloaked to lead to court action. The *People's Advocate* initially urged Negroes to concentrate on fair play: instead of suing white proprietors for refusing them accommodation, first file complaints against Negro barbers who refused to serve other colored men. Two years later the editor doubted the wisdom of those tactics. "A respectable colored lady or gentleman, unless it happens to be a man like Frederick Douglass, John F. Cook, or Register Bruce [former United States Senator from Mississippi], is not readily accommodated, if at all, in the eating establishments, no matter how genteel he may be in appearance or in manners." The result was "more or less friction between the keepers of these saloons and a class of our citizens rapidly growing in wealth and intelligence." Washington Negroes nevertheless still relied upon patience to destroy prejudice.[2]

In the summer of 1883 a Negro visitor from Connecticut sued a Washington restaurant owner under the criminal section of the federal Civil Rights Act. Newspapers throughout the country discussed the case, partly because it was only the second criminal suit to be brought under the act of 1875, partly because the argument for the defense had an ominous logic: a government which sanctioned separate colored schools could not reasonably require a restaurant proprietor to seat Negroes in a dining room with whites; he had offered to serve the colored man in the pantry. The judge reviewed all earlier decisions in local civil rights cases, noted that several verdicts had been adverse to the plaintiffs, but in this case found against the defendant and fined him $500.

John Dollard, *Caste and Class in a Southern Town;* Albion Davis and G. and M. Gardner, *Deep South.*

[2] *People's Advocate,* 5 Jul, 15, 29 Nov 1879, 10 Jul 1880, 6 Aug 1881 (hereafter cited as *Advocate*).

It was at best a Pyrrhic victory. It strengthened white animosities already heightened by the discovery that federal courts outside the District of Columbia rarely heard civil rights cases, and it inspired pronouncements that the judge's interpretation of the law would force restaurant owners either to accept an exclusively black clientele, or see their business ruined, or both. Negroes native to the District were ironically rewarded for their past forbearance by repeated statements citing their eight-year failure to sue under the federal law as proof that the color line was unobjectionable to them. Two months after the decision of August 1883, the United States Supreme Court declared the Civil Rights Act unconstitutional in the states, although it might still be binding in the District of Columbia and United States territories. Ignorant blacks were badly frightened, expecting to see the whipping post brought back at any moment. Educated Negroes in Washington were angry. Frederick Douglass, with more passion than accuracy, called the decree a deliberate repudiation of a law that had won general public acceptance. Only George Richardson, a teacher in the colored high school, told the Bethel Literary and Historical Association that the court ruling, however distressing to colored people, was "severely and equitably just." Negroes would have to count on demonstrating to the states that colored people were citizens worthy of the same treatment as whites. In any case, the local laws were in force. But no one favoring racial legal equality pretended that the court decision was not a serious setback.

The Bethel Literary and Historical Association, founded in 1881 by Bishop Daniel Payne of the African Methodist Episcopal Church, frequently debated the question of what course Negroes should pursue. Alexander Crummell, rector of St. Luke's Episcopal Church, whom many people considered the foremost Negro intellectual of his time, in 1875 had called it a "heresy" for colored Americans to forget "that they ARE colored people." On coming to Washington in 1873 after spending twenty years as a missionary in Liberia, he had discarded his advocacy of colonization, but he preached a gospel of Negro uniqueness. Negroes, " 'a peculiar people' in this land," must strive for racial organization as a distinct entity in the nation. Other speakers at Bethel Literary sessions insisted that racial solidarity and economic chauvinism were destructive, underscoring Negro differences from other Americans; colored people ought rather to aim at obliterating the factors that set them apart and seek social assimilation into white America. But John Cromwell of the *Advocate* in addressing himself to the thesis of Negro advancement by self-improvement pointed out that "the material defect in the individual development theory is that the white people will not let you get rid of the idea of race."

The Negro press took special note of Frederick Douglass' about-face. In 1866 he had told white paternalists to leave the Negro alone to find his own level; by the mid-1880's he had become convinced that the race problem was the white man's problem which Negroes could not and should not have to solve. When he married a white woman in 1884 and some of his associates angrily accused him of lacking pride of race, he brushed their criticism aside as an impertinence. Race pride and race solidarity he contended were fallacies. He wrote in the AME *Review* in 1889: "Our union is our weakness," breeding a cultural provincialism in an oppressed people. "A nation within a nation is an anomaly. There can be but one nation . . . and we are Americans." Yet in the capital most colored leaders veered increasingly toward a form of Negro nationalism.[3]

Between 1884 and the turn of the century most of the few civil rights suits filed in the District of Columbia were dismissed; only two or three were successful, such as the case against a lunchroom proprietor who had not posted a

[3] *Ibid.*, 3 Mar, 25 Aug 1883; Washington *Bee*, 4 Aug, 8 Sep 1883, 28 Apr 1884; *Star*, 7, 13, 16, 18, 24 Aug, 17, 24 Oct 1883; John Cromwell, *History of the Bethel Literary and Historical Association;* August Meier, *Negro Thought in America, 1880-1915*, pp. 42-43, 53-55, 75-77.

price list and had overcharged a Negro outrageously by demanding fifty cents for three eggs, two biscuits, and a cup of coffee. In the 1880's barrooms generally served colored customers, but lunchrooms and ice cream parlors usually excluded them, a source of particular irritation to "genteel" Negroes. The genteel plainly indicated their readiness to have vulgar blacks denied service. Petitions submitted to Congress in 1886 asked for stronger local laws extended to areas not covered in the municipal and territorial acts, but new laws seemed unlikely to improve white tempers. Congress dismissed all proposals for racial legislation, whether bills forbidding miscegenation or those demanding a change in the District Medical Society's discriminatory rules. In 1896 the Supreme Court struck a deadly blow at all American Negroes by ruling in the famous Plessy versus Ferguson case that separate but equal accommodations met every requirement of the Fourteenth Amendment. Four years later a suit against the owner of the Washington Opera House for refusing to let a colored man occupy the orchestra seat he had paid for netted the plaintiff damages of one cent.[4]

Nor were Negroes guiltless. A number of Negro-owned barber shops and some hotels and restaurants run by colored men would not accept Negro customers. A circular of 1888, for example, announced: "Preston's Pension Office barber shop, first class in every particular. Devoted *Strictly to White Trade*. The rumor that this shop has been serving any Colored Trade is false in every particular." The white press called attention to such incidents. "The refusal is based, of course," remarked the *Star*, "not on color prejudice, but on the business consideration that the best paying class of customers can be retained only by excluding those

---

[4] *Star*, 8, 22 Nov 1884, 4 Feb, 10 Dec 1887, 18 Feb 1888; *Cong Rec,* 47C, 1S, pp. 1408-10, 1839; ptn, S49A-H63, 28 Jan 1886; S. Rpt 1050, 52C, 1S, Ser 2915; *Bee*, 1884-1899, 24 Nov 1900. As virtually every issue of the *Bee* carried items relevant to the topics discussed in this and in the next chapter, citations represent a mere sample.

who for any reason are objectionable to their fastidious notions."[5] After the founding of the short-lived Afro-American League in 1890, a Washington branch sent delegates to its national conventions, but disunity, lack of a positive program to combat racism, and the magnitude of the problem stripped the organization of effectiveness. Its successor, the Afro-American Council, which came into being in 1898, was largely controlled by Booker T. Washington, whose seeming subservience to whites alienated Negro militants. As Jim Crow laws began to multiply in the Southern states, Negroes in the District realized they were far better off than most of their race; but they saw that the local antidiscrimination laws had come to be more honored in the breach than in the observance.

Chance, moreover, played into the hands of segregationists. In 1901 Congress accepted the first part of a codification of District law but left "the second or municipal part" to be revised and adopted later. Although Congress specified that existing police regulations, unless expressly repealed, should continue in force—a stipulation that meant the civil rights laws were still valid—the fact that the published code contained no mention of the antidiscrimination ordinances encouraged white men to ignore them.[6]

Washington's old, well-established colored families such as the Cooks and the Wormleys had reason for a time to believe that they and distinguished later arrivals such as Frederick Douglass and ex-Senator Blanche K. Bruce could enjoy some rights not specifically protected by law. Good manners, professional status, and money made them acceptable residents of any locality provided they did not obtrude

[5] *Star,* 12 Dec 1887; *Bee,* 21 Jul 1888.
[6] *Colored American,* 9 Apr 1898; *Bee,* 16 Nov 1889, 27 Aug 1898; August Meier, "Booker T. Washington and the Negro Press," *Journal of Negro History,* xxxviii, 85, n; *Cong Rec,* 56C, 2S, pp. 3497, 3586, 3603; Walter S. Cox, "Attempts to Obtain a Law Code for the District of Columbia," CHS *Rec,* iii, 127-32; Phineas Indritz, "Post Civil War Ordinances Prohibiting Racial Discrimination in the District of Columbia," *Georgetown Law Journal,* xlii, 196-201.

themselves socially upon white people. But cultivated Negroes, even those who looked almost white, discovered that each passing year made it harder for them to purchase or rent comfortable houses without paying exorbitant prices; by the 1890's they could rarely buy at all in a conveniently located, orderly neighborhood. In 1892 John Lynch, a successful building contractor, put up a handsome house for himself in the most fashionable section of New Hampshire Avenue, but Mary Church Terrell's *A Colored Woman in a White World* tells of endless humiliations in the course of her house hunt. Yet her husband was a *cum laude* graduate of Harvard, a respected lawyer, principal of the M Street High School, and after 1896 a member of the Board of Trade; she herself was a graduate of Oberlin, an accomplished linguist, and one of two women before 1900 to be appointed to the school board.

Rising rentals hastened the exodus of Negro householders who in the seventies had lived along 16th Street a few blocks above Lafayette Square and out beyond Scott Circle. As the real estate boom in northwest Washington gained momentum, colored people moved farther from the center of the city. Whether sheer economics or, as rumor had it, combinations of real estate agents kept respectable Negroes from moving into desirable localities, the result was the same. It did not mean that clear-cut solid black belts arose outside of which Negroes could not find housing; some intersprinkling of white and Negro dwellings continued down into the 1930's. But by 1900 the barrier of caste, seemingly collapsing in the late 1860's, had become stronger than ever. The one notable exception lay in the Board of Trade, the city's principal business organization: James T. Wormley was a charter member; Dr. Charles Purvis, head of Freedmen's Hospital, George F. Cook, superintendent of the colored schools, and Robert Terrell were elected in the mid-1890's.[7]

[7] *Advocate*, 8 Sep 1883; *Star*, 4 Feb 1887; Edward Ingle, *The Negro in the District of Columbia*, in *Johns Hopkins University Studies in*

Disregard of civil rights as a rule affected only upper-class Negroes. The workings of the criminal law, on the other hand, touched the lives of countless blacks living on a bare subsistence level. Of those some were undoubtedly vicious; and some, though vaguely well-intentioned, took to thieving, drunkenness, and disorderliness as the easiest way to blunder through a world that offered them at best very little. In a city where only one person in three was colored, the number of Negro arrests exceeded the number of white every year after 1889. People as ignorant of their rights as of their obligations were, to be sure, in some measure at the mercy of the police, and police brutality was all too common. The *Bee*, founded in 1882, asserted that policemen, particularly the Irishmen on the force, frequently clubbed Negroes savagely when arresting them, and the dark-skinned man was always the first suspect when a crime occurred. Officers "delight in arresting every little colored boy they see on the street, who may be doing something not at all offensive, and allow the white boys to do what they please." The severity of the sentences magistrates imposed on Negro misdemeanants seemed often to reflect white men's aversion to the entire race. Calvin Chase, editor of the *Bee*, as a boy having seen his father shot down in cold blood and his white assailant go unpunished, was vitriolic about Washington police methods. But more temperate men than he believed that racial equality before the law had largely disappeared by the end of the century.[8]

Historical and Political Science, 11th Series, nos. III and IV, pp. 50-51, 90 (hereafter cited as Ingle, *The Negro in D.C.*); Coroner's maps in Comrs Rpts, 1882, p. 508, 1890, p. 826, 1900, p. 826; Joseph W. Moore, *Picturesque Washington,* p. 139; Mary Church Terrell, *A Colored Woman in a White World,* pp. 113-19; membership lists in *Rpts B/Tr,* 1897, 1899; *Colored American,* 26 Mar 1898; *Bee,* 1898-1901.

[8] *Star,* 15 Mar 1882, 27 Oct 1887, 1 Jan 1897; *Chronicle,* 10 Mar 1895, 7 Jun 1896; *Sentinel,* 15 Oct 1892, 25 Nov 1893; *Bee,* 6 Aug 1887; Ingle, *The Negro in D.C.,* pp. 100-01; William J. Simmons, *Men of Mark, Eminent, Progressive and Rising,* pp. 118-19; Elizabeth M. Chapin, *American Court Gossip, or Life at the Nation's Capital,* pp. 36-40.

Despite the decline of Negroes' legal position, political preferment for colored men fell off surprisingly little. Frederick Douglass kept his post as Marshal of the District through President Hayes' administration, while the lucrative position of District Recorder of Deeds continued to go to Negroes. President Garfield, moreover, appointed ex-Senator Bruce of Mississippi Register of the Treasury, a place that would be filled by a Negro for the next thirty-two years. Garfield's assassination and President Arthur's failure to give colored men much consideration, it is true, hurt their prospects and shut off talk of appointments to the Cabinet, but during the 1880's a half-dozen Negroes had administrative assignments of some importance, and more clerkships and custodial jobs than formerly went to colored men. Both before and after the introduction of competitive civil service examinations, colored employees feared for their jobs when a new administration took over, but even the shake-up anticipated during Grover Cleveland's first term did not cut the number of Negroes on the federal payroll; on the contrary, scrupulous fairness in grading examinations enabled more Negroes than ever before to enter government service. In 1891 out of 23,144 federal employees in Washington, nearly 2,400 were colored; they held 337 of the 6,120 jobs in the Interior Department, and 127 ranked as copyists, "transcribers," and clerks. At the Library of Congress Daniel Murray was one of nineteen assistant librarians, only seven of whom drew an annual salary larger than his $1,400. Negroes rarely encountered overt hostility from fellow white employees. Negroes got far less consideration from the District commissioners. In 1879 one appointment out of fifty to the police force was colored, none to the fire department. Later policy gave Negroes some of the jobs but never established a stable ratio of colored to white. Outside the colored school system, in 1891 Negroes held only 25 District positions above the rank of messenger and day laborer.

Cleveland's second administration, troubled as it was by countrywide unemployment, saw a drop in Negro preferment and the dismissal of "surplus" Negro clerks. Republican prosperity, launched with the election of William McKinley, failed to restore the earlier proportion of colored employees, in spite of the liberal attitude of Secretary of the Treasury Lyman Gage and his top assistants. The falling off in other departments, if less pronounced than white men expected, was at once a bitter disappointment to Negroes and a gloomily foreseen development in keeping with trends in other areas of American life.[9]

Negro pride was badly hurt, moreover, when the new president of Howard University filled seven out of nine faculty vacancies with whites. A worse humiliation befell at the outbreak of the Spanish-American War. Independent companies of colored Civil War veterans had organized in the late 1860's and 1870's, formed into battalions in the mid-1880's, and had been incorporated into the District National Guard in 1887. Until then they had paid all their own expenses, recruited student cadets, and periodically held competitive drills. Thus a dozen times a year every old soldier relived the glory of the days when he had served his country on active duty. When the commanding general in 1891 mustered out the colored battalions as supernumerary, an appeal to the President had reinstated them, whereupon they were consolidated into the First Separate Colored Battalion of the District National Guard. That the battalion appeared at every drill and ceremonial occasion thereafter made the rebuff harder to bear when in 1898 General George Harries refused to enroll the unit for active service with the District regiment sent to Cuba.

[9] Laurence John Wesley Hayes, *The Negro Federal Government Worker, A Study of His Classification Status in the District of Columbia, 1883-1938*, pp. 22-25 (hereafter cited as Hayes, *Negro Govt Worker*); Cleveland *Leader*, 7 Nov 1884; *Nation*, xcvii, 114; *Sentinel*, 10 Apr 1880; *Advocate*, 3 Dec 1881; *Bee*, 1882-1901; *Star*, 9 May 1883, 2 Feb 1887; Ingle, *The Negro in D.C.*, pp. 48-49; Rpt Sec/Int, 1895, p. 724, Ser 3383; *Official Register of the United States*, 1891, p. 18.

Colored men felt that their loyalty and efficiency had been impugned.[10]

The collapse of earlier hopes for political and legal equality might have distressed Negroes less had their economic opportunities widened consistently. With the District's colored population growing from the 59,000 of 1880 to 90,000 twenty years later, Negroes trained in the professions seemingly should have found abundant openings. Besides more than four hundred colored teachers, Washington in 1900 had fifty qualified physicians, ten professionally trained dentists, over ninety ministers, and some thirty lawyers. The colored press usually put the totals in each category very much higher. Negro doctors, barred from the District Medical Society, formed the Medico-Chirurgical Society in 1884, the first Negro medical association in the United States. But except for the pastors, including those without much schooling, colored professional men faced hard sledding. About ten applicants for every teaching post in the school system created intense competition. Relatively few Negroes could afford to pay doctors', dentists', and lawyers' fees, no matter how modest, and a discouragingly large proportion of the colored people of means preferred to deal with white men. The *Colored American,* in 1898 the *Bee*'s new competitor, observed that colored people in Washington went to a colored doctor "only when we wish to run a bill we do not intend to pay." Conversely, several Negro physicians refused to attend impoverished colored patients, "the back door trade." Inexperienced lawyers, in a frantic scramble to find clients, hawked their services about the Police Court.

Colored business enterprises also suffered from Negroes' reluctance to patronize men of their own race. The failure of the Freedmen's Bank in 1874, although due primarily to white exploitation, had shattered confidence in their

[10] Hilyer, *Directory,* pp. 150-57; Capt George W. Evans, "The Militia of the District of Columbia," CHS *Rec,* xxviii, 95-105; *Bee,* 3 Jul 1897, 13 Jan 1900; Fleetwood Mss.

capacity to handle finances. A colored savings bank opened in 1888 increased the list of its depositors yearly, but for commercial purposes Negroes used white banks. As in other American cities, Negro merchants had enormous difficulty in competing with white for the colored trade and could rarely cater successfully to both races.[11] The career of John A. Gray, a restaurant owner and one-time member of the territorial governor's council, illustrates some of the hazards. "He kept one of the first houses in the city," reported the *Bee*. "He first opened it for white people and was having a success until the Negroes kept clamoring for a respectable place to go. He opened his house to the high-toned colored people and in less than a year they broke him up." Undeterred by the refusal of white merchants to employ Negro clerks, colored families persisted in trading at white shops. Prices were often lower there, and service and the selection of goods better, but investigation revealed a more basic and pettier reason: in the city's colored business world the "great impediment has been jealousy and a dislike to see each other succeed."

Caterers were one of the few groups able to avoid the complications of seeking mixed or purely colored patronage, for the business, unique to Washington, depended solely upon a white clientele. Unlike the modern term, catering in the capital of the 1880's and 1890's meant delivering hot meals twice a day to people living in rented rooms who wished to escape from the restaurant or dismal board-

[11] *Colored American*, 14 May 1898; W. Montague Cobb, "Washington, D.C.," in Dietrich C. Reitzes, *Negroes and Medicine*, pp. 193-94; Walter L. Fleming, *The Freedman's Savings Bank*, pp. 53-99, 129-30; W. E. B. DuBois, ed., *The Negro in Business, The Report of the Fourth Conference for the Study of Negro Problems, held at Atlanta University, 30-31 May 1899*, pp. 13, 28-29, 56-61 (hereafter the special studies and the reports of the proceedings of the conferences at Atlanta University every May from 1896 to 1916 are cited only by title, conference number, and date); *Advocate*, 30 Aug 1879; *Bee*, 31 Jul 1886; Ingle, *The Negro in D.C.*, pp. 91-92; John H. Harmon, Arnett G. Lindsay, and Carter G. Woodson, *The Negro as a Businessman*, pp. 34, 51-55; Hilyer, *Directory*, pp. 4, 38, 62, 73-74.

inghouse table by breakfasting and dining in their rooms. The best caterers charged from $25 to $30 a month per person. Those with fast teams of horses could deliver well-cooked dishes in specially constructed double-racked tin containers before the food cooled. A skillful caterer with a clientele of fifty to a hundred families could clear a considerable sum in a year, despite the decline of his business in the months between congressional sessions. Since the enterprise, however profitable, smacked of menial service, white men rarely competed.

A few Negroes made money in fields considered wholly dignified, notably real estate, building, and selling life insurance or shares in benefit and relief associations. James Wormley, owner of the famous Wormley House, left an estate of over $150,000; his sons, after nearly doubling their inheritance, so gossip said, by betting on President Harrison's election in 1888, put the family fortune into the construction business. Negroes who had owned local real estate before the war and had hung on to it through the disasters of the board of public works era and the Freedmen's Bank failure might be very well off indeed, although the number whose holdings were ever extensive was certainly small. District tax collector John F. Cook, himself said to be the largest taxpayer of his race, reported in 1887 two local colored men worth $100,000, two worth $75,000, a flour merchant worth $50,000, and some forty men with property valued at a figure between $10,000 and $25,000.[12]

While the lack of racial solidarity hurt the Negro professions and business enterprises, the increasing hostility of white workingmen and the bars erected by labor organizations severely handicapped the lower-class Negro. An analysis of 1881 attributed the troubles of Philadelphia's

[12] *Bee,* 22 Oct 1887, 17 Nov 1888, 12 Jan 1889, 12 Jul 1890; Cleveland *Leader,* 5 Jan, 7 Apr 1883; *Star,* 23 Oct 1884, 18 Apr 1926; Simmons, *Men of Mark,* pp. 249-50; Harmon et al., *Negro as Businessman,* p. 91; Hilyer, *Directory,* pp. 3-4, 104-09.

colored workmen to foreign immigrants: "Southern cities were built by colored mechanical labor. In this city twenty years before the late war, it was no unusual thing to find a majority of colored mechanics engaged in all the leading trades. . . . But Irish emigration [sic] was destined to strike a blow at the colored mechanic, from which it will take years for him to recover." Negroes in Washington looked upon Irishmen as enemies, but foreign immigrants in the capital were too few in the last decades of the century to be a determining factor in the local labor market.

In the early eighties the local carpenters' union drew no official color line, and one of the two mechanics' unions had mixed membership, but white mechanics made life for their colored fellows miserable in a dozen ways, and, by refusing to accept colored apprentices, the unions gradually excluded all Negroes. A colored lodge of the Knights of Labor, organized in 1884 as the Thad Stevens Assembly, fell apart before the Haymarket tragedy in Chicago two years later undermined the national brotherhood. In 1886 a Negro waiters' union appeared, but within a decade colored men found that occupations "which by common consent were regarded as belonging to them, such as waiters and the like, are now being monopolized by the whites." Booker T. Washington's exhortations to Negroes to think less about political equality and more about acquiring competence as workers fell on sterile soil in the District; here economic independence appeared to be unattainable merely by hard work.[18]

To combat trade union discrimination, "the curse of which has more than any other, fettered the energies of the colored people," and to recapture civil rights, non-segregated schools still seemed to some Negroes the first essential; only early association of the races would induce a "more generous spirit" in white men. But the opposition of other Negroes strengthened as the colored school system

[18] *Advocate*, 21 Apr 1882; *Bee*, 1 Jan 1897, 8 Oct 1898; *Star*, 26 Jul 1885; Simmons, *Men of Mark*, pp. 270-72; *Sentinel*, 30 Mar 1889.

expanded and the number of teaching posts grew. The opening of a colored high school nine years before the city had a white high school weakened the integrationists' contention that the white schools invariably provided a quality of education superior to anything available in the colored. In actuality the Miner Fund, not tax money, initially supported the colored high school as well as the Negro normal school. The question of mixed schools revived in 1881 and 1882 when the school trustees allowed two or three very light colored children to attend white schools. While Negro advocates of separate systems insisted that more money and Negro trustees less prone to toady to whites and less ready to show favoritism would correct every shortcoming in the colored schools, the *Star* declared school integration a "purely sentimental" notion:

There is a small sprinkling of colored children in the white schools, but for the most part the colored people prefer to have their separate school organization with a superintendent and teachers of their own race; just as they prefer to maintain their own . . . benevolent and social associations. The colored schools get their full share of school moneys; and in proportion to numbers are supplied with better school accommodations than the whites. For various reasons the colored children get on better in schools of their own. One is that they are spared the disadvantageous competition with white children of their own age who have had greater opportunities at home and elsewhere for advancement in their studies. Again were the schools to be merged it would necessarily throw 165 colored teachers out of employment, as it could not be expected that the white school population of the District—outnumbering the colored about two to one—should give up their teachers to make room for colored teachers. . . . Better let well enough alone.

Somewhat later, at two lively sessions of the "Bethel Literary," George W. Cook of Howard University, George

T. Downing, and Dr. Charles Purvis vainly opposed John Cromwell and other proponents of ethnocentrism.

The census figures on the percentage of adults unable to write suggest the handicap under which the children of hundreds of Negro parents labored:

	1880	1890	1900
White	5.4	2.67	1.86
Colored	59.3	39.4	30.47

From the mid-1880's onward one group of colored people argued that vocational training was a wiser goal for the Negro schools than a more literary education; a curriculum like that of the white schools should wait until the economic level of the average colored family had risen enough to enable Negro children to benefit from academic courses. In the 1890's Booker T. Washington, by then head of Tuskegee Institute in Alabama, began to popularize that thesis among white people who saw in it a way to create a permanent, docile working class. Dissidents in Washington, although believing the plan equivalent to giving up the fight for racial equality and accepting a position of inferiority for decades to come, had to abandon the campaign for integrated schools. The issue dropped out of sight in Washington for fifty-odd years. But more than one colored aristocrat, unwilling to subject his children to a segregated system, had them taught at home and then sent them to boarding schools and colleges in New England.[14]

Meanwhile Negroes who were determined to develop an independent school system as good in every particular as the white vigilantly watched the school board's every act. Hypersensitive to any possible slight, they criticized so persistently, and sometimes so unfairly, that the board president in 1899 resigned in protest at their nagging. But

[14] *Advocate*, 25 Feb 1882; *Star*, 14 Sep 1881, 22 Feb 1882; *Bee*, 30 Dec 1882, 10, 17, 24 Mar 1884; *Rpt School Trustees*, 1882, pp. 29, 33, 67; Booker T. Washington, *Up from Slavery*, p. 91; Ingle, *The Negro in D.C.*, pp. 34-37, 103; Cromwell, *History of the Bethel . . . Assoc*, pp. 5-7.

the fact remained that salaries were nearly 10 percent lower and teaching loads heavier in the colored than in the white schools. At an annual salary of $750 a colored high school teacher earned $74.54 less than his, or more often her, white counterpart, and the differential for grammar and primary grade teachers was as great or greater. In 1890 white classes averaged forty-one children to a teacher, the colored forty-seven. Otherwise the two systems ran generally parallel. In 1892 a well-equipped, roomy colored high school rose on M Street. Despite Negro complaints about favoritism in teaching appointments on the part of Superintendent George F. Cook, some of the Negro schools made a good showing. Insofar as the limited resources at his disposal permitted, he introduced the innovations in teaching methods begun by Superintendent William Bramwell Powell in the white schools in the late 1880's. Like Powell, Cook sought to encourage pupils to reason rather than depend solely upon memory; he added classes in nature study and manual training to the curriculum and arranged field trips for pupils and teachers to the Library of Congress, the Smithsonian Institution, the zoo, and other places where children could learn by observation. Thanks to the insistence of a group of colored women, in 1896 the school board opened both Negro and white kindergartens.

Lower standards obtained in the colored grade schools than in the white, but in examinations given all high school students in 1899, the colored high school scored higher than either the Eastern or the Western high schools. At the M Street High School a dedicated and stimulating faculty fostered students' intellectual ambitions. Twenty of the thirty regular teachers had degrees from top-flight Northern colleges and universities and five others had graduated from Howard, a far larger proportion of highly trained talent than the white high schools could claim. Still when Congress reorganized the entire system early in 1901, Negroes acquiesced in having a white superintendent

137

put over the head of the colored school system. Fortunately, the new assistant superintendent, Winfield Scott Montgomery, a Phi Beta Kappa of the class of 1878 at Dartmouth and a gifted teacher, spent no time in protecting his own dignity. Under his enlightened direction the colored schools during the next decade would achieve an excellence well beyond that of Negro schools in other cities.[15]

Unhappily, in the late nineteenth century relatively few Negro children stayed in school beyond the fourth grade, and of those who finished the eighth grade, still fewer, especially of the boys, went on. "There are inducements to keep white children in the white High School," remarked the *Bee*. "Our colored citizens should see to it that some effort be made to keep their boys in the schools." Quite apart from their poverty, the seeming futility of acquiring more than an acquaintance with the three R's deterred many Negro families from making the effort. They saw well-educated girls, barred from suitable occupations by an inflexible caste system, drift into the life of the *demi-monde* and Negro college graduates forced for want of something better to take jobs as waiters and hotel bell boys. It is not surprising that 325 of the 367 undergraduates at Howard University in 1898 were enrolled in its secondary school; as none of the 42 taking the college course were white, the original ideal of a biracial institution vanished.[16] And the university had only partly recovered from the financial reverses of the mid-1870's.

Long before the Negro intelligentsia saw that public schooling in itself was unlikely to elevate greatly the general level of Negro society, Washington's colored aristocrats

[15] Lofton, "Separate but Equal," pp. 164-87; *Bee,* 11 Feb 1888, 20 Aug 1897; *Rpts School Trustees,* 1890, 1892, pp. 153-202, 1899, pp. 273-97; Hilyer, *Directory,* pp. 161-63.
[16] *Rpts School Trustees,* 1880, p. 152, 1886, p. 13, 1892, p. 17; *Report of the Board of Education of the District of Columbia,* 1901, pp. 140-43 (hereafter cited as *Rpt B/Ed*); *Bee,* 14 May 1887; W. E. B. DuBois, ed., *The College-Bred Negro* (Fifth Atlanta Conference, 1900), p. 16.

had begun to detach themselves from the Negro rank and file; for their own reassurance they felt they had to sharpen class distinctions. Educated colored men in other cities also defended the thesis that the social equality of all Negroes was a concept destructive to racial progress. In 1880 a letter to the *Advocate* declared that Frederick Douglass, John F. Cook, and others to whom the community had once looked for leadership "have shown conclusively how little they care whether other colored men sink, as long as they swim." Calvin Chase of the *Bee*, not himself one of Washington's "first families" but occupying a place in the upper stratum of the rank just below, alternately defended the "exclusive set" and attacked it for a snobbery that he believed originated in the determination of the Lotus Club after 1863 to force contrabands to keep to themselves. Later societies heightened that snobbery. "The Monday Night Literary is a cast organization," wrote Chase. "There is more intelligence excluded than there is in the association . . . there are few holding clerkships who belong." Members had ceased to give New Year's Day receptions because they did not want to meet "objectionable upstarts."

The Negro press repeatedly insisted: "There is more discrimination among the colored people than there is among the white against the colored." A petition complained to Congress in 1896 that only daughters of "the favored few" were admitted to the colored normal school. "The would-be leaders, . . . John M. Langston excepted, have taken no interest in the general welfare of the masses of our people; political office by all means, after that, their wish is total exclusion from their race and to be white." Yet many of that small group composing the highest circle of Negro society were indeed nearly white, and a number of them had personal distinction as scholars, officeholders, and professional men. They were certainly culturally closer to the white community than to the lower-class Negro. In displaying an ungenerous attitude toward their inferiors, they were behaving like most self-made white men who reached positions of eminence in the face of enormous obstacles.[17]

The *Sentinel,* Washington's German-American newspaper edited by a former abolitionist, presented the tolerant white man's view of the Negro's position in 1883:

> The colored people of Washington enjoy all the social and political rights that law can give them, without protest and without annoyance. The public conveyances are open to them, and the theatres, the jury box, the spoils of party power are theirs. Many of these men are wealthy. . . .
>
> But the color line is rigidly drawn in what is known as society. Wealth, learning, official place, give no colored family the right or privilege of entering the best or the commonest white society on terms of equality or endurance. In this respect the colored race lives as separate and exclusive a life as in the days of slavery, and as a drop of African blood was once held to make a man a negro, so now it taints him and makes an immutable barrier against social recognition.
>
> Blanche K. Bruce lives in a handsome house that he owns on M Street. It is richly furnished. . . . Mrs. Bruce is a handsome woman, with not a suggestion of her race in her face, and whose manners are regarded as the consummation of ease, grace and courtesy. She dresses as richly and handsomely as any woman in the city. In official circles Mr. Bruce is received in courtesy and as a political equal, but there the line is drawn.

Envious Negroes, averred the *Sentinel,* considered this exclusive set not good enough for whites and too good for its own race, but the next lower rank of Negro society was

[17] *Advocate,* 4 Dec 1880; *Star,* 11 May 1880; *Bee,* 10 May 1884, 18 Sep 1886, 18 Sep 1887; ptn, H54A-H7.6, 2 Jun 1896; see illustrations accompanying the articles on Washington Negroes in Simmons, *Men of Mark;* Richard Bardolph, "The Distinguished Negro in America, 1770-1936," *American Historical Review,* LX, 527-47.

equally cut off from the class below. Government clerks formed the basis of the second stratum. "They are well dressed, seem to prosper and are happy. For the great bulk of the colored population—the servants, laborers and the poor—they have sympathy, but have no more social relations than a white family would." Those at the base of the social pyramid "in the main are thriftless, living from hand to mouth; happy if they do nothing, happy if they get a job. Their social instincts are gratified by the organization and maintenance of societies of all sorts, benevolent, patriotic, social and economic. There are nearly one thousand of these organizations, supported almost entirely by the laboring colored people." [18]

That portrayal, if in any degree fitting the Washington of 1883, was too simple and too cheerful in tone to describe the Negro community a decade or more later. Before the end of the century the class structure resembled a pyramid less than a truncated cone capped by a needle. From the strata below, the Negroes who danced on the point of the needle appeared to be not angels, but scarcely more accessible than heavenly creatures. Of the District's 700 octoroons and 1,100 quadroons, those who had, in addition to light color, the qualifications of antiquity of family, money, education, and honorable occupation belonged to the aristocracy; "honorable occupations" included the professions, political posts of more than trivial importance, banking, real estate brokerage, and businesses not tinged with menial service. Washington's Negro "Four Hundred," as the *Bee* dubbed the aristocrats, probably numbered not more than ninety to a hundred families.

The middle class in the 1890's apparently derived mainly from the District's 18,000 mulattoes. Only less fully than the Four Hundred with their very light skins and generally non-Negroid features were the mulattoes conscious of gradations of color: those of "doe-nut or ginger-cake color . . .

[18] *Sentinel,* 22 Dec 1883.

said those blacker than themselves should be ignored." The relative flexibility of the middle class permitted the occasional acceptance of exceptionally able, ambitious, full-blooded Negroes. But even a well-qualified government clerk, if a newcomer to the city, could not hope for immediate entree to upper-middle-class circles. Whether the barber, the caterer, the livery-stable man, the oyster-house owner, or the proprietor of any other small business was acknowledged as upper or lower middle class evidently depended upon the extent of his business success as well as his nativity and his complexion. Warnings frequently appeared in the *Bee* about unsuitable marriages between scions of established families and those of doubtful antecedents who wormed their way into the "social circle" by joining a "tony" church, by enrolling for a few weeks in one of Howard University's professional schools, or by making a specious show of great wealth. Differentiations among the "masses," that is, chiefly the city's thousands of full-blooded Negroes, were not a topic the press bothered to explore.[19]

Nor did any observer analyze the family structure of colored Washington. The infrequent mention of colored women except in the *Bee*'s society columns suggests that the matriarchy common among Negroes in the Southern states had slight hold in the District. Apparently during the Reconstruction era colored men able to support their families had been the acknowledged heads of their own households and, as voters and sometimes officeholders, had commanded a status as clearly denied their wives and mothers and daughters as in the white family of the Victorian era. When hard times and racial prejudice left Negro workingmen unemployed, their women could usually still find work as domestic servants, and, as the family breadwinners, might then assume matriarchal authority, just as they were obliged to do when husbands or fathers deserted

[19] *Bee*, 30 May 1885, 8 Jun 1889; W. E. B. DuBois, ed., *The Negro in Business* (Fourth Atlanta Conference, 1899), pp. 13, 19-20; *Eleventh U.S. Census*, 1890, *Population*, I, 397.

them. But not until social workers began to report upon what they found when they walked into colored homes in the late 1890's did the role of the colored woman as the backbone of the indigent colored family evoke comment.

From 1884 to 1898 Washington's Negro press was the *Bee.* It prided itself on its sting aimed at the shoddy and evil. Yet back-biting and destructive jealousy of one class and of one Negro toward another was a striking feature of the paper's reporting. Let anyone get his head ever so little above his associates, and his individual accomplishments and former services were forgotten in vitriolic attacks upon his real or imagined self-seeking. Instead of applauding a colored man who won recognition, especially from whites, his fellows at once set to work to belittle him and accuse him of sycophancy and putting on airs. The *New National Era* had eschewed that line, and the *People's Advocate,* which ceased publication in 1884, pursued it very little. The *Bee,* without wholly abandoning a crusading point of view, indulged in more sweeping condemnations of individual Negroes and organizations the longer it ran. Its publisher obviously thought scandal and malicious gossip sold better than other news. A comment on a problem affecting Washington as a whole was a rarity.

Booker T. Washington, after some months at the Baptist Wayland Seminary in 1878-1879, decided that Washington was no place for a Negro who wished to dedicate his life to helping his race; here false standards and selfishness predominated. Among immigrant minorities and among the Jews in the District, mutual helpfulness was the rule. Not so among Negroes. The pressures of caste which kept the gifted colored man from going as far as his talents would otherwise permit split colored Washington into jealously competing fragments, with results damaging to every Negro. Congress, noted a Philadelphia journal, was naturally disinclined to do anything for Washington's colored people because their squabbling made them ridiculous: rivals claimed "that this one's father was a horse thief, that one

143

doesn't know who his father was, another is too black, another is too light and therefore does not represent the race, another does not belong to the best families and still another is an interloper." Bitterly the *Bee* asked in 1887: "Who of our so-called colored representative men can point to a single thing of a public character beneficial to the colored people established and fostered by them? To their shame and to the humiliation of the race the record is a blank, and with all our boast about our wealthy . . . men the race is dependent upon the charity of whites." Yet if "you talk to our people about an excursion down the river in August, or a cake walk in December, they will listen to you and will no doubt purchase several tickets." And a large part of the funds of the mutual benefit societies, in which much of the social life of working-class Negroes centered, went for elaborate funerals rather than help for the living.[20]

The assertion that well-to-do Negroes never lifted finger for the needy was, of course, an exaggeration. John F. Cook, for years an active member of a citizens' relief committee, was also a trustee of the Home for Destitute Colored Women and Children, while a dozen public-spirited Negro women served on the board of manageresses. Caroline Taylor, who founded the Home for Friendless Girls in 1886, also organized an Aid Society at the Berean Baptist Church. About the same time, two or three Negro women opened a free kindergarten and day nursery for the children of working mothers, and in the 1890's the newly organized Colored Women's League expanded the program. Although Alexander Crummell, rector of St. Luke's, was more concerned with developing character in his people than with their material progress, he raised a considerable sum of money for the

[20] Jesse Lawson to Booker T. Washington, 6 May 1902, Booker T. Washington Mss; Washington, *Up from Slavery*, pp. 88-90; *Cong Globe*, 41C, 2S, p. 842; Ingle, *The Negro in D.C.*, p. 109; Philadelphia *Odd Fellows Journal* quoted in *Bee*, 23 Feb 1901; *Bee*, 15 Jan 1887, 12 Nov 1898.

Episcopal Freedmen's Aid Society by sale of copies of one of his sermons. In 1887 the Colored Baptist Home Mission Society was "putting shoes on the feet of the poor, clothing on them, and giving immediate aid," but $95.72 represented the total sum collected in the course of several months from Washington's thirty-five colored Baptist churches and the members of the society.

In 1893 a severe depression again swept over the United States. As was true in the mid-1870's, Washington's colored people were hit harder than white. Negro volunteers worked with the Associated Charities, and the "Hill Group" on 6th Street, moved by the suffering of the poor at the foot of the hill, distributed food and fuel in that neighborhood. A good many relatively well-to-do individuals gave help without working through any organization, just as desperately poor Negro families often took care of the children of even poorer neighbors. From a mother-child center, opened in 1895, came the Southwest Social Settlement, and that year Miss Amanda Bowen, assisted by funds from the Metropolitan African Methodist Episcopal Church, launched the Sojourner Truth Home for Working Girls. Three years later the Colored Women's League undertook "rescue work" among young women. A study prepared for a conference on Negro problems held in Atlanta in 1898 listed thirty-eight Negro churches in Washington which spent $4,300 for charity, contributed to the support of eighty-three benevolent and missionary societies, and supplied twelve workers in the slums and the jail. The individual generosity of Professor William Hart of Howard University made possible the Hart Farm School for colored boys. And in 1900 a colored woman started the Stoddard Baptist Home for aged Negroes.

Yet the overall record of Negro charities, while not "blank," was distinctly thin. The impressively long list of welfare projects at the end of the century was deceptive, for most of the undertakings were small-scale and short-lived unless white people came to the rescue. Unhappily, numberless whites were extraordinarily myopic; prone to think charity must go only to the "worthy" lest it nurture pauperism, they were chary of helping struggling Negro organizations. The white women whom Mrs. Grover Cleveland interested in the Home for Friendless Colored Girls raised only $150 for it in two years of soliciting. The uncooperativeness of many well-to-do Negroes annoyed ordinarily open-handed whites. "We all know," a white woman told a congressional committee, "that a good deal of what was good in the race has gone and they are now in a state of transition." What exasperated whites failed to take into account was that the social pressures that fostered philanthropy in the white community could not operate effectively among people who felt their precarious position in the city's overall social structure progressively and inescapably weakening. And white people probably attributed larger resources to prosperous Negroes than they actually possessed.[21]

Negro pastors and Negro churches which in earlier years had not only provided spiritual leadership but taken an active part in lightening parishioners' material distress apparently lost sight of both goals as congregations vied with each other in building big, costly edifices. Between the worldliness of the sophisticated churches and the excessive otherworldliness of those wedded to a somewhat primitive, highly emotional religion teaching that only heaven or hell

[21] Katherine Hosmer, "What Women Have Done in Washington City Affairs," *Municipal Affairs*, II, 514; W. E. B. DuBois, ed., *Some Efforts of Negroes for Their Own Social Betterment* (Third Atlanta Conference, 1898), pp. 14, 36-37, 57-59; *Bee*, 14 May 1887; Cleveland *Leader*, 29 Feb 1884; *Advocate*, 5 Feb, 20 Nov 1881; *Anl Rpt of the Home for Destitute Colored Women and Children*, 1891; Inabel Lindsay, "Participation of Negroes in the Establishment of Welfare Services, 1865-1900, with special reference to the District of Columbia, Maryland and Virginia," pp. 124-59, 164, 170-73 (dissertation, Univ of Pittsburgh, 1958); S Doc 185, 55C, 1S, Joint Select Committee to Investigate the Charities and Reformatory Institutions in the District of Columbia, Pt. I, pp. 56, 100-01, 155, 197, 310-17, 396-402, 554, Ser 3565. For a fuller account of white neglect of Negro needs, see Green, *Washington, Capital City, 1879-1950*, pp. 67-74.

in the hereafter mattered, the efforts of the handful of selfless civic-minded Negroes met with defeat. Proposals to turn over to the National Colored Home the proceeds of Emancipation Day celebrations fizzled because the money from ticket sales went into the pockets of "sharks" or for the rental and elaborate decoration of floats for the parades. Lack of funds threatened to close the Sojourner Truth Home three years after it opened. A small indebtedness, which modest gifts could have wiped out, shut down the colored YMCA. According to one critic of his people, when Negroes contributed to any good works their motive was notoriety, not Christian charity. Such behavior was characteristic of the *nouveaux riches* the world over, but the small public-spirited minority in colored Washington sadly admitted that the generosity that had once distinguished the community was rarely in evidence at the end of the century.[22]

Negroes with means could scarcely plead ignorance of the want existing about them, for destitution was nearly as widespread as in post-Civil-War years. In the early nineties, amid the enormous prosperity of much of the city, 16,000 persons, the great majority of them colored, were without visible means of support; in 1870 the number had been little greater. Until 1897 the police were responsible for reporting cases of illness and desperate want and for distributing relief; Negro distrust of the police was an obstacle, but the health department defended the system on the grounds that it hastened investigations of complaints and lessened demands upon doctors to care for malingerers. The police found Negro families eking out existence by picking spoiled food from garbage cans and dumps. Households in the Negro slums were ridden with illness; a report of 1891 described a one-room shanty in which beside a dead infant lay five adults and six children stricken with in-

[22] Lindsay, "Negro Welfare Services," pp. 105-18; *Advocate*, 5 Apr 1884; *Bee*, 1887-1901; Ingle, *The Negro in D.C.*, pp. 95-100, 107; Carter G. Woodson, *The History of the Negro Church*, pp. 224-30; Hilyer, *Directory*, pp. 30, 136-48.

fluenza. Four fifths of the patients at Freedmen's Hospital were indigents; of the 17,048 persons to whom the District's seven public dispensaries ministered in 1891, over 12,000 were colored. The most conscientious physician could do little more than palliate momentarily the miseries he encountered daily.

In twenty years the colored death rate dropped to 28.12 per thousand from the 40.78 of 1876, but Negro mortality always greatly exceeded and in most years was double that of whites. Infant mortality, high for whites, was 338.5 per thousand for Negroes in 1890 and in 1900 was still 317. The occasional charge that Negro "ignorance and indifference" was to blame was a part-truth. A larger cause, the health officer argued, was the foulness of the alley tenements in which thousands of Negroes lived.[23]

Neither poverty nor illness, however, prevented Negroes from enjoying themselves at times. The gift of laughter, that capacity to create and delight in moments of gaiety in the midst of suffering and want, is a Negro characteristic that down to the present day confuses and baffles white people. As W. E. B. DuBois sardonically put it, "that we do submit to life as it is and yet laugh and dance and dream is but another proof that we are idiots." With a light-heartedness that sober-sided white Washingtonians called irresponsible, colored families not always able to feed themselves joined in church sociables and in club and fraternal society celebrations. The lower down the economic ladder, the more pleasure members of a society took in giving it a high-sounding name, such as "Grand Ancient Order of the Sons and Daughters and Brothers and Sisters of Moses of the USA and the World at Large." A funeral, always an occasion, usually called for lavish spending on carriages and

---

[23] *Star*, 15 Mar 1882; Comrs Rpts, 1887, pp. 16-17, 1889, p. 14, 1890, pp. 639, 756-57, 845-47, 1895, pp. 9-13; H Ex Doc 1, 51C, 1S, p. 94; *Chronicle*, 11 Sep 1899; *Eleventh U.S. Census*, 1890, *Population*, I, Pt. II, 20; *Twelfth Census*, 1900, *Population*, Pt. II, 22; W. E. B. DuBois, ed., *Mortality among Negroes in Cities* (First Atlanta Conference, 1896), pp. 8, 18-19, 20-28.

clothes. Noisy picnics complete with bands to furnish music took place on Sundays, in the 1880's frequently at the "Manor," once the house and grounds of a wealthy mayor of the city, where the National Red Cross Headquarters now stand; when a proprietor of the beer hall there closed the place in 1887, colored picnickers were allowed to use the Schuetzenverein park. Mutual benefit societies arranged excursions down the Potomac until the steamboat lines, adopting the pretext that every boat was already chartered, refused to sell Negroes tickets.

For lower-class Negroes the great event of the year was the annual District Emancipation Day parade on April 16. Every colored organization in the District usually took part. Despite a downpour of rain, in 1883 the procession was a mile and a half long; among the scores of societies parading in dress array were the Chaldeans, the Knights of Moses, the Osceolas, the Galilean Fishermen, the Sons and Daughters of Samaris, the Solid Yantics, the Lively Eights, and the Celestial Golden Links. White onlookers, watching the elaborately decorated floats and the thousands of Negroes marching on foot to the accompaniment of twelve brass bands, were impressed, amused, or indignant at the money poured into the display. Sophisticated Negroes sensitive to white ridicule protested now and again that a church service would mark the day more fittingly. "The thought is already gaining ground," wrote Frederick Douglass in 1886, "that tinsel show, gaudy display and straggling processions, which empty the alleys and dark places of our city into the broad day-light of our thronged streets and avenues, thus thrusting upon the public view a vastly undue proportion of the most unfortunate, unimproved, and unprogressive class of the colored people, and thereby inviting public disgust and contempt, and repelling the more thrifty and self-respecting among us, is a positive hurt to the whole colored population of this city. These annual celebrations of ours . . . should bring into notice the very best elements of our colored population." But

149

until the school board voted in 1899 not to dismiss the colored schools for the day, the parade on April 16 was more important to most of colored Washington than the Fourth of July and Christmas and New Year's combined.[24]

Few middle-class Negroes were in a position to carp at the extravagances of their social inferiors, for display was an essential ingredient in most of their own pleasures. Below the thin top crust all Negro society was as intent upon keeping up with the Joneses as were ambitious, socially insecure whites. Booker T. Washington spoke with dismay of seeing "young colored men who were not earning more than four dollars a week spend two dollars or more for a buggy on Sunday to ride up and down Pennsylvania Avenue in, in order that they might try to convince the world that they were worth thousands." Plug-hatted "dudes" carrying canes swaggered about the streets to impress their fellows. Clothes were all-important. At a club party "young gentlemen and ladies in and just leaving their teens, assembled, dressed in full reception style, the young gents in full dress suit, the ladies in every ornamentation art or fancy could give. One lady of family remarked, 'they are all plebians, too!'" Plebeians as well as aristocrats still attended the theatre occasionally, but, as time went on, evening parties at home or concerts at the churches became a more customary form of entertainment. Athletics had not yet begun to loom large, although Negro bicycle clubs appeared in the eighties, and in the nineties colored cyclists held races at the Park Cycle Track. The Cadet Corps drills, begun in 1883, invariably attracted large crowds.

After the Lotus Club disappeared, for a year or two the Monday Night Literary Society embraced the most distinguished of the Negro intelligentsia, but the Bethel Literary and Historical Association soon overshadowed the older clubs by supplying the principal forum for enlightened dis-

[24] W. E. B. DuBois, *Dusk of Dawn,* p. 147; Ingle, *The Negro in D.C.,* p. 106; Cleveland *Leader,* 19 Apr 1883, 28 Sep 1884; *Advocate,* 28 Apr 1882; *Bee,* 21 Apr 1883, 24 Mar 1888.

cussion of race problems; the most notable Negroes in the country spoke before it. On three or four occasions learned white men, such as the meteorologist Cleveland Abbe of the Weather Bureau, lectured on scientific topics, but racial themes, including Negro history, were more compelling. As the sessions were open to every interested person, they gave unknown newcomers a chance to try their wings. There Kelly Miller, in the mid-1880's a student at Howard, emerged from obscurity by challenging some of the radical statements of the eminent Bishop Benjamin Tanner. Indeed the three factors which, despite manifold discouragements, made Washington a center of Negro civilization were government employment, Howard University, and the Bethel Literary and Historical Association. The creative and performing arts, on the other hand, played a minor part in community life, although proponents of an all-inclusive cultural nationalism sometimes talked of Negro artistic potentialities. The church choral societies earned modest fame, and the Treble Clef Club, founded in 1897, stimulated interest in classical music, but local talent focussed its attention chiefly on practical affairs.

The Negro newspapers gave a great deal of space to society weddings; the list of presents, often with the donors' names attached, might fill over a column. The gowns, "a Worth dress of canary silk" or a "crimson velvet entrainee," were described in the same detail with which white society reporters wrote of the costumes at White House receptions. Even after discounting the braggadocio of the Negro press, the evidences of Negro wealth and taste were unmistakable —beautiful jewelry, handsome clothes, well-furnished houses tended by Negro servants, and expensive summer holidays. Every June the exodus began with "Saratoga trunks" packed for Newport, Harpers Ferry, and Cape May. In 1886 the *Bee* reported: "Mr. Richard S. Locke of Washington who spends his summers at Nonquitt Beach [Massachusetts] has sold his beautiful yacht; Mr. Locke is the only gentleman

151

of color that ever owned a yacht at Nonquitt." By and large, the higher a Negro's social standing, the more exactly his diversions corresponded to those of white people of similar position. Well-bred colored people in the mid-1880's some-times joined the gatherings on the White House lawn on summer afternoons to hear the Marine Band play, but by the 1890's they avoided mingling with whites even on such informal social occasions.[25]

In 1900 Andrew Hilyer of the then eight-year-old business-promoting Union League compiled a "directory" to take stock "after a generation of freedom . . . [to] see just what is the actual status of the colored population of Wash-ington, the Capital of the Nation, . . . where the condi-tions are the most favorable, to see what is their actual status as skilled workmen, in business, in the professions, and in their organizations; in short, to make a study, at first hand, of their efforts at social betterment." Frankly in-tended to overcome Negro hostility to Negro enterprise, the slim booklet assembled a wealth of specific information and offered a judicious appraisal of what fuller cooperation thenceforward could mean. But while seeking to encourage by pointing to past accomplishments, the analysis was too honest to hold out golden hopes.

Washington Negroes whose memory stretched back into the late 1860's had little cause for optimism. Since the days when they had shared in governing the city and the territory and the wall of caste had appeared to be crumbling, their bright prospects had darkened and then all but vanished in the shadows of a new and mounting racism. The *New National Era* had marked 1870 as the high point for the Negro community and saw the shrinkage of its horizons as

[25] Cleveland *Leader,* 7 Apr 1884; Washington, *Up from Slavery,* pp. 88-89; *Advocate,* 1880-1884; *Bee,* Apr 1883 and 1884-1901; Francis Cardozo, Jr., to Booker T. Washington, 8 Aug 1902, Booker T. Washing-ton Mss; Cromwell, *History of the Bethel . . . Assoc;* Mrs. E. T. Williston, "History of the Treble Clef" appended to program, *Treble Clef Club,* 16 May 1923 (Music Div., L.C.); *Post,* 3 Aug 1902.

beginning with the creation of the territorial government.[26] Witnessing the inexorable narrowing of their world after 1874, the wisest colored people doubtless knew that the splintering into mutually jealous groups had further reduced the elbow room for all contestants and had multiplied the difficulties of combatting white prejudice. Washington's reviving racism was the harder to fight because the white community, increasingly oblivious to the existence of any other, recognized no opponent. The few white Washingtonians who acknowledged Negro citizens' potentialities were prone to dismiss the possibility of any injustice by declaring the capital "the colored man's paradise."

The very light-colored Negro with three-fourths or seven-eighths white blood might find an answer for himself by passing permanently into the ranks of whites. Miscegenation, not unlawful in the District of Columbia and far more common than most people realized, eased the process for the stranger, but for a member of any well-known local family passing was difficult. In any case, it left the larger problem unsolved: how Negroes were to live with dignity in a white world. Voluntary isolation might protect individuals from some humiliations but would scarcely ensure long-term progress for the race. Preoccupation with these questions stripped colored Washington of interest in the well-being of the city as a whole.

In 1901 for white Washingtonians the future stretched out in an ever-widening vista of prosperity and orderly living in a beautiful city whose national and world importance could only expand. The difference between that picture and what perceptive Negroes could envisage for their own people was heightened by the contrasts between their status then and that of a quarter century before. True, some families had made money in the interval, and others had achieved a modicum of financial security. Negroes who worked in government offices usually received civil, if im-

[26] Hilyer, *Directory*, pp. 3-5 and *passim; New National Era*, 25 Jun 1874.

personal, treatment from their white fellows. Moreover, a careful unobtrusiveness permitted well-dressed Negroes to hover in the background at the reception celebrating Washington's centennial. But sensitive men and women found that concession a poor substitute for friendliness. Fortunately they could not foresee that events in the next fifteen years would force colored aristocrats and middle-class Negroes into a psychological ghetto along with ambitionless blacks.

While the most easily observed factor in the progressive disintegration of Washington's Negro world was the failure of economic opportunity to keep pace with the growth of the colored population and with the spread of education, that material loss was itself rather a manifestation than a cause of the change. The wealthy Negro knew all too well that financial security provided no safeguard against endless humiliations and frustration. The deterioration of Negro status sprang from a complex of causes, but the common denominator was the steady paring down of incentive. With the dwindling of the attainable external rewards for continuing the struggle, only the strongest individual able to draw upon deep inner resources could withstand the ceaseless battering of his self-respect.

CHAPTER VIII

THE BEGINNINGS OF ORGANIZED

PROTEST, 1901-1916

In the Deep South the exclusion of Negro voters from the polls in state after state had begun with Mississippi in 1890 and extended to six others before 1902. Determination to establish white supremacy on an immutable basis had multiplied Jim Crow laws and confined Negro education largely to the vocational and manual training deemed suited to a servile labor force. From Texas through the Gulf states and up into North Carolina, lynchings of Negroes had grown in frequency during the 1890's. In his farewell speech to Congress in January 1901, Representative George White of North Carolina, for the next thirty years the last colored man to occupy a seat in the House, told his colleagues: "You may tie us and then taunt us for our lack of bravery, but one day we will break the bonds. You may use our labor for two and a half centuries and then taunt us for our poverty, but let me remind you we will not always remain poor." To most of his race his words pictured a future infinitely distant. The United States in the next two decades would see a spate of books and articles purporting to be careful scientific and historical studies of race which "proved" the innate inferiority of the Negro. The doctrine, justifying Jim Crow, would win credence in the North as well as the South.

Washington Negroes had not faced lynchings or overt intimidation. Here the black masses at the bottom were little worse off in 1901 than in the 1880's; in fact, with luck on jobs, consistent good health, and three or four years of schooling, hard workers might rise a peg or two into the

155

ranks of the Negro lower middle class. It was the upper middle class and the aristocrats whose status and pride had suffered and from whom either courageous leadership or corrosive despair must emanate. During the preceding twenty years their role had become increasingly negative. Yet at the turn of the century colored Americans throughout the country still looked to the privileged members of that group to act as standard-bearers for them all.

Contrary to later, often quoted Republican claims, the position of Negroes continued to worsen during the Roosevelt and Taft administrations, although subtle changes rather than admitted shifts in official policy marked the decline. Theodore Roosevelt, as President Harrison's first Civil Service Commissioner, had exercised scrupulous fairness in putting the merit system into effect in government, but the Colonel of the Rough Riders had deeply offended colored men by belittling the heroic services of the Black Cavalry at San Juan Hill during the Spanish-American War. As President, the vigorous Teddy for a time seemed to colored Washington to be a staunch friend: one of his first acts was to invite Booker T. Washington to dine at the White House to discuss Negro appointments to office. Hopes built on that unusual gesture quickly shriveled under arch-conservative Republican wrath. Within six months the Washington *Bee* was speaking of "the Negro political decapitation dinner." [1] The President stuck by his guns long enough to win Senate concurrence in several Negro appointments, and he retained a number of colored men McKinley had put into office, but thereafter he made no further overtures. On the contrary, in 1906, when Negro troops in Brownsville, Texas, were involved in a brawl in which a

[1] Paul Lewison, *Race, Class and Party*, University Library ed., 1965, pp. 79-97; *Cong Rec* 56C, 1S, p. 1636; I. A. Newby, *Jim Crow's Defense: Anti-Negro Thought in America, 1900-1930*, pp. 19-82; Republican National Committee, *Republican Campaign Textbook, 1912*, p. 278; *Bee*, 15 Oct 1898, 19 Oct 1901, 8, 22 Feb 1902, 5 Aug 1905; Hayes, *Negro Govt Worker*, p. 22; Monroe N. Work, ed., *Negro Year Book, An Annual Encyclopedia of the Negro, 1912*, pp. 75-76.

white man was shot, presidential severity in approving the dishonorable discharge of the entire battalion for refusing to identify the guilty person alienated Roosevelt's colored supporters. His appointment of two Negroes to the Homes Commission in 1908 won him no applause, since all members of the commission gave their services.

President Taft stirred up fewer animosities than his predecessor. Avowing belief in the Tuskegee philosophy of Negro economic advancement before enlargement of Negro political power, Taft declared himself unwilling to appoint colored men to posts in the South where white resentment would create friction. But he selected colored men for several "offices of essential dignity at Washington," on the principle that it was better to give "large offices to well-equipped Negroes of the higher class" than to scatter "a lot of petty ones among the mass of their race." Rather apologetically he wrote to Robert Terrell: "I have not done all I ought to do or all I hope to do in the matter of the recognition of colored men, but positions are hard to find. Nobody resigns and nobody dies." However sound his reasons, Taft's policies offered the city's colored people meager encouragement.[2]

Up to a point colored Washingtonians rejoiced at any Negro's receiving a responsible federal post, but they were dismayed at the Presidents' consistently passing over well-qualified local Negroes even for the office of Recorder of Deeds, which handled only local transactions. The profound respect in which all colored Americans held Washington's upper-class colored community heightened the grievance. Upon Booker T. Washington's recommendation, President Roosevelt appointed Robert H. Terrell to a municipal judge-

[2] As in Chapter VI, citations of the *Bee* are reduced in this chapter to a sample, since relevant comments appear in almost every issue. *Bee*, 17, 24 Sep, 31 Dec 1904, 17 Mar, 21 Apr, 1, 8 Dec 1906, 4 May 1907; William F. Nowlin, *The Negro in American National Politics*, pp. 114-15; *Negro Year Book, 1912*, pp. 30-31; *Star*, 20 Jun 1909; President Taft to Judge Robert Terrell, 2 Mar 1910, Mary Church Terrell Mss.

ship, but colored Republicans from the states won the other six major federal assignments in the capital to go to Negroes, the posts of Register and Deputy Register of the Treasury, Assistant District Attorney for the District of Columbia, Auditor of the Navy Department, District Recorder of Deeds, and Chief Surgeon at the Freedmen's Hospital. President Taft added two more, the office of Collector of Customs at Georgetown and, still more gratifying, the position of Assistant Attorney General of the United States, a plum which fell to William H. Lewis, a prominent colored lawyer from Boston. At those nine, Negro preferment stood till 1913.

The significance all Negroes attached to those nine offices seems at first out of proportion to their number or intrinsic importance. But between 1901 and 1913 they represented far more to colored people than sops to racial ambition. As white-collar jobs in the federal government for the past thirty years had offered greater security with dignity than any other open to Negroes, protection of those places loomed large. In the 1880's and 1890's colored civil service employees had looked to Negro congressmen as their bulwark within the federal establishment. Now, with no colored man sitting in Congress, departmental clerks counted on the President's Negro appointees for help when civil service rules swayed precariously in the winds of a stiffening racism. In 1910 a Negro journalist jokingly called the nine men Taft had selected "the Black Cabinet." The name stuck, and with some reason: although their intervention was not always successful, it sometimes had the desired effect.[3]

Nevertheless the civil service held fewer opportunities for intelligent Negroes than in the 1880's and 1890's. The commission's rules had always allowed a department or division chief a choice among the three top candidates

[3] *Bee*, 19 Apr 1909, 23 Feb, 25 Mar, 11 Sep 1911, 29 Mar, 12 Apr 1913; William McKinley Clayton to Woodrow Wilson, 19 Mar 1915, Wilson Mss; *Negro Year Book, 1912*, pp. 70-71; Hayes, *Negro Govt Worker*, pp. 26-27, 32-35.

whose examinations qualified them for a vacancy, but after the turn of the century that latitude, Negroes believed, increasingly came to be a weapon of racial subjugation. Certainly promotions became fewer and fewer for Negroes; more often white associates of lesser education and experience and therefore presumably of lesser competence were pushed ahead of them. By 1908 not more than three or four colored men had advanced into supervisory positions, and all colored federal employees in Washington had dwindled from the 1,537 of 1892 to 1,450, about 300 of them clerks, the rest messengers or common laborers. Until 1909 the State Department had no colored employee ranking above a messenger, and the lone Negro who then attained a clerk's rating achieved it, he later explained, because his personal friend, the incoming Secretary of State, insisted that the merit system recognize merit. While Republican campaign literature of 1912 claimed that the federal government then had more than 4,100 colored employees in Washington earning over $4 million a year, those figures were manifestly exaggerated and in any case made little impression upon educated Negroes who knew that the color of their skins would keep them in the bottom grades of government service.

In the District government civil service rules did not apply at all. The wishes of members of the House or Senate District committees might determine who was hired or promoted, and, when congressional patronage did not interfere, the preferences of individual commissioners or their immediate subordinates were the deciding factor. The *Bee* insisted that the engineer commissioners never approved of Negroes in any but menial jobs, and of the civilian commissioners only Henry West, a Roosevelt appointee, displayed no "colorphobia." In 1908, out of a clerical force of 450 in the District Building, only 9 were Negroes; among 731 policemen and 498 firemen 39 and 9 respectively were colored; 79 clerks and 55 mail carriers were colored out of

881 city post office employees; 460 colored schoolteachers selected chiefly by the assistant superintendent completed the list of the District's Negro employees in white-collar jobs. The pay scale put the yearly income of all but a very few at less than $1,000. Four years later a city containing some 94,000 colored inhabitants and 20,000 colored taxpayers had about 900 Negroes on the payroll, nearly half of them rated as unskilled laborers at wages of $500 or less a year.[4]

At the same time jobs open to Negroes in other fields, especially domestic service, shrank in number. Judge Terrell put the blame for householders' shift to white servants upon his own people; for too often, he said, they skimped their work while making unwarranted demands upon their employers. He viewed the refusal of Negroes to work for other Negroes as particularly serious in a city where he estimated a tenth to a fifth of the colored people were jobless; he told the National Negro Business League in New York of a colored woman who, having advertised for a washwoman, was informed by a colored applicant: "Lady, I can't work for you; I'm in society myself." The overcrowding of the professions in colored Washington, pronounced in the late nineteenth century, now intensified. In spite of the efforts of the local branch of the recently organized Negro Business League, and in spite of a few isolated examples of modest success—an insurance company, a shoe store, and several drug stores—Negro business enterprises made no progress. In 1903 Washington's one Negro savings bank failed; attempts to organize another came to nothing. While

---

[4] Hayes, *Negro Govt Worker*, pp. 125-30; *Republican Campaign Textbook, 1912*, pp. 71-72; Osceola Madden, "A Color Phase of Washington," *The World Today*, XIV, 549-52; *Bee*, 22 July 1905, 11 May, 16 Nov 1907, 2 Oct 1909, 4 May 1912, 20 Feb 1915; Kathleen Dudley Long, "Woodrow Wilson and the Negro, 1912-1916" (M.A. thesis, Bryn Mawr College, 1956), pp. 14-17; H Committee on Reform in the Civil Service, 63C, 2S, "Hearings on Segregation of Clerks and Employees in the Civil Service," pp. 4-5; Sherman's *Directory and Ready Reference of the Colored Population of the District of Columbia, 1913*, pp. 388-417.

the *Bee* improved its appearance, gave better news coverage, and adopted a more dignified tone, the *Colored American,* which Booker T. Washington had largely financed, ceased publication in 1904 after a losing six-year struggle for existence. The *Bee,* in turn, ran into financial difficulties in 1908 when a rival, the Washington *American,* appeared. Calvin Chase's repeated attacks upon Mr. Washington's "Uncle Tomism" notwithstanding, the educator came to the *Bee*'s rescue, for he considered a vigorous Negro press an important weapon in the fight for advancement, and the national capital above all must have Negro newspapers.[5]

Accompanying the growing economic pinch was a gradual tightening of the cordon excluding Negroes from any slight share in a common social life of the city. The one exception was the children's annual Easter Monday egg-rolling contest on the White House lawn when for a few hours white and colored children intermingled, "all beaten up as it were in a social omelette. Eggs of every color are rolled back and forth . . . and there are just as many shades, if not as many colors, of skin as of egg shell." The rest of the year race prejudice seeping down from parents poisoned the relations between white and colored youngsters. As Joe Gans, the Negro prize fighter, won fame in the ring whenever a championship bout was scheduled, a boy of either race who ventured alone into Washington's streets beyond his own immediate neighborhood risked a beating up from a gang of the enemy intent upon upholding the honor of Gans or his white rival. One very light-colored, red-haired Negro boy faced double jeopardy, since colored contemporaries outside the Negro section of Foggy Bottom took him for a white, while white boys pounced on him as a Negro. Jack Johnson's victory over Jim Jeffries later made matters worse.

[5] *Star,* 20 Aug 1905; *Bee,* 26 Aug, 25 Nov 1905, 27 Mar 1909, 15 Feb 1913; *Rpt B/Ed.,* pp. 207-08; Booker T. Washington to Judge Robert Terrell, 19 Feb 1906, B. T. Washington Mss; *Negro Year Book, 1912,* pp. 170, 175; August Meier, "Booker T. Washington and the Negro Press," *Journal of Negro History,* XXXVIII, 68, 88, 89.

Athletic prowess, which in post-World-War-II years would begin to bridge racial cleavages, merely widened the gulf.

The rapidity with which the breach developed in the first decade of the century is astonishing. In 1902 the Washington *Post,* with an unusual display of interest, devoted a half-column to praise of the city's upper-class Negro society, "the Negro scholar in silk hat and frock coat," the well-to-do Negro lawyer, the half-dozen colored members of the Washington Board of Trade, the colored women graduates of Wellesley, Smith, Oberlin, and Russell Sage, the Treble Clef Club, "organized for the study of classical music," the Samuel Coleridge-Taylor Oratorio Society with its 225 voices, and the church choirs which "won golden opinions." Two years later the *Post* was deploring the unseemly ambition of Washington's colored leaders to get "the ballot, recognition, admission to theatres and restaurants, monopoly of the public parks and other like prerogatives," instead of pouring their efforts into establishing colored vocational and manual training schools as Negroes in the Deep South were doing. White residents overlooked the steady decline of illiteracy among Washington's adult Negroes; in 1910 it stood at less than 17 percent. The *Star* suggested that white people should not draw the color line in giving Christmas charity; otherwise, save for an occasional friendly notice in the Washington *Times,* after 1903 the city's white press confined its favorable comments on Negro activities to applauding Booker T. Washington's Tuskegee program with its implied acknowledgment of Negroes' inherent racial inferiority. White people now and again went to Sunday evening services in colored churches that had exceptionally fine choirs; the intruders, who as a matter of course would have refused seats in their own churches to Negroes, assumed that colored congregations were flattered by that form of white patronage. Foreign visitors as curiosity-ridden as H. G. Wells about American modes of life rarely met any Negroes but lackeys and hence seldom had any comment to offer on Negroes in the capital.

No white host thought of taking a guest to Howard University, where he might have talked with some of the ablest Negroes in the country. A dispassionate appraisal of race relations in the capital of 1908 led an observant social worker to conclude that in Washington "the separation of the races is more nearly complete than in any other city of the Union. The better class of white and colored people know absolutely nothing of each other."

The "better class" of Negroes, particularly those who had lived for years in the city, were painfully aware of what was happening. An anonymous article entitled "What It Means to be Colored in the Capital of the United States" listed for readers of the *Independent* some of the new manifestations of racism: in January 1906 the Columbian Debating Society at George Washington University had argued the question: "Resolved that a Jim Crow law should be adopted and enforced in the District of Columbia"; the affirmative won; a few months later a bill for Jim Crow street cars was introduced into Congress with a citizens' association endorsement; until 1900 the colored schools had had colored directors of music, art, cooking, sewing, manual training, and physical culture; now all were white. "For fifteen years," wrote the author, "I have resided in Washington, and while it was far from being a 'paradise for colored people' when I first touched these shores, it has been doing its level best ever since to make conditions for us intolerable." [6]

Mounting white antagonism had its effect: from 31 percent of the total population in 1900, colored Washington dropped to 28.5 percent in 1910 and would be only 25 percent by 1920. Knowing themselves unwelcome, the colored members of the Board of Trade resigned. At the

---

[6] Mrs. R. Kent Beattie, "Easter Egg-Rolling," *Crisis*, xi, 313-14; *Bee*, 19 Feb 1916; Washington *Post*, 3 Aug 1902, 9 Jan 1904; *Star*, 14 Dec 1903; Madden, "A Color Phase," p. 549; "What It Means to be Colored in the Capital of the United States" and "Our Washington Letter," *Independent*, lxii, 181-86, 1012.

request of the local chapter of the Women's Christian
Temperance Union, Negro women withdrew in 1908 to form
a Jim Crow unit. While the severity of sentences imposed
on colored misdemeanants increased, white supremacists
talked openly of reestablishing the whipping post to check
Negro crime or of forcing all "niggers" out of the District.
Northern newcomers fell easily into the habit of using only
the Christian name in speaking of or to a Negro, no matter
how distinguished he might be. In her published *Recollections,* so kindly a person as Mrs. William Howard Taft
alluded to her indebtedness to Arthur Brooks, a major in
the colored unit of the District National Guard; but,
perhaps because he was also a messenger in the War
Department, she wrote of him as "Arthur," never "Major"
or "Mr. Brooks"; every white person mentioned, except
the Taft children and the uneducated Irish coachman, was
dignified by his surname and title. Such minor slights were
unimportant save as never-ending reminders to colored
people that they had won scant respect from whites.

Probably a better gauge of the strengthening of the caste
barrier lay in the attitude of white churchmen. At the
Congregational Church, which had welcomed Negro members in the 1870's, a congressman from Maine received an
ovation when he stated that colored men should never have
been enfranchised *en masse,* but rather one by one as each
proved himself ready. Episcopal Bishop Henry Satterlee
went further. Giving Negroes equality through suffrage
when they were not in fact equal, combined with the
growth of the Negro population, he said, had promoted
racial hostilities. Although he supported Christian missions
for colored people, he thought Negroes "morally and in-
tellectually a weaker race, and . . . even if they should
become great landowners, men of wealth and of education,
race antagonism would only become stronger and more
sharply defined." Washington's Negro intelligentsia no
doubt saw some truth in these pronouncements, but the
Bishop's repudiation of education, wealth, and political

164

power as means of closing the gap between the races and his statement that a solution must depend upon every Negro's winning for himself "a strong, robust Christ-like character" were profoundly discouraging. Seemingly, white men could remain devils, but colored must become saints. Told by white men year after year of the virtues of Booker T. Washington's subservient philosophy, Negro aristocrats listened without enthusiasm to the sage of Tuskegee when he informed them at the colored YMCA that the eyes of the world were upon them and they must set an example by ridding the city of loafers, drunkards, and gamblers. Washington, himself plebeian-born, distrusted the aristocrats as much as they doubted his wisdom.

Perhaps the most deadly blow the city's white churches dealt their dark-skinned Christian brethren came in 1910 with the assembling in Washington of the sixth World Sunday School Convention. The local committee on arrangements refused to seat local colored delegates or permit them to march in the parade because they were not members of the District Sunday School Association although they belonged to the World Association and had taken part in earlier conventions. The *Star* reported all "wrinkles . . . smoothed out" by a vote of the organization to make Booker T. Washington a life member, but as Mr. Washington represented "Uncle Tomism" to many local Negroes, the *Star*'s account smacked of belittling the issue.[7] Manifestly the separate colored churches which Negroes had proudly begun to establish eighty years before as evidence of Negro self-reliance had now turned into barriers to social assimilation of colored people into the larger community.

More alarming to colored Washingtonians were the multiplying instances of racial segregation in government

[7] *Annual Report of the Board of Charities of the District of Columbia,* 1901, p. 269 (hereafter cited as Rpt. *B/Ch*), *Bee,* 11 Feb, 10 Dec 1905, 8 Feb 1908; *Post,* 18 Apr 1904, 7 Nov 1910; *Star,* 11 Jan 1905, 10 May, 20 Jun 1909, 20, 24 May 1910; Mrs. William Howard Taft, *Recollections,* pp. 279-80; *Times,* 14 Jul 1907; *Rpt. B/Ed,* 1905, pp. 105-15.

offices. A "Jim Crow corner" first appeared in 1904 in the Bureau of Engraving and Printing. The *Bee* noted in 1905 "a systematic effort inaugurated to Jim Crow the Negro. The fever is spreading. . . . The Negro is afraid to complain." Race prejudice, having once gained a foothold under a Republican regime, quickly widened its reach. Before 1909 separate locker and washrooms and separate lunchroom accommodations had become the rule in several sections of the Treasury and the Department of the Interior, and, although the scheme did not spread far during the next four years, the administration made no move to check or forbid it.

What Republican officials saw fit to allow set the pattern for private concerns. In 1910, at the invitation of the Federation of Citizens' Association, ten recently organized Negro neighborhood groups attended a meeting only to have their hosts then vote to exclude them from federation membership; the Negroes thereupon took the name Civic Associations and formed their own federation. The local civil rights acts still stood unrepealed, but restaurants, barber shops, and hotels now barred Negroes as a matter of course, theatres admitted them only to "nigger heavens," and railroads and buses carrying passengers into the District from Virginia and Maryland enforced Jim Crow seating. As a suit, if won in court, meant at most token damages for the plaintiff, Negroes ceased to invoke the law.[8] Indeed a good many of them obviously shrank from public complaint lest it feed fuel to the campaign to institute new restrictions. White extremists might persuade Congress not only to destroy the last flimsy legal safeguards against racial discrimination in the District of Columbia but to make segregation mandatory.

From 1907 on, bills for Jim Crow cars in the District came up in the House of Representatives at intervals. While a new congressman from Georgia announced his determina-

[8] *Bee,* 3 Sep 1904, 11 Feb 1905, 7 May 1910, 4 May 1912.

166

tion to force all Negroes out of government service, agitation for a District antimiscegenation law made headway. In February 1913 the House passed the bill in less than five minutes; only Senate inaction stopped it. When the Negro Register of the Treasury and a colored guest lunched in the House Office Building restaurant, five congressmen threatened a boycott that would close it down if such an affront to white manhood ever recurred; the manager assured them it would not. With lynch law rampant in the Deep South, Negroes in Washington had some reason to think the moment inopportune to protest the curtailment of their own civil rights. Possibly only a few men understood the seriousness of the trend in the capital; before the summer of 1913 perhaps the rank and file were not apprehensive for themselves. But over a ten-year span the evidence the *Bee* assembled and published periodically indicated clearly that Washington Negroes, although spared lynchings, were already subject to most of the discriminations imposed upon colored people elsewhere in America.

The city's upper-class Negroes, however, reacted with growing militance to the accelerating racism of white Washington. Booker T. Washington kept many close friends in the capital, but educated colored people who accepted his program of "racial solidarity, self-help, and economic chauvinism" increasingly rejected his methods and his disregard of political action. His conciliatory policies, his anxiety to avoid friction with whites, and his stress upon patience led to a break between him and a group of Negro radicals in 1906 when some twenty-nine "rebels" headed by the brilliant, young W. E. B. DuBois of Atlanta University and William Monroe Trotter, editor of the Boston *Guardian,* launched the so-called Niagara Movement with a manifesto of Negro rights and aims. Four Washington Negroes took part in the first Niagara conference. Inspired by that example, leadership long dormant in colored Washington began to reassert itself.

Kelly Miller, professor of mathematics and later dean at

Howard University, George W. Cook, treasurer of Howard, the Reverend Samuel Carruthers of the Galbraith AME Church, Francis J. Grimke of the Fifteenth Street Presbyterian Church, three or four other local pastors, Mary Church Terrell, the first president of the National Association of Colored Women, Calvin Chase of the *Bee,* and a score of other men and women who commanded prestige now abandoned the tactics of suffering indignities in silence and began a campaign of outspoken protest against social injustice. Few of them openly criticized Booker T. Washington. On the contrary, Mrs. Terrell, while serving on the board of education, rebuked a Negro newspaperman for objecting to the "Tuskegee idea" of Negro education, although she herself advocated giving the colored child in the District the same schooling as the white. Like others who shared that view, she welcomed the opening of the Armstrong vocational high school in 1902, partly because a white technical high school was built at the same time, and doubtless partly because the separation of pupils seeking vocational training from those aspiring to professional careers enabled the M Street High School to concentrate upon the gifted college-bound student. But irrespective of their feelings about Mr. Washington, all of the group joined in publicizing the fact that colored people were not content to be hewers of wood and drawers of water and that whites were deluded if, like the New York *Times,* they thought "the Negroes of the United States are doing very well." [9]

Although Washington's Negro militants constantly gained adherents, the city was not initially in the front of the fight, perhaps because the District's voteless status gave political leadership to New York, Boston, and Chicago,

[9] H Rpt 8072, 59C, 2S, Ser 5065; *Star,* 14 May 1909; *Herald,* 21 May 1907; *Post,* 11 Feb 1913; *Crisis,* v, 270-71; Hayes, *Negro Govt Worker,* p. 33; W. E. B. DuBois, *Dusk of Dawn,* pp. 88-89, 92-95; August Meier, "Booker T. Washington and the Negro Press," pp. 75, 79, 80-81; *Bee,* 25 Nov 1905, 25 Apr 1906, 26 Nov 1910, 29 Jul 1911; Mary Church Terrell to H. G. Pinkett, 9 Sep 1906, Terrell Mss; *Rpt B/Ed,* 1902; New York *Times,* 18 Apr 1913.

perhaps also because colored people in the largest Negro city in the country, having escaped the excesses of "lily-white" agitation that the Deep South was experiencing, were wary about forcing an issue locally lest it boomerang violently. If, as one scholar avers, Booker T. Washington's greatest ascendency, which spanned the first decade of the century, "coincided with the period of greatest oppression Negroes have faced since the Civil War," the birth of the National Association for the Advancement of Colored People in New York City in 1909 must be recognized as marking the beginning of the slow march upward. Started by a handful of earnest white people, the association from the first was intended to be interracial. But of its national officers and staff only W. E. B. DuBois was a Negro, and radicals such as William Trotter of Boston distrusted it too deeply to join or work with it. In Washington, caution and inertia combined to delay until the spring of 1912 the organization of a local branch of the NAACP. But within a few months it was one of the largest in the country and counted 143 dues-paying members, among them so distinguished a white man as Chief Justice Stafford of the District Supreme Court. But, unlike the New York group, white members were few. Here the most able of the upper-class Negro community took charge, bending their first efforts to providing legal aid for victims of discrimination.[10]

Grim as things looked for all American Negroes in 1912, gleams of hope were visible in Washington. They derived principally from the changing point of view of the city's professional social workers and the volunteers they trained as visitors in the slums. First-hand exposure to the conditions under which honest hard-working colored families had to live taught fair-minded investigators a good deal

[10] Meier, "Booker T. Washington," p. 88; *Negro Year Book, 1912,* p. 134; *Third Annual Report National Association for the Advancement of Colored People,* p. 23 (hereafter cited as *Anl Rpt NAACP*); Flint Kellogg, "Villard and the NAACP," *Nation,* CLVIII, 137-40; *Crisis,* VI, 190.

about the obstacles confronting the city's Negroes. The report of President Roosevelt's Homes Commission and an eye-opening study by the United States Labor Department presented evidence that starvation wages and destitution were directly related. White businessmen occasionally talked as if lowering the Negro death rate was important only because high mortality interfered with favorable advertising for the city, but few men sounded as sure as once they had that Negro "shiftlessness" lay at the root of the problem. Anyone who had looked could see that the squalor existing in the fetid overcrowded alley dwellings which, for lack of other low-cost housing, several thousand colored families had to call home was not solely the product of laziness.

White assumptions that upper-class Negroes lacked civic-mindedness received a jolt when a compilation of scattered data revealed that Negroes had initiated and carried on several projects for their people, notably a day nursery for infants of working mothers. Of the $50,000 collected in Washington for a colored YMCA, colored people contributed $27,000. Conferences between Negro workers at the colored Southwest Settlement House and white philanthropists came to be "remarkably free from race consciousness, the one thought on both sides being the common welfare." Negroes thus brought into touch with whites active in Washington charities could feel the lightening of the atmosphere of censoriousness.[11]

Inasmuch as white men's respect, not their charity, was the goal of Negro leaders, any sign that a segment of white Washington was ready to work with them for the common good assumed importance. Reform was in the air throughout the United States as the presidential election

[11] Annual Report of the Associated Charities, 1903, p. 23 (hereafter cited as ACRpt); *Crisis*, III, 51; *Rpt B/Tr*, 1910, p. 8; *Times*, 5 May 1911; Sarah C. Fernandis, "In the Making," *Charities*, XVI, 703-05; *Bee*, 13 Apr 1907, 17, 24 May, 5 Jul 1913; Washington *Sun*, 12 Feb, 14 May 1915.

of 1912 approached, and, noting the fervor with which white muckrakers and Progressives talked of the far-reaching social and political changes that must come, thoughtful colored men dared think reform might extend to race relations. None of the candidates made explicit promises, but while Republicans pointed to President Taft's record of Negro appointments and Theodore Roosevelt denounced "brutal" Democratic and "hypocritical" Republican racial policies, Woodrow Wilson preached the "New Freedom" with its guarantees of "fair and just treatment" for all. The *Bee*, wary of trusting any Democrat, urged its readers when the election was over to have faith in the assurances of Wilson's influential colored supporters that the incoming President would not countenance continued discrimination and segregation.[12]

Negroes in the capital waited eagerly for word of new appointments and measures that would wipe out the Jim Crow sections in government offices. March and most of April 1913 came and went. Confidence in the New Freedom gave way to uneasiness. Then piece by piece the world of colored Washington fell apart. Within the next few months the President dismissed all but two of the Negroes whom Taft had appointed "to offices of essential dignity at Washington" and replaced them with white men. He nominated a colored lawyer from Oklahoma for Register of the Treasury with the intention of making the Register's section an all-Negro unit, but when the nominee, intimidated by fierce opposition in the Senate, withdrew his name, Wilson appointed an American Indian. The District Recordership of Deeds, a colored preserve since 1881, went to a white man in 1916. By then the only Negro to hold an appointive position in Washington was Robert Terrell, confirmed in April 1914 for another term as a municipal

---

[12] Long, "Woodrow Wilson and the Negro," pp. 14-32; *Republic Campaign Text Book, 1912*, p. 238; Theodore Roosevelt, "The Progressives and the Colored Man," *Outlook*, CI, 909-12; *Journal of Negro History*, XXXII, 90; *Bee*, 12 Dec 1912.

judge. Disillusioning though these snubs were, they were pin pricks compared to the segregationist policies officially sanctioned in government departments in the summer of 1913.

"Segregation," reported a white officer of the NAACP, "is no new thing in Washington, and the present administration cannot be said to have inaugurated it. The past few months of Democratic Party control, however, have given segregation impetus and have been marked by more than a beginning of systematic enforcement." As soon as the Virginia-born President was installed in the White House, a group of Negro baiters calling themselves the National Democratic Fair Play Association had undertaken to stir up trouble in order to get Negroes out of the civil service, to restrict them to menial jobs, or at the very least to keep white and colored workers separate. A Fair Play committee busily poking about in various offices had elicited complaints from "Democratic clerks and other white employees of the government who are inimical to the Negro," and had obtained the backing of officeseekers who declared it intolerable for white people to work in proximity to Negroes, let alone under their supervision.[13] The President, apparently convinced that racial friction was rife in the executive departments, was anxious to check it if only because it might imperil his legislative programs.

In view of the Southern background of Postmaster General Albert Burleson, Secretary of the Treasury William McAdoo, and Secretary of the Navy Josephus Daniels, perhaps segregation would have become standard throughout their departments without the impetus supplied by outside agitation and the shocked disapproval of Mrs.

[13] *Bee*, 29 Mar, 26 Jul, 25 Oct, 15 Nov, 6 Dec 1913; *Nation*, xcvii, 114; *Crisis*, vi, 9, 60-63, xii, 198; New York *Times*, 19 Feb, 25 Apr 1914; L. H. Pickford to Joseph Tumulty, 12 Jun 1916, Wilson Mss; *NAACP Report*, 13 Aug 1913, and "Segregation in Government Departments," *NAACP Report of an Investigation*, 1 Nov 1913, Wilson Mss (hereafter cited as *NAACP Rpt*, 1 Nov 1913); *Post*, 30 Apr 1913.

Woodrow Wilson at seeing colored men and white women working in the same room in the Post Office Department. There the change had gone into effect before the end of July 1913, and by autumn the Treasury, after cautiously watching public reaction, had consigned the colored employees of most divisions to separate rooms and forbidden all Negro employees to use the lunch tables and the toilet facilities that for years past they had shared with their white fellows. Similar rules applied in the Navy Department as well as in all federal offices where segregation had obtained under Republican rule.

"The effect is startling," the NAACP report noted. "Those segregated are regarded as a people apart, almost as lepers." White clerks, seemingly without personal convictions, now said they approved. To endorse the new arrangement had become "the thing to do." Yet ever since President Cleveland had quashed every proposal of segregation, the *Bee* pointed out, "Afro-American clerks" had worked side by side with white in "peace and harmony." In the summer of 1913 Booker T. Washington wrote a friend: "I have never seen the colored people [of Washington] so discouraged and so bitter as they are at the present time." Many of them refused at first to believe that the author of "The New Freedom" knew what was afoot, but in late October when a delegation led by William Monroe Trotter of Boston begged him to intervene, the President's evasive answer dissipated doubts: Jim Crowism in the federal government had his approval. A mass meeting to protest "the officializing of race prejudice" overflowed the Metropolitan AME Church, but for the moment Negroes in the government service dared go no further lest they precipitate a drastic change in the civil service law which would extend segregation into every federal department and be far harder to rescind than the word-of-mouth orders of departmental chiefs.[14]

[14] *Post*, 2, 20 May 1913; Ralph Tyler to President Wilson, 12 May, Booker T. Washington to Oswald Garrison Villard, 10 Aug, enclosed

Members of the local NAACP realized that "almost every man employed by the government and by the schools risks his position when he stands on our militant platform," but they believed that only a united front could stop the spread of racial discrimination. In November they organized a speakers' bureau to go from church to church, society to society, and lodge to lodge, "to arouse the colored people themselves to their danger, to make them feel it through and through, and at the same time to make them willing to make sacrifices for the cause." The response, said Archibald Grimké, president of the Washington NAACP branch, was "nothing short of a miracle." In a city notoriously rent by "all sorts of factions, school teachers whom you would not believe cared for anything but pleasure, society women, [and] young men" joined in the campaign. At the M Street High School a group of exceptionally inspiring teachers passed on the torch to their students; for them W. E. B. DuBois became a symbol of liberty. By the early months of 1914 the Washington NAACP had over seven hundred dues-paying members and had sent nearly $4,000 to national headquarters.[15]

Personal letters from influential white men pleading with the President to alter his course and indignant articles in the liberal magazines and newspapers failed to persuade Mr. Wilson to reverse his position. On the contrary, his resistance stiffened. When a second Negro delegation, again led by William Monroe Trotter, reminded him of his earlier promise to see justice done, Wilson lost his temper and told the delegation he was not to be high-pressured. The remonstrances, however, were almost certainly instrumental in preventing the wholesale adoption of segregation through-

---

in ltr, Villard to Wilson, 18 Aug 1913, and Villard to Wilson, 29 Sep 1913, Wilson Mss; *Bee,* 10, 17 May, 26 Jul, 6 Sep, 15 Nov 1913; Arthur Link, *The New Freedom,* pp. 245-54; *Crisis,* VI, 220, 289-99, VII, 89; *NAACP Report,* 1 Nov 1913.

[15] *Crisis,* VII, 192-93, VIII, 32-33; Dr. Rayford Logan to the author, 9 Mar 1960.

out the government. In March 1914 when the House Committee on Civil Service Reform held hearings on two bills calling for mandatory racial separation of government employees, a Louisiana sponsor of the bills argued that to put a member of "this inferior race" in a position of authority over Caucasians was unrighteous. By the stamp of color the Lord had decreed a lowly place for Negroes. When Congressman Martin Madden of Illinois asked, "Who can say the Almighty decreed it?" the Louisianan replied: "History, experience, and first-hand knowledge." Northern representatives killed both bills in committee.

Mrs. Wilson's frequent excursions into the Negro slums and her zeal in working for legislation that would eliminate alley-dwelling did little to lessen colored people's resentment of the President and the First Lady. To them her explanation that her Christian upbringing had instilled in her a sense of charitable duty toward Negroes sounded sanctimonious. Even colored people who recognized the importance of slum clearance as a weapon against disease and hopelessness found her brand of philanthropy intolerably patronizing. Neither her death nor the passage of the Alley Dwelling Act in the autumn of 1914 modified their feelings.[16]

In the meantime a Supreme Court ruling that the federal Civil Rights Act of 1875 was unconstitutional not only in the states but also in federal territories opened the door to new discriminatory laws in the District of Columbia. But fresh attempts to exclude Negroes from government service, District antimiscegenation and Jim Crow streetcar bills, and a segregated residential bill patterned on a Baltimore ordinance of 1913 all met with defeat. Pressures in fact

[16] O. G. Villard, "The President and the Negro," *Nation*, xcvii, 114; Villard, "The President and the Segregation at Washington," *Independent*, lxxx, p. 275; *Herald*, 16 Nov 1914; *Times*, 13 Nov 1914; *Crisis*, ix, 119-27; *Negro Year Book, 1914-15*, pp. 34-36; H Comee on Reform in the Civil Service, 63C, 2S, *Segregation of Clerks and Employees in the Civil Service*, 6 Mar 1914, pp. 3, 7; Grace Vawter Bicknell, "The Home Maker of the White House, Mrs. Woodrow Wilson's Social Work in Washington," *Survey*, xxxiii, 19-22.

eased slightly in 1915 when the Supreme Court in an un-
foreseen reversal of earlier opinions refused to allow nearby
Maryland to write a "grandfather clause" into her constitution.

"More than seventy-five percent of the present segregation," the *Bee* reminded its readers in 1915, "was trans-
mitted to President Wilson by the Republicans," and the
editor noted more Negro promotions in the civil service
than in years past. But although the transit companies
were not allowed to introduce Jim Crow cars, other District
corporations and individual white citizens interpreted the
administration policy to mean that short of open violence
they could carry discrimination virtually as far as they
chose. Informal agreements between sellers and buyers
effectively strengthened the residential color line. In 1914
an eminent Boston lawyer persuaded the American Bar
Association to rescind its recent ruling that no Negro could
be elected to membership, but the substitute provision that
applicants must state their race served the same purpose.
While not all white Washingtonians shared the prevailing
colorphobia and Chief Justice Wendell Stafford fought it
in the District Supreme Court, most of the white community
took it for granted that colored teachers should be excluded
from a teachers' lecture series held in the Congregational
Church and that Negro civic organizations should not be
invited to join with the fifty-six white groups in planning
better correlation of the city's recreational activities.[17]

The attacks and the disheartening indifference of white
people, however, had the effect of maintaining the new
solidarity in the Negro world. In Washington's triple-
tiered colored community a sense of cohesiveness, lacking

[17] *Crisis,* VII, 117, 142, 169, 252-53; *Negro Year Book, 1914-15;* pp.
30, 34-35, 39; *Times,* 3 Dec 1914; *Bee,* 4 Oct 1914, 27 Feb, 5 Mar, 15
May 1915; *Sun,* 26 Mar, 30 Apr, 25 Jun 1915; H Rpt 1340, 63C, 3S,
Ser 6766; H Dis Comee, 64C, 1S, Hrgs, "Intermarriage of Whites and
Negroes in the District of Columbia, and Separate Accommodations in
Street Cars for White and Negroes in the District of Columbia."

for nearly thirty years, had begun to emerge before 1911;
it strengthened extraordinarily during the crisis of 1913 and
1914. Although, as the struggle against race prejudice
dragged on, the failure to make headway might well have
dissolved the new bonds, they endured. In Northern cities
also, upper-class Negroes, the "talented tenth" upon whom
W. E. B. DuBois pinned hopes for the race, saw they could
not remain detached from the lower-class black, no matter
how superior they knew themselves to be and no matter
how uncongenial they found his society. But the growth
of "group-identification" among all classes of Washington
Negroes had special significance, both because elaborate
class distinctions were older here than in most cities and
because much of colored America still thought of Washington as the center of Negro culture.

The new attitude of the *Bee* supplies an index to this
change. Where the paper had once carried scathing accounts
of Negro discrimination against Negro and had sneered
at any colored man who achieved distinction, the editorials
and news articles gradually took on a constructive character.
The addition to the editorial staff of the wise, public-
spirited George H. Richardson gave the *Bee* new dignity;
his opinions carried weight. Calvin Chase, whose attacks
on Booker T. Washington had stopped in 1908, lashed out
periodically at W. E. B. DuBois, arch opponent of Mr.
Washington's teachings, but after the death of the Tuskegee
leader in November 1915, those explosions ended. Chase
and Richardson saw fit to needle colored men who sought
their own advantage at the sacrifice of principle. Editorials
called attention to the destructive selfishness of Negro
candidates for office under the proscriptive Democratic regime. "Woody," one article declared, "believed his segregation policy was approved by the black gentry because so
many of them were anxious to serve under him, segregation
or no segregation." Sarcastically the *Bee* observed that no
local colored men had had the courage to ask the President
in person to define his position on race questions as William

Monroe Trotter of Boston had twice obliged him to do, first in November 1913 and again a year later. Yet in taking cowards and the mean-minded to task, the *Bee* also accorded praise to colored men of firm convictions and larger vision. Scoldings at Negro shortcomings became progressively fewer and turned instead into exhortations to push on with the work of establishing a self-respecting, self-sufficient Negro Washington within the larger community.[18]

Four other Negro publications were appearing regularly in Washington in 1914 and 1915—the short-lived *Sun,* put out by a talented but erratic protégé of Booker T. Washington, the *American,* the *Odd Fellows Journal,* and the *National Union,* organ of a Negro insurance company. In 1915 the *Journal of Negro History* began its long and useful career. The *American,* an uninspired, rather shabby sheet, and the ably edited *Sun* pursued the same line as the *Bee* in less bellicose language: buy colored, support colored charities and colored civic enterprise, take pride in Negro achievements, and don't be "Jim Crowed" by patronizing places where Negroes are segregated. Andrew Hilyer at the turn of the century had preached three quarters of that fourfold program. Now the fight against Jim Crow gave it strength. Businessmen and nonprofit groups began to talk of what Negro solidarity had accomplished. The Howard Theatre, for example, since reverting to colored management, staged good plays, amusing minstrel shows, and musical hits like those of the "Black Patti Troubadours"; by renting the premises for amateur performances now and again, the theatre also served as a kind of community cultural center. There and at the Majestic vaudeville theatre and the two new Negro movie houses colored audiences never had to face Jim Crowism. The eight or nine hundred colored families that had managed to

[18] *Negro Year Book, 1914-15,* pp. 43-45; Arnold M. Rose, *The Negro's Morale, Group Identification and Protest,* pp. 57-95; *Bee,* 21 Nov 1914, 27 Feb, 5 Mar 1915; Colonel Campbell C. Johnson to the author, 9 Jun 1960.

178

rent or buy houses in the one-time exclusively white home-owners' cooperative in LeDroit Park could enjoy a similar freedom by giving their custom to the Negro-owned grocery store there. The *Sun,* remarking that the local Negro Business League had gone "to sleep" in 1913, began in 1915 to carry a directory of reliable Negro business firms in the city. A colored department store in a building on 14th Street employed only colored help and met a long-felt want. U Street in northwest Washington was becoming the colored Connecticut Avenue. In southwest Washington the new Douglass Hotel offered colored tourists and conventions comfortable accommodations. The Negro press insisted on use of the capital *N,* and after 1914 frequently capitalized "colored" also; doubtless in the interest of racial harmony, colored newspapers practically dropped the term *black.* Despite the militance of the new propaganda, it was refreshingly free of the braggadocio that formerly had often accompanied attempts to boost Negro enterprise.

Indeed, there was more in which to take pride, as the social disorganization that had long characterized colored Washington began to yield to community effort. Progress, begun even before the disasters of the Wilson era added impetus, was particularly noticeable in the realm of charities and civic undertakings. By the spring of 1913 the recently opened colored YMCA, built brick by brick by Negro workmen, was able to meet its first year's operating costs of $8,200 and show a $.56 balance. "The fraternal spirit existing between the Y and the local ministry is happily shown in the use by a number of the churches of the great swimming pool for baptismal purposes." The Y became the meeting place of the local branch of the NAACP, the Public School Athletic League, the Christian Endeavor Union, the Federation of Civic Associations, the Negro medical society, and other organizations. The colored YWCA expanded its program and paid off all but a small indebtedness during 1913. While public-spirited Negroes admitted that too few well-to-do families contributed to

179

charity, a new determination to carry on without white philanthropy went far toward obliterating the earlier attitude: let whites shoulder the burden, since they are responsible for the colored man's plight. At the annual meeting of the Colored Social Settlement in December 1913, after paying tribute to Dr. John R. Francis, Washington's leading colored physician, for his tireless work in launching this center for "social uplift," the assistant superintendent of the colored schools spoke of the importance of teaching colored children about the great men of their own race; only thus would the younger generation escape being overwhelmed by white prestige and avoid impairment of colored initiative. In much the same vein the newly organized Oldest Inhabitants Association (Colored) of Washington announced its purpose to be the fostering of Negro civic pride.[19]

It would be untruthful to picture colored Washington in 1915 and 1916 as a unified community free of the old divisive jealousies and destructive backbiting, its individual members now singlemindedly working all for one and one for all. Leaders faltered, quarrels persisted—particularly over teaching appointments and promotions in the school system—and self-contempt, shown in the sheer meanness of Negro to Negro, continued to interfere with the important task of raising the economic level of all classes. While the *Sun* argued that the cost of racial disunity was as high for the light-colored Caucasian-featured person as for the black-skinned Negroid-looking, few of the former were willing to discard class distinctions based largely upon degree of color. Moreover, the tightening of the net drawn by strengthened white hostility, while binding courageous colored people together in a common purpose, strangled the will of the weak and timid; circumstances that awak-

[19] *Bee*, 17 May, 6 Dec 1913, 2 Oct 1915, 25 May 1916; *Sun*, 8 Jan, 12 Mar, 23 Apr 1915; *Crisis*, XI, 90-94; John H. Paynter, *A Souvenir of the Anniversary and Banquet of the Oldest Inhabitants Association (Colored) of the District of Columbia, April 16, 1914.*

ened a fighting spirit in some of the race stripped others of the capacity to hold up their heads at all. Nevertheless the energy with which Washington's Negro leaders fought lynching in the South and racial discrimination everywhere was impressive.[20]

W. E. B. DuBois later wrote of the early years of the Wilson administration: "Quite suddenly the program for the NAACP, which up to this time had been more or less indefinite, was made clear and intensive." The Washington branch forestalled adverse legislation, got a few Negroes reinstated in government jobs, and induced Congress to continue appropriations for Howard University and its 300 college students. Besides a vigorous separate University chapter, by 1916 the Washington branch of the NAACP, with 1,164 members, was the largest in the United States, and, according to national headquarters, constituted "really a national vigilance committee to watch legislation in Congress and lead the fight for Negro manhood rights at the capital of the nation." [21]

Differences of opinion inescapably arose over both long-term strategy and more immediate local tactics. For example, in which direction should Washington Negroes lean when the discussion of District home rule revived in 1916? The colored press had argued that popular elections were essential to the progress of the Negro community, but, as Henry West had always treated Negroes with exemplary fairness and, rather surprisingly, Woodrow Wilson's three commissioners showed no racial prejudice, might not colored people be better off under the rule of men like those than under officials chosen by a two-thirds white electorate?

[20] *Sun,* 12, 26 Feb 1915; M. C. Terrell to Robert Terrell, n.d., Terrell Mss. Practically every issue of the *Bee* carried some complaint about Negro school administrators' injustices.

[21] W. E. B. DuBois, *Dusk of Dawn,* pp. 235-36; *Sun,* 15 Jan, 12 Mar 1915; *Crisis,* IX, 217, XI, 35, 256, XII, 197; see also list of Washington members at the 1916 conference at Amenia, New York, *Programme,* Terrell Mss.

Most colored men side-stepped the question; if white citizens persuaded Congress to restore the franchise, then would be the time for Negroes to seek their share of local political power. Again, what was the wise course to pursue when "The Birth of a Nation" began its long run in Washington movie houses? Some men, seeing it as an incitement to race hatred, wanted to demand that the commissioners ban the picture, just as they had barred the prize fight film of Jack Johnson beating Jim Jeffries; other colored people believed that a petition for censorship would merely advertise the offensive D. W. Griffiths film more widely.

While Negro leaders in the national arena examined alternatives as the presidential campaign of 1916 opened, in the voteless capital the question about working with whites for "national preparedness" caused uncertainty. In June 1916 the colored men who marched in a big preparedness parade were "Jim Crowed with a vengeance" and two days later were greeted with a formal segregation order from the War Department. At the request of a New Jersey congressman whose reelection hung in the balance, the order was later rescinded, but before the end of October the all-Negro battalion of the District National Guard was on the Mexican border. Six months later the United States' declaration of war upon the Central Powers would force upon all American Negroes a decision of whether to be Americans first and Negroes second or to let white Americans carry on without voluntary help from the people they treated as second-class citizens.[22]

Still, every Washingtonian daily rubbed elbows with or at least was aware of the presence of people not of his own race. Scores of Negroes were as acutely concerned with municipal taxation, civic betterment, and artistic

[22] *Bee,* 14 Nov 1908, 1 Apr, 17, 19 Jun, 9 Sep, 21 Oct 1916; *Sun,* 9 Apr 1915; Rose, *The Negro's Morale,* pp. 38-39; *Seventh Anl Rpt NAACP,* 1917; *Crisis,* XII, 194, 268; W. E. B. DuBois to Woodrow Wilson, 10 Oct 1916, and Memorial, Boston Branch Negro Equal Political Rights League, 20 Apr 1917, Wilson Mss.

growth as were their white-skinned neighbors. Whether they would or no, some give-and-take resulted. An experiment of 1913 in publishing a Negro city directory was not repeated. Colored Washington, largely separate and wholly unequal in status, had not yet become a completely secret city.

CHAPTER IX

WAR, RACE RIOTS, AND NEW

NADIR, 1917-1928

Negroes the country over were depressed at President Wilson's reelection in 1916, but as the war clouds darkened in the early months of 1917, the younger generation in Washington turned its thoughts to what lay ahead. Unlike colored radicals in several Northern cities, few colored men in the capital considered putting race before country. On the contrary, when the United States declared war on Germany in April, most of them looked upon the fight to come as their opportunity to win recognition as loyal Americans and upon the inevitable postwar readjustments as a unique chance to establish themselves permanently in a sound economic position. The relative stability of the local colored population heightened the chances of success. Whereas industrial cities like Detroit and Chicago were inundated with Southern Negroes who moved north to take jobs in war plants, Washington faced no comparable colored in-migration. The intelligent local Negro community consequently was not submerged by a wave of ignorant farm hands from the rural South.

The District NAACP early declared that patriotism did not require colored men to put up with injustice or to remain silent about lynchings in the South and unprovoked attacks such as those in East St. Louis, but, from the spring of 1917 till the return of colored troops of the AEF two years later, complaints about racial discrimination in Washington dwindled. The local Negro press underscored every instance of fair behavior from whites and exhorted

184

colored people to make the most of the new openings which wholehearted cooperation would bring. However flimsy the foundations of that counsel of hope, colored Washington built on it.

Thus the District's colored candidates for officer training swallowed their dismay at being sent to an all-Negro camp at Des Moines, Iowa; there they at least might have a better chance to prove their worth than in a mixed camp. George Richardson of the *Bee* warned colored servicemen not to write home about every slight they endured; their record would speak for them upon their return. Signs of white recognition seemed to be multiplying: Herbert Hoover appointed a Negro science teacher from the Dunbar High School to head the colored bureau of the Food Administration; Secretary of War Newton Baker made Emmett J. Scott, Booker T. Washington's former secretary, an assistant in the War Department, and the local chapter of the Red Cross asked Scott to serve on the finance committee; the Labor Department assigned George Haynes, a competent economist, to a responsible position, and Secretary of the Treasury McAdoo proposed sending fifty colored men across the country to explain national war aims to Negroes. Even the archconservative Oldest Inhabitants' Association invited the Oldest Inhabitants' Association (Colored) to visit the white headquarters in the old firehouse at 19th and H streets northwest. Furthermore, labor scarcities opened up jobs for colored workmen and netted them higher wages than they had had in peacetime.[1]

Yet proofs of white antagonism were also numerous: new congressional proposals for residential segregation and other Jim Crow bills which, though shelved, were a slap at the Negro war effort; the three-year sentence imposed by court martial on a Negro sentry for shooting a white man who disobeyed the command to halt; the failure of government

---

[1] *Crisis*, XIV, 4, 304, XVI, 217-19, XVII, 182-84, 194; *Bee*, 14, 21 Apr, 26 May, 2, 30 Jun, 28 Jul, 25 Aug, 1, 15 Dec 1917, 13 Apr, 4, 11, 18 May, 7 Sep 1918; *Star*, 21 Oct 1917, 1 Oct 1918.

offices to hire colored people qualified by civil service examinations and of the District police department to take on colored patrolmen; in the face of a dearth of white motormen and conductors, the refusal of the street railway companies to employ Negroes to fill some five hundred jobs; and Red Cross segregation of colored volunteers from white. Despite the serious shortage of living quarters for the city's war-swollen population, District officials and Congress rejected a housing plan for alley-dwellers when Negro builders sought a loan to enable them to put up low rental apartments. When the president of Howard University retired, the trustees again elected a white man. And during the war for the first time Negroes heard themselves called "darkies" in a District courtroom.[2]

Negro leaders knew that some white Washingtonians, like those who joined the local branch of the NAACP, deplored the continuing discrimination and fully appreciated what Negroes were doing for their country. Colored families suffered every deprivation that white residents had to endure, and in the bitterly cold winter of 1917-1918 the coal shortage imposed hardships upon Negro slumdwellers far more severe than any known to the occupants of better built houses. Negro families faced the same anxieties as whites about fathers, sons, and brothers serving in training camps and on the battlefields of France, and Negroes had the added burden of withstanding racism within the American army. The most generous element in colored Washington, however, counted on the perceptive element in the white community to insist upon racial justice in the postwar world. Were that hope to materialize, colored people were ready to dismiss wartime discomforts as insignificant. What happened when peace came was all that mattered.

In December 1918 Archibald Grimké as president of the

[2] *Star,* 2 Sep, 25 Dec 1917, 3 Jan, 18 Jul 1918; *Bee,* 3, 10 Nov 1917, 2, 9, 23 Feb, 9, 23, 30 Mar, 28 Sep 1918; *Crisis,* XIV, 139, XVII, 116; H Rpt 420, 65C, 2S, Ser 7304.

American Negro Academy told his colleagues: "I am glad to say that associated with us . . . are a number of leading white men. We do not have to fight this battle alone." About the same time John R. Hawkins, financial secretary of the AME Church, presented to the Washington NAACP fourteen points, paralleling President Wilson's fourteen points for world peace, which alone would give meaning to the word *democracy* in the United States. Although Mary White Ovington, one of the white founders of the National Association, wrote in *Crisis* that "the last place to which the returning colored soldier can look for justice is Washington, the very foundation of the Government he has so faithfully served," she added: "The power of numbers, but *organized* numbers, is the power that wins the battle. Every oppressed group . . . is engaged in a separate struggle to secure something of value for itself in the chaos that comes at the close of a great war. Now, . . . while systems are fluid, before the structure of society becomes rigid again is the opportunity to win the reality of democracy." [3]

Colored Washingtonians won a first minor victory in January 1919 when District Commissioner Brownlow established an all-Negro platoon in the fire department, an arrangement that ensured promotions for the department's four colored veterans of twenty years' service and gave new appointees a chance to prove their competence under men of their own race. Equally helpful to colored morale were several articles in the *Star* describing the valor of the District's "famous old 1st Separate Battalion" in action in France. Of the battalion's 480 Washingtonians, 25 had been awarded the Croix de Guerre, and the officers of the French regiment to which the battalion was attached had nothing but highest praise for the entire unit. The *Star* correspondent remarked that the city would surely want to stage a

[3] Corcoran Thom to Mary Church Terrell, 25 Nov 1918, and Jane Ogle to M. C. Terrell, Terrell Mss; *Star*, 26 Dec 1918; Mary White Ovington, "Reconstruction and the Negro," *Crisis*, xvii, 169-70, 172; *Bee*, 16 Nov 1918, 4, 18 Jan, 15 Feb, 21 Jun 1919.

187

homecoming demonstration for these troops, for "every citizen of Washington—in fact of the United States—should feel proud of them." The chief secretary of the national Salvation Army said he had "a pretty complete record" of the conduct of the colored soldiers and that "something ought to be done to show their courage and fidelity were appreciated." He had rented a building in the capital to house them when they returned late in March 1919.[4]

That was the last expression of general good will in Washington. The parade of returned white soldiers, led by President Wilson, took place before the 1st Separate Battalion reached home. As if alarmed by the praise already meted out to the colored heroes, after February 1919 Washington's white newspapers had nothing more to say of them or of Negroes' part on the home front. By late spring *Crisis* reported that influential Americans were repeating comments supposedly originating with high-ranking officers of the AEF to the effect that "the Negro officer is a failure" and the behavior of colored troops in France had been cowardly in battle and improper in social contacts with French people. W. E. B. DuBois, after three months in Europe spent in collecting facts for a "History of the Black Man in the Great War," concluded that "no person in an official position dare tell the truth" about the shabby treatment the American army had accorded colored soldiers.[5]

While most of colored Washington was smarting with indignation over the widespread white "conspiracy of silence" about Negro war service, further signs of white blindness to the interests of the Negro community were to be seen in the conduct of a local campaign for District representation in Congress and an accompanying, less widely supported drive for the return of an elected city government.

[4] *Star*, 18 Jan, 14, 15, 17, 28 Feb 1919; *Bee*, 8, 22 Mar, 14 Jun, 19 Jul 1919.
[5] *Crisis*, XVII, 111-12, XVIII, 9-11, 63-67; *Bee*, 14 Dec 1918, 15 Feb 1919.

Incensed at accusations circulating throughout the country that during the war all Washingtonians had been "rent sharks" and profiteers, a large part of the white community endorsed one or both proposals as means of giving the city a voice in national and local administration. But for all their enthusiasm, whites made no overtures to enlist the cooperation of their colored neighbors. Negroes, already angry at white disregard, volunteered no help. Thus a chance to bridge the forty-year-old gulf between the races and promote a cause useful to both was lost. Instead, racial cleavages widened.

About the same time another episode, trivial in itself, fanned the smoldering embers of racial antagonisms, when a group of colored families launched a fight with the school board over its refusal to dismiss Assistant Superintendent Roscoe Conkling Bruce. The Parents' League, representing perhaps six or seven hundred colored parents, accused Bruce of favoritism in promoting teachers and, worse, lack of vigilance in what came to be known as the "Moens affair." Acting upon a recommendation from the Dutch embassy, Bruce had given a Dutch anthropologist by the name of Moens permission to photograph some of the city's colored school children in order to obtain comparative anthropological data. Moens, so the stories ran, had then taken advantage of innocent children and indulged in indecent behavior with one of their teachers. White members of the school board and Mrs. Coralie Cook, a colored member, upheld Bruce and labeled the tales about Moens as gross, if unwitting, exaggerations or lies. Still Negro women, obsessed by the idea that official inaction was based on indifference to Negroes' good names, picketed the Franklin School week after week whenever the school board met at its offices there. Only a small minority of the Negro community took stock in the unsavory rumors spread by the League, but lily whites in the city considered the agitation proof that all Negroes were emotionally unstable

189

and lacking in judgment.[6] Racists would have been incredulous had they heard the American anthropologist Ernest Hooton of Harvard telling New England audiences of colored Washington's extraordinary culture about which white people knew nothing.

The "Red Scare," which was sweeping the entire country in the spring of 1919, meanwhile was frightening Washington. In June a bomb set off in the house of the new attorney general convinced conservative citizens that "Bolsheviks" were about to destroy the entire fabric of American society. "It is unsafe," announced the *Star,* "to wait for specific proof of individual criminality. It is dangerous to delay until jury-proof cases can be found." Although no one came out flatly with the accusation that colored Washington was one of the "red centers" in the United States, anxieties lest radicalism eat its way into Washington's working classes, at the bottom of which stood the city's black masses, undoubtedly increased racial animosities.

On top of the Red Scare came a wave of public hysteria over recurring street robberies and attacks upon women. White newspaper accounts generally conveyed the impression that Negroes alone were responsible. At one point the *Post,* then owned by the playboy "Neddy" McLean, accused the Negro press of "a plot" to stir up race hatred. By July a series of sex crimes, most of them, later evidence established, committed by a single colored man, had whipped the city into a fury of alarm and rage. While a Negro bishop assured whites that colored people would join in the manhunt, the *Bee,* aware that the temper of white Washington might lead to punishment of innocent colored people, insisted that the criminals were not local men and that an all-Negro-officered precinct in the undermanned police department would be useful in bringing the assaults to an end. At the same time the local NAACP warned the city's white

[6] *Rpt B/Tr,* 1918, pp. 59-68, 1919, pp. 11, 128; J. D. Kaufman, Scrapbooks on Washington Home Rule, Jan–Jul 1919; *Bee,* 29 Mar, 12, 26 Apr, 28 Jun 1919; *Star,* 10 Jun 1919, 1 Jan 1920.

dailies that further "inflammatory headlines and sensational news articles" would encourage race riots. Hundreds of servicemen stationed in and about Washington roamed the streets during those hot July evenings and added to the pervasive sense of restlessness. In a situation already explosive, the more so because military police had been withdrawn from Washington in June, their presence served as a fuse requiring only a minor episode to trigger violence.[7]

The first overt acts of race warfare occurred on a Saturday night, July 19: "Men in Uniform Attack Negroes" announced the Sunday papers. "As a climax to the assaults on white women . . . a band of more than a hundred soldiers, sailors and marines last night invaded southwest and beat several colored persons before they were finally dispersed by a provost guard, a detachment of marines and reserves from three police stations." Worse followed. On Monday morning the Washington *Post,* after describing Sunday's fighting, carried an alarming article under a huge headline, *Scores are Injured in More Race Riots:*

It was learned that the mobilization of every available service man stationed in or near Washington or on leave here has been ordered for tomorrow evening near the Knights of Columbus hut, on Pennsylvania Avenue between Seventh and Eighth streets.

The hour of assembly is 9 o'clock and the purpose is a "clean-up" that will cause the events of the last two evenings to pale into insignificance.

Whether official cognizance of this assemblage and its intent will bring about its forestalling cannot be told.

If, as Commissioner Brownlow concluded, "these white ex-servicemen were frauds, paid to provoke the trouble they began," and if the Washington *Post* deliberately fanned the

---

[7] *Bee,* 16 Feb, 12 Jul 1919; *Crisis,* XVIII, 242. From mid-April to the end of July practically every issue of the *Star,* and all during July the *Post,* carried stories on Negro crime; equally frequent items on the Bolshevik threat began in February 1919.

fires, the scheme succeeded. "That night, the race riot swept over Washington. If it had not been for the good work of police and soldiers who kept the large mobs from contact, the city would have been a shambles. During the week the race riots in Chicago and Knoxville followed and the month of July ended with a feeling of apprehension and disturbance."

In Washington colored people, convinced that the time for meekness had passed, fought back. Guns brought from Baltimore and distributed at 7th and T streets provided weapons for men trained to their use by war service. Colored men then and later believed that it was the killing of whites by Negroes that brought the riot to an end within five days. Reinforcement of the police by some four hundred cavalrymen from Fort Myer and four hundred marines from Quantico unquestionably helped. But the restoration of outward order at the end of the week did not cool Negroes' anger, for, although every eye-witness of the opening fights testified that white men had been the aggressors, only eight or nine of the hundred-odd persons arrested were whites, and of those only one was convicted for carrying a concealed weapon. Soothing words in the white press to the effect that the "colored residents of Washington are law-abiding people, good citizens and dependable in all crises" came too late to allay bitterness.

Years later, Commissioner Brownlow spelled out the reasons for his belief that the riot had been a put-up job skillfully arranged by two or three outwardly respectable, unscrupulous men who were determined to make trouble enough to force him and the chief of police to resign. The 1918 increases in tax assessments, Brownlow explained, and his refusal to exempt from the law persons who had long considered themselves entitled to special privileges had won him enemies, among them individuals not above employing a race riot to undermine his authority and thus escape prosecution under the Mann Act. The *Post*'s inflammatory article of July 21 with its allusion to "official cognizance"

192

of an "assemblage" that no one had heard of until the paper announced it lent some plausibility to the conspiracy theory. The *Survey* tentatively attributed the trouble to antiprohibition forces which "welcomed and, to some extent, planned a 'crime wave' in the nation's capital to illustrate the appalling consequences of the bone-dryness since July first." [8] Viewed from the distance of the 1960's, explanations based on the immediate circumstances of 1919 look too simple. Washington was reaping the whirlwind of nearly forty years of disregarding a third of the community.

Colored leaders displayed extraordinary restraint. A week after the first night's outbreak Judge Terrell and Dr. Emmett J. Scott, former special assistant to the Secretary of War, issued a statement to Negro newspapers in the rest of the country pointing out that, whereas white servicemen were to blame for the Washington riots and Negro retaliation was natural, the most important fact was that "white and colored citizens freely counseling together in the interest of law and order" had successfully reestablished peace and that henceforward all efforts must be directed at preserving the "gains of mutual war-time sacrifices." James Weldon Johnson, the NAACP investigator sent down from New York, shared Brownlow's private opinion that the Washington *Post* had had a large part in fomenting the violence. His report in *Crisis* contained humorous touches: the city editor of the *Post,* assuming that Johnson had come to tell Washington Negroes "to be good," had welcomed him cordially but had then suffered near-panic upon discovering that the NAACP might ask the Attorney General to bring action against Washington's white newspapers, the *Post* above all, for inciting to riot. Johnson averred that Negro courage had saved the day in Wash-

[8] *Post,* 21-23 Jul 1919; Louis Brownlow, *A Passion for Anonymity,* p. 84; Comrs Rpt, 1920, I, 223; Rayford W. Logan to the author, 9 Mar 1960; *Star,* 20-25, 27 Jul 1919; *Bee,* 26 Jul 1919; Edgar M. Gray, *The Washington Riot, Its Cause and Effect* (mcf pamphlet, Arthur A. Schomburg Negro Collection, New York Public Library) ; "The Darkest Cloud," *Survey,* XLII, 675.

ington. By fighting "in defense of their lives and homes" instead of running, they had prevented Washington's being "another and worse East St. Louis." Indeed, he concluded, bad as things had been, whites' shame over the shocking events in Washington and Chicago "mark a turning point in the psychology of the whole nation regarding the Negro problem."

That overly optimistic note appeared justified in the months immediately following. Washington's white press, perhaps frightened by the consequences of its earlier propaganda, ceased to harp on Negro criminality. In December at a meeting called to raise money for a war memorial to colored heroes, white response was heartening. Secretary of War Newton D. Baker and Secretary of the Navy Josephus Daniels both spoke, and "the tabernacle quaked from the acclamation of approval" when Judge Stafford challenged the crowd: "Cite me a case of a Negro traitor"; "show me a Negro anarchist"; "let me see a Negro bolshevist"; "the only red rag the Negro ever carried was when his shirt was stained crimson by the sacrificial blood he gave for America."

The single most penetrating analysis of the Negro's situation in Washington and in Chicago came from the pen of George E. Haynes, director of Negro economics in the United States Department of Labor. His article entitled "Race Riots in Relation to Democracy" recognized the role of sensational journalism in contributing to racial hostility but pointed to three other, equally significant factors. First was the lack of mutual understanding that resulted from the loss of contact between the races: "The lack of contact has increased with the years. Older residents of Washington and Chicago tell you of the growing racial antagonism with the growth of separation. Only a few weeks before the riots in both cities, some leading people of Washington were discussing the fact that in former years the white and colored representatives of various philanthropic and community agencies were accustomed to meet more frequently than now for the exchange of views and plans on matters

194

of community interest. The holding of such meetings has grown more difficult and less frequent." Second was the new Negro militance. Years of seeing the unequal enforcement of law had led the colored man to believe "his safety demands that he protect himself and his home," a conviction strengthened by a new conception of liberty which accompanied the higher standard of living that war had brought to thousands of colored families. Although well-to-do, well-dressed Negroes had been a familiar sight in Washington for forty years past, other observers than Haynes remarked upon white irritation at Negroes' improved economic status: "Everywhere one can hear expressions of disgust at the expensive clothes of successful Negroes, their owning automobiles, etc." The third factor was the realization by both white and colored Americans that the United States as a great world power was now "face to face with the problem of dealing with the darker peoples of Asia, Africa, Central and South America." Those peoples would judge the United States by the treatment white Americans accorded darker-skinned citizens within its borders. That an Abyssinian mission had been in the national capital during the riots was an uncomfortable reminder that race relations here had a wider bearing than a purely domestic local question.[9]

While much of the colored community benefitted from better paid jobs during and immediately after the war, schoolteachers and government clerks, who composed the backbone of the middle class, had suffered, like their white counterparts, from the pinch of rising living costs and minor or no salary increases. Even at the peak of employment the number of appointments to professional and clerical posts in Washington fell far short of the number of Negro candidates qualified either by graduation from the Miner Normal School or by civil service ratings. Assistant Superintendent

[9] *Star*, 27 Jul, 16 Dec 1919; *Crisis*, XVIII, 241-43; *Bee*, 2 Aug 1919; "The Darkest Cloud," and George E. Haynes, "Race Riots in Relation to Democracy," *Survey*, XLII, 675-76, 697-99.

Bruce, while fighting to get better salaries for colored teachers, implied in 1919 that those willing to leave Washington now had larger opportunities than formerly because of the prosperity the war had brought to Negroes in other cities. The opening of a colored Industrial Savings Bank on U Street and a new well-built, well-furnished Negro hotel indicated that, in spite of inflation, Negro business enterprises here also had enjoyed some success, and the wider support of charitable projects suggested that many Negro families had more financial leeway than ever before. But the NAACP and the *Bee* repeatedly reminded colored people that racial solidarity was essential to a continuing advance.[10]

In the autumn of 1919, while colored Washingtonians wondered whether they had gained more than they lost by the race riots, white business leaders worried briefly about whether the outburst had given the city a bad reputation for uncontrolled racial violence and for being a hotbed of Negro radicalism. But a large part of white Washington soon ceased to think about the riots at all. Senate ratification or rejection of the Versailles Treaty, plans, quickly quashed, for a District policemen's union affiliated with the American Federation of Labor, wage strikes that threatened Washington's white building trades, and the intensifying conflict throughout the United States between capital and industrial labor preempted white men's attention. Although, like Americans everywhere, people here were frightened by the bogey of red infiltration into the ranks of organized labor, in a predominantly white-collar city fear of a red-infected local black proletariat had relatively little to feed upon. Neither the local business community nor federal officials could link Washington's race riots to labor radicalism. Although nine men had lost their lives in the street fights and more than thirty men later died from

[10] Comrs Rpts 1919, IV, 238, 1920, IV, 323-39; *Star,* 19 Mar 1920; *Crisis,* XIII, 168, 174-76, 280, XIV, 89, XVII, 116, XVIII, 154; *Bee,* 29 Mar, 26 Apr 1919.

injuries, Congress saw no cause to investigate. Thus re-assured, whites banished from memory the uncomfortable events of July as representing no more than an unfortunate episode best forgotten as quickly as possible. The wish to forget the unpleasantnesses of "the intense, restless, disturbed year," as a Board of Trade committee described 1919, nevertheless had long-lasting consequences; it gradually reinforced white prejudices, deepened the obliviousness of much of white Washington to the needs of a biracial city, and for nearly two decades defeated the attempts of an enlightened minority to collaborate with Negro citizens.[11]

During 1920 and early 1921, however, neither Negro nor most of white Washington foresaw a worsening of race relations. On the contrary, racial toleration seemed to be regaining some of the headway lost after the Reconstruction era. Two biracial organizations came into being in 1920, Community Services, Inc., a group of civic-spirited volunteers, and the Council of Social Workers, composed of white and colored professionally trained employees of the police department, the Juvenile Court, the U.S. Public Health Service, the Visiting Nurse Association, the Associated Charities, the white and colored YMCA's, the NAACP, the Boy Scouts, and a half-dozen more. By exchanging information on common problems and meeting sociably over the luncheon table from time to time, social workers hoped to breach the color line. Community Services planned to open neighborhood recreation centers which white and colored people could enjoy together. Unfortunately, to archconservatives fearful of social change, such

[11] *Rpt B/Tr*, 1919, p. 128; *Star*, 28 Nov 1918, 29 Jul, 29 Sep 1919, 1, 3 Jan 1920; Brownlow, *Passion for Anonymity*, pp. 84-89; Robert K. Murray, *Red Scare, A Study in National Hysteria, 1919-1920*, pp. 148-256; Gray, *The Washington Riot* (Schomburg Collection). Further evidence of local whites' unconcern about race relations derives from interviews with people living here in 1919 and from the disappearance of newspaper items about local Negro radicalism and all Negro ideas. See also Lloyd M. Abernethy, "The Washington Race War," *Maryland Historical Magazine*, LVIII, 309-24.

proposals smacked of Bolshevism; the Board of Trade considered them dangerously radical. Community Services, Inc., thus denied businessmen's financial support, withered before it was well started, and the Council of Social Workers within a matter of months became a small, rather ineffectual colored gathering as white members dropped out. Still Negroes refused to believe that racism would strengthen after Warren G. Harding became President. The campaign rumor that he had Negro blood in his veins had some currency in the colored community and not improbably increased colored men's faith in the President-elect. Joyfully they heard him announce in his inaugural address that American Negroes "have earned the full measure of citizenship bestowed; that their sacrifice in blood on the battle-fields of the Republic has entitled them to all freedom and opportunity, all sympathy and aid that the American spirit of fairness and justice demands." With those words ringing in its ears, colored society celebrated that night with a large reception and a dance.

Although government offices had dismissed some 16,000 wartime employees, the city's permanent population between 1917 and the end of 1920 had increased about 25 percent; the building trades were booming in consequence, and the Red Scare fizzled out in the spring of 1921. When a business recession accompanied by wage cuts and unemployment overtook the capital in mid-summer, Negroes, letting hope triumph over experience, still counted on the new administration to set its face against the racial discrimination and segregation that had taken root under Woodrow Wilson. True, Harding's North Carolina-born commissioner of public buildings and grounds had recently decreed that colored people could use the new golf course in East Potomac Park and the tennis courts on the Washington Monument grounds only on Tuesdays. True also, the President delayed month after month to name Negroes to the federal offices they had expected of him. But in November, when the capital welcomed Marschal Foche,

French hero of the Marne, and Howard University conferred upon him a honorary degree while "scores of veterans of colored regiments who had served under the French military leader in the World War stood at attention," Negroes half believed that white onlookers had been sufficiently impressed to prod the President into keeping his promises to colored Americans.[12]

It was a year after the inauguration before politically naïve colored people admitted that they had been leaning on a man of straw. In that twelve-month Harding had assigned only three Negroes to appointive posts in Washington; Negroes in the civil service were more fully segregated and all Negroes more rigidly excluded from the city's public recreational facilities than during the Wilson regime; neither Congress nor the white press had demurred at the forming of a District Ku Klux Klan; white newspapers had allotted two lines at most to the "silent parade" of 1,500 Negroes in wordless protest against lynchings in the South. Full realization of the situation came at the dedication of the Lincoln Memorial on Decoration Day in 1922. Dr. Robert Moten, president of Tuskegee Institute, had been invited to speak at the unveiling of the statue of the Great Emancipator, but, instead of being placed on the speaker's platform, he was relegated along with other distinguished colored people to an all-Negro section separated by a road from the rest of the audience; and the language of the ill-tempered Marine who herded the "niggers" into their seats caused well-bred colored people as much indignation as the segregated seating itself. Chief Justice Taft's later explanation that the arrangement had not had official sanction failed to modify colored Washington's view: no Negro could hope to be treated as a full-fledged American citizen

[12] *Rpts B/Tr,* 1920, 73-74, 183-86, 199-210, 1921, pp. 21, 50-51; *Bee,* 1 Jan, 12 Mar 1921; *Tribune,* 21 May, 25 Jun, 16 Jul 1921, 18 Feb 1922; *Star,* 6, 9 Mar, 17 Nov 1921; Minutes, Council of Social Agencies, 14 Feb 1921, typescript in possession of the Health and Welfare Council of the National Capital Area (hereafter cited as Min CSA).

TABLE IV
POPULATION OF THE DISTRICT OF COLUMBIA, 1880-1960[a]

	1880	1890	1900	1910	1920	1930	1940	1950	1960
TOTAL	177,624	230,392	278,718	331,069	437,571	486,869	663,091	802,178	763,956
% increase in 10 years	34.9	29.7	21.0	18.8	32.2	11.3	36.2	21.0	−4.8
WHITES	118,006	154,695	191,532	236,128	326,860	353,914	474,326	517,865	345,263
% increase in 10 years	33.7	31.1	23.8	23.3	38.4	8.3	34.0	9.2	−33.3
Native	101,026	136,178	172,012	211,777	298,312	323,982	440,312	478,368	311,875
% native to D.C.	55.4	52.1	48.5	46.7	38.0	39.6	33.2	31.4	27.4
% native to Md. & Va.	21.3	21.8	23.5	23.9	22.0	23.6	20.1	16.5	
% native to South exclusive of Md. & Va.	2.9	4.1	5.4	5.7	9.4	10.1	14.6	15.6	
% native to North and West	20.5	20.9	22.3	23.0	29.5	25.8	31.2	33.5	
Foreign-born	16,980	18,517	19,520	24,351	28,548	29,932	34,014	39,497	33,450
% of total population	9.7	8.1	7.2	7.5	6.7	6.3	5.3	5.5	4.4
% of white population	14.3	11.9	10.2	10.3	8.7	8.5	7.2	7.6	9.7
NEGROES	59,596	75,572	86,702	94,446	109,966	132,068	187,266[b]	280,803[b]	411,737[b]
% increase in 10 years	37.3	26.8	14.7	8.9	16.4	20.1	41.9	49.9	46.1
% of total population	33.6	32.8	31.1	28.5	25.1	27.1	28.2	35.0	53.9
% native to D.C.	41.6	41.9	41.9	42.8	42.4	39.8	39.4	40.4	44.4
% native to Md. & Va.	54.1	51.9	50.8	46.3	42.3	35.4	27.3	20.9	⎫ 43.1
% native to South exclusive of Md. & Va.	2.4	3.4	5.2	7.3	11.3	20.2	28.9	32.1	⎭

[a] Compiled from *U.S. Census*, Tenth through Eighteenth

[b] Negroes only; the nativity percentages are computed from subtotals which include all nonwhites, but the number of nonwhites other than Negroes was negligible.

as long as the White House, Congress, and the overwhelming majority of the city's white residents looked upon him as a creature apart and inferior.[13]

That state of affairs underwent little change under President Coolidge. Only three colored men received desirable federal posts, and one of those appointees, James Cobb, merely succeeded to the municipal judgeship that Robert Terrell held till his death. After attempting to segregate the picnic places in Rock Creek Park, in 1925 the federal commissioner of public buildings and grounds allowed the National Ku Klux Klan to stage a showy parade of 25,000 capped white-robed marchers and to hold a formal ceremony at the Washington Monument. And the *Star* played up the event as if it were a national celebration. Representative Martin Madden of Illinois, chairman of the House Committee on Appropriations, was one of the few whites to fight the rising tide of racial segregation. When the commissioner of public grounds barred Negroes from the public bathing beach at the Tidal Basin, Madden insisted that Congress cut off funds and close the beach altogether. Doubtless other Northerners sometimes deplored the needless hurt to the pride of a distinguished colored man, the lack of care provided for the small Negro orphan, the persistent stifling of Negro ambition, but, like native Southerners, they apparently thought the existing social order immutable. Newcomers unfamiliar with the city of earlier years readily assumed that the capital had always endorsed the arrangement.

Except for the haunts of bootleggers and other elements of the underworld, by 1923 the only places in Washington where racial segregation did not obtain were on the trolleys and buses, at Griffith Stadium, and in the reading rooms of the public library and the Library of Congress. When one of the "Senators" knocked out a home run, white and black rooters in the stadium bleachers delightedly slapped

[13] *Tribune*, 27 May, 10, 13, 17 Jun 1922, 24 Jan, 14 Apr 1923; *Herald*, 9, 25 Jan, 16 Jul 1923, 4 Dec 1924.

each other on the back and together discussed the team's prospects. Although no Negro player was allowed on the team, when Washington won the pennant in 1924, the colored *Daily American* wrote: "Long live King Baseball, the only monarch who recognizes no color line." In the libraries, Negroes might read and study in peace alongside whites, a circumstance, a Washington-born Negro scholar recalled, that alone had prevented his pursuing the path of a Richard Wright in his hatred of all white America.

Had the ratio of Negro to white inhabitants risen sharply during and after the war, the tightening of segregation in Washington might be easier to explain. Between 1910 and 1920 Chicago's and Detroit's colored populations had grown respectively nearly seven and six times as fast as their white, and the change had been only less pronounced in four or five other Northern cities. All of them confronted an unfamiliar social and economic problem. For Washington a large Negro population was no novelty. Here, moreover, the proportion of Negroes to white had dropped since 1910 and, with the exception of 1920, the 27.1 percent of 1930 was below the figure shown in any census since the Civil War. White fears of being swamped in a black metropolis therefore had little validity. Possibly Negroes' slightly improved economic position threatened to lessen the supply of cheap domestic and unskilled labor and, by enlarging the Negro middle class, to jeopardize the social status of lower-class whites. Whatever the reason, whites chose to build an invisible wall about all colored Washington and then strove to forget about what a contributor to *Crisis* called the Secret City. Its inhabitants unexpectedly gained two infinitesimal advantages from this sedulous ignoring— a slight decline in white bullying and an accompanying reduction of newspaper talk about Negro crime.[14]

At the end of 1926 the *Tribune*, by then Washington's

[14] *Star*, 25 Jul 1925; *Washington Daily American*, 9 Oct 1924, 13 Oct 1925; *Fifteenth Rpt NAACP*, 1924, pp. 21-23; Louise V. Kennedy, *The Negro Peasant Turns Cityward*, p. 34; *Crisis*, XXXIX, 185.

principal colored paper, declared that segregation had "grown to the dimensions of a national policy." It was in full force in the government departments, and "it remains only to observe that the Negroes themselves have about reached the stage of acquiescence in the practice." Colored civil service employees, fearful of losing their jobs, refused to lodge complaints, leaving NAACP officials without provable grounds for protest. The major gratification the colored intelligentsia had that year was the Howard University trustees' selection of a Negro president, Mordecai Johnson. What had begun as a biracial institution had long ago become wholly Negro.

Uneasiness lest an organized Negro vote in the Northern states put "Al" Smith into the White House led to a slight relaxation of departmental segregation rules in 1928, but civil service policies did not change. The Department of Labor published statistics contrasting the number of the government's Negro employees in 1928 and 1910: some 51,880 in 1928 at salaries totaling nearly $64,484,000 compared to fewer than 23,000 paid less than $12,456,000 in 1910. *Crisis* promptly noted that laborers, charwomen, and messengers, earning on the average $1,243 a year, still made up the bulk of the list; well-paid jobs for Negroes were actually fewer than in 1910. At the Library of Congress Armstrong Claytor made a unique place for himself, for as the Orientalia Division began to acquire rare volumes of Chinese philosophy and literature written in ideograph which scarcely fifty men in the United States could read, Claytor, who unpacked the shipments, taught himself enough Chinese to identify and catalog the books. But a single swallow did not make a summer, and no colored man now held a position at the Library equal to that Daniel Murray had occupied at the turn of the century. When Oscar De Priest of Chicago was elected to the House of Representatives, colored morale rose a little; and it rose higher when Mrs. Hoover invited his wife to a White House reception with a small, carefully chosen group of other congressional wives. Otherwise the first Negro to be elected to Congress in the twentieth century could do little for the local community. When at long last a published code of laws for the District of Columbia appeared, it did not mention the sixty-year-old ordinances and the territorial acts prohibiting racial discrimination, although those had never been repealed or declared unconstitutional. The NAACP's drive that stopped Senate confirmation of Judge Parker of North Carolina as an Associate Justice of the Supreme Court seemed to colored Washington a negative triumph, at best a block to new inroads upon civil rights.[15]

In the eyes of Washington's upper-class Negroes a peculiarly invidious new restriction on their liberties had only recently received the blessing of the Supreme Court when a ruling of 1926 upheld the legality of voluntary covenants among white property-owners aimed at preventing Negroes from purchasing or occupying houses in white neighborhoods. The battle against restrictive municipal ordinances had been won before the war in a case originating in Baltimore; now voluntary compacts seemingly negated that victory and threatened to confine all Negroes in the capital to a true ghetto. Whites endorsing the covenants displayed as much passion as the Negroes who sought to halt them. Professor Kelly Miller of Howard University contended that since white people were determined to prevent racial intermarriage, the "destiny of the Negro population in large cities is clearly foreshadowed. The Negro is to live and move and have his social being in areas apart from the whites." Yet, as Miller himself pointed out, tempting offers from colored men sometimes overcame white resistance: only a year after the Supreme Court verdict the "very block that was the subject of the test case in Washington is now

---

[15] *Tribune,* 2 Jul, 31 Dec 1926, 25 Jan, 14 Jun 1929; *Crisis,* xxxv, 337, 369-87, 418, 427, xxxvi, 298-99; Walter A. White, *A Man Called White,* pp. 110-11; Indritz, "Post Civil War Ordinances," *Georgetown Law Journal,* xlii, 201; William H. Jones, *Recreation and Amusements among Negroes in Washington.*

occupied by negroes, in uncontested tenancy, although the court decision forbids persons of negro blood to buy or live in that block for a period of twenty-one years." Long afterward, Campbell C. Johnson, in the 1920's secretary of the colored YMCA, looked back upon the fight against residential segregation as a constructive move, for the men who sued for their right to live wherever they could afford raised a banner around which other colored Washingtonians gathered. But their defeat evoked a smoldering anger in them deeper than that caused by any other one episode of the past. Housing in actuality would be the last category of discrimination in Washington to yield to the enlightened pressure of the 1960's.

Members of the Washington Federation of Churches were sufficiently troubled by the mutual ill will the housing covenants had generated to sponsor a study of Negro housing in the city. The resulting book completed in 1929 by William Jones, a young Howard sociologist, contained both a survey of existing residential patterns and an analysis of what underlay the objections of whites to living alongside Negroes. In the tabulation of answers to his inquiry, real estate brokers' stock contention that property values dropped when a Negro family moved into a neighborhood found a predictably conspicuous place, but other replies spoke of colored people's noisiness and untidiness. Without attempting to demolish the fallacies upon which much racial prejudice rested, Jones offered one conclusion that probably startled his readers. Negroes, he stated, although superficially products of the same environment as white Americans, were culturally different. Whites seeking to resolve tensions without taking those differences into account would merely multiply problems.[16]

[16] *Crisis*, XXVIII, 271-72, XXIX, 19, 27; *Tribune*, 1 Nov 1924, 9, 16 May 1925, 8 Jan 1926, 2, 9 Mar 1928, 18 Jan, 25 Oct 1929; Kelly Miller, "The Causes of Segregation," and Herbert J. Seligman, "The Negro Protest against Ghetto Conditions," *Current History*, XXV, 827-33; William H. Jones, *The Housing of Negroes in Washington, D.C.*; Bernard H. Nelson, *The Fourteenth Amendment and the Negro since*

While most of what colored Washington underwent in these years of near despair was forced upon it by white laws, white bigotry, or white thoughtlessness and stupidity, citizens of the Secret City themselves determined part of their fate, bad and good. The jealousies and quarrels that had splintered the community before 1915 again took command. If the fight against the housing covenants created a measure of unity, it did not reach down to families whose poverty precluded their trying to live in comfortable white neighborhoods. Certainly Washington's high yellow society did not recapture its wartime zeal to "close ranks" with its social inferiors. On the contrary, civic-minded Negroes encountered among their educated fellows the same kind of indifference to the welfare of the black masses as public-spirited white people met with in high white society. Altruism did not flourish in the "Age of the Golden Calf."

The Washington NAACP was no longer powerful. Some Negroes thought it too radical, others too conservative and too prone to appease; a good many gave it no thought at all. With a few rare exceptions, young men upon whom leadership might logically have fallen lacked the will or had lost faith in their capacity to win a respected place for their people. Negro real estate brokers and firms building Negro apartment houses made some money, and the National Life Insurance Company with three hundred employees in its home office on U Street paid a 10 percent dividend in 1928, but confidence in other Negro enterprises waned. When a Harvard graduate after a distinguished but heart-breaking career in the AEF became a convert to the necessity of never-ending Negro militance, he started the Washington *Daily American,* the second Negro daily in the United States; despite its excellence, the paper was unable to get enough advertising to survive. The *Tribune* absorbed it. Between the lines of newspaper exhortations

---

1920, pp. 23, 31, 34; interview, Col. Johnson; "Housing of Negroes in Washington, D.C.," *Monthly Labor Review,* xxx, 972.

to "buy Negro," give to Negro charities, and build up a self-sufficient community ran hints that calls for racial solidarity fell on deaf ears.

Upper-class families, tired of making common cause with needy blacks, washed their hands of every group but their own. Lightness of color was necessarily a bond, for where light-skinned people could move about in a white world with some freedom, the acceptance of a dark-skinned person into the group circumscribed the activities of all. It was a fact of life white people never had to face. Whites prone to think Negro social distinctions absurd lost sight of the obvious truth that the cultivated Negro had no more in common with the lower-class black than the white society leader with the white ditchdigger. The creed of the high yellow elite ran: let the uninformed masses applaud Marcus Garvey, "the Black Moses," or gather adoringly about "Papa Divine." Let the vulgar loaf on 7th Street, that "bastard of Prohibition and the War," where, sang Jean Toomer,

> Money burns the pocket, pocket hurts,
> Bootleggers in silken shirts,
> Ballooned, zooming Cadillacs,
> Whizzing, whizzing down the streetcar tracks.

All that need not touch the aristocracy. The very light-colored group, on the other hand, was frequently involved with "passing." Former associates of the person who chose to pass were at pains not to betray him, and, if envious, did not openly criticize him. The joke after all was on the white folks. Morality was in no way involved. Tacit agreement among old friends decreed that each must decide what was right for himself. Passing was so common in the twenties that the National Theatre employed a black doorman to spot and bounce intruders whose racial origins were undetectable by whites. And no Negro despised the doorman for earning his living in that fashion; a job was a job.

Still, passing tended to disrupt the solidarity of the top level of Washington's colored world.[17]

Snobbery pervaded all upper-class Washington. Among whites the "cave-dweller" had come to occupy the most envied place in the social hierarchy; his status rested on three or more generations of established position in the community where his forebears had disdainfully kept themselves apart from the *nouveaux riches* and vulgar onhangers of official society of the Reconstruction era. Cave-dwelling was equally entrenched in colored Washington of the 1920's. A long line of respected Washington ancestors was an essential ingredient of distinction and as much a prerequisite for the Negro as for the white cave-dweller. Elegantly dressed colored ladies spent afternoons playing bridge and five-hundred with other cave-dwellers, their husbands took flyers in the stock market and bought expensive cars, and all the well-to-do gave select evening parties in their homes to which the personable newcomer could not hope to be invited. The person born on the wrong side of the tracks or whose Washington antecedents were obscure could never outlive that handicap. In other respects too the behavior of high yellow society was a replica of high white, except that whereas the white woman invested in tightly curled permanents and, at least if young, cultivated a deep sun tan, the colored woman used bleach lotions and Mrs. Walker's "Anti-Kink" or the equivalent.

Like whites, all Negroes also made some obeisance to wealth. "When Washington Society 'Turns Out' " described that aspect of the colored city's life to readers of the *Tribune:* "There are two events in the District of Columbia which attract the undivided support of the 'well-known' and 'exclusive' Washington society. They are the Howard-Lincoln football game and the annual cadet corps drill.

---

[17] *Tribune,* 11 Apr 1925, 12 Aug, 30 Dec 1927, 18 Jan, 9, 30 Mar 1928, 1, 25 Nov 1929; *Crisis,* XXXI, 11-16, XXXIII, 186-87, XXXIV, 193, 212, 224; Eugene Davidson, *Black Boy on a Raft;* Jean Toomer, *Cane,* p. 71; Caleb Johnson, "Crossing the Color Line," *Outlook,* CLVIII, 526-27.

Just as the pretty school 'marms' exhibit their raccoons, chinchillas and sable skins at the gridiron classics, so the cadet drill occasions the display of the choicest most elaborate and scantiest spring frocks." When Washington's and Baltimore's "smart set" barred darker-skinned Negroes from the summer colony which Frederick Douglass' son had founded in the 1880's at Highland Beach, Maryland, the ensuing fued matched in intensity the battles in white society.

At the end of the 1920's Langston Hughes, grandson of colored Washington's idol of the 1870's and 1880's, lashed out at the city's high yellow elite. Poems sketching the porter "climbing a great big mountain of Yes Sirs," the "Black Gal" crying "I hate them rinney yaller gals," and the "loud laughers in the hand of Fate" had won him some literary fame, but the disregard of his Washington neighbors angered him. They overlooked talent; they objected to Jean Toomer's *Cane* and Rudolph Fisher's *City of Refuge* because the main characters in both books were so "black." Many of the "best people" were newly rich, and many were not cultured at all. A true picture would reveal their "pseudo-culture, their slavish devotion to Nordic standards, their snobbishness, their detachment from the Negro masses and their vast sense of importance to themselves." [18]

Other gifted young men also found the atmosphere surrounding "the best people" stifling. As the "Harlem Renaissance" gained momentum about 1925, writers and musicians aspired to leave Washington for New York, where they would not be throttled by the dead hand of a past, imagined or real. If relatively few followed the example of a Jean Toomer, a Duke Ellington, and a Louis Armstrong in making names for themselves in the North, and more felt obliged simply to forget their artistic ambitions, by the mid-1920's Washington had nevertheless lost most of the attrac-

[18] Dixon Wecter, *The Saga of American Society*, p. 418; *Tribune*, 22 Apr 1927, 26 Oct 1929; Langston Hughes, *Fine Clothes for the Jew*.

tion she had once held for the creative Negro. Unlike Harlem, the Secret City remained "undiscovered" by the rest of the world, partly because there was less talent to discover here. Thirty years later the city had still not recaptured the prestige she had commanded in the colored world at the turn of the century. Howard University drew exceptionally able students in law, medicine, and sociology, and colored scholars in many fields were glad to teach at this, one of the two or three institutions of higher learning that could offer them chances of professional advancement. Men of the caliber of Kelly Miller, the young economist Abram Harris, the eloquent Alain Locke, apostle of the "New Negro," and Ralph Bunche, in 1928 starting the university's first political science courses, lent the faculty distinction. But undergraduates entering from high schools outside the District all too often received from classmates native to Washington the same kind of patronizing treatment as cave-dwelling parents accorded older outsiders.[19]

The college preparation a student could get at the Paul Dunbar High School was unquestionably better than that obtainable in other cities with segregated systems. Just as families had sometimes moved to Washington in order to enter their children in the deservedly famous M Street High School, so Dunbar, which replaced it in 1916, maintained exceptionally high standards. The list of its graduates would include an astonishingly large proportion of the names in a *Who's Who* in Negro America of the 1950's. The Armstrong High School, committed as it was to vocational training and business courses, usually enrolled students of more limited horizons, but its graduates were not openly labeled inferior to those of the white McKinley Technical High

[19] The data in this paragraph and, except where documentary sources are cited, in the rest of this and succeeding chapters derived from interviews with knowledgeable colored people familiar with the community of the years under discussion. The biographical notes appended to V. F. Calverston's *Anthology of American Negro Literature* indicate how large a proportion of notable Negro writers in 1929 had either studied or taught at Howard University.

School. Indeed Assistant Superintendent Garnet Wilkinson, in 1922 successor to the controversial Roscoe Conkling Bruce, contended that the entire colored school system was the best in the United States—not, unhappily, a mighty boast. Certainly colored Washingtonians fought vigorously to have their schools duplicate every improvement introduced into the white. While a statistical unit kept tabs on enrollments, attendance, truancy, and the issuance of "work cards" for pupils over fourteen who had to work during part of the school day, a new research department inaugurated achievement and aptitude tests and checked on the effectiveness of novel methods of teaching. The white Superintendent Frank Ballou placed considerable stress on teachers' conferences, but, as a white teacher regretfully observed some years later, the separation of black from white denied to both the benefits of comparing notes on common problems. White advice probably could not have furnished answers to the question of how to keep colored children in school beyond the eight years required by law after 1924, but free interracial discussion of that abiding difficulty might conceivably have inspired the board of education and Congress to investigate the causes. Colored teachers, however, generally preferred to be free of white "snooping," even at the cost of missing out on sound ideas.

Two other impediments interfered with the functioning of the colored schools as much as did their intellectual isolation. The first was inadequate accommodations, in spite of a multi-million-dollar building program authorized by Congress in 1925. The white schools also suffered from overcrowding and insufficient physical equipment, but Negroes had to watch new schoolhouses go up in white neighborhoods while thirty- and forty-year-old buildings in areas formerly white were turned over to Negro use. Economy, the board of education explained, alone dictated the transfers when shifts in the racial character of neighborhoods occurred; the new buildings had to be placed in once thinly populated sections of the city where residents—

211

almost invariably white—were multiplying rapidly. But the explanation did not account for the lack of assembly halls, gymnasiums, athletic fields, and playgrounds for the schools converted to Negro use. The second deterrent to progress, on the other hand, the constant friction within the colored educational establishment, only Negroes themselves could eliminate.[20]

Considering the emphasis most of colored Washington put on education and the pride it took in its schools, the petty feuding that went on at every level, from the Howard University faculty to the teachers and supervisors of the public kindergartens, was as startling to the outsider as it was disastrous to the community. The reason for it is plain enough: where opportunities were so limited, only the most generous individual would dream of letting a rival snatch a coveted prize from him without fighting, and the fight was unlikely to proceed by the Marquis of Queensbury rules. As a newspaperman sardonically observed of the white capital in 1929: "One of the charming things about Washington is that it is almost never without a social, diplomatic, or matrimonial war,"[21] but the backbiting there did little damage to the white city as a whole, whereas the vituperative exchanges among colored school administrators and teachers tended to heighten white contempt for the entire race. When, for example, Kelly Miller chose the occasion of a Howard University trustees' dinner to voice a vitriolic attack on President Mordecai Johnson, congressmen were not inclined to increase the appropriation for the institution. Anything that undermined white support for Negro education hurt all colored people, even those who had concluded that schooling that led nowhere was futile.

---

[20] *Rpts B/Ed,* 1926, pp. 81-82, 1930, "School Achievements in Ten Years, July 1, 1920 to June 30, 1930"; Mary Hundley, *The Dunbar Story; Crisis,* xxv, 376; Garnet C. Wilkinson, "Washington Is Easily the Foremost Center of Negro Education in America," *School Life,* xi, 114. See also discussion in Green, *Washington, Capital City,* pp. 340-53.

[21] *Washington Merry-Go-Round,* p. 10.

Where white people placed in the circumstances surrounding colored Washington might have either soon sunk into sullen despair or resorted to open warfare, Negroes managed to find pleasure in their own society, mutual jealousies and envy notwithstanding. With their gift for laughter, they got genuine amusement out of the antics of the complacent white—his stiff-jointed contortions, for example, in trying to master the rhythms of the Charleston, that import from Cat Fish Alley, or his manifest expectation of a cordial welcome of a Sunday when he visited a revivalist colored church in order to be entertained by the breast-beating and hallelujahs of repenting sinners. While crap games and evenings in a black speakeasy offset some of the frustrations of "low-life" Negroes, people further up the economic and social ladder turned to music and dancing for recreation. Jazz bands, in demand for white debutante balls, generally played with greater abandon and artistry in the colored dance halls. Certainly Washington's "reputation for syncopation" did not stem from whites. Music, in fact, whether popular, classical, or spiritual, was a cultural bond in the Secret City. The passerby might hear as much singing and merrymaking in a Negro neighborhood as in the purlieus of the most affluent and carefree whites.

Yet every Negro in the District of Columbia felt hemmed in. The pattern of the late 1920's closely resembled that of the years following the collapse of Reconstruction, but this time disillusionment bit deeper and carried a kind of dreadful finality. In the 1880's and 1890's the federal government still offered colored people chances in Washington. Indeed they pinned their future on political preferment until the Wilson administration knocked that prop out from under them. Thereupon anger, abetted by the indignation of white liberals, had pumped adrenalin into the colored community creating a solidarity that promised to produce noteworthy results. Patriotism and patience during and after the war for a time had held out further prospects which survived even a race riot. Then piece by piece the edifice of hope

213

had crumbled. The national government took the line of the Deep South, and white people as private persons now looked upon Negroes scarcely as citizens at all. Negro endeavors to break into Washington's business world had largely failed. Skilled Negro craftsmen had found themselves nosed out of job after job and occupation after occupation until their skills had all but atrophied. The higher a Negro's place in the colored social hierarchy the more pronounced his resentment at banging his head on the underside of the lid that ceiled him in. Better no doubt to be at the top than further down within the caste, but was the difference in elevation worth much, where head space was at best so cramped? The courage that had enabled men of fortitude to rise above the bitter defeats of a generation before and undertake a second assault on the bastion of prejudice now appeared to have exhausted itself. Hope deferred maketh the heart sick. Hope annihilated meant the death of every ambition.

CHAPTER X

THE UPWARD TURN, 1929–1939

The social disorganization characterizing the District of Columbia during most of the 1920's, setting apart white from Negro, Gentile from Jew, businessman and civil service employee from the workingman, clique from clique, and cave-dweller from upstart, left the capital of 1928 little more than a geographic expression. Yet in almost miraculous fashion late that year a nascent community spirit began to emerge. It grew out of plans for a Community Chest, a scheme long urged by the handful of white people concerned with "civic betterment." Once converted to the idea of having a single body manage an annual money-raising drive for all the city's charities, the Board of Trade decided that business efficiency must prevail in setting it up and making it function. The board asked Elwood Street, an experienced fund raiser from St. Louis, to take charge. While some professional social workers and some of the volunteers directing the then eight-year-old Council of Social Agencies had hoped from the first to bring Negro organizations into the campaign, that possibility had certainly not occurred to most Washingtonians. The Board of Trade itself had not thought about it until Street specified his conditions for accepting the assignment.

The effect of Street's arrival and the public announcement of his plan of action was electrical. To the dismay of lily-whites, he stated that this must be a united effort of the entire city, not of white Washington working apart from colored Washington; representatives of both races must meet and participate as equals. Confronted with Street's insistence, objections that such an arrangement would run counter to long established local mores fell flat. At the

215

initial organizing luncheon, prominent white Washingtonians for the first time in the memory of most people present sat alongside leading colored Washingtonians. As the luncheon was ending, a Negro heard one white man mutter to another: "I don't see why we have to sit at table with Jews." But no one then or later protested at the racial mixing.

The mixing in itself gave the undertaking an element of drama. Frederic A. Delano, uncle of Governor-elect Roosevelt of New York, accepted the presidency of the Chest, Kelly Miller the vice-presidency. Equally valuable in creating a sense of common purpose as preparations moved forward was the exchange of information that went on week after week among organizations anxious to join the Chest. The benefits of that give-and-take long outlasted the fund-raising campaign. Well-intentioned white volunteers and self-protective Negroes learned a good deal about each other's problems. At the gala dinner held at the Mayflower Hotel to wind up the campaign, Elwood Street bowed to local custom: Kelly Miller did not dine with his white associates but, dressed in tails and white tie and accompanied by Mrs. Street, he came in afterward to make his report. Although the first drive did not quite go over the top, the heady discovery that the city could unite even briefly was exhilarating.

The change, to be sure, was neither so sudden nor so profound as ill-informed optimists believed. Years of work by a dedicated few had prepared the way. The Associated Charities and from 1921 onward the Council of Social Agencies had maintained a narrow, somewhat unsubstantial bridge between white and colored Washington; individuals had tried to widen it. In December 1928 two hundred delegates representing some eighteen social service and interracial organizations throughout the country had met in Washington under the sponsorship of the Social Science Research Council to discuss the statistical data assembled

216

on race relations by Graham Taylor of Chicago and Charles S. Johnson of Fisk University, but the sessions had ended without producing any positive scheme of action. Although the Washington Federation of Churches in 1927 had commissioned William H. Jones' study of Negro housing, the federation rejected the arguments of Canon Anson Phelps Stokes of the National Cathedral, Robert W. Brooks, Negro pastor of the Lincoln Congregational Church, Walter H. Brooks of the Nineteenth Street Baptist Church, Francis J. Grimké of the Fifteenth Street Colored Presbyterian Church, and some ten other ministers of both races who urged the admission of colored churches to membership. The Community Chest scored its chief triumph in pricking the conscience of white people and arousing in colored people a deeper interest in Negro charities, but the immediate effect of the campaign on interracial collaboration was slight.[1]

Too many white people merely displayed condescension in new form, marveling at their own broadmindedness in recognizing human attributes in the Negro. That he might respond to the question "What do colored people want?" with the blunt answer "Get out of our way" was an idea well-meaning whites could not yet grasp. Six months after the first Chest drive ended, Robert Brooks summarized Washington's situation as he saw it: economic conditions were uncertain, morals "blatantly corrupt," and race relations marked by more mutual ill will than ever. Yet thirty years later wise men, both white and colored, averred that the launching of the Community Chest had cleared the way for the interracial contacts that would multiply

---

[1] Min CSA, 14 May 1928 to 11 Nov 1929; Min As Ch, 1928-30; "Street Accepts the Challenge," *Survey,* LX, 507; "Local and National," *ibid.,* LXI, 429; *Tribune,* 18 Oct, 1 Nov 1929; *American Journal of Sociology,* XXXV, 902. Throughout this chapter and the three that follow much of the data derives from interviews with people familiar with the local scene at the time but whose qualifications for speaking with authority would require an inordinate amount of space to explain.

during the 1930's and eventually demolish the wall about the Secret City.[2]

When the stock market crash of October 1929 set off the worst depression the United States had ever experienced, Americans began to reexamine earlier premises about the nation's basic economic and social structure. Doubts about the place assigned to the Negro stirred slowly in many parts of the country. During the next three years church publications and left-wing magazines gave race relations increasing attention, sometimes suggesting that patronizing attitudes common even among civic-minded whites might be as destructive as overt racial antagonism. In Washington the Associated Charities, whose social workers were in closer touch with indigent colored families than were other organizations, finally took the long discussed step of electing two Negroes to the board of directors and for its 51st annual meeting asked President Mordecai Johnson of Howard University to give the principal address. Several interracial social work conferences took place in 1931 and 1932; the Metropolitan Police dispensed with segregation at the department's annual Christmas party for the city's needy; and very occasionally Northern college alumni associations invited Negro graduates to social gatherings. Twice the Nineteenth Street Baptist Church was host to white congregations. In 1932 the Young Communist League sponsored the first biracial dance to be held in Washington since President Grant's inauguration in 1873. Yet throughout the 1930's every step toward mutual understanding and cooperation was followed by half a step backward.[3]

The depression which sharpened awareness of social

[2] *Tribune*, 15 Nov 1929.

[3] *Tribune*, 10 Jan, 14 Feb 1930, 5, 19 Feb 1932; Min As Ch, 10 Dec 1930, pp. 4, 6, 50th Anniv Mtg, 12 Jan 1932, p. 7, 51st Anniv Mtg, 31 Jan 1933; *News*, 7 Nov 1932; *Negro Status and Race Relations in the United States, 1911-1946, The Thirty-five Year Report of the Phelps-Stokes Fund*, pp. 73-79. For typical exhortations about race relations, see *Christian Century*, XLVII and XLVIII, especially Hubert C. Herring, "An Adventure in Black and White," XLVII, 1526-29.

injustice also created new strains. It early killed traditional "Negro jobs," as white men, asserting their superior claims to work they had formerly considered beneath them, supplanted Negroes as janitors, bell-hops, waiters, elevator operators, and barbers. While Washington suffered far less than most cities, private building operations dropped during 1930 to less than a third that of 1929, a number of small businesses failed, and, with the spread of unemployment, appeals from the Associated Charities for help for destitute families began to take on a note of desperation even though the Community Chest drive that autumn reached its goal. Fortunately a vast federal building program furnished jobs for about nine thousand men, and authorization in February 1931 of an $8 million District public works project provided work for more. But contractors engaged in putting up some of the buildings for the new Federal Triangle complex frequently brought in outside labor, so that local workmen, however badly in need of jobs, often had to look elsewhere. Several hundred Southern Negroes, imported in 1927 to work for 25 cents an hour on the Department of Commerce building, became a public charge when the unskilled heavy work on the job was finished in 1931. By the end of that year Washington was feeling the depression acutely. Furthermore, as bank failures swallowed up families' life savings and mortgage foreclosures multiplied throughout the country, citizens of every state in the Union began to look to the national government for help. Twice during the winter of 1931-1932 bands of two to three thousand jobless and desperate men staged a "Hunger March" on Washington in a futile endeavor to high-pressure Congress into inaugurating national unemployment insurance.[4]

The next months, instead of marking the start of the

[4] Comrs Rpts, 1931, p. 58, 1932, p. 42, 1934, p. 46; Min As Ch, 12 Feb, 19, 21 Mar, 18 Jun 1930, 12 Jan, 11 Feb, 8 Apr 1931; *Star*, 1 Jan, 11 Dec 1930, 4, 11 Oct 1931; "Washington's Chest Expansion," *Survey*, LXVI, 99; Fleta Campbell Springer, "Glassford and the Siege of Washington," *Harper's Magazine*, CLXV, 641-45.

economic recovery the Hoover administration believed would develop automatically, saw the United States plunge deeper into depression. That spring, jobless World War I veterans pinned their hopes of relief on a congressional bill calling for immediate payment of a war-service bonus due them by law in 1945. When a group of Oregonians concluded that the best way to lobby for the bill would be by a mass march on the capital, the "Bonus Expeditionary Force," as they named it, set out in May, gathering reinforcements as it moved eastward. By early June some 20,000 men had collected in Washington, and nearly twice that number arrived later. With official sanction, they took up quarters in empty warehouses, in buildings scheduled for early demolition on lower Pennsylvania Avenue, and in an improvised camp adjoining the city dump on the mud flats across the Anacostia. Visitors to "Camp Marks" were impressed by the self-discipline and good humor prevailing among its occupants, but what most astonished Washingtonians was the discovery that the white veterans, from Alabama and Mississippi as well as from the Northern and Western states, shared billets, rations, and chores with the 2,000 Negroes of the BEF in complete amity. Not a trace of Jim Crow in the entire Bonus Army during the days of waiting, or the evening when the Senate defeated the bill, or in the weeks thereafter during which some 10,000 dejected "bonuseers" stayed on in stubborn belief that Congress would come to their rescue. When the War Department undertook at the end of July to expel them forcibly as a menace to the security of the federal government, the use of tear gas, an intimidating show of tanks, and the burning of Camp Marks shocked Americans, most of all the local citizens who helplessly watched the ruthless performance.[5]

[5] Springer, "Glassford," pp. 645-55; Walter W. Waters, with W. C. White, *B.E.F., The Whole Story of the Bonus Army*, pp. 56, 63-64, 149-98; *Post*, 1, 3, 5, 8-10, 12-17, 21-29 Jul 1932; *Star*, 27-30 Jul

Washingtonians were immersed in trouble that fall and winter, none of it, as far as they could see, of their own making. Four local banks went into receivership. A congressional act cutting government salaries by 15 percent, RIFs—reductions in force—in the executive departments, and obligatory furloughs without pay directly affected one family in every three and crippled all local business. President Hoover's announced plan of slicing another $700 million from the federal budget for the next fiscal year spelled doom to the federal building program which had been Washington's economic mainstay during the preceding two years. A $350,000 emergency appropriation for unemployment relief in the District, spent chiefly in hiring men to tidy up the debris at Camp Marks, was exhausted by December. By then estimates put the number of people out of work in the tens of thousands; to keep an exact tally of the unemployed had become impossible. Although Congress voted the welfare board on New Year's Eve another $625,000, the committee in charge of disbursing the funds felt obliged to exclude from public assistance some five categories of needy: all single men, all families with less than eighteen months' residence in the District, families in which the unemployed wageearner was over sixty years old, families with part-time earnings, however small, and all cases where other social problems complicated unemployment. Because Negroes, always "the last hired and first fired," had lesser reserves than impoverished whites, the want in the city's colored sections was appalling, grim though it was also among whites. Like the shipwrecked seamen about whom the traditional old lady refused to worry because "sailors are accustomed to drowning," Negroes, in the view of a good many whites, were so inured to unemployment and near-starvation that they could

---

1932; *News,* 30-31 Jul, 18 Aug 1932; *Tribune,* 29 Jul, 5, 12 Aug 1932; "The Human Side of the Bonus Army," *Literary Digest,* CXIII, 25 Jun 1932, pp. 28-30; Roy Wilkins, "The Bonuseers Ban Jim Crow," *Crisis,* XXXIX, 316-17. See also Green, *Washington, Capital City,* pp. 364-79.

manage on next to nothing. Undernourishment and con-
comitant illnesses that winter filled both Gallinger and
Freedmen's hospitals to overflowing.[6]

Self-help schemes fostered by the Council of Social
Agencies were useful on a small scale. In plots laid out in
vacant lots several hundred families raised enough vegetables to feed themselves till fall. Agreements between
prospective tenants and landlords who were willing to reduce
or forego rent in exchange for free renovations undertaken
by the former provided a certain amount of housing, but
the *Monthly Labor Review* noted: "little co-operation has
been received from the real estate group as a whole." Elder
Lightfoot Michaux, a recently arrived Negro evangelist,
arranged the largest single housing deal: he got the use,
rent-free, of a big building at T and 7th streets, which his
followers at the "Church of God" repaired, and there he
installed some forty Negro families evicted from their
former quarters for nonpayment of rent. In the meantime,
as the Community Chest drive fell nearly $500,000 short of
its goal, member organizations had to curtail their services
at the very moment they were most needed.[7]

While hard times and apprehensions of worse to come
revived a sense of unity within white Washington, the
strands of common interest which the Community Chest
had begun to spin in 1929 between white and colored
people were still too frail to bind the city into a single
community. Indeed in the last months of the Hoover
administration, intensifying competition for jobs, white
people's fears for their own future, and mounting hopelessness in colored Washington virtually nullified the effect of

[6] *News,* 13 Aug, 22, 26 Nov, 6, 7, 10 Dec 1932; Comrs Rpts, 1932,
p. 25, 1933, pp. 82-83; Min As Ch, 9 Mar, 15 Apr, 12 May, 14 Dec
1932; interview, Elwood Street, director of the Washington Community
Chest, 1928-1934, 2 May 1962.

[7] *News,* 4, 28, 30 Nov, 3, 6, 24, 30 Dec 1932, 9 Mar 1933; Min
As Ch, 10 Feb, 12 Oct, 10 Nov 1932, 31 Jan 1933; *Monthly Labor
Review,* xxxv, 1038; Comrs Rpt, 1933, pp. 83-84, 87; *Pictorial Review
of the Church of God,* pp. 26-27.

any reciprocal friendliness. Contractors for the new British embassy on Massachusetts Avenue had to abandon plans to hire some colored builders because the AFL raised a row about the use of nonunion labor. Only forty of the thousand-man police force in January 1933 were Negroes. The fire department's all-Negro platoon, in 1919 a welcome innovation, had become a means of keeping Negro recruits to a minimum and confining Negro promotions solely to places within the platoon. While white directors of charities deplored Negro unresponsiveness to appeals, Negro social workers resented assignments to routine tasks which denied them the broad professional experience demanded for important posts in the welfare agencies. Victor Daly's *Not Only War*, a new novel by the colored Washington real estate dealer who thirty years later would hold a key position in the United States Employment Service, dealt with the all-too-familiar theme of the careers of educated Negroes doomed to look in vain for "the elusive altruism which they imagined they had found in college." [8]

Discrimination took all the old forms. Under the District's system of aid to mothers of small children, *Crisis* declared, white social workers set one standard for the budget of white families, another for colored. "The white visitors insisted on calling colored mothers by their first names, discouraged them in the education of their children, and suggested sleeping apartments in cellars." Nor were churches above discrimination: a Roman Catholic priest interrupted the prayers of a Negro woman kneeling in the white section of the Immaculate Conception Church and hustled her off to the gallery. A War Department regulation covering the pilgrimage of Gold Star mothers to Europe decreed segregated transportation and assigned colored women to converted cattle ships. With Congressman Madden safely in his grave, Colonel U. S. Grant, III, commissioner of public

---

[8] *Tribune*, 17 Jan, 28 Feb 1930, 8, 15 Jan, 5, 19, 26 Feb, 11, 25 Mar, 10 Jun, 15 Jul, 30 Sep, 2, 9 Dec 1932; *Crisis*, xxxix, 187, 234, 343-44, 362; Victor Daly, *Not Only War*.

buildings and grounds, enforced segregation in picnic areas of Rock Creek Park. Congress and the school board earmarked 80.4 percent of the new building fund for white neighborhoods and a sizable part of the remaining 19.6 percent for converting to Negro use the badly located Business High School erected in the 1890's for white students.

Yet Carter Woodson, founder and director of the Association for the Study of Negro Life and History, and in the past not an outspoken proponent of Negro separatism, talked of the "blessings" of the economic disaster which forced every Negro to depend upon his own people and to "indulge in serious thinking." Some of that thinking found expression at a meeting called by Campbell C. Johnson, secretary of the colored YMCA, at which Colonel West Hamilton, printer and publisher, J. A. G. LaValle, editor of the *Tribune*, Mary Church Terrell, Lucy D. Slowe, dean of women at Howard University, and other leaders discussed methods of coordinating Negro welfare services. At the same time a newly formed Committee on Improving Industrial Conditions among Colored People in Washington undertook an educational campaign to combat the factors that interfered with Negroes' getting and keeping jobs: intractability, lack of skills, unreliability about reporting for work after Sunday and pay days, lack of cleanliness, and refusal or inability to work under Negro bosses. "Possibly for the first time in years," said a member of the Associated Negro Press, "our local politicians, high-hatters, low-brows, schemers and general hustlers found something that requires their attention to a greater degree that they have been faithfully and joyfully giving to their favorite pastime of trying to unload a President of Howard University or an assistance superintendent of the public school system." Common troubles were submerging the old divisiveness. The *Tribune*, to be sure, complained about the lack of a "representative militant organization": the Parent-Teacher Associations had no drive, and "the civic associations are made up of pussy-footing government employees and scared school teachers." But although the editor dismissed the NAACP as a bruised reed to lean upon, a delegation of the shrunken local chapter persuaded the Bureau of the Budget to transfer $315,000 from the white to the colored schools.

Colored Washingtonians were gratified to find white people joining them in a huge demonstration at the Capitol when the Supreme Court was preparing to order a new trial for seven Negro boys charged with rape in Scottsboro, Alabama, but few Negroes in the capital nursed illusions about the final outcome of the second trial. The Alabama court again found the boys guilty. On the eve of the inauguration of a new administration Washington's colored intelligentsia perceived little fundamental change in the white city's point of view. When the National Theatre announced a "special" performance of *Green Pastures* on March 2, 1933, which would be "open to all," Negroes assigned no enduring importance to the overture.[9]

Vague gestures of good will were not enough in March 1933. While all Americans awaited inauguration day with anxiety, colored people remembered the past: Franklin Delano Roosevelt's campaign speeches promised a "New Deal," but so had Woodrow Wilson's "New Freedom." On March 4, with every bank in the United States closed, nearly 13 million people out of work, and the local resources of every community in the country seemingly exhausted, the nation had reason to be fearful. But was the new administration not the more likely therefore to concentrate upon other national problems and ignore the plight of that special segment, colored America? Negroes who attended the ceremony on the Capitol grounds that raw March morning felt the upsurge of hope that swept the crowd as the President assured his audience that "we have nothing

---

[9] *Crisis,* XXXIX, 187, 316-19; *Tribune,* 1 Apr, 17 Jun, 23, 30 Dec 1932, 3 Mar 1933.

to fear but fear itself," but his intelligent dark-skinned listeners recognized the fallacies in the comforting words; colored men still had to fear white racism. Any remedies the New Deal might contrive for the stricken nation would extend, colored men suspected, last of all to Negroes. Two days after the inauguration the Metropolitan Police deepened their forebodings: billy clubs, curses, and arrests were the means used to disperse some six hundred local unemployed marching to the White House to petition for help—"mostly colored people under communist leadership," the District commissioners blandly explained. But at least the white press expostulated at the senseless brutality.[10]

Within a fortnight all Washington faced fresh troubles, for a new Economy Act reduced the pensions of some 17,000 residents, sliced another 15 percent from all federal salaries and, in order to spread jobs, stipulated that no one with a spouse in government employ could remain on the federal payroll. The last provision alone cut in half the income of many a family; husband and wife had to choose between his job and hers. In spite of thankfulness for the establishment of a United States Employment Service, a new Banking Act that halted bank failures, and a Home Owners' Loan Act that staved off mortgage foreclosures, by late summer Washingtonians were again enveloped in gloom. The jobs opening up in the new federal agencies went to new arrivals, rarely to local applicants, Negroes least of all. Although young New Dealers pouring into the capital and needing living quarters lessened the decline in the real estate market, suspension of federal building projects lowered the dollar value of building operations to less than half the figure for 1932. At the end of October several of the District's savings banks were still in receivership and depositors' prospects of reclaiming more than a fraction of their $12.5 million were dim. At the same time some 28,000 pieces of real property, the District

[10] Arthur M. Schlesinger, Jr., *The Coming of the New Deal*, pp. 1-21, 105, 182; Comrs Rpt, 1933, p. 72; *News*, 9, 13 Mar 1933.

assessor announced, were to be auctioned off unless the $1.2 million to $1.5 million in back taxes were paid before Thanksgiving.[11]

Expansion of New Deal programs and enlargement of the federal establishment during the next two years nevertheless restored vigor to Washington's white business community. The 63,000 government jobs of March 1933 grew to about 93,000 within twenty-one months, two thirds of the 15 percent pay cut of 1933 was restored in mid-1934, the rest nine months later, demands for office space and housing mounted steadily, and a stream of industrial executives, come to confer with government representatives on working codes for every major American industry, filled the hotels. According to one of the District commissioners, 40,000 people arrived daily at the Union Station in 1936. Every two weeks cash from the $8.5 million in federal and the $1 million in District government pay checks circulated in Washington shops and markets. "Effective buying income," asserted a magazine writer, averaged $3,782 in Washington, $2,000 in other American cities. National unions, encouraged by New Deal friendliness to organized labor, began to set up permanent headquarters here. While the value of private building operations rose in two years from the $7 million of 1934 to about $24 million, the federal public works program resumed and broadened. Whereas the population of all but eight or nine American cities declined during the decade, Washington's increased by 36 percent. Before midsummer of 1940, the number of federal employees in the city had risen to about 166,000.[12]

[11] Cmrs Rpts, 1933, pp. 37, 46, 49, 1934, p. 46; *Rpt Comptroller/Currency*, 31 Oct 1933, pp. 224, 229-30, 402, 590-92; *News*, 14 Apr, 22 Sept, 1, 2 Nov 1933; *Star*, 1 Oct 1933; Wilson Record, *The Negro and the Communist Party*, p. 153.

[12] Rpts B/Tr, 1934-1936, *passim*, 1937, p. 10; *Star*, 21 Sept 1941; George E. Allen, "Washington, A Capital that Went Boom," *Nation's Business*, xxv, 32-33; Cmrs Rpts, 1939, pp. 88-89, 1941, p. 78; Oliver McKee, Jr., "Washington as a Boom Town," *North American Review*, ccxxxix, 177-83; David L. Cohn, "Washington, The Blest," *Atlantic Monthly*, clxiii, 609-13.

Colored businessmen had little share in this mounting prosperity. Although the nearly 42 percent increase in the Negro population outstripped the 34 percent white increase, Negro purchasing power rose relatively little, if at all, during the decade. For after the upturn in white business, Negroes were seldom able to reclaim the places from which white competitors had ousted them. The building trades unions, the bulwark of organized labor in Washington, kept them out of skilled construction jobs, and hopes that the Capital Transit Company would hire Negro platform workers collapsed when the Transit Union threatened a walkout if a single Negro were employed. Year after year, moreover, an unrecorded number of practically destitute Negro families arrived from the Southern states to swell the District's unskilled labor supply. Although thirty-five new Negro-owned retail stores opened between 1929 and 1935, the volume of business was too small and payrolls were too thin to take up the slack in the Negro labor market. Advertising in the *Tribune* shrank month after month, and the paper gradually lost most of its readers to the Baltimore *Afro-American*.

The spirit of rebellion against the old order and the faith in a new which had infused vitality into the New Deal's "first 100 days" meanwhile inspired a group of professionally trained young Negroes to try a new form of self-help. Some twenty-two national Negro organizations had already set up a Joint Committee on National Recovery with headquarters in Washington in an endeavor to induce the new federal agencies to adopt nondiscriminatory policies. But as the committee was making no perceptible progress, a more direct approach to the problem of jobs seemed essential to younger Washingtonians—John Aubrey Davis, later a professor of philosophy at New York's City College, William Hastie, soon to become a federal judge, Charles Houston, famous a decade later as special counsel of the NAACP, Robert C. Weaver, destined to be the first Negro to become a member of the President's Cabinet, and two or three other lawyers of exceptional ability. They concluded that the best weapon available to the colored community was the boycott, which, by using the power of the Negro consumer, might check discrimination in employment. Abetted by several seasoned NAACP fighters such as Eugene Davidson, they formed in the fall of 1933 the New Negro Alliance to organize and carry on the struggle. Their first move was to picket a U Street hot-dog stand whose owner employed only white men, although his customers in that solidly Negro area were colored. A week or two without Negro patronage persuaded the proprietor to hire colored help. The mere prospect of a similar boycott brought a change in the hiring policies of the proprietors of the scores of small Jewish-owned shops in the vicinity. By 1934 the great A & P chain had taken on a few Negro clerks in its branches in colored neighborhoods.

For a time some of the Howard University faculty objected that the movement represented an unwholesome racism certain to boomerang by alienating all recently won white sympathizers. Twenty years later E. Franklin Frazier's *Black Bourgeoisie* would publicize his thesis that middle-class Negroes endorsed economic chauvinism solely because they profited from it, not because of race pride, but Alliance leaders from the beginning denied any connection with an aggressive Negro nationalism. "Buy where you work," whether in a white-owned or a Negro-owned establishment, simply amounted to using Negro purchasing power to give Negroes an equal chance with whites. Earlier "buy colored" campaigns had not helped much because Negro merchants had never managed to satisfy the Negro purchaser. The new plan required a careful campaign of educating the local public. An Alliance weekly newspaper, *New Negro Opinion,* not only reported progress in the nonviolent fight and printed full accounts of Alliance meetings, but reiterated at intervals the do's and don't's necessary for effective action. Negro criticism subsided as small successes multiplied: in two years nearly 300 jobs filled by Negroes in stores formerly manned only by whites convinced the community of the utility of the "consumer strike" and led Negroes in other cities to try it.

In proportion as the Alliance made its power felt, white merchants undertook to break it. The Sanitary Grocery Company, later renamed Safeway, Inc., filed a suit to enjoin the Alliance from organizing boycotts of the company's stores where about 95 percent of the customers were Negroes. The District Court granted the injunction, and the Court of Appeals upheld it, but when the case reached the Supreme Court in 1938, the justices reversed the decision. The court ruled that the Norris-La Guardia Act prohibiting injunctions in labor disputes also outlawed the injunction against Negroes who were seeking to end racial discrimination by means of boycotts and dissemination of information. The decision was recordmaking, although at the time not widely recognized as such. The confidence it gave colored men in the efficacy of appeals to the highest court paved the way to the larger triumphs of the 1950's. True, fifteen months of picketing two branches of the Peoples Drug Store located in the Negro business center failed to persuade the company to hire colored clerks or to yield to the "sit-down" challengers at the soda fountains. But the heavy financial loss sustained by the drug store chain discouraged emulation by lesser companies. And the presence in the picket line of Mary McLeod Bethune, President Roosevelt's special advisor on minority affairs, supplied the Alliance cause with valuable publicity.[18]

Until Mrs. Bethune's appointment in 1936, and indeed after, the New Deal did less for colored people than they had expected. The District Recorder of Deeds, a municipal court judge, and the minister to Liberia, as for years past,

[18] *Tribune*, 13 Jul, 5 Oct, 23 Nov 1933, 3, 31 May 1934, 6 Dec 1935; *Afro-American*, 28 Jan 1939; *New Negro Opinion*, Oct 1933-Apr 1936; *New Negro Alliance Yearbook*, 1939; interview, Eugene Davidson, 9 May 1962, Judge Marjorie Lawson, 6 July, and Belford Lawson, 26 July 1965; 303 U.S. 552.

were colored men; William Hastie received the federal judgeship for the Virgin Islands; some forty-odd minor administrative posts in Washington went to Negroes, and in 1935 a new analysis section of the Labor Department took on forty more. As early as 1934 Secretary of the Interior Harold Ickes appointed an advisor on racial matters connected with public works and later inserted in all contracts a clause requiring contracting companies to follow nondiscriminatory employment practices. When the new Interior Department building opened in 1937 its cafeterias were completely nonsegregated. Nor was a color line recognized in the federal Works Progress Administration when it came into being in 1935 or in the provisions written into the new social security acts. Unskilled colored laborers, like white, got manual jobs under the WPA and a group of Negroes on the Federal Writers' Project put together for the WPA *Guide to Washington* a useful chapter on the colored city's history and contributions to the life of the capital. But in 1938 of the 9,717 Negroes regularly employed by the federal government in Washington, 90 percent held custodial jobs for which the top annual pay rate was $1,260; only 9.5 percent had clerical jobs, and only 47 men had subprofessional rank. In the matter of promotions, the merit system was as inoperative as in earlier years.

Furthermore, if neither WPA nor District welfare administrators deliberately sanctioned racial discrimination, regulations intended to spread help evenly among the needy bore far harder on colored people than on white. Severe cuts in appropriations forced the District welfare board in 1936 to adopt a hard and fast rule that no financial aid was to go to any family that included an employable person, and in 1938 the WPA decreed that no one could stay on its rolls more than eighteen months whether or no he had any other source of livelihood. "A family is classified as employable," Washington's Council of Social Agencies explained indignantly, "even if the only potential wage earner is an adolescent boy or girl who not only has no

231

job but has had no training or experience to equip him for qualifying for a job." Irrespective of the consequences for hundreds of colored families, Negroes were to be treated like everybody else. Demonstrably they were not in several respects.

A first blatant exhibition of racial discrimination under the New Deal occurred in launching the Civilian Conservation Corps. That imaginative program, inaugurated in 1933, called for collecting jobless boys of seventeen through nineteen from town and city streets throughout the country and placing them in camps under trained directors to improve roads, drain swamps, clear trees of tent caterpillars, and undertake a score of other chores useful to the public. But Southern states insisted on separate camps for colored boys, and in the North the proportion of Negro boys admitted to mixed camps was small compared to white enlistees. The colored camp for the District of Columbia had great difficulty in opening at all because white people objected to having it in the vicinity. So a magnificent opportunity was lost. The colored youths who were enrolled got better food than they had at home, enjoyed far better surroundings, and probably learned a great deal from the camp experience. White prejudice and acquiescent or timid corps leadership nevertheless denied the experience to thousands of future colored citizens.

At the District Employment Center, set up under the U.S. Employment Service, a second form of discrimination went hand in hand with segregation to victimize the Negro in fashion that whites outside the center rarely comprehended. Negro applicants for work had to go to a separate building lest their presence in the same waiting room with white job-seekers offend white sensibilities, but it was the differences in procedures at the two centers that made the arrangement peculiarly invidious. Whereas job listings for whites included every category of work, those at the Negro center were confined almost wholly to domestic service and common labor. An expert Negro typist would never find a place through the Employment Center. Negroes with special skills and talents quickly learned to apply there only as a desperate last resort.[14]

The third major area in which Negroes got little or no help was in housing. Yet of all the enduring improvements New Deal legislation promised the District of Columbia, none gave local do-gooders greater initial satisfaction than passage of the Alley Dwelling Act of 1934. It authorized a small body of housing experts to raze the worst of the alley tenements, and relocate their occupants in new or remodeled buildings in better neighborhoods. The alley slums had worsened since 1917 when the war had first postponed and later events had canceled the plan Mrs. Woodrow Wilson had struggled for in 1913 and 1914. Unhappily the new act, in the opinion of the agency director, came too late to be effective; had it passed when drafted in 1930 he believed that private builders would have cooperated in putting up inexpensive housing for the displaced "alley families," but by 1935 the building boom was in full swing, and projects on which profit would be narrow no longer interested contractors. To a man, they opposed public housing, and the Alley Dwelling Authority spent most of its first two years fighting law suits aimed at stopping its acquisition of suitable sites, especially for Negro developments. In that interval rising prices limited the agency's purchasing power. Consequently Negro alley-dwellers who had hoped to move into respectable low-cost quarters had to stay on in the slums.[15]

[14] Hayes, *Negro Govt Worker*, p. 104; John P. Davis, "A Black Inventory of the New Deal," and Abraham Epstein, "The Social Security Act," *Crisis*, XLII, 141-42, 334-38; *Crisis*, XLIII, 168, 204, XLVI, 271; John A. Salmond, "The Civilian Conservation Corps and the Negro," *Journal of American History*, LII, 75-88; working papers of the National Committee on Segregation in the Nation's Capital, 1947-1948.

[15] *Herald*, 28-30 Mar 1934; "Private Agencies Are Still Needed in the Research Field," *Council Bulletin*, I, Nov 1936, pp. 1-2 (official organ of the Council of Social Agencies); Schlesinger, *Coming of the New Deal*, 293-96; CSA, 17th Anl Rpt, "Research," *Community Service*,

In 1937 some 9,000 houses were still lighted only by oil lamps, 7,000 multiple-family tenements were without inside water taps, and 11,000 families had no inside toilets. One of the worst alleys debouched into the street within a hundred yards of the new air-conditioned office of the Federal Housing Administrator. "Behind the marble mask," in the words of a horrified journalist, the capital concealed an incredible squalor in which Negro and white families often lived side by side. Nor did the alleys alone contain wretchedness. The tourist might drive along streets lined with what appeared to be respectable middle-class houses and never dream that behind the front doors fifteen to twenty families, white as well as colored, were packed into space designed for one. In fact the outer presentability of those rows of houses was a deterrent to reducing their excess population and making them livable. By 1940 construction of about 3,000 public housing units, including a 286-family Negro development on Benning Road, marked the total accomplishment of six years' work; over four fifths of the beneficiaries were indigent whites. When careful studies showed that Negro mortality from all causes was 70 percent higher than white and stressed the direct relationship between the incidence of fatal disease and the occupance of alley slums, private citizens speaking through the newly organized Washington Housing Association vainly sought to redress the balance. But although the two Sanitary Housing companies of the early years of the century had proved to be "a philanthropy that pays dividends," at the end of the thirties only the federal government could finance a larger-scale program. And Congress considered other goals more pressing.

In meeting the housing needs of people in somewhat higher income brackets, the differential between white and Negro opportunities was still more pronounced. As the

II, Apr 1938, pp. 2-5; *First Report of the Alley Dwelling Authority for the District of Columbia*, 15 Dec 1935.

Federal Housing Authority guaranteed loans approved for private housing projects, and the Resettlement Administration set about building for middle-income white families a carefully planned "Greenbelt" town in the countryside of nearby Maryland, a white exodus to the suburbs began. While real estate developers put up a series of multiple-family dwellings in Clarendon, Virginia, and a rash of new, privately financed houses turned Arlington into a burgeoning albeit unpretentious suburb, the opening of two units of the National Institutes of Health encouraged a migration into Bethesda, Maryland, and pushed the growth of the small city of Silver Spring. But none of this outward movement benefited Negroes. Virginia and Maryland property-owners, real estate dealers, and builders stood fast against renting or selling to colored families irrespective of their financial resources. Relying on a clause in the Federal Housing Act stipulating that guaranteed loans must be confined to projects that would not disrupt neighborhoods, banks refused to make Negroes loans for houses outside predominantly colored areas. Hence a steady shrinkage in the percentage of nonwhites in the suburban population and a proportionate rise in the District of Columbia's followed. And within Washington neighborhoods changed character.[16]

The most dramatic shift took place in Georgetown. While a number of her beautiful eighteenth and early nineteenth century houses had been kept up over the years, a good many buildings, especially the smaller and simplest, had

[16] *News*, 15 Sep 1933; Rpt B/Tr, 1935, p. 11; John Ihlder, "Housing in Washington," *Council Bulletin*, I, Oct 1936, pp. 8-12; *Community Service*, I, Mar 1937, p. 9, May 1937, pp. 3, 6, and Paul B. Cornely, "Health Problems of the Negro in Washington," p. 5; "The United States and District of Columbia Housing," *ibid.*, Sep 1937, pp. 3-4; "We Can Get Rid of the Slums," *ibid.*, II, Feb 1938, p. 6, and "Alley People," May 1938, p. 9; Comrs Rpt, 1938, pp. 173-74; National Capital Planning Commission, *Washington Present and Future*, Monograph #1, 1950, p. 21; "Behind the Marble Mask," *Collier's*, CII, 3 Sep 1938, pp. 11-14; *Star*, 13 Oct 1935; Federal Housing Authority, *Underwriter's Manual*, 1938.

TABLE V

PERCENT OF NONWHITE POPULATION IN SUBURBAN JURISDICTIONS OF
METROPOLITAN WASHINGTON AND THE DISTRICT OF COLUMBIA, 1930-1960

	1930[a]	1940	1950	1960
Montgomery County, Md.	16.8	11	6	4
Prince Georges County, Md.	23.3	19	12	9
Arlington County, Va.	12.5	9	5	6
Fairfax County, Va.[b]	19.0	16	10	5
Alexandria, Va.	20.3	16	12	12
Falls Church, Va.[b]	—	—	2	2
District of Columbia	27.1	28.2	35	54

[a] Negro only
[b] Falls Church included in Fairfax County before 1950

fallen into disrepair before the turn of the century. In 1930 over two fifths of her inhabitants were poverty-stricken Negroes, most of them occupying substandard dwellings, some without running water or electricity. Yet the convenience of the location and the abiding charm of the shabby little village had begun to have its effects in the late 1920's. The remodeling started then had proceeded slowly until it gained sudden momentum about 1934. Impecunious young New Dealers moved into the cramped little houses when restored, while real estate brokers hastily played down their decades-old argument that once a neighborhood had become part Negro, it deteriorated with inexorable rapidity. Colored homeowners found the prices white dealers offered for Georgetown property hard to resist, and tenants often could not afford the higher rentals demanded after adjoining property had undergone renovation. But as relocation across Rock Creek was difficult, some Negroes stayed on, thus keeping for Georgetown a biracial quality that permitted Negro and white children to play side by side in the nearby public parks.

In the rest of Washington the complexion of several erstwhile white neighborhoods darkened—the area around the Morgan School above Florida Avenue, for example—while rows of jerry-built little boxes in remote stretches of Northeast began to fill with up-rooted colored tenants. Kelly Miller observed that residential segregation, so far from easing, had increased under the New Deal. Black ghettoes, even while spreading a little geographically, became more tightly packed, the congestion worsened by in-migrants from the Deep South who continued to come, undeterred by the fact that thousands of colored people native to the District were out of work. Whereas the nearly 120,000 white newcomers of the New Deal era were generally well-educated upper-class citizens qualifying for government posts, most of the 55,000 Negroes added to the population stood at the bottom of the social and economic scale. When the Resettlement Administration proposed to help middle-class colored city-dwellers by relocating a number in Negro Greenbelts, the Washington *Tribune* blasted the plan as a sign of a deliberate policy of cutting Negro Americans off from the main body of American life.[17]

Similarly, the hypercritical wondered why the National Youth Administration should have a separate unit for Negro affairs instead of handling them as part of all youth problems. Consensus, however, was general that Mary McLeod Bethune, founder and former head of a colored girls' school in Florida, was the person to take charge of the Negro division. Although nuances indicated a faint irritation among some of Washington's colored elite at her keeping herself somewhat apart from the local community, they quickly realized that her breadth of knowledge, her perceptiveness, her political finesse, and her direct access to the President were invaluable to the Negro cause. In dealing with her white associates, one young man recalled, her pronouncedly Negroid appearance in itself helped. With her deep-chocolate-colored skin, her heavy build, and rather prognathous jaw, she seemed like a product of darkest Africa—until she spoke. Then the exquisitely musical voice offering sagacious counsel in a perfect Oxford accent carried an impact that

[17] Census Tracts, D.C., 1930, Bureau of the Census; Eunice Grier, *Understanding Washington's Changing Population;* pp. 10-13.

left no one in doubt that here was an extraordinary woman to whom any sensible person would listen with respectful attention.

To some colored Washingtonians more important from the first than any political appointee or any New Deal agency was Elder Lightfoot Michaux and his Church of God. Such confidence as they had in the President perhaps stemmed from the evangelist's assurance that Franklin D. Roosevelt was the Lord's chosen instrument. Not long after the Elder came to Washington in the depths of the depression, he managed, no one knew quite how, to get money for a daily radio program to tell listeners to lean on Jesus. Every morning at seven o'clock the "Happy Am I" preacher explained over station WJSV that W stood for willingly, J for Jesus, S for suffered, and V for victory over the grave. His tub-thumping exhortations helped him quickly collect a following as devoted as that of "Papa" Divine. Outwardly little different from the scores of other store-front churches mushrooming in the Georgia Avenue neighborhood, the Church of God under Michaux turned into an institutional church that fed the hungry and housed the homeless. When the millionaire Bernarr McFadden, appalled by the pilferage from the penny lunchroom he had been financing, turned it over as a gift to the Elder, the preacher appealed to his radio audience for help; local people out of work gave their services, and, when they got paying jobs, contributed money to the "Happy News Cafe," where day after day for several years thousands of hungry people paid a penny a meal for hot food. As a coast-to-coast network picked up the evangelist's broadcasts, one of his publications noted, "the people began to clamor for him to come out into the open and fight his War on the devil. Elder Michaux was himself eager to go directly to the front and boldly let the people eat right out of his hands the spiritual food they needed to keep the devil on the run." So the Elder organized the Cross Choir of 156 trained singers to stage elaborately executed programs of choruses and marches, usually at Griffith Stadium.

The preacher won the ear of politically influential people. When the congregation of the Church of God elected five honorary deacons, District Commissioner George E. Allen, Major Dwight D. Eisenhower, "Steve" Early, personal secretary to the President, Clark Griffith, principal owner of Washington's baseball team, and Harry Butcher, vice president of the Columbia Broadcasting Company, all accepted the honor and a Bible each to seal the covenant. Upon hearing that a congressman, possessor of a race horse named "Not Worth Owning," was about to propose legalization of horse racing in the District and revival of the old race track on Benning Road, the evangelist, pointing out that gambling was not pleasing to God, persuaded the congressman to drop his bill and sell his horse also. Michaux then inveigled his convert into helping him buy the track at a bargain price. There in the future he would put up Mayfair Mansions, a luxurious 596-unit Negro housing development. Until 1938 he engaged an excursion boat every summer to convey people awaiting baptism down the Potomac, but that year Honorary Deacon Clark Griffith arranged to have a large canvas tank set up at the ball park, where the pastor, clad in a black robe, high rubber boots, and a black skull cap, baptized his flock in water imported from the River Jordan. New Dealers prone to ignore all other local affairs and other local citizens looked upon him as a personage, the one Washingtonian, white or colored, to excite their interest.[18]

If nobody begrudged Elder Michaux his triumphs, neither were many colored Washingtonians willing to accept his brand of religious fervor or adopt his tactics. On the contrary. No doubt a number of white people were genuinely moved by his oratory and impressed by his good works, but the delighted amusement his methods provoked in much

[18] *Church of God, A Pictorial Review*, pp. 6, 23, 26-27, 46, 51, 58, 60; Caroline Ware to the author, 21 May 1962.

of white Washington contained the seeds of a derisiveness damaging to all colored people. The elements in American society which twenty years later would form the core of white citizens' councils naturally looked approvingly upon the Elder as the epitome of the old-style camp-meeting Negro whose militance was directed at the devil, not in seeking equality with white men, a Negro to be patted on the back, helped when convenient, made use of, and ridiculed. Whether or not highly educated colored Washingtonians saw a potential threat in the racial image Elder Michaux presented, they looked for other paths than his to their goals. Few of them were concerned about a new religious sect that appeared in 1938, for the Black Muslims whose scarlet robes and fezzes could be seen in Georgetown on Mohammedan holy days made relatively little impression on the Secret City. If the doctrine that all evil sprang from whites was easy enough to accept, repudiation of Christianity in favor of the belief that only black followers of Mohammed could inherit the earth was impossible for most of colored Washington.

While Mrs. Bethune and Elder Michaux both stimulated white people's interest in Negro talents and Negro problems, it also grew independently, sometimes out of sheer curiosity, more often from philanthropic contacts under Community Chest aegis. The *Star*, which for fifty years had rarely printed any but derogatory or facetious stories about colored people, in 1933 carried a long account of a meeting of the Association for the Study of Negro Life and History, and at intervals thereafter the white press published news items that implied, as one man put it, that "Negroes are people." Although Negro quotas in Chest drives were miniscule— less than $5,000 in 1934—Chest funds supported the three Negro settlement houses, the Stoddard Baptist Old Folks Home, St. Ann's Home, and the colored YM- and YWCAs. Collaboration widened a little when, after six years of backing and filling, in 1935 the Washington Federation of Churches invited Negro churches to join, and, not without

21. Dedication of the Lincoln Memorial, May 1922. The segregated area for Negroes was at the far left.

22. Ku Klux Klan parade, 1925.

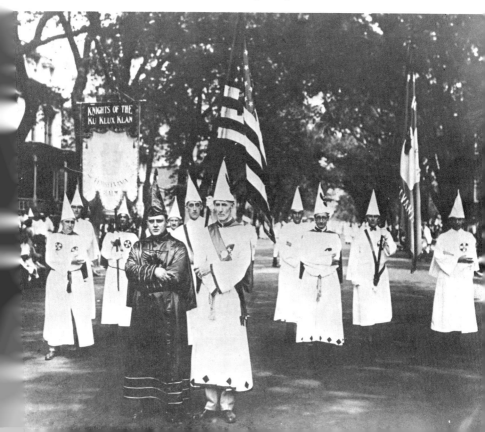

23. Negro tenements of the 1930's.

24

26

29

NEGRO NOTABLES. 24. Archibald Grimké, president of the Washington chapter of the NAACP and of the American Negro Academy. 25. Dr. Walter H. Brooks, pastor of the Nineteenth Street Baptist Church, 1882-1939. 26. Mary Church Terrell, first president of the National Association of Colored Women. 27. Kelly Miller, dean of Howard University. 28. Carter G. Woodson, founder of the Association for the Study of Negro Life and History. 29. Garnet C. Wilkinson, assistant superintendent of schools, 1922-1949.

28

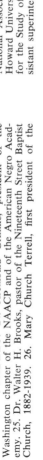

27

30. Water from the River Jordan, consigned to the Elder Lightfoot Michaux, 1938.

31. Elder Michaux baptizing his sheep at Griffith Stadium, 1938.

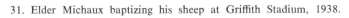

32. Marian Anderson singing at the Department of Interior Building four years after the famous concert at the Lincoln Memorial.

33. White playground, 1949.

34. Separate but equal. Volunteers clearing vacant lot
for a Negro playground, July 1952.

35. Parent-Citizens' Committee for Better Schooling picketing
at Franklin Square, December 1947.

36. Picket line at the Capitol Theatre, 1949.

37. Parents' Day at Powell Elementary School, November 1955. Secretary of Agriculture Ezra Taft Benson, center rear, with his daughter in front of him.

38. An honors class at McKinley Technical High School, February 1957. "Superiority," ran the newspaper caption, "is not a racial characteristic."

some hesitation, four Negro congregations accepted, doubtless chiefly because its new biracial committee on race relations seemed likely to reach further into strongholds of local prejudice than other organizations could. While a racially mixed group inaugurated a self-help cooperative in northeast Washington, white and colored people together raised the money to open the Northwest Settlement House on M Street, and, in response to a plea from the *Tribune*, an interracial committee conducted a drive to combat the excessively high tuberculosis death rate among Negroes. In 1938 the recently organized chapter of the National Conference of Christians and Jews began to seek Negro members. And when the District Suffrage League launched a new drive for an elected city government, campaigners, instead of ignoring colored Washington as they had in 1919, urged Negroes to vote in the unofficial plebescite and carried the question to potential future voters in the colored high schools.[19]

A more significant break in the color line occurred at Catholic University in 1936: the admission of a Negro to the school of social work. Oddly enough, the event occasioned little comment. Several months later the faculty of the graduate school at American University voted unanimously to admit Negro students. The decision came in answer to an application from a graduate of the Howard University Law School who explained that she wanted to take a Ph.D. in political science, and Howard neither offered sufficiently advanced courses nor conferred doctoral degrees. When the president and the most influential of the trustees endorsed the faculty vote, only one of the nearly 2,000

[19] *Star*, 22 Oct 1933, 22 Apr, 6, 30 May 1938; Minutes of the Board of Managers of the Family Service Association, 8 May, 8 Dec 1937 (hereafter cited as Min FSA); *Tribune*, 19 Jul, 13 Oct, 17, 24 Nov 1934, 6, 27 Dec 1935, 22 Nov 1937; Washington Federation of Churches, *Yearbook*, 1936; *Council Bulletin*, I, Oct 1936, p. 13; Mrs. William Kittle, "Fiftieth Anniversary of the American Social Settlement Movement," *Community Service*, I, Feb 1937, pp. 2-3; Cornely, "Health Problems," *ibid.*, May 1937, p. 5; *Post*, 1 May 1938.

graduate students withdrew. The new policy at American University was peculiarly important to colored students because most graduate classes met at night when people with daytime jobs could attend. Still Negro enrollment was not heavy. Some of the colored students found the standards of scholarship hard to meet, and professors were troubled now and again at having to give discouragingly low grades, but most of the candidates eventually completed the work for masters' degrees, and several won doctorates with distinction.

Still more important to the Negro rank and file was the establishment of CIO unions in the District after the Congress of Industrial Organizations split off from the AFL in 1937, for the CIO affiliates opened membership to all workers. CIO picnics with softball games, races, soccer, touch football, and square dances were always interracial; several times the Industrial Union Council held nonsegregated dances in its own buildings or at a commercial hall. Red-baiting politicians were inclined to regard such overtures to Negroes as a sign of communist infiltration, but such party members as Washington's CIO unions contained talked and behaved like socialists, not subversives. And here, as indeed throughout the country, Negroes were astonishingly resistant to communist doctrine. "Democratic racial harmony," said the council president, marked local CIO union meetings. The AFL, on the contrary, generally clung to its color bars, and, as it comprised all the building trades, its numbers were larger and its power greater in the city than the CIO's.[20]

Another approach to interracial conciliation looked promising to a handful of Negroes and a small group of earnest whites who, at the suggestion of Assistant School Superin-

[20] Interview Ernest Griffith, in 1937 dean of the American University Graduate School, 6 May 1962; "Statement of Robert Sherman, President, Washington CIO Industrial Union Council," in Statements or Excerpts of Committee against Segregation in Recreation before the Board of Education, 17 Jul 1945 (mimeo); Record, *The Negro and the Communist Party*, pp. 146-183.

tendent Garnet Wilkinson, founded a local Urban League in December 1938. That it appeared twenty-seven years after New Yorkers and Chicagoans had established a National League attests to colored Washington's long preoccupation with political maneuvers and NAACP court action. The league worked on the premise that persuasion was the only effective way to end racial prejudice and give Negroes economic opportunities. A gift from Canon Anson Phelps Stokes of the National Cathedral provided funds for a first year. But the new organization, later to be a vital force in the city, made little headway at first. Ultraconservative whites and, conversely, left-of-center Negro leaders considered the program of biracial conferences little more than talk and more talk. And talk opened no doors, not even to the movie theatres showing "Abraham Lincoln in Illinois" to which a colored man who had won a contest as the person looking most like Abe was refused admission. Negro indignation ran high at Mrs. Roosevelt when, avowed champion of colored people's rights that she was, she walked through the picket line at the theatre to see the film.

Inevitably in a city where two generations of white people had thought of Negroes primarily as servants, or at least as human beings of a distinctly lower order, the new contacts made through charity board sessions and university classrooms were generally formal, often marred by white condescension, and usually lacking in personal warmth. Sixty-odd years of sitting side by side at school board meetings had failed to create close ties between white and colored members; now conferences to discuss common welfare problems deepened mutual understanding considerably less than white enthusiasts supposed. Indeed to much of colored Washington the olive branches extended by white philanthropists and civic leaders seemed too spindly to lean upon heavily. But what else was there to rely on? The local NAACP, unable to work with "the rowdy element," had become virtually a cipher. The New Negro Alliance, however successful in opening up jobs, could not ensure fair

243

wages; after winning its case before the Supreme Court, it gradually ceased to function; *New Negro Opinion* disappeared. In 1936 when the brilliant and respected John Preston Davis, during NRA days executive secretary of the Joint Committee on National Recovery, issued a call for a Negro congress to formulate a national racial policy, delegates from Washington had attended the first meeting in Chicago with high hopes. But, like the Afro-American Council of the early years of the century, the convention arrived at no constructive plan of action, and at a second session held in Washington in 1940, when Davis advocated the Communist Party line, most of his followers repudiated him. The National Negro Congress lost its appeal to inhabitants of the Secret City.[21]

Meanwhile doubts about what course to pursue also subtly affected Negro attitudes toward the school system. Although the heightened difficulty of getting jobs probably strengthened lower-class Negroes' convictions that any schooling beyond the legal minimum was useless, enrollments in the junior and senior high schools rose somewhat. At the same time upper-class Negroes began to pose questions about the quality of education available to them. "To some of us who got our schooling before the present-day reign of fads, futilities and 'activities' so-called," the *Tribune* had complained in 1933, "it is no surprise to observe the shocking deficiency in the fundamentals—the three R's, if you please—of the present-day high school pupil." School officials generally ignored the protests, either on the principle of least said soonest mended or else because administrators honestly believed that fault-finding about the "watered-down curriculum," the stress on high school athletics, and the lowering of teaching standards sprang merely from parental yearnings for "the good old days." In 1935

[21] Address, Garnet Wilkinson at Twentieth Anniversary of the Founding of the Washington Urban League (ms, in League files); *Tribune*, 22 Nov 1937; *Afro-American*, 7, 14, 21 Jan, 25 Feb 1939; Record, *The Negro and the Communist Party*, pp. 153-162.

Dr. Howard Long of the colored school research unit decided to check on the validity of complaints by comparing the Intelligence Quotient scores made by Negro children over a period of years with the results of their achievement tests. But as his findings were not completed until 1943, dissatisfied parents unfamiliar with research data already published elsewhere could only guess at the causes of weaknesses in the schools.[22] If conscientious elementary grade teachers attributed the high proportion of "slow learners" in their classes to the extremely limited cultural background of children whose families had recently come from the Deep South, teachers did not discuss their suspicions with laymen. Assistant Superintendent Wilkinson did not welcome criticisms that might reflect upon his competence even when they grew out of circumstances he could not change. After all, Washington's colored public schools since their founding in the 1860's had had to contend with the problem of in-migrants.

Unlike the tacitly sanctioned policy in the white schools of concentrating upon children of average or below average mentality and those with physical disabilities, Negro school administrators and teachers believed their first obligation was to the most able of the colored school population. To the distress of some members of the board of education, many colored principals and teachers appeared to take the position that truants, pupils who fell behind in their work or got into other trouble, the emotionally disturbed, and mentally retarded children were not entitled to special attention, for it would necessarily be at the expense of their more competent fellows. Since school resources were limited, and all Negro children faced discrimination in a predominantly white world, those able to make effective use of edu-

[22] *Tribune*, 10 Mar 1933; Howard Long, "Intelligence and Achievement of Colored Pupils in the Public Schools of the District of Columbia," Part II (mimeo 1948). Otto Kleinberg's *Negro Intelligence and Selective Migration*, published in 1935, established the thesis which Long's study later verified for Washington.

cation must not be sacrificed to the less promising. If teaching methods were faulty, changes to adapt them to handling the lame ducks were less important than improvements aimed at gifted children. While nothing in official reports acknowledged such a philosophy, it was a natural point of view in so class-conscious a community as colored Washington, where teachers, themselves occupying an enviable place in the social structure, would understandably want to preserve it intact.

Only a very small, unvociferous minority of Washington Negroes saw any advantage in school integration. The rest, if concerned about education at all, aimed at full recognition of the accomplishments of the colored schools and a larger, juster share of funds with which to better past records. The editors and contributors to the 1935 Yearbook issue of the national *Journal of Negro Education* concerned themselves only with overcoming "the flagrant discrimination in the provision of public education for Negroes" the country over; "not even the NAACP," Charles H. Thompson noted seventeen years later, "envisaged a direct attack on segregated public schools." When the Miner Teachers' College, outgrowth of the earlier normal school, won an "A" rating from an official of the American Association of Teachers' Colleges, who declared that his survey had upset his settled conviction about the inferiority of Negro institutions, colored Washingtonians felt they had proved their ability to run their own show. The admission of Negroes to two of the local university graduate schools was gratifying but affected very few people directly. Most Negroes preferred to maintain a Negro teaching preserve at the lower educational levels. Not improbably distrust of Superintendent Ballou, whom they considered tainted with racism, strengthened their determination to keep their schools free of white interference. The superintendent had approved the use of a white school building for a citizens' association meeting called in the 1920's to tighten restrictive housing covenants; he repeatedly, Negroes perhaps mistakenly believed, betrayed a dislike of colored people; and even after the board of education created a biracial citizens' advisory committee on vocational training, apart from appointing a few colored teachers to committees manned largely by whites, Ballou set himself against any modification of segregated schooling. At least as long as he was in charge, if Washington's dual system were to be discarded, *Crisis* observed, it would be at the insistence of economy-minded whites in the face of Negro opposition.[23]

Knowledgeable Negroes in early 1939 were still skeptical about any nascent conversion among whites to the doctrine, let alone the practice, of racial equality. Certainly the idea had little impact on the Hill. When Elwood Street, as head of the District's welfare department, sought out Congressman Ross Collins of Mississippi, chairman of the House Subcommittee on District Appropriations, to ask his help in solving an acute local problem, the result was predictable. For several years past, Street explained, Negro girls of fourteen, fifteen, and sixteen, unaccompanied by their families, had been pouring into Washington from the South. Prepared only to live on the streets, many of them quickly landed in the colored unit of the National Training School for Girls. Segregated by law, the school was overflowing; more space and more skilled supervisors were needed if any of the young inmates were to be salvaged. Representative Collins, looking the social worker straight in the eye, said, "If I went along with your ideas, Mr. Street, I'd never keep my seat in Congress. My constituents wouldn't stand for spending all that money on niggers." [24] Mississippi's racial views thus controlled correctional work in the nation's capital. Unquestionably a great many members of Congress thought economy more important than voting appropriations to redeem erring Negroes or to forestall worse condi-

[23] Robert Haycock, "The Capital's Unique School System," *School Life,* XVII, 102-03; *Tribune,* 25 Oct 1929, 5 Feb 1932; *Crisis,* XXXIX, 39, XLVI, 170-71; *Journal of Negro Education,* XXI, No. 1, pp. 1-2
[24] Interview, Elwood Street, 7 May 1963.

tions for the future, just as an unknown number of the city's permanent residents still dismissed all racial questions as a nuisance unconnected with either moral or humanitarian issues.

Few whites indulged in soul-searching about Negro equality. White proponents of the Negro cause concentrated rather upon Negroes' rights as citizens. White House policies, if somewhat noncommittal, helped, and Mrs. Roosevelt's warm interest in colored people as people was reassuring. At her invitation distinguished Negro musicians gave several concerts at the White House, and other colored people occasionally had tea with the First Lady. "Old Curmudgeon" Secretary of the Interior Harold Ickes and Assistant Secretary Oscar Chapman from the first were fighters for democratic fair play and were wholly colorblind, Harry Hopkins of the WPA only slightly less so. And yet had the administration completely ignored race relations, the change in attitude that had begun to emerge in Washington early in Hoover's presidency would probably have spread. That the admission of Negro graduate students to American and Catholic universities made no stir in itself suggests that racial toleration was growing without political forcing. The chief outside stimulus to a reexamination of second-class citizenship was the shock of observing the application of race doctrines in Nazi Germany.

Chance gave a dramatic turn to events in the spring of 1939. The national limelight suddenly focused on racial discrimination in the capital when the DAR refused to allow the famous contralto Marian Anderson to sing in the DAR-owned Constitution Hall. The board of education, after pondering the subsequent request for use of the white Central High School auditorium, hung its permission on Superintendent Ballou's proviso that this was to be an exception, not a precedent. The furor aroused in the city and throughout the country exceeded any outburst of indignation within the memory of Washington's oldest inhabitants. White people were jolted out of their assumption that Negroes with ambition and talent could make their way anywhere, here was a woman of utmost distinction being treated as an obnoxious nonentity. Marian Anderson revealed to the nation the depths into which white ignorance and prejudice had forced all Negroes. Secretary of the Interior Ickes immediately authorized the use of the Lincoln Memorial, and there on Easter Sunday afternoon the concert took place at the feet of the "Great Emancipator" before an audience of 75,000 people. No one present at that moving performance ever forgot it. It was the turning point, one man averred, in Washington Negroes' seventy-year-old fight against discrimination. And it was no longer a local affair only. Race relations in the capital thenceforward were a matter of interest to Americans everywhere.[25]

[25] Victor Daly, "Washington's Minority Problem," and John Covell, Jr., "Washington Fights," *Crisis*, XLVI, 170, 276-77.

CHAPTER XI

A NEW ALIGNMENT, 1939–1945

As Negroes in the capital discovered that they had more white allies than anyone had suspected in early 1939, a life-giving sense of confidence coursed through the colored community. Optimistically the secretary of the recently reconstituted local branch of the NAACP wrote of the change taking place in the colored city's upper strata; in the past too eager for white recognition to bother about the lower classes, the Negro intelligentsia, now encouraged by signs of white interest, was joining with the "common man" of the Negro world to create a new era. In spite of the shortage of jobs and in spite of local custom that perpetuated segregation, Victor Daly remarked in turn, colored people here after six years of Roosevelt's administration were better off "economically, socially and culturally" than Negroes anywhere else. The "phenomenal culture" of Negro Washington's 191 doctors, 72 dentists, 98 lawyers, and nearly 600 public school and university teachers gave the city a unique opportunity: the equivalent of an Age of Jackson might lie ahead for colored Americans, provided they did not falter, and provided that the conscience of white America did not dissipate its force on other causes.[1]

Both conditions, however, soon looked unattainable. The NAACP estimate notwithstanding, rigid class distinctions still prevailed within the colored community. At Howard University the scions of cave dwellers looked down their patrician noses at black classmates from other parts of the country or from the lower ranks of local society. During leisure hours the Secret City was almost as remote from

[1] John Covell, Jr., "Washington Fights," and Victor Daly, "Washington's Minority Problem," *Crisis*, XLVI, 170, 276-77.

white Washington as in the 1920's. Cultivated colored people generally preferred it that way; as long as their children could not associate with white children in school, why seek artificial bonds with adults? Old families, though readier than formerly to share in civic responsibilities, were, if possible, more than ever inclined to exclude from their social life any outlander, the white person above all. Twenty years later social psychologists would point to the necessity of constant massive contacts if white and colored Americans were to build a hierarchy of social values which would recognize racial prejudice as too costly to sustain. But at the end of the 1930's all Americans had a long road to travel, and two immediate obstacles to progress troubled colored leaders and discouraged their followers, namely continuing widespread unemployment and, after the outbreak of war in Europe, the diversion of influential white men's attention from domestic to foreign affairs.

Contrary to cheery predictions of local businessmen and to the congressional majority's fixed convictions about local prosperity, unemployment in this nonindustrial city was as severe as in 1938 and ran a third again as high as the average for the rest of the country. In August 1939 the District Employment Center had 62,000 applicants for jobs, and families who were trying to live on earnings of as little as $6 to $7 a week from part-time work perhaps tripled the number in want. Of those, according to educated guesses, two thirds were Negroes. And since many young adults had never had jobs, they were ineligible for employment insurance. Much of colored Washington consequently thought more about where the next meal was to come from than about a promised land lying a year or a decade or a quarter century in the future. The needy white householder naturally did not concern himself about the indigent black. In September the Nazi invasion of Poland distracted official Washington. By winter, it is true, belief that the European war was "phony" and in any case need not involve the United States as a belligerent again focused congressional thinking upon domestic problems, but the spring and early summer of 1940 dispelled the first illusion and shook faith in the second. With the fall of France in mid-June, American preparations for national defense relegated questions of race relations in Washington to a place of minor importance.

In America's big manufacturing centers employment had picked up as soon as modification of the Neutrality Act in January 1940 permitted companies to accept orders on a cash and carry basis from British and French purchasing commissions. That quickening of activity had had little effect on Washington's working classes. Among colored males in the labor force over 10 percent were unemployed at the time of census taking in March, and over 22 percent of those with jobs had had no work for at least four of the preceding twelve months. Even in mid-summer, when large-scale military planning and the subsequent creation of offices of price stabilization and consumer protection promised to open up places for several hundred clerks, stenographers, and people with some administrative experience, blue-collar jobs in the capital outside the building trades were hard to come by. The AFL building trade unions still refused to take Negro apprentices, and the District Employment Center's segregated listings of available jobs still confined Negro applicants largely to common labor or domestic service. Almost 70 percent of employed Negroes held jobs in the lowest paid categories. Fortunately, passage of the Selective Service Act in September, the drafting of the first quota of young men a few weeks later, and the start of special training classes in carpentry, metalworking, and machine-shop skills for Negro as well as white youths combined to reduce the roster of the District's able-bodied unemployed to some 27,000 before November. By February 1941, the Family Service Association reported, all semi-skilled workmen in the city had found jobs. The demand for office workers during the next four and a half years was such that even well-to-do women who had never before held any kind of paid job became full-time government employees.[2]

A job did not of course necessarily mean a congenial occupation or pay commensurate with a person's abilities. Whether he were a military draftee or worked as a civilian in a government office, an industrial plant, or for a company providing some other kind of service, the Negro early concluded that discrimination in placement and promotion was still in effect. The Washington edition of the *Afro-American* had argued in June 1940 that with Hitler master of continental Europe, the United States could not and would not allow color bars to continue in America's armed services. A few months later the army was putting only white officers in command of colored draftees, the air corps and the Marines refused to accept any Negro, and in the navy colored men could hope for nothing better than menial assignments. Memories of the humiliations Negro officers and troops had suffered in World War I fanned the anger of colored Washingtonians. The promotion of Colonel Benjamin O. Davis to the rank of Brigadier General seemed to them the merest gesture. In civilian offices discrimination, far from withering away as optimists had expected in 1939, widened its reach with the appearance of new defense agencies. Doubtless the colored typists and file clerks sprinkled into newly organized offices sometimes imagined slights; few of them admitted that their more limited background and education rather than prejudice might deny them equality with their white associates. But white supervisors intent on getting the job done generally felt justified in placing Negro typists in separate rooms and separate stenographic pools assigned to the least exacting work. By the end of 1940 Negro militants in and out of the capital concluded the time ripe to dramatize their demands for nondiscriminatory treatment.

[2] Min FSA, 10 May, 13 Sep, 11 Oct 1939; 19 Jun 1940, 19 Feb 1941; *16th U.S. Census*, 1940, *Population, The Labor Force*, 3rd Series, pp. 47-50.

Early in 1941 Eugene Davidson, one of the founders of the New Negro Alliance, reminded A. Philip Randolph, head of the Brotherhood of Sleeping Car Porters, that the Alliance picket lines had opened up several hundred jobs in Washington shops to Negroes during the Depression. Now that the government and American industry badly needed competent workers, the two men and NAACP leaders agreed that similar action on a national scale should produce wider results. Randolph sent out a call for 50,000 Negroes to march on Washington in July to present to the President and Congress colored Americans' protests at job discrimination. By April, as colored men throughout the country pledged themselves to march, high-ranking government officials began to ask: "What'll they think in Berlin?" Still, apparently unable to believe that a Negro army bigger than the Bonus Expeditionary Force and possibly more militant in temper might actually descend upon the capital, federal department heads took no positive action. When the United States Employment Service proposed to modify the segregation that obtained at the District Employment Center, a threat from an influential Georgian on the House Appropriations Committee to cut off the agency's funds perpetuated the discriminatory and wasteful arrangement of the past. Plans for the march went on. In early June, with the demonstration impending in less than a month, Mayor La Guardia of New York arranged a meeting between Negro leaders, Mrs. Roosevelt, and government representatives. The white men urged patience. Mrs. Roosevelt suggested that in the long run the march would heighten the racism of Southerners in Congress and provoke disastrous retaliation. Randolph replied that, as the mere prospect of the march had already netted Negro rights more serious attention than had decades of verbal appeals, colored Americans preferred to chance revenge rather than drop the mass protest in exchange for mere promises. And any acceptable agreement would have to include government offices and installations as well as private industry.

Six days later a conference took place at the White House. There Randolph, Walter White, executive secretary of the NAACP, and two associates faced the President, William Knudsen and Sidney Hillman of the Office of Production Management, La Guardia, and Aubrey Williams of the National Youth Administration. Three of the white men wielded enormous power over American industry; the names of the other two were familiar to several million Americans. People interested in race relations had heard of the author of *A Man Named White;* railroad officials and operatives dimly recognized the stature of Randolph; the other two Negroes were relatively unknown in white America. White people who got wind of the White House confrontation expected the colored delegation to capitulate quickly. In return for calling off the march, the President offered to set up a group to study the situation and recommend the ruling with the "teeth in it" that Randolph declared essential. But a study was not action; the Negro leaders refused to cancel the march.

At a second White House meeting on the morning of June 24 La Guardia produced a plan proposing a commission to see that government contractors adhered to specified rules of nondiscrimination in hiring and promoting. The Negroes took the draft, said they would examine it during lunch, and return with their decision. Early that afternoon they informed the outwardly incredulous white conferees that the plan would not do: it was too vague and did not include government establishments. The response was immediate. At four o'clock an Executive Order on Fair Employment Practices was ready for the President's signature, laying down rules of nondiscrimination for all plants with defense contracts and all federal offices and agencies; a committee within the War Manpower Commission was to check on compliance and recommend to the President measures necessary "to effectuate the provisions of this order." The President signed the paper on June 25. For the first time since the Emancipation Proclamation of 1863 a President of the United States had issued an official order protecting Negro rights.[3]

While the new policy minimized fears that foreign affairs would completely submerge consideration of racial problems, satisfaction in colored Washington was tempered by events in areas to which the Executive Order did not apply. It did not touch many of the city's private employers or the unions with whom they dealt. When the stage production of *Native Son,* directed by Orson Welles, was opening at the National Theatre, Richard Wright walked into a restaurant in the company of one of the white producers and a white woman, only to be told that the management would have to serve the distinguished author in a car at the curb. Seemingly the Marian Anderson triumph might never have occurred. As the American Red Cross began to enlarge its professional staff and volunteers thronged into the District chapter offices to offer their services, colored women were given to understand that, provided someone could be found to give them the necessary training, they might be used as Canteen or Home Service workers or as nurses aides in connection with colored units. In fact, so far from ending Negro resentments, the Executive Order appeared, as time went on, to increase Negro hostility in Washington. Colored people reasoned that since the administration was ready to recognize them as first-class citizens, all white Americans should do so; because they did not, Negro belligerence tended to mount. By December a scathing article in *Harper's Magazine* entitled "Washington: Blight on Democracy" declared: "Negroes who have lived in many parts of the country say that nowhere else in America is there such bitter mutual race hatred." With a pronounced increase in violent crime in the city, Negroes believed that, as always, the police and the white public held them responsible.

[3] *Afro-American,* 8, 22 Jun, 12 Oct 1940; Earle Brown, "American Negroes and the War," *Harper's Magazine,* CLXXXIV, 545-52; *Times-Herald,* 28 Apr 1941; H Com on Appropriations, 75C, 3S, Hrgs; Louis Ruchames, *Race, Jobs and Politics,* pp. 87-99.

Yet the official nondiscrimination policy had some effect in Washington. Although Pearl Harbor and America's immersion in global war intensified pressures upon everyone and shortened tempers, efforts to work together amicably increased. A story describing an inspection tour the President and Harry Hopkins made of the partly completed Pentagon told of their astonishment at finding four huge washrooms placed along each of the five axes that connect the outer ring to the inmost on each floor of the building; upon inquiring the reason for such prodigality of lavatory space, the President was informed that nondiscrimination required as many rooms marked "Colored Men" and "Colored Women" as "White Men" and "White Women." The differentiating signs were never painted on the doors. Opposition to racism, moreover, drew strength from the constant influx of people from parts of the country where anti-Negro feeling had never had wide currency. In a half dozen agencies exceptionally able colored men, ranked as government messengers in 1941, gradually moved up in grade and a few would eventually win the coveted "P" or professional rating. Ralph Bunche, formerly a little-known Howard University political scientist, would become head of a policy-making section in the State Department at the end of the war. In the Office of Price Administration, where morale was consistently high, no color line of any kind existed.[4]

As an executive rather than a congressional creation, however, the committee charged with watching over fair employment practices lacked authority to subpoena witnesses and to enforce its decisions with all the powers of law behind it. And political opposition and the fear of strikes arising from workingmen's resentments at having

[4] Alden Stevens, "Washington: Blight on Democracy," *Harper's Magazine*, CLXXXIV, 50-51; Foster Rhea Dulles, *The American Red Cross, A History*, pp. 419-21; National Committee on Segregation in the Nation's Capital, *Segregation in Washington*, pp. 62-63 (hereafter cited as Ntl Comee on Seg, *Rpt*).

Negroes move into well-paying jobs formerly reserved for whites repeatedly undercut FEPC effectiveness. Ruefully the chairman later remarked that Southern "bludgeon-wielders" in Congress flayed at the committee as if it were "a poisonous snake." The segregated system at the District Employment Center continued because, as the head of the War Manpower Commission explained to an NAACP representative in 1944, "the Appropriations Committee instructed this agency that . . . if we operate on any other basis there would be no money appropriated for this operation." The FEPC's most "conspicuous failure" to make nondiscriminatory employment work in Washington occurred in a three-year battle with the Capital Transit Company. The case assumed peculiar importance because, the FEPC chairman noted, the colored community looked upon "the promotion of its race to trolley platforms as the test of government sincerity in promising equal opportunity to all Americans."

Although privately owned, the public utility chartered by Congress came under the surveillance of the President's committee. Responding to complaints filed in July 1942 that Capital Transit was refusing to hire Negroes as streetcar operators, the committee issued a directive to the company in November and obtained paper compliance to the extent of getting one Negro platform worker on the payroll. Sixteen white motormen promptly walked out but were reinstated a day or two later. The Negro trainee was dropped. In February 1943 fifty to sixty indignant citizens organized a Minorities Workshop, one of the earliest of a succession of somewhat similar biracial groups that would appear during the next decade. Transit company executives continued to advertise for several hundred white operators, while public interest in better service and in less racial discrimination led to the formation of a biracial Committee on Jobs for Negroes in Public Utilities, a group headed by an AFL hotel-workers' organizer. As negotiations between the FEPC and the company bogged down over whether or not the transit-workers' union would strike, the citizens' group decided to dramatize the fight and enlist public support for the Negro cause by picketing at the bus and trolley stops, placing white pickets in conspicuous downtown locations, and winding up a week's activities with a "Capital Transit Trek" to a mass meeting in Franklin Square on May 8. Earlier in the week sympathizers surveyed the company's car barns and garages every morning to tally and publicize the number of idle vehicles standing there. Meanwhile as a good many of the Committee on Jobs were known to be politically left of center, word went out over the grape vine that the purpose of the rally was to set off a race riot as part of a subversive plot. Although the *Star* and the *Post* endeavored to quash the rumor by facts, common sense, and ridicule, President Roosevelt's adviser on race relations reportedly was so frightened that he seriously considered asking the President to order cancellation of the parade and the meeting. The chief of the Metropolitan Police saved the day, for he himself marched at the head of "Trek," and the large crowd was orderly throughout the rally.

The demonstration settled nothing. As the company insisted that white workers' prejudices were insuperable and officials of Local 689 declared that the union itself was not opposed to Negroes' employment, the FEPC agreed to suspend further action while the company engaged an expert to make a survey of operators' attitudes. The survey completed in January 1944 stated that 72.8 percent of the people questioned believed a wildcat strike would follow upon the hiring of Negro platform workers, but the nature of the questions put to the operators cast doubt on the validity of the findings. Prolonged by anxieties over D Day and by a struggle to obtain a congressional appropriation for FEPC, an eleven-month stalemate ensued. Everyone in the city suffered in the interim—people dependent on inadequate public transportation to get to and from their jobs, overworked motormen, Negroes barred from well-paid employment, and harried FEPC staff and company officials. Hearings held in January 1945 at last produced directives issued to the company in April, but as the committee's prestige had dwindled seriously by then, enforcement in the face of objections and exceptions proved impossible. Indeed a severe cut in appropriations in June and the approaching end of the war imperilled FEPC's very existence. A last chance occurred in the autumn when a strike put company operations into the hands of the government, but for unknown reasons the White House forbade the issuance of a new FEPC order; Charles Houston, able Negro member of the committee, resigned; and six months later FEPC expired. Capital Transit carried on as a lily-white employer until its demise in 1956.[5]

While congressional hostility, company ineptitude, and committee timidity wrecked the transit negotiations, nondiscrimination worked surprisingly well in some instances. With price controls and ration coupons for foodstuffs, shoes, fuel oil, gasoline, and tires, white people and colored shared alike in purchasing such goods as were available to civilians. Although closer daily contacts in government offices sometimes heightened mutual antipathies between the races, the association frequently tended to bridge social gulfs. More than one young white woman discovered with astonishment that the Negro girl at a nearby desk had hair as soft and skin as smooth-textured as her own, and the colored girl's amusement at her white neighbor's surprise relieved the embarrassment of both. Colored members of the staff, if invited and persuaded to stay for an occasional office party, often lessened rather than heightened the artificiality of its gaiety. But give-and-take on the job usually stopped at the office threshold. Government cafe-

[5] Ltr, Paul V. McNutt to Leslie M. Perry, 2 Sep 1944, cited in working papers of the National Committee on Segregation in the Nation's Capital; working papers, Ntl Comee on Seg; *Star*, 2-9 May 1943; *Post*, 2-9 May 1943; Malcolm H. Ross, *All Manner of Men*, pp. 156-62, 170-79, 241-63; Ruchames, *Race, Jobs*, pp. 199-213.

terias, following the example of the Department of the Interior, were open to everyone, but white and colored employees seldom chose to lunch together. Segregation in other realms interfered with the growth of personal friendships.

Discrimination in housing, more pronounced than in the 1930's, presented a major barrier to interracial social intercourse if only because of the geographical distance between white and Negro quarters. While rent controls, imposed in January 1942, saved the purse of newcomers, no regulation supplied enough living quarters to accommodate them all. Dormitories put up for white "government girls" and Slowe and Carver halls built for incoming Negro federal workers scarcely scratched the surface of what was needed. In 1943 many Negro war workers were literally homeless when the National Capital Housing Authority, successor to the Alley Dwelling Authority, prepared to undertake a large development for them in Southeast Washington. The Congress Heights Citizens' Association protested and, by means of a carefully organized campaign directed behind the scenes by the Home Builders Association of Washington, succeeded in blocking the project. Congressional hearings in January 1944 revealed that the government agency had scheduled four times as many temporary war housing units for whites as for Negroes, and, of the 30,700 dwelling units for which private builders had obtained priorities, only 200 had been completed for Negro occupancy. Public housing for any but government employees did not materialize at all. Controversy about what tactics to use defeated the efforts of the Washington Housing Association to make more and better accommodations available to Negroes. One group advocated reliance on moral suasion to induce the all-powerful Real Estate Board to abandon its transactions in "exclusive," that is, racially restricted, property, while another group wanted to stage an open fight both on that issue and over placing a Negro on the board of the National

261

Capital Housing Authority. One rabbi insisted that the association must take a strong stand against discrimination aimed at any minority, Negro, Jew, or other; a second rabbi passionately asserted that to lump Jews with Negroes was to increase unwarrantably the handicaps with which Jews were already saddled. Elder Michaux, to the accompaniment of veiled charges that he was lining his own pocket, managed to put up on the old race track site a complex called Mayfair Mansions into which 596 well-to-do Negro families moved in 1944, but otherwise virtually no comfortable living units were available to self-respecting Negroes.[6]

Segregated recreation was another handicap to widening mutual understanding. The city's one legitimate theatre, most movie houses, restaurants, bowling alleys, skating rinks, and white dance halls excluded Negroes. In 1939 Secretary of the Interior Ickes, under whose jurisdiction the National Park Service fell, had begun to reverse the rules that had been in effect since the mid-1920's, first by opening the picnic grounds in Rock Creek Park to biracial use, in 1940 by ordering the admission of Negro players to the lighted tennis courts in West Potomac Park and on the Mall, and in 1941 by making the federally operated golf courses similarly available to everyone. There and wherever else permitted, adults and children of both races amicably shared recreational facilities. The District Community Centers and school playgrounds, on the contrary, continued to maintain color lines. Six months after Pearl Harbor citizens' protests persuaded Congress to omit from an act creating a new District recreation board a clause that would have made segregated facilities obligatory, but three of the four members appointed to the board by District Commissioner Guy Mason favored that policy,

[6] Ntl Comee on Seg, *Rpt*, pp. 22-32, 68-74; Subcomee, S Dis Comee, 78C, 1S, "Investigation of the Ntl Cap Housing Authority," Hrgs, pp. 130, 1138, 1142, 1267; see also clippings filed under "Housing," Washingtoniana Room, D.C. Pub Library.

and of the three ex-officio members, only Irving Root of the National Capital Park Service opposed it. Commissioner Mason, it is true, in asking Mrs. Alice Hunter to serve, explained that the enabling act contained no racial restrictions whatsoever, nor, except for the school acts of the 1860's, did any congressional law or the District legal code. The gentle, soft-spoken colored woman consequently would be free to impress her view upon fellow board members. What they expected of her was unwittingly revealed by the chairman at an early meeting when, despite the formality generally observed, he turned to her and asked: "Don't you agree, Alice?" Unruffled by the disrespectful form of address, Mrs. Hunter replied equably, "Why no, Harry, I don't." From the first, a majority of the board professed to believe itself bound by arrangements established by the National Park and Planning Commission. When Major General Ulysses S. Grant III, the recently named chairman of the commission, supplied maps prepared in 1929 delineating the approved "Recreation System Plan," the clearly marked designations of specific areas for whites and for Negroes fortified the position of the confirmed segregationists. Mrs. Hunter's objections seconded by the National Park Service representative failed to move the rest of the recreation board. Still, through ignorance or defiance of the board's rules, white and colored people made joint use of several playgrounds.

If those who had fled to the Virginia and Maryland suburbs took racial segregation for granted, some Washingtonians and many newcomers to the wartime capital found the illogicalities of the situation in the District baffling and unreasonable. It naturally drew attention to school grounds and to the Metropolitan Police Boys' Clubs and the newer privately sponsored Washington Boys' Clubs. White and colored children could play scrub ball or cops and robbers together in Rock Creek Park but must separate if they wanted to use the basketball stands in a school yard. The Boys' Clubs were as rigidly segregated as the schools. Started in 1934 by the chief of police who saw a way of reducing juvenile delinquency by giving boys a place of their own to gather for sports and games under rules which the boys themselves would agree to and abide by, the first two clubs had been for white boys only; the colored Boys' Club had been an afterthought of 1936. The Washington Boys' Clubs had no unit for Negroes at all. White men's regulations forbade casual exchanges between the groups. As neither the Metropolitan Police, nor the board of education, nor the recreation board wanted any upheaval, and wartime exigencies complicated matters, critics of the regimented nonintercourse felt obliged to wait. But its unsuitability in a city pledged to winning a war for a free world did not go unnoticed.[7] Thoughtful men, furthermore, were troubled about potential racial conflicts likely to arise in such a setting.

The uneasiness awakened by the rumors about the "Capital Transit Trek" and in June 1943 a race riot in Detroit sharpened memories of the summer of 1919 in Washington and brought into being a Citizens' Committee on Race Relations headed by white ministers, lawyers, educators, and two or three prominent Negroes. Its purpose was to hold a watching brief and, by factual publicity about sources of racial tensions, reduce or eliminate them, whether springing from Negroes' anger at the segregation of Negro blood from white at Red Cross blood donor centers, from job and housing restrictions, or from white people's exasperation at Negroes' tendency to attribute their own inadequacies solely to white exploitation. Although the committee had to measure its achievements in terms of what did not happen rather than what did, its

[7] 56 Stat 261; "Statement concerning Administration of the D.C. Recreation Department since June 1, 1942," 17 Jul 1945 (duplicate); Greater Washington Area Council of the American Veterans Committee, correspondence, 1947-1953, on segregated playgrounds, Am Vet Comee files; interview Mrs. Alice Hunter, 19 Aug 1965.

mere existence was useful. In 1944 the founding of a local Roman Catholic Interracial Council also helped, while the Minorities Workshop looked for vulnerable spots at which to attack racism. At the same time, as police methods in dealing with Negroes were an ever-present bone of contention, the Washington branch of the National Conference of Christians and Jews pursued a plan initiated in 1940 by the director, Verna Linzel, to provide scholarships to local officers to attend police schools offering courses or seminars in "human relations." The plan remained a plan during the war, but, like many another sound idea, would bear fruit only later.[8]

Rather surprisingly, considering the heavy demands the war put on congressional time, in December 1943 the Senate Judiciary Committee decided to conduct hearings on a bill for "Reorganization of the Government of the District of Columbia." Angry complaints about the ineffectiveness and the autocratic nature of the existing governmental system had been multiplying since 1938 and reached such volume in 1941 that some people had counted on a prompt restoration of a popularly elected city council. Over the years colored men had shown a rather passive interest in home rule; those who endorsed it doubtless suspected they would do the cause more harm than good by freely voicing their opinions. One of the few Negroes to testify in 1941, a teacher at the Armstrong High School, had declared the one measure that would better the lot of his people would be a massive, federally financed program of education for Negroes throughout the South; until that occurred, colored Washington would not benefit from local enfranchisement. If other Negroes shared his view, reflecting as it did an apprehensiveness about the effects of the unbroken flow of illiterate, unskilled Southern Negroes into

---

[8] *First Annual Report of the Citizens Committee on Race Relations,* Jul 1944, and *Second Annual Report,* Sep 1945; interviews Mrs. Hunter and Russell Bradley, director, Ntl Conference of Christians and Jews, 19 Aug and 22 Sep 1965.

the city, it probably accounted for the thin Negro attendance at the 1943 hearings.[9]

Senator McCarran opened proceedings by asking for forthright discussion of citizens' attitude toward Negro suffrage, a subject that "people say you cannot talk about." One colored witness deplored "the injection of the race theme into the matter of local voting," but the inseparability of the two evoked outspoken objections to the bill from several people who regarded themselves as friends of both races. The gentle Clinton Howard, great-nephew of a founder of Howard University, dealt the bill for an elected municipal government deadlier blows than any racist delivered, for he argued that intensifying racial antagonisms in wartime Washington made the moment peculiarly unpropitious to talk of enfranchising "the under-privileged, illiterate, proletarian class who would at once possess the balance of power and, in the near future, a majority of the voting citizenry." In this, "the most southern city north of Richmond," where, he contended, the Negro population was permanent, the white largely temporary, "the law of fecundity" would rule. At his annual Christmas party in 1942 for all the children living in the square directly to the east of the Senate Office Building, there were no longer any white children in the houses adjoining his on Northeast B Street, whereas in Schott's Alley at the rear were ninety-nine colored children, all of whom, scrubbed and well-behaved, came to his party. "Now that is Washington tomorrow. . . . The alley will dominate the avenue." By a touch of historical irony, within fifteen years the alley would have turned into a beautifully kept mews lined by small gardens and dwellings occupied chiefly by congressmen, while the marble mass of a new Senate Office Building and a parking lot would dominate the traffic-packed avenue.

Suffrage advocates flared out angrily during the hearings at the worshipers of "The God of Things as They Are."

[9] S Dis Comee, 77C, 1S, Hrgs on S Jt Res 35, pp. 69, 99, 140, 166-69, 212-15, 234-35. See also Green, *Washington, Capital City,* pp. 428-40.

The president of the Federation of Citizens' Associations pointed out that the federal Treasury was now paying less than 10 percent of the cost of running the city and Congress was giving less time than ever to her problems. But members of the Judiciary Committee were clearly swayed more by Howard's testimony; Senator Bilbo would quote phrases from it later when he was campaigning for reelection in Mississippi. In vain a labor leader explained that the well-intentioned Howard simply did not know what he was talking about when he forecast disaster for a self-governing Washington. The committee, sympathetic though its chairman was to the interests of the city's humble people, shelved the bill as untimely. It had aroused disappointingly little public attention; most people in the wartime capital saw no direct connection between local suffrage and defeating the Axis powers. Home rulers would have to wait till the war was over.[10]

How many Negro in-migrants moved to Washington "for the duration" is unknown. The number probably constituted a smaller addition to the colored population of 1940 than the percentage increases in most of America's big industrial cities. But in the District of Columbia, its limited area encircled by suburbs that would not permit the rise of "dark towns," the arrival of every new colored family caused immediate problems and foreshadowed future complications for householders long rooted in the capital. Perhaps wisely, when Dr. Howard Long presented his eight-year study of Negro school children's intelligence and achievement tests to the assistant superintendent, Garnet Wilkinson chose not to reveal its contents. Long reported no discernible loss in intelligence ratings but observed "a general downward trend in the achievement of pupils on all grade levels from year 1935 to 1943," with the sharpest drop after 1937. He attributed some of it to "ineffectual instruction" but added that he placed "a great deal of

[10] S Dis Comee, 78, 1S, Hrgs "Reorganization of the Govt of D.C.," pp. 7, 9, 141, 169-73, 227, 243-56, 287-304, and *passim*.

emphasis on the effects of cultural socio-economic status of the pupils." And the IQ of those born in Georgia, South Carolina, and other parts of the Deep South averaged five points below the 97.31 median of children native to Washington.[11] If Wilkinson's pigeonholing of those findings forestalled a furor in a city already seething with discontents and racial hostilities, his silence did not prevent some colored people from thinking about inadequacies in the "separate but equal" school system. Too many colored Washingtonians trained in the local schools and now employed in war agencies were finding that they could seldom compete on equal terms with their white associates.

Dismissing inferior native intelligence as an explanation still left the questioner with only three possible reasons for the Negro's relatively poor showing. The first was of course white prejudice that refused to recognize colored capability or which put the Negro employee on the defensive and thereby undermined his needed confidence. The second was gaps or superficialities in Negro education. The limited vocabulary which the colored typist too often exhibited and the faulty spelling and punctuation about which the *Tribune* had complained in 1933 suggested shortcomings in schooling. That half as many Negro boys as girls were enrolled in the colored high schools indicated another serious weakness. Furthermore, how could the graduate of the Howard University School of Engineering and Applied Sciences offer the educational qualifications that would open to him a place in any of the scientific research units under the aegis of the Office of Scientific Research and Development? If not yet clearly manifest to the ambitious colored man, the meagerness of training in any scientific field except medicine and biology would become increasingly evident in the postwar era. The third explanation was the Negro's childhood and later environment of intellectual isolation

[11] Howard A. Long, "Intelligence and Achievement of Colored Pupils in the Public Schools of the District of Columbia," Parts II and III (mimeo, 1948).

from the white world into which the Negro white-collar worker was now plunging; that impoverished background was a scarcely less severe handicap in the armed services. Any or all of those factors might obtain, but the analytically minded person saw that something was very much amiss. If, as he had supposed, Washington's separate colored schools were the best in the United States, their very separateness prevented their supplying what life in a truly open society required.

Such reflections may have helped to undercut the disdainful sense of superiority long dominating the attitudes of the city's colored cave dwellers. At Howard University, where for forty years undergraduates drawn from old Washington families had kept at arm's length the heavy-featured black without social pedigree, a new cordiality began to penetrate lecture and seminar rooms. It appeared to be less an expression of an aggressive racial solidarity than a willingness to weigh human rather than class or color values. In the eyes of people anxious to foster an all-inclusive community consciousness in Washington, the change augured well for the future.

Slight as the Negro advance seemed to colored people, it looked excessive to whites who considered segregation a natural arrangement. The most moderate of them believed social innovations were proceeding too rapidly; extremists wanted to revert to the pattern of the 1920's. In their opinion the unrest in the city was due not to racial injustice but to unwholesome pampering of Negro aspirations and the promotion of colored people to positions for which they were not qualified. Before D Day white consensus ran that further change, whether directed to a restoration of the past or to building a new social order, would have to be postponed. But by the autumn of 1944, as victories in overseas theatres indicated an early end of the war, archconservatives began to lay careful plans for peacetime. Covert hostility to Negroes increased, while worried liberals strove to contain it. Cleavages within the community deepened accordingly. Every important question touching upon Washington's future took on racial overtones—housing, recreation, police procedures, municipal government, private employment, and public education. In some degree, it is true, race had entered into these problems for eighty-odd years. What gave the situation a different look now was a new alignment of opposing forces. From 1879 to 1929 colored people and a gradually diminishing array of white altruists had stood side by side against the rest of the city. For the next fourteen or fifteen years a modest albeit steady shift in white opinion had strengthened the pro-Negro ranks. Now an uncounted but unquestionably greatly enlarged body of people drawn from every walk of life was preparing to confront the old guard and timid, vascillating mugwumps.

For several months fresh anxieties awakened by the Battle of the Bulge, grief over President Roosevelt's death in April 1945, and uneasiness about how Harry S. Truman would carry his new responsibilities diverted Washingtonians' thoughts from District controversies. And rejoicing over V-E Day lightened the skys in May. But two months before V-J Day an announcement of the recreation board jerked District citizens back to awareness of conflicts at home. On June 12 the board formally adopted a byelaw which nailed down the segregationist policy long endorsed by a majority of members. Ostensibly the matter had come to a head when the District playground director complained that she and her staff could not handle the racially mixed groups that were using various public recreation centers with or without official sanction. Henceforward, the board decreed, all facilities under its control were to be divided into two mutually exclusive categories, those for whites and those for colored; only white persons could obtain permits for use of the former, only Negroes permits for the latter.

The indignation with which many white people, as well

as Negroes, greeted the edict probably startled its authors. While individuals wrote angry protests, a racially mixed Committee against Segregation in Recreation representing twelve civic groups, nine labor organizations, and four churches demanded and got a public hearing before the board of education, inasmuch as the dual school system had been used to justify segregation at the community centers and hence in other recreation areas. Lawyers exposed the flimsy legal basis for the new policy, political scientists pointed to its damaging effects on American foreign relations, Civic Association leaders explained its inequities, and the spokesman for the 10,000 members of the local United Federal Workers of America, CIO, declared that the Jim Crow order would cripple their recreational programs. One of the most unanswerable protests came from an army lieutenant colonel:

> For the past two years we and our children have been playing tennis on the courts in Georgetown [Rose Park Playground]. Under the supervision of the most able and agreeable Negro playground superintendent, we have taken our turns with our neighbors, some Negroes and some white.
>
> Now we can no longer use these courts. . . . I do not know how to answer the questions of my children when they say they want to go over to the tennis courts. Shall I tell them that the Government has said we may not share the facilities with Negroes? They won't believe it, because they know that the Negro children with whom they frequently play welcome them. They ride the buses, go to the movies and to concerts in the company of Negroes. They have been told by their parents and teachers and Government that this frightful war is necessary in order to assure freedom, the equality of men— that their Negro and Chinese brothers have been fighting and dying bravely for the cause of humanity. They have been told that they should judge people not by pigmenta-

271

tion but by qualities of character, honesty, kindness, ability.

How can we explain to these children that they must not enter the playground with Negroes, even if the colored children invite them? How can you explain your position to me? Some of my best assistants in the Army are Negroes. We eat in the same Government cafeterias, ride the same streetcars, enjoy the same entertainments. . . .

At the very moment when the peace of the world depends on emphasizing the brotherhood of man, we would . . . exalt the foundation of fascism, racial intolerance.

If the Nation's capital permits segregation in recreation, I say we have fought this war in vain.[12]

On V-J Day several hundred citizens interrupted their celebration of the end of the war against fascism abroad to stage a second mass protest against the recreation board's brand of fascism at home. But the board ruling stood. For antisegregationists the defeat brought one wry comfort: the rising tide of anger among people who until then had not committed themselves to the fight. And although individuals would play a progressively lesser role than organizations, every fighter would be needed as the city turned to long-range peacetime problems. The Board of Trade and the real estate board, with its representatives from twenty-five banks, insurance and title companies, and building and loan associations, had already defined their policy of tightening racial segregation and controlling the city's pattern of growth by every financial and political means at their command. Their adversaries covered a far broader spectrum: alongside all colored people, a strangely assorted aggregation of whites, some wealthy individuals, a few small businessmen, CIO officials and wage earners, members of organizations such as the Urban League and the National Conference

12 Citizens Committee against Segregation in Recreation, Presentations to Bd/Ed, 17 July 1945; interview Mrs. Hunter.

of Christians and Jews, a dozen newspapermen reporting on city affairs, social workers, and a heavy sprinkling of the city's ministers and rabbis. To imagine that such a heterogeneous group united only by belief in a moral principle could successfully challenge powerfully entrenched right-wingers and people reluctant to risk any nonconformity to a familar "norm" required an act of faith.

CHAPTER XII

THE LEGAL BATTLE

FOR WASHINGTON, 1946–1954

World War II had put American Negroes in a less precarious position than they had ever held before, chiefly because white men who served with them overseas and at home had seen at close quarters for the first time what discrimination meant and had come to respect its victims. The planned March on Washington in 1941 had shown colored people how much power they possessed when they acted as a body, and in 1945 the creation of the United Nations, with a charter pledging members to recognize the rights of all races, foreshadowed the ever-increasing influence the dark-skinned peoples of the earth would exercise in international affairs. America's political leaders after World War I had soon dismissed race relations at home and abroad as a matter of minor importance. Now astute men realized that they dare not again take white domination of the world for granted or strive with impunity to maintain it.

Yet in the District of Columbia reaction had already set in. The mounting racism which had alarmed anti-segregationists as early as 1943 looked formidable at the end of 1945. Destined to become the most fundamental problem confronting the city during the next eight years, the conflict anticipated by half a decade the turmoil that engulfed the rest of the country in the late 1950's. Perceptive Americans nevertheless saw before the end of the 1940's that what happened to race relations in the capital must in time affect every community in the United States. The earlier assumption of many of Washington's temporary

274

residents that here was a local feud that need not concern them would fade rapidly after 1948. Ultimately the contest was to be settled in the courts and in the halls of Congress. Initially the arena was the offices of District administrators, of the National Capital Park and Planning Commission, and of the big corporations that controlled most of the city's private enterprise.

Although the civil rights of an American minority were always the central issue, the struggle in Washington took place in six fairly distinct areas, all of them at first in the public domain, most of them later directly involving private interests as well. And because a voice in the management of the city's affairs was important to people who wanted to change the *status quo,* the question of home rule cropped up periodically. Whether at any given moment the particular conflict commanding foremost public attention was housing, employment, welfare and police procedures, recreation, biracial patronage of restaurants and places of public amusement, or the dual school system, a victory, a defeat, or a stalemate in one realm affected the fight in every other. Campaigns, however, did not proceed on every front at once. The legal thickets were too thorny and experienced leaders as yet too few to hack through the obstructions in more than one or two fields at a time. Indeed, until a specific new threat to Negro housing arose in 1947, a good many white recruits to the antisegregation cause thought the battlefield lay almost entirely within the confines of the public playgrounds and the privately owned halls used for athletic meets.

Various imponderables cluttering the stage delayed action at the opening of the postwar drama. Federal demobilization officials had estimated at the end of October 1945 that 8 million Americans would be out of work in 1946 when troops returned from overseas received their discharges and an anticipated business recession followed on the heels of cutbacks in industrial production. Reductions in the work force of government agencies, already taking effect in

Washington, would aggravate unemployment in the months ahead. The huge national war debt was likely to heighten congressional reluctance to vote large appropriations for the capital. With the expiration of tire and gasoline rationing, the flight of well-to-do white families to the suburbs would resume, leaving District budget experts fearful lest it eventually cripple the city whose income derived chiefly from real estate taxes on privately owned office buildings and residential property. Nearly half the land within the District's limits was tax exempt because it was owned by the United States or foreign governments, by the District itself, or by eleemosynary and educational institutions. If prosperous whites were to move en masse to nearby Maryland and Virginia, abandoning Washington to impecunious colored people, where was the money to come from to maintain public services? Without money, slum clearance, highway construction, new school buildings, and a host of other needed improvements would have to go by the boards. Simultaneously business would shrink severely. Visions of such disasters fortified the determination of white supremacists to hold the color line. Inasmuch as racists as extreme as Senator Theodore Bilbo of Mississippi now dominated the District committees in Congress, some support for that position would come from the Hill. And as the White House had failed to back up the Fair Employment Practices Committee in its showdown with the Capital Transit Company, the FEPC's power had evaporated.

Irrespective of ideas about the rightful place of colored people in the scheme of things, everyone interested in Washington's well-being agreed that prompt action was essential to redeem the city from blight. In August 1946 Congress passed a long-delayed District "Redevelopment Act of 1945," creating a five-member Redevelopment Land Agency but instructing the National Capital Park and Planning Commission to prepare a "land-use" plan to guide the rebuilding of Washington's slum-ridden areas, to locate new highways, parks, and playgrounds, and to specify the sites for new public buildings. The program briefly outlined by Major General U. S. Grant III sounded splendid, but until the commission completed elaborate surveys, the general public could know little of the details. And once the plans were announced and approved, execution would take several years.[1]

In the interim, the housing squeeze continued, despite a steady white exodus to the suburbs. Negro newlyweds and young couples with small children were forced to double up with relatives or acquaintances in the city. As real estate brokers and rental agents clung to the rules they had maintained for a quarter century, Negro hopes of deriving solid advantages from urban redevelopment dwindled. At the same time, partly because of multiplying RIFs in government offices and more largely because Congress starved the FEPC out of existence by denying it funds, Negroes were having utmost difficulty in getting any but menial jobs. Certainly the overall record for 1946 was not conducive to optimism. The Greater Washington Area Council of the newly formed American Veterans Committee, AVC for short, was setting up committees to fight all racial discrimination; publicity put out by a new Committee for Racial Democracy in the Nation's Capital had induced the Secretary of Labor to require integrated services of the District Employment Center; the citizen's Committee against Segregation in Recreation had persuaded the Washington *Post* and the *News* to come out against racial bars in the Golden Gloves amatuer boxing matches; the Secretary of the Interior ordered the opening of the tourist camp in East Potomac Park to biracial use; and in December the Council of Social Agencies released a detailed report on the scandalous living conditions which white bias imposed

---

[1] Citizens Comee on Race Relations, *2nd Anl Rpt*, pp. 8-9; Malcolm Ross, *All Manner of Men*, p. 162; Final Report of the NAACP Committee to the Citizens Committee against Segregation in Recreation, 20 May 1948; Committee for Racial Democracy, correspondence and minutes, 1946-1947, in possession of Miss Ida Fox, executive secretary (hereafter cited as CRD files).

on the city's colored residents. That month President Truman appointed a Committee on Civil Rights to draft recommendations, and some ninety-nine influential Americans, with financial backing from the Julius Rosenwald Foundation of Chicago, formed a National Committee on Segregation in the Nation's Capital. But two years after V-J Day the visible progress made by friends of the Negro still looked insignificant.

In the opposing camp confidence ran high. Avowed racists and, more numerous and more influential, men moved by an unemotional conviction that Washington's economy would suffer irreparably from a discarding of decades-old social mores were busily perfecting schemes whereby all colored people would be housed in a geographical ghetto and their isolation reinforced by narrowed job restrictions. Now, while official redevelopment plans were going down on paper, was the time to fix the city's social pattern for generations to come. Tacit endorsement came from stand-patters who persuaded themselves that Negroes would benefit from the arrangement as much as whites. Many of the men who objected to basic change, moreover, were in most respects charming and cultivated individuals with warm friends in Congress and government agencies. The unusually large number of high-ranking army and navy officers in postwar Washington also lent support to the extreme right, and their prestige had never stood higher. Although they avoided openly expressing opinions about District affairs, the archconservatism of the armed services, their unmistakable anti-Negro bias during the war, and the class tradition inbred at West Point and Annapolis tended to push them into the white supremacist fold. Probably the single greatest bulwark of that position was the unawareness of what was at stake that persisted among thousands of lazy-minded white people.

The segregationist triumph looked assured in mid-1947. The *Star* remarked that "the Confederacy, which was never able to capture Washington during the course of that war, now holds it as a helpless pawn." In May the United States Appellate Court for the District of Columbia sustained a lower court in declaring restrictive housing covenants enforceable by law; Judge Henry Edgerton's vigorous dissent to the majority decision in Hurd versus Hodge made a stir in legal circles without changing the outcome. If the casual newspaper reader was startled at Mrs. Hodge's declaration that she would rather live next door to a white convict, "because he is white and I am white," than to a Negro family, "no matter how educated or cultivated," much of the white public shrugged it off as merely an exaggerated expression of a familiar prejudice. More meaningful at the moment to the man on the street was a statement from General Grant in discussing the completed plans for Washington's redevelopment. To the city whose elected municipal officials had enacted two antidiscrimination laws during President Grant's first administration, his grandson announced that the National Capital Park and Planning Commission would see that "the colored population dispossessed by playgrounds, public buildings, parks and schools," was relocated in a remote section "in the rear of Anacostia." In short, a magnificent white metropolis was to rise with the servants quarters at the rear. "Segregation," explained a National Capital Housing Authority official, "is the accepted pattern of the community."

Such pronouncements immediately produced an outraged protest from eminent colored men and quickly obliterated within the Negro community the last vestiges of social distinctions based on degree of color. And when the report of the President's Committee on Civil Rights appeared in October 1947 its recommendations and its rebuke to the nation for the "failure of democracy" in the capital infused fresh courage in fighters for minority rights. To the consternation of the old guard, Congress saw fit to subject the Planning Commission's layout to protracted scrutiny and in January 1948 to refuse to grant the Redevelopment Land

Agency the appropriations necessary to start operations.[2]

Long before this impasse in the urban renewal program developed, home rule advocates and adversaries had known that a popularly elected city government would induce changes in the leopard's spots. In 1945 the Washington *Post* had taken an informal poll of its readers; although the responses were too few to represent citywide opinion, 80 percent of the replies had favored District voting. A year later the Board of Trade sponsored a much-publicized plebiscite. The turnout was puzzlingly small; the results showed 70 percent of the adult participants supporting home rule—a more than 15 percent drop since 1938—and nearly 60 percent of the white high school students and a scant 3 percent of the colored against local self-government. "Opposition to suffrage is on the increase," reported the *Times Herald.* The *Post,* commenting on the corrosive effect of deep-seated social ills, called Washington's disenfranchisement "a poisonous thing." Still in 1946 a group of well-informed citizens dedicated to combating local apathy organized a biracial Washington Home Rule Committee, replacing the by then defunct District Suffrage Association. Members felt encouraged when the House and Senate District committees opened joint hearings in July 1947 on a bill introduced by Congressman James Auchincloss of New Jersey for District governmental reorganization.

The hearings, begun at a time when the real estate board was asserting its domination of the District's future, halted for six months but resumed in February 1948 when the urban renewal program was under fire. The committee listened attentively to expressions of every shade of opinion, even to ideas on the management of the District dog pound. Unlike the testimony presented in 1943, arguments about

---

[2] Clipping file on Housing, 1945-1952, Washingtoniana Room, D.C. Pub Library; Hurd *v* Hodge, 162 F(2d) 233, 26 May 1947; Ntl Comee on Seg, *Rpt,* pp. 39-53, 82-84; and Comee working papers; President's Committee on Civil Rights, *To Secure These Rights,* pp. 87-95, and *passim; Star,* 4 Sep 1946.

the dangers of Negro suffrage were surprisingly few and carefully camouflaged. Protests at a "dual" voting provision that would give local suffrage to temporary nontaxpaying residents drew from the president of Washington's recently formed chapter of Americans for Democratic Action the comment that, whereas once Americans had fought against taxation without representation, now the conflict appeared to be over representation without taxation. Witnesses pointed out that a second poll conducted by the Washington *Post* that winter had tallied only 70 percent of the respondents interested in local voting.

From the first the joint committee's primary purpose was to design an act that would relieve Congress of the time-consuming chores of running the District; an efficient system responsive to local citizens' wishes was a secondary desideratum. Two years of intensive work on the part of an able committee staff produced a bill that met those specifications: Washington residents, dual voters among them, were to elect a nonvoting delegate to the House and a city council whose general legislation should come under the review of a joint Senate and House committee and be subject to presidential veto; the federal government was to pay the lesser of two amounts, either $15 million or 14 percent of the city's yearly operating costs; with a few relatively minor exceptions, all other powers were to be vested in the twelve-man council, four members chosen at large and two from each of the four geographical divisions of the city. The wishes of the bulk of local citizens would thus be paramount. Approved by eight of the fourteen men on the House District Committee, the bill reached the floor of the House in mid-May 1948.

For the first time in seventy years the lower body of Congress undertook to pass upon a revision of the Organic Act of 1878. The moment the debate opened, Representative Oren Harris of Arkansas demanded that the entire ninety-page document be read out word for word. Hour after hour the intoning voice of the clerk droned in the ears of congress-

281

men oppressed by the volume of legislation awaiting action before adjournment. At the end of two days the filibuster technique accomplished its purpose. Impatient members shelved the bill. One perverse man, representing, Congressman Auchincloss estimated, the views of scarcely 50,000 citizens, had defeated the will of over 300,000 people.[3] For the next seventeen years the House would not again debate a home rule bill.

Throughout the abortive attempt to secure self-government, the delay in starting on urban renewal kept the race issue very much alive in the city. When Congress held up funds, General Grant hastily declared that there had been a serious misunderstanding of the Planning Commission's proposal. More land, it is true, was available for housing on the outer fringes of Southeast Washington than nearer the heart of the city, and razing the rat-ridden, unsanitary little tenements, corner stores, and warehouses in Southwest would open up space near the river front, some of which might well be converted to parks and playgrounds. Some locations near the Mall, moreover, would obviously be suitable sites for new public buildings. But General Grant could not explain away his flat statement about a wholesale transplanting of the displaced colored population to a relatively inaccessible area; nine people out of ten interpreted his words as presenting an official policy of shoving Negroes out of sight and hence out of mind. Objections cropped up also to the new highway layout which projected elevated throughways and many-laned bands of concrete cutting through fine old residential neighborhoods as well as decayed sections of the city. To many Washingtonians, white and colored alike, it looked as though their own comfort was to be sacrificed to the convenience of tourists and

[3] Washington Home Rule Committee files, 1947-1948; H and S Dis Comees, 80C, 2S, Jt Hrgs on "Home Rule and District Reorganization," *passim* and App. 429-45 (hereafter cited as Home Rule Hrgs, 1948); H Rpt 1876, 80C, 2S; interview, George Galloway, comee staff director, 16 Nov 1962; Comee Recommendations on H 6227, 80C, 2S.

suburban commuters. While would-be contractors for new highways, slum clearance, and rebuilding fumed at post-ponements, and disinterested citizens worried lest nothing useful materialize at all, congressional dissatisfaction with the original proposal forced the National Capital Park and Planning Commission to rework its plan.

Prospects of obtaining a nondiscriminatory redevelopment program brightened in May 1948 when the Supreme Court, in a decision of utmost importance, reversed the rulings of the lower courts on the legal enforceability of restrictive housing covenants. One lawyer familiar with the problem later declared that, in interpreting constitutional protections in line with Judge Edgerton's dissent in Hurd versus Hodge in the United States Appellate Court for the District, the justices took the fork in the road that led on to the civil rights decisions of the 1950's and 1960's. Had the Supreme Court chosen the other fork, legal safeguards for minorities would have vanished for a generation or more. Thus the significance of the decrees in Hurd versus Hodge and in the simultaneous Missouri case of Shelley versus Kraemer equaled that of the Dred Scott decision of ninety-one years before. The results were quickly visible: the 1950 census showed that of the 3,887 residential blocks in the city, nonwhite accommodations had spread into 459 more than in 1940, and the number of exclusively white blocks had dropped from 2,041 to 1,956. Most of that change occurred after the decision of May 1948.

When the Planning Commission's revised version of urban renewal appeared in 1949, it further quieted some fears, inasmuch as it included provisions for low-cost housing in Southwest Washington and stressed human as well as monetary values. The expiration of General Grant's term as commission chairman at the same time removed a hazard. Still the governmental machinery ground slowly. Two years later, demolition of perhaps a third of the slum dwellings stretching from South Capitol Street westward toward Fort McNair and beyond to the Department of Agriculture buildings near the Mall sharpened public realization of the plight of the dispossessed. With the termination of rent controls in mid-1951, living quarters within their means became scarcer month by month. As rebuilding in Southwest had not yet started, doubling up in existing colored neighborhoods accelerated, some of it occurring across the Anacostia, more of it in the black crescent reaching from the Navy Yard to Rock Creek in an arc about the central business district. Voluntary adherents to housing covenants, though no longer enforceable in the courts, still severely limited the areas into which Negro families could move, and, quite apart from restrictive agreements, the prices of real estate in Georgetown virtually completed the decoloration of that section. Despite the completion of some public housing developments for colored families, urban renewal seemed to be merely substituting new Negro ghettoes for old.[4]

Much of the dilemma of course sprang from Negroes' economic insecurity. Secretary of Labor Schwellenbach's order to integrate services at the District Employment Center had eased matters a little, but employers rarely accepted a Negro if a white were available. The veteran discharged from the armed services had a better chance than the civilian, especially in finding a slot in the civil service, but until the Korean War began in the summer of 1950, government jobs were far fewer than in 1944 and 1945. Furthermore, if hired, even the college-trained Negro in 1947 had one chance in six compared to the white man of winning a promotion. The openings for young Negroes newly arrived at an age to enter the labor market were, to be sure, better than in 1940, since the CIO unions and the integrated AFL Hotel Service Industry local widened Negro oppor-

---

[4] Shelley *v* Kraemer and Hurd *v* Hodge, 334 U.S. 1, 24, 3 May 1948; Clement E. Vose, *Caucasians Only, The Supreme Court, the NAACP and the Restrictive Covenant Cases*, pp. 187-211; National Association of Intergroup Relations Officials, *Civil Rights in the Nation's Capital, A Report on a Decade of Progress*, pp. 39-43 (hereafter cited as NAIRO *Rpt*, 1959); National Capital Park and Planning Commission, *Washington: Past and Future*, 1950.

tunities. But in 1948 the counselling service of the Urban League succeeded in placing only 156 out of 612 job-seekers, although three-quarters of them were under 29 years of age, and 285 of them had some college training. The bulk of Negro jobs, moreover, still lay in the lowest paid categories —common labor, wholesale delivery truck driving, laundry work, domestic service, and the menial tasks connected with the public utilities. On-the-job training given new employees of such corporations as the Chesapeake & Potomac Telephone Company was never offered colored people. The Capital Transit Company still refused to employ any Negro platform workers.[5]

President Truman, however, after receiving the report of his Committee on Civil Rights, undertook to recapture the initiative he had lost in November 1945 when he or members of his staff refused to uphold the Fair Employment Practices Committee in its final attempt to bring the District transit facilities into line. He made his position abundantly clear in a message to Congress in February 1948 and more emphatically on July 26 in a new executive order on nondiscrimination within the government. Every executive department was to appoint a special officer to supervise compliance with the principles enunciated in the Roosevelt order of 1941, to receive and act upon complaints, and to interpret to employees of his agency the meaning of the regulation. The Civil Service Commission, in turn, was to establish an advisory fair employment board to assemble data on the workings of the order and to report violations or shortcomings to the President. At the same time the President issued an order on Equality of Training and Opportunity in the Armed Services. Some evasions and numerous hitches occurred in carrying out both orders. Civilian officials were wary about choosing a colored person from

---

[5] Ntl Comee on Seg, working papers; D.C. Welfare Dept, "Surveys of Income," 1947 and 1950 (mimeo); NAIRO *Rpt,* pp. 30-32; Bureau of the Census, *Current Population Reports, Labor Force,* Series P-51, No. 1, p. 5 (1947).

among the three candidates with highest civil service ratings, because if the Negro, his rating notwithstanding, proved ill-suited to the job, transferring him or dropping him involved a great deal of red tape and unpleasantness. Yet by 1950 the executive departments in Washington were generally abiding by the new regulation, and the armed services had gone most of the way toward implementing the order to them. They continued to observe it despite Senator McCarthy's virulent charges of communist infiltration of the army and the State Department. The presidentially appointed District commissioners, on the other hand, took no notice whatsoever of the President's instructions. The District government proceeded as before. The battle for Washington was not to be won merely by a message from the White House.[6]

A more effective attack on the local regime and its supporters came from the report prepared under the aegis of the National Committee on Segregation in the Nation's Capital. Founded when the forces of reaction were exhibiting an ever-growing strength, in 1947 the national committee engaged a competent research staff headed by Joseph Lohman of the University of Chicago sociology department to pin down the facts of what Negroes in the capital were up against and to spell out the consequences for all America. Clarence Pickett of Philadelphia, director of the American Friends Service Committee, Marshall Field, millionaire Chicago newspaper owner, Bishop G. Bromley Oxnum of the Methodist Episcopal Church, Hubert Humphrey, mayor of Minneapolis, Walter Reuther of the United Automobile Workers, Eleanor Roosevelt, Washington-born actress Helen Hayes, and half a hundred other notables scattered from California to New York were not to be intimidated by a

---

[6] Ex Orders 9980 and 9981, 26 Jul 1948, 15 *Federal Regulations* 4311 and 4313; Col Campbell C. Johnson, *Fifty Years of Progress of the Armed Services* (reprint from a 1950 series in the Pittsburgh *Courier*).

small, tight-knit group of archconservatives in Washington. Of the committee's ninety-odd members, only three of the thirteen who lived in the District of Columbia were Negroes. It was an impressive array of men and women without any personal ax to grind, intent only on reversing a trend that, left alone, they believed, would fasten a caste system upon the entire country. Over a period of eighteen months the staff collected a mass of irrefutable evidence. The findings, condensed for publication in popular form, covered every phase of the pressures, old and new, which threatened to reduce Negroes in Washington to a servile status from which they could not escape without the help of energetic white people.

Despite the impassioned language of the report and its somewhat oversimplified presentation, a check on its sources forced the serious reader to conclude that here was an essentially truthful summary. Articles in the Pittsburgh *Courier* and the releases of the Committee for Racial Democracy and its successor, the Council for Civil Rights, had set forth the current facts, but when *Segregation in Washington* appeared in print in December 1948, it had special impact. Too painful, too shocking to become table talk in official society, the report repeatedly emphasized that the pattern set in the capital would shape that of every community in the United States. The review of the steady degradation of Negroes from the 1870's on, if not news to colored Washingtonians, dumbfounded many whites and worked upon the conscience of people who would have preferred to forget. Unlike earlier accounts, the survey, E. Franklin Frazier observed, searched out "the dynamics, . . . the reasons and factions responsible for the system." The text pinned the guilt primarily on the Board of Trade, the real estate board, and the Park and Planning Commission.[7] Although the report did not

[7] Ntl Comee on Seg, *Rpt;* Pittsburgh *Courier,* 18 Dec 1948, 1 Jan 1949; CRD files; correspondence of the Council for Civil Rights in the Nation's Capital, 1948-1950, in possession of Ida Fox, exec sec 1948.

kill the local anti-Negro movement outright, it accomplished more in breaking the hard core of racism in Washington than any other one instrumentality.

The conditions described in *Segregation in Washington* in themselves explained why the incidence of crime and juvenile delinquency ran higher in the Negro ghettoes than in the rest of the city. Frustrated, idle blacks hung about the street corners, shot craps, got into the rapidly spreading "numbers racket," beat up wives, begot illegitimate children, assaulted and stole from passers-by, burglarized, and sometimes finished off brawls with manslaughter. The story was the same in other big cities. Boys with nothing better to look forward to than their fathers knew made careers of vandalism before graduating to worse, while girls of fourteen and fifteen bore them babies. As long as lawbreakers, old or young, confined their activities to colored neighborhoods, the press paid little attention to them. But gradually horrified adults discovered that juvenile delinquency was by no means solely a product of the Negro slums. It invaded the white suburbs as well as the city and infected children of well-to-do white families as well as the underprivileged. Car stealing for joy rides went on everywhere. The violence on the streets throughout the city which would later damage Washington's name had not yet reached the crescendo of 1961, but it appeared to be spreading before 1950. Much of the white public, however, was slow to recognize the situation. Police officers dealt with it as they saw fit, too many of them attributing it chiefly to innate Negro depravity.

Active supporters of such organizations as the Washington Urban League and the National Conference of Christians and Jews from 1946 onward watched police methods with growing apprehensiveness. Granting that amorality was distressingly widespread in the bottom layers of the colored population, experienced social workers believed nothing was to be gained by bullying tactics in making arrests and interrogating colored misdemeanants and suspects. Granting also that a larger police force might forestall a good deal of trouble, enlightened criminologists and thoughtful laymen put greater emphasis on better trained officers able to perceive nuances in human behavior and to see that a black skin was not a sure sign of the lawbreaker. In 1950 the NAACP persuaded the District commissioners to hold a hearing at which Negroes presented a bill of particulars against the chief of police; the character of the charges helped win converts to plans for special schooling for policemen. That year the Conference of Christians and Jews with help from the biracial Council of Church Women started a "workshop on human relations" for some of the Metropolitan Police and provided scholarships to send three officers to Michigan State University's police school. Four years later several other organizations were supporting the scheme on a larger scale, and an originally skeptical police chief was acclaiming its utility.

Just as a better-staffed juvenile court obviously would help steer a larger proportion of young delinquents on to a straight course, so Washingtonians saw in the Boys' Clubs and wholesome recreation the means of combating juvenile crime. In 1946 Oliver Cowan, an officer attached to the juvenile division of the police force, started the Junior Police and Citizens' Corps in a notoriously tough precinct. There, under his imaginative tutelage, Negro boys and white together took on the unfamiliar and satisfying role of helping instead of baiting other people, tidying up the neighborhood instead of committing depredations, and arranging competitive sports and games among each other. Not improbably much of the drop in Negro juvenile delinquency between 1951 and 1955 may be attributed to the corps: while the number of Negroes seventeen years old and younger increased by 13 percent in those four years, arrests of colored boys dropped by 3 percent. Successful as the corps was, directors of the Boys' Clubs made no move to follow its example of racial integration. Before 1952 all Boy Scout troops similarly remained segregated.[8]

Meanwhile, with an ever-lengthening list of supporting organizations, the Citizens' Committee against Segregation in Recreation carried on its campaign in the face of repeated defeats. The National Theatre after surviving a law suit and weeks of picketing in 1947 closed its doors to all legitimate stage productions in 1948 rather than accede to the demands of the Actors' Equity that Negroes be admitted to the house; outraged lily-whites thereupon excoriated Negroes for depriving the capital of the pleasures of seeing Broadway plays. Although the Citizens' Committee that year won the fight to open to colored members of the Amateur Athletic Union the boys' boxing matches and track meets held at the privately owned Uline Arena, every plea for biracial use of public playgrounds failed, even when a careful tally counted in an entire week only ten white children using the spacious New York Avenue playground while across the street a thousand Negro girls and five hundred Negro boys at the Dunbar High School had no play space at all. The sight of dark-skinned children peering wistfully through the fence at a well-equipped white playground in their neighborhood disturbed the equanimity of white parents as nothing else could.

In answer to every appeal the recreation board asserted that mandates from the board of education and the National Park and Planning Commission fixed its racial guidelines. But three months after President Truman issued his nondiscrimination order, the school board flatly denied that it was compelling adherence to any special racial policy outside the school system itself. Congressman Arthur G. Klein of New York, inspired by members of the AVC, thereupon asked General Grant to explain whether, and if so why, the planning commission assumed authority to

[8] Interviews, Russell Bradley, ex dir National Conference of Christians and Jews, and Mrs. Alice Hunter, 19 Aug and 17 Sep 1965; Ellis O. Knox, *Democracy and the District of Columbia Schools*, pp. 25-26.

dictate a segregation rule to the recreation board. The chairman's reply was legalistic and evasive. Yet in April 1949, when the Assistant Secretary of the Interior requested the planning commission to remove all racial designations from the maps of its recreation system plan, the commission complied. At that point the Interior Department offered to turn over operation of its public swimming pools and golf courses to the recreation board, provided the board run all its facilities on a nondiscriminatory basis. Copies of the correspondence and of many private appeals went to President Truman.

For weeks the local press daily discussed what the recreation board would or should do, while commentators talked of the oddity of having high-ranking federal officials, ranging from the President of the United States to minor functionaries in the Justice Department, concerning themselves about whether white and colored children could play together on public playgrounds and whether their parents might make joint use of community centers and public school buildings after school hours. Seemingly the recreation board no longer had a legal leg to stand on in insisting on segregation. But the diehards died hard. They rejected the Interior Department's offer. Instead, they announced a policy of "gradualism." As a great concession they opened several tennis courts to Negro players, agreed to let the American Friends Service Committee take charge of supervised recreation for children of both races at two playgrounds during the summer, and reluctantly acquiesced in allowing mixed groups of responsible adults to use school buildings after school hours. That done, the chairman contended that further "study" and "experiment" were necessary before ending segregation in other areas.[9]

[9] Final Rpt NAACP Comee to Citizens' Comee against Seg in Recr, 20 May 1948; Ntl Comee on Seg, working papers; Maj Gen U. S. Grant III to Assoc Dir Ntl Park Service, 31 Aug, and to Arthur G. Klein, 19 Oct 1948, 31 Jan 1949, Klein to Grant, 2 Oct, 23 Nov 1948, 7 Mar 1949, Sec/Int J. A. Krug to Pres Truman, 4 Apr, and enclosure to ltr, Mastin G. White to Asst/Sec/Int C. Girard Davidson, 28 Apr,

The swimming pools were a particularly touchy question. In spite of medical testimony exploding the notion that biracial use would spread infection, a number of white people shied away from the very idea of "mixed" swimming. Because of white hostility, until 1949 Negroes had not tried to use four of the six nonsegregated pools run by the Interior Department, but shortly after the Assistant Secretary reiterated in June 1949 that the large Anacostia pool was open to both races, fifty Negro boys paid the small fee and attempted to enter. The lifeguards employed by the District recreation board refused to admit them, and white bullies chased them off, while the Park Police looked the other way. That evening an angry crowd collected, Negroes and white friends to protest at broken promises, segregationists to protect their own assumed "rights" against intruders. Although the demonstrators confined themselves to name-calling and threats, mounted police dispersed the crowd. The upshot was the closing of the pool for the rest of the summer. Aware that the inattention or indifference of Park Police had permitted the situation to develop, the National Capital Park Service engaged Joseph Lohman in August to conduct a police training course in human relations, while committees of the Jewish Community Council and the American Veterans Committee drafted a series of procedures to follow when the pool reopened. The results showed in 1950. The new Secretary of the Interior, Oscar Chapman, announced that all six pools under his jurisdiction would continue to operate without segregation. No trouble of any kind ensued. While a member of the recreation board growled that white attendance at the pools dropped from the 346,275 of 1948 to about 146,400, he failed to note that much of the summer of 1950 had been

---

Klein to Dis Comr J. R. Young, 27 May 1949, all in CRD files; *Post,* 8 May, 12 Jun 1949; *Star,* 27 Jul 1950; Henderson *v* E Street Theater Corporation, Mun Crt App, D.C., 76 *Washington Law Reporter,* 1165, 4 Nov 1948.

cool and rainy. The recreation board kept its two pools for whites only.[10]

The playground controversy meanwhile dragged on. At the end of the summer of 1949 the Community Relations Group of the American Friends Service Committee published a full report of its experiences in managing integrated programs at Rose Park in Georgetown and the Garfield playground in Southeast Washington. Wherever the directors had small children to handle, friction had been minimal; with young teenagers some difficulties had arisen but not insuperable ones; but games between white and colored teams made up of seventeen-year-olds and older had often turned into "grudge games" and had to be dropped. "Catch 'em young" was the principal lesson the summer taught.

That autumn a Negro parent lost a suit aimed at forcing the recreation board to let colored children use a playground in Northeast which both whites and Negroes had enjoyed together until the board put a director in charge to keep it "white only." The constantly swelling chorus of protest in 1951 brought about the transfer of two playgrounds to colored use and, more significant, in 1952 the opening of three without any racial restriction. Two of the three, however, had no equipment, no planned program, and no director, so that children there, unable to join in citywide competitions, felt that there was "something wrong with integration." At the third, the playground director was so hostile to the colored children that the Washington *Post* suggested he was trying to sabotage the "experiment." In the three years since the announcement of a policy of gradualism, racial designations had disappeared from 9 of the District's 137 recreation areas. At that rate, one Negro observed, playground desegregation would take forty years.

---

[10] Statement of E. B. Henderson, director physical education for the Colored Schools, 27 Jun 1949; Fellowship of Reconciliation (FOR) and Congress of Racial Equality (CORE), Bulletin of Summer Interracial Workshop, 1949 (mimeo); memo, Asst/Sec/Int Davidson to Sec/Int Krug, 15 Jul 1949, all in Int Dep files; *Post*, 12, 26 Jun, 26 Jul 1949, 10 Sep 1950; *Star*, 14 Jun, 25 Jul 1949.

Of the confusing and frustrating circumstances surrounding the long fight, one of the most exasperating to liberals was the District commissioners' refusal to commit themselves in any way. Instructions from them could have put an end to the resistance of the recreation board at any time. And when President Truman's order of July 1948 appeared, they had ample justification for interpreting nondiscrimination as a federal policy that applied to more than hiring and firing employees. But just as they failed to appoint fair employment officers in District departments, so they chose to ignore pleas from local citizens to carry out the clear intent of the presidential order. Although the makeup of the board of commissioners changed several times between 1946 and 1953, only Commissioner Joseph Donahue openly expressed a personal wish to see segregation curbed in Washington; whether the others preferred the old order remains a matter of inference. The reason for their silence is not far to seek. Whatever their individual convictions about race, none of them lost sight of the fact that congressional committees held the District's purse strings, and Southerners exercised control of the House District Committee and the Subcommittee on District Appropriations. In 1951 the head of Gallinger Hospital agreed to accept some Negro interns, but otherwise, except for a few half-hearted gestures from the chief of police and the attempt of the far-sighted fire department chief to integrate the fire companies—an order at which the firemen's union balked and which Congressman Davis of Georgia succeeded in blocking—the District government stood pat. Not until President Eisenhower prodded his appointees in November 1953 did the commissioners respond by instructing their subordinates to observe the presidential order.

Still the interracial workshops started by several citizens' organizations were gradually spreading the gospel of cooperation and, in the process, deepening the mutual respect white and colored participants were developing for each other. The *Post*, by 1952 the city's most widely read paper, became increasingly critical of the recreation board's obduracy, and, although the *Afro-American* and the *Courier* accused the *Star* of always straddling on all racial issues lest it offend the real estate interests, the *Star's* news columns conveyed less assurance than once they had that the "best people" wanted to preserve segregation. In the spring of 1953 the recreation board itself chose by a four to one vote to permit biracial use of the swimming pool at Rosedale playground. As events moved rapidly that year toward desegregation in other realms, the board went further: it authorized for all playground employees inservice training in handling racially mixed groups. The finale of this about-face occurred on May 17, 1954.[11]

In the battle to end the exclusion of Negroes from restaurants and other places of public accommodation, the federal executive departments had made the first moves, initially in the government cafeterias and then at National Airport. Located on the Virginia side of the Potomac, the airport came under the jurisdiction of the civil aeronautics administrator. The concessionaire of the airport restaurant from its beginning in the 1930's had refused to serve colored people in the dining room and cocktail lounge; when challenged by two lawsuits in early 1948, he defended his stand on the grounds that a Virginia statute tied his hands. That act, born of fantastic circumstances, had been passed in 1926. The preceding autumn of 1925, when the North Carolina College glee club was to give a concert at Hampton Institute, the president of Hampton had courteously extended invitations to white people in the vicinity to attend, but some of the white guests on arrival had been incensed at finding that they would have to sit

[11] Am Friends Service Comee, Rpts, Community Relations Program, nos 1-23, 1949-1954 (mimeo, hereafter cited as AFSC Rpts Comty Rel Pg); *Post*, 31 Aug 1949, 11 Oct 1950, 22 Sep 1952, 15 Apr 53; Rpts, Wshg Intrcl Workshop, 1 Nov 1951, and Summer Intrcl Workshop, Jul 1952 (mimeos); ltrs, briefs in two suits against Int Dep, and AVC memos, 1949-1952, AVC counsel's files.

alongside Hampton students and their friends. Convinced that here was proof of a "pernicious" spirit of racial equality emanating from the Institute, the assemblyman from the district had introduced at the next session of the state legislature and pushed through a law making it a criminal offense to intermingle whites and Negroes in the seating in any public hall in Virginia. For sixteen years, in the absence of formal federal action, that law had been in force at the airport. On December 27, 1948, the civil aeronautics administrator, backed unobtrusively by the Department of Justice, issued an order to desegregate the airport facilities. The concessionaire sued, but in mid-January the federal judge for the Virginia district ruled that on federal property federal regulations superseded state laws.

Heartening to civil rights fighters as the airport decision was, it did not affect privately owned restaurants in Washington. The campaign for those started after the report of the National Committee on Segregation drew attention to the "lost" antidiscrimination laws of 1872 and 1873. In the spring of 1949 sixty-one civic, religious, labor, and charitable organizations set up a biracial Coordinating Committee for Enforcement of the District Antidiscrimination Laws.[12] In September attorneys of the Washington Lawyers Guild submitted to the District commissioners the results of extensive research showing that the two territorial acts had never been repealed or declared unconstitutional and were therefore still valid. After reviewing the findings, the corporation counsel agreed. As the Washington Restaurant Association wanted a court ruling, the District commissioners undertook to institute a test suit against the John R. Thompson Restaurant Company, owner of a cafeteria at E and 14th streets. Lawyers representing the

[12] Richmond *Times-Dispatch*, 26 Jan 1926; Pittsburgh *Courier*, 8 Jan 1949; Air Terminal Service, Inc., v Rentzel, 81 F. Supp 611, D.C., E.D. Va, Alex Div, 1949.

American Veterans Committee and other organizations as friends of the court conducted most of the legal research, while members of the citizens' Committee for Enforcement assembled statistics on how many out of ninety-nine restaurants in downtown Washington denied service to well-behaved colored or racially mixed groups, how many accepted them, and in either case what the proprietors' reasons were and how white patrons reacted. Under the guidance of Annie Stein, an energetic young white woman, and inspired further by nonogenarian Mary Church Terrell, the surveying groups, each composed of three or four people, were at pains never to argue with waitresses or managers and left quietly if they were rebuffed. They concluded that few white people had objections to the admission of colored patrons, and that most owners of the sixty-nine places that refused were merely fearful of losing business to competitors; were the courts to rule the antidiscrimination acts in force, customers and proprietors would accept the order without boggling over it.

In July 1950 Municipal Judge Frank Myers declared the 1872 and 1873 territorial acts repealed "by implication" and quashed the case against the John R. Thompson Company. Although the Municipal Court of Appeals reversed Judge Myers' decision, the District commissioners announced they would not act on the ruling until further appeals settled the case beyond any question. During the next two years, however, orderly sit-ins accomplished a good deal. The Hecht Company opened its lunchroom to Negroes in November 1951, other department and drugstores along lower 7th Street a few months later. About the same time, sale of the National Theatre brought a change there also: the theatre reopened to Broadway productions staged before racially mixed audiences. But when the Thompson Restaurant case reached the United States Court of Appeals, a five to four verdict overrode the earlier reversal. Fortunately the United States Supreme Court agreed to review the case. In June 1953 the justices unanimously affirmed the validity of the eighty-year-old Equal Service Acts.

Probably relatively few white people fully understood why the decision mattered so much to Negroes except insofar as it recognized a principle of justice. What whites failed to take into account were the bodily discomforts to which racial barriers had subjected colored citizens. For fifty years any Negro who worked downtown, out of reach of a government cafeteria, had to travel several miles to get a bite of lunch. And as long as eating places excluded Negroes, rest rooms which colored people could use were few and far between. For that reason, colored parents had rarely taken their children to shop in the big well-supplied downtown stores. Now with the ban lifted, merchants found their clientele expanding and, as the Coordinating Committee had foreseen, white customers quietly acquiescing in the new scheme of things.[13]

Every advance counted, but knowledgeable Washingtonians from 1950 onward realized that as long as the dual school system endured, rapport between the races could not achieve sturdy growth. That realization had been slow to mature even among Negroes whose faith in Washington's colored schools had been shaken during the war. In the spring of 1946 the Washington edition of the Pittsburgh *Courier* had carried a forthright exposition of the weaknesses of the colored schools and declared the dual system the root of the trouble. A year later an article in the *Journal of Negro Education* presented facts and figures describing "the breakdown of the separate but equal con-

---

[13] *Times Herald,* 22 Feb 1950; *Post,* 1 Mar, 12 Jul, 1, 3 Sep 1950; *Star,* 12 Jul, 20 Aug, 1, 3 Sep 1950; D.C. *v* John R. Thompson Company, Inc., Criminal No. 99150, Mun Crt, D.C., 10 Jul 1950; *Afro-American,* 27 Nov 1951, 28 Jan, 19 Feb, 23 Aug 1952; Case No. 987, AVC, *amicus curiae* brief, Mun Crt App; D.C. *v* Thompson, 81 At (2d) 249-65, 24 May 1951; AVC et al, *amici curiae* brief, 30 Jun 1951; Thompson *v* D.C., 92 U.S. App. D.C., 203 F(2d), 579, 593, 22 Jan 1953; D.C. *v* Thompson, 346 U.S. 100, 10 Jun 1953.

cept" in Washington. Based on the proportion o
school population to the Negro, the division of
by Congress had become increasingly inequitab'
because enrollments in the white public schools ..
steadily, whereas the colored had risen. (See Table VI.,
Hence by 1947 the annual per pupil expenditure for Negro
children was $120.52 compared to $160.21 for white. The
white junior high schools had 1,851 unused spaces; the
colored had to accommodate 2,234 more pupils than the
buildings were intended for. In the senior high schools
the disparity was only slightly less pronounced. Classes in
the white elementary schools averaged 34.5 pupils to a
teacher, in the colored 38.8. Since 1942 a number of white
and colored teachers had worked together to better elementary education, but apart from heightening their respect
for each other, they had made little headway. In May 1947
the board of education transferred two white elementary
school buildings to the colored division, approved the hiring
of seven additional Negro teachers, and later in the year
turned over four more white school buildings to Negro use.
The maneuvering managed only to slow the rapidly accelerating deterioration visible throughout the colored school
system.

The consequences were predictable: parental appeals to
the board of education to allow colored children to attend
partly empty white schools in their neighborhood and,
when those petitions failed, lawsuits based on the manifest
violation of the congressional acts of the 1860's guaranteeing
Negroes educational privileges equal to whites. But the outcome of a fight in the courts was highly doubtful in a
community where, with three exceptions, no one had challenged the existing system since J. Sella Martin in 1869
and three colored men in 1881 and 1882 had enrolled their
children in white schools. In 1910 District judges had ruled
that a child with a sixteenth-part Negro blood could not
attend a white school; in the last year of World War II

two other adverse verdicts had prevented a white student from taking courses in the colored vocational high school and a Negro pupil from entering a white junior high school. Although the Pittsburgh *Courier,* the *Afro-American,* and several far-sighted Negro leaders were urging legal action in 1946, parents hesitated. Not until the President's Committee on Civil Rights spoke out in October 1947 did litigation appear to have any chance of success, and even then an attack upon anything beyond the abuses in particular instances looked precarious.

In the autumn of 1947, when the father of Marguerite Carr sued the superintendent of schools for denying Marguerite a transfer from the grossly overcrowded Browne Junior High School to the thinly attended white school nearby, the brief focused mainly on the glaring inequality of accommodations; if remedies were unobtainable under segregation, mixed schooling must replace it. A second suit filed shortly afterward by the PTA of the colored school took the same line. Because the board of education hastily contrived to find space in an abandoned building for the overflow from Browne, in 1948 the court declared the plaintiffs' pleas satisfied. As numberless inequalities remained, particularly in the teacher-pupil ratios, the complainants chose to appeal. Still most of the organizations supporting the protests directed their campaigns not at abolition of the dual system but at persuading the board of education to turn over partly empty white schools to Negro use, to build new colored schoolhouses, and to engage about 320 additional colored teachers. Although for fiscal year 1949 Congress voted a bigger appropriation for buildings and equipment than in any year since 1931-1932, the total was still far too small and, in any case, did nothing to relieve the acute shortage of colored teachers. At this stage of the battle, in the opinion of an investigator for the National Committee on Segregation, Negro school officials maintained a self-protective detachment from the controversy whenever it veered toward any suggestion of integration. Instructions from the Roman Catholic hierarchy in 1949 to desegrate Washington's parochial schools aroused astonishingly little comment in the city.[14]

Meanwhile, in order to get a clearer picture of the situation, the congressional subcommittees on appropriations requested a team of experts headed by George D. Strayer of Columbia University to undertake a survey of the condition of the public schools of the District of Columbia. Publication of the Strayer report in early 1949 drove home to formerly oblivious whites many unpalatable facts. The most revealing dealt with the quality of schooling provided at every level in both the white and the colored divisions. The experts found numerous things wrong with the white schools, but the colored, though as good as those in other cities with segregated systems, were so far inferior to the white that the Strayer group recommended for a start allotting to the former three quarters of the entire budget for physical plants. Although the investigators did not accept without qualification the interpretation that the head of the colored school research unit had put upon the IQ and achievement tests he had tabulated before and during the war, they observed the downward trend in colored children's achievements and the drag created by Southern in-migrants. Counseling service, introduced in 1943, began with the seventh grade and was intended to give junior high school pupils guidance in their school work and help those with personality troubles. But the Strayer team considered the number of counselors too few and their consultations therefore too hurried to be of any real value; whereas the average in the white schools was 390 pupils for each counselor, in the colored schools, where

[14] Pittsburgh *Courier*, 16 Feb, 4 May 1946; Mary A. Morton, "The Education of Negroes in the District of Columbia," *Journal of Negro Education*, XVI, 325-39; Wall *v* Oyster, 1910, 36 App D.C. 50; Pres. Comee, *To Secure These Rights*, pp. 90-91; Ntl Comee on Seg, working papers; *Post*, 8 Jun, 31 Oct, 12 Nov 1947.

guidance was most needed, the ratio was 690 to 1. The miracle lay in the colored schools' making as good a showing as they did.

The matter-of-factness and lack of moralizing of the report added to its impact on white readers. Tax-conscious citizens, moreover, got a new understanding of the monetary costs of supporting a dual system. And the Strayer data verified a central thesis of the National Committee on Segregation, that the separate schools underlay the city's entire social structure. They formed the basis upon which the local universities built in maintaining racial bars. In 1948 only Catholic University had opened all its schools to Negroes. George Washington, Georgetown, the under-graduate college of American University, the National University law and medical schools, all refused admission to colored students, and, although Howard University did not exclude whites, only special circumstances occasionally led a white student to enroll there. Thus day by day association between young people of the two races never occurred.[15]

As a mountain of documentary evidence buried the myth that the separate school systems were or could be equal, the old legal defenses for segregation crumbled. Try as one might, nobody even remotely concerned with education in the city of 1950 could altogether avoid examining the possibility of eventual integration. Blandly putting the cart before the horse, the acting superintendent of schools had stated earlier that so drastic a step would have to wait until Negroes were sufficiently "advanced" to justify it. Judge Henry Edgerton lashed out at that credo in 1950 when the United States Court of Appeals reviewed the decisions in the Carr and the Browne Junior High School

[15] *The Report of a Survey of the Public Schools of the District of Columbia, George D. Strayer, Director;* Knox, *Democracy and the D.C. Schools,* pp. 12-13; brief for plaintiffs, Carr *v* Corning, and Browne Jr. High School PTA *v* Magdeburger, Mun Crt, D.C., Apr 1948; Carr *v* Corning and Browne Jr. High School PTA *v* Magdeburger, 14 Feb 1950, 86 U.S. App. D.C., 173, 191-92.

PTA cases. "Independent of objective differences between white and colored schooling," declared Judge Edgerton, "school segregation means discrimination against Negroes for two distinct reasons. (1) By preventing a dominant majority and a depressed minority from learning each other's ways, school segregation inflicts a greater economic and social handicap on the minority than on the majority. It aggravates the disadvantages of Negroes and helps to preserve their subordinate status. (2) School segregation is humiliating to Negroes. . . . Both whites and Negroes know that enforced segregation in schools exists because the people who impose it consider colored children unfit to associate with white children." As the defendants had argued that congressional acts of the 1860's made segregated schooling mandatory in the District and, until Congress itself rewrote the laws, change was legally impossible, Judge Edgerton concluded: "In my opinion the Constitution does not permit the courts to wait for Congress to act." His, however, was still a dissenting voice. Its chief effect for the time being was to spur the board of education on to more vigorous efforts to meet the needs of the separate colored schools and, despite the transfer of the big Central High School, when little improvement was discernible seven months later, to inspire Negro parents again to sue for redress.

Neither course of action produced immediate rewards. The District court dismissed the new suit, Bolling versus Sharpe, in April 1951 on the grounds that the law provided no relief for the plaintiffs. While the complainants prepared to appeal, the school board continued to flounder about helplessly seeking solutions for troubles that half measures could not correct. Every newspaper in the city was discussing school problems almost daily. Curiously enough, no paper made a point of the desegregation of Washington's Roman Catholic parochial schools the year before. The *Post*, by 1951 openly espousing integration, struck out at the District judges for appointing to the board of education persons unresponsive to local public opinion; conservative judges selected conservative citizens for their conservatism, not for their wisdom or ability to keep abreast of the community's needs. In reply, a municipal judge wailed over the paucity of public-spirited residents willing to accept so thankless an assignment. But according to one ardent integrationist, any Negro appointee who displayed any readiness to fight for a new approach to old problems never received a second appointment.

All school board members, however, were in an uncomfortable position. "They were living in a goldfish bowl," wrote one of the staff of the American Friends Service Committee. "Since community opinion was sharply divided, they could take no step without serious criticism. They were guided by the opinion of the corporation counsel that they were operating under a mandate from Congress to operate a dual school system, yet there was no escape from the problems of operating such a system." Questions arose in legal circles about the correctness of the corporation counsel's interpretation, but the board of education, like the District commissioners, believed in playing safe: appropriations after all came from the Hill. While the board temporized, Assistant Superintendent Carl Hansen prepared a "Handbook on Intergroup Education," which forward-looking organizations in the city eventually persuaded the board to adopt; informing under any circumstances, it should be invaluable if and when desegregation occurred.

In the interim matters were going from bad to worse in the colored schools. Enrollments there in 1950 for the first time had exceeded those in the white division, and the disproportion was still mounting. At the Payne school conditions had become so intolerable that in December 1951 pupils staged a four-day walkout. As the transfer of ten additional buildings to the Negro division failed to stem the citywide crisis, the superintendent of schools suggested shifting surplus white teachers with tenure to the understaffed Negro schools. President Walter Hager of the white teachers college had already proposed a merger with Miner College, and several other indications pointed to white teachers' willingness to move into Negro classrooms. Colored people, on the contrary, objected; the scheme would do Negro candidates for teaching posts out of jobs unless the interchange were two way. The board of education dared not sanction such an arrangement: it would be tantamount to acknowledging that the sacrosanct principle of segregation was neither sacred nor useful. The decision about what the law permitted would have to come from the United States Court of Appeals in its expected review of the Bolling versus Sharpe case. And the *Star* reminded its readers that, despite the clamor of a highly vocal minority, a great many Washingtonians thought school desegregation would be a disaster.[16]

Throughout the protracted and often heated discussion of whither public education in Washington, few people followed developments in a struggle launched by Negro parents with AVC aid to enter their deaf children in the Kendall Green school for deaf-mutes. Since 1857, when Congress chartered the quasi-public institution, federal subsidies had enabled white deaf-mutes to attend the school where Edward Gallaudet had introduced sign language in teaching. For the District's colored deaf, on the other hand, under an eighty-year-old plan originated by the Secretary of the Interior, the government paid the tuition at a Maryland or a Pennsylvania institution. Partly because sending children so far from home meant added expense and inconvenience for parents and partly because the Kendall Green school offered better instruction, Negroes rebelled in 1950. When petitions to the Federal Security Agency and the board of education netted them nothing, several colored parents sued. In deciding the case, District Judge

[16] *Post,* 3 Sep 1950, 2 Jan 1951, 18, 26 Jan, 20, 28 Feb, 28 Aug, 15, 23 Sep, 31 Oct 1952; *Star,* 13 Oct, 8 Dec 1951, 18, 22 Jan, 1 Jun 1952; *Afro-American,* 5, 19, 26 Feb, 27 May 1952; AFSC Rpt Comty Rel Pg, 1 Mar 1952; NAIRO *Rpt,* 1959, p. 68.

David Pine relied upon a Supreme Court ruling of 1938 declaring that states could not meet their constitutional obligations by shipping students to schools beyond the state borders. The analogy was exact. In June 1952 Judge Pine ordered the admission of Negro deaf children in the District to the local institution. The president and trustees had no objection, but the contract drawn up that summer stipulated, at the insistence of the corporation counsel, that the colored children were to be taught in segregated classes. The arrangement failed to satisfy Negro parents and caused the school's administrators considerable trouble. When Kenneth Miller's mother complained that as a day pupil he was receiving only six hours of instruction five days a week, and was barred from vocational training, physical education, and recreational activities, President Elsted could only reply that he was bound by the terms of the contract. As he explained later to a AVC representative, the Kendall Green staff found the colored pupils six or seven grades behind their age level, and inasmuch as vocational training began in the seventh grade, they were not yet able to benefit from that program. Like public school pupils, Negro deaf children had to wait for a decision to desegregate all public education in the District of Columbia.[17]

Welcome or not, belief in the inevitability of school integration in the not-too-distant future had spread through much of Washington by the autumn of 1952. Exactly when and how the change might come about was still a moot question. During the preceding year the Community Relations Program inaugurated by the American Friends Service Committee had converted a number of doubting Thomases to faith in the feasibility and desirability of prompt measures. A small biracial vacation school conducted during

---

[17] Paul Cooke, AVC, to Oscar Ewing, FSA, 8 Dec 1951; AFSC Rpt Comty Rel Pg, Jun 1952; Contract between Bd/Ed and Columbia Institution for the Deaf, 29 Jul 1952; Louise B. Miller to Col. Institution, 16 Feb 1953; President James Elsted, Col. Institution, to Paul Cooke, 11 Dec 1953.

part of two summers jointly by the Friends Service Committee and the Unitarian Social Action group had shown what could be done by volunteers alone. Through a Joint Committee on Education, delegates from parent-teacher associations, the NAACP, the Urban League, the Consolidated Parents, Inc., churches, clubs, and a score of other organizations had sponsored workshops for school principals and teachers, conducted forum and panel discussions, and fed to the press quantities of material on constructive interracial activities in the city. A fraction of Washington's population though these people were, their work subtly influenced the thinking of many others. A conference held at Howard University in April 1952 disposed of activists' remaining doubts about how to proceed.

Significantly, the announced topic of the Howard conference was "The Courts and Racial Integration in Education." Seventeen years before, a similar conference had confined itself to "The Courts and the Negro Separate Schools." The nearly two hundred educators and lawyers from all sections of the country who spoke at the 1952 sessions and the attentive guests who managed to squeeze into the conference rooms were of one mind about what they wanted. The discussion revolved chiefly around tactics. The final consensus ran that the time had come to strike at the heart of the problem: when suits reached the courts, instead of pleading on the grounds of the demonstrable inequities in particular cases, the attack must be directed at the unconstitutionality of all state and local laws requiring segregated schools.[18]

Washington integrationists did not have to fight alone. Suits brought in Kansas, South Carolina, Delaware, and Prince Edward County, Virginia, were pending in the Supreme Court before hearings on the District of Columbia case had begun in the United States Court of Appeals.

[18] Knox, *Democracy*, p. 10; AFSC Rpts Comty Rel Pg, 1953; *Post*, 22 Oct 1952; *Journal of Negro Education*, xx, pp. 1-6; NAIRO *Rpt*, 1959, pp. 68-70.

As the principle involved in each was one and the same, the Supreme Court took the unusual step late in 1952 of proposing that Bolling versus Sharpe bypass the intermediate court and be argued with the other four cases before the nation's highest tribunal. The argument before the Supreme Court opened in December. Unlike the state cases, the local suit rested first on the contention that no law applying to the District of Columbia had ever made segregated schooling mandatory. Separate schools had endured through the 1870's and after because both races in Washington had been content with the arrangement. In the second place, even if Congress had intended to decree segregation, any such law would be unconstitutional, a denial of rights guaranteed by the Fourteenth Amendment. The evidence included long extracts from the *Congressional Globe,* the *Congressional Record,* citations from the *Journal of the Washington City Council* and the territorial journals, the text of statutes passed between 1862 and 1906, and a mass of supplementary twentieth century data. It comprised, in fact, a historical summary of civil rights in the national capital. Furthermore, the reply brief for the petitioner and several *amici curiae* briefs outlined the programs under way in the community to prepare for integration. The volume and the quality of the testimony reduced the appellees' arguments to dust.[19]

When the Supreme Court handed down its momentous decision on May 17, 1954, school officials were ready to carry out the order. In spite of his earlier fumbling, in 1952-1953 the superintendent had requested citizens to send him suggestions about how to ease the transition he believed impending even then; he had received some forty constructive responses. The board of education itself, though still fearful of transgressing the law, had resorted to joint examinations of white and colored candidates for physical

[19] Bolling *v* Sharpe, 347 U.S. 497, 1954; U.S. Supreme Court, *Records and Briefs,* 1954, cases 1-5.

TABLE VI
School Enrollments, 1920-1960[a]

	1920	1931	1935	1937	1941	1944	1948	1950	1955	1960
TOTAL	77,355	92,706	106,876	107,723	109,345	103,780	109,198	112,810	124,754[b]	139,838
WHITE										
Public	45,775	53,175	59,582	58,793	55,777	49,500	47,801	46,736	38,165[b]	24,982
Catholic		9,599	11,224	11,822	13,410	12,971	14,088	13,851		12,034
Non-Catholic private		1,907	1,565	1,549	2,287	2,448	2,508	2,682		
Public welfare					46	95	120	76		
Subtotal		64,681	72,371	71,164	71,520	64,919	64,440	63,351		37,016
% of white students enrolled in public schools	79.1	82.1	82.3	82.6	78.0	76.2	74.2	72.2		67.5
% change in white public school enrollment from previous year listed		13.9	12.0	-1.3	-5.1	-11.2	-3.4	-2.2	-18.3	-34.5
COLORED										
Public	19,523	26,974	33,498	34,625	36,666	37,768	43,264	47,980	68,877	97,897
Catholic		969	777	691	917	1,018	1,182	1,226		4,925
Non-Catholic private		82	86	72	63	75	146	117		
Public welfare			144	171	179	188	172	136		
Subtotal		28,025	34,505	35,559	37,825	38,861	49,758	49,459		102,822
% colored of all public school enrollment	28.9	33.6	35.9	37.0	39.7	43.3	47.6	49.6	64.3	71.5
% Catholic enrollment of all school enrollment		11.4	11.2	11.6	13.1	13.5	13.9	13.4	11.5	9.9

[a] The 1920 figures derive from the *Comrs Rpt*, 1920, I, 20 and from U.S. Comr of Ed, *Biennial Survey of Ed*, 1920, pp. 50, 126, 144, in which private school data are estimated. The rest of the tabulation is from the official records of the statistics dept. of the D.C. public schools. Roman Catholic includes parochial and private Catholic schools. In 1950 school records show 263 children in Hebrew and 96 in Seventh Day Adventist schools, and in 1955, 317 in Hebrew, 88 in Seventh Day Adventist schools, and in 1960, 334 and 236 respectively, who are shown here as entered in private schools. The board of public welfare entry refers to schools at centers maintained by the board for children in its care.
[b] Exclusive of 603 white students in Americanization classes.

education posts. The biracial AFL Teachers Union optimistically declared that the indoctrination of teachers in methods of handling racially mixed classes had eliminated anxieties on that score in 1953. During that spring and autumn the AFSC Community Relations Program had included teacher seminars from which almost all of the participants had emerged with a good working knowledge of the dos and don'ts of multiracial class situations. School administrators at the end of the year had conducted a series of one-day workshops to discuss ways of handling problems likely to arise. No one pretended in May 1954 that opposition to desegregation had evaporated or that a changeover would be painless, but the white community as a whole accepted the Supreme Court decree with greater equanimity than worried citizens had expected. Negroes and their friends in Washington, however confident of their ultimate triumph, greeted with elation the announcement issued by the board of education on May 25 that desegregated schools would open in the city at the start of the new school year.[20]

Nine years after the launching of the playground fight, every bastion of racial prejudice in Washington had given way, not completely by any means, but at least stripped of its statutory defenses. On the evening of the Supreme Court decision of May 17, 1954, the recreation board had signed a statement, prepared in advance, that thenceforward all public recreational facilities in the District were to be available to everyone. Two and a half years before, the new owners of the National Theatre had adopted that policy, and by mid-1953 movie houses and most other privately owned places of public entertainment had followed suit. The Thompson Restaurant case had put an end to the exclusion of Negro customers, and President Truman's and President Eisenhower's executive orders on nondis-

[20] *Ibid.*

criminatory employment within the government had had wide effect. Police procedures, yielding to the influence of education in human relations, had lost much of their one-time high-handedness. Although segregation, by congressional fiat, continued in the District's Industrial Home School and other correctional institutions, there also a less biased attitude prevailed than formerly. Housing, the first area to be freed of legal racial restrictions, had lagged behind developments in other realms, but in June 1953 a resolution of the National Housing Authority had quashed plans for segregated public housing units, and in October a District contract compliance order had upheld it. Manifestly, a social revolution further-reaching than that of the Reconstruction era was in the making.

Three features of the long struggle were particularly noteworthy. First was the absence of violence, a sharp contrast to what was to occur a decade later in other American cities where racism had a strong hold. Although Washington in mid-1947 had appeared to be unalterably set in a segregationist pattern, opponents of that scheme had demolished it piece by piece without resorting to violent means at any point. The second notable element was the method of social action evolved by citizens of widely disparate backgrounds and interests. Techniques of persuasion, mediation, sit-ins, peaceful picketting, petitions, letters, and working programs, such as those conducted by the American Friends Service Committee and CORE, had all come into play. Scores of organizations had informally divided amongst themselves the fields on which to concentrate, each group learning from the mistakes and the successes of the others. Finally that people of both races worked together harmoniously and together made victory possible was a fact almost as significant for the future as the court decisions themselves. From the NAACP and civic associations composed exclusively of Negroes, to the Urban League whose supporters were both white and colored, to

311

the AVC, about 90 percent white, and the entirely white Jewish Community Council, singleness of purpose bound civil rights workers together. The achievements were the fruits of biracial effort.

CHAPTER XIII

LAYING THE FOUNDATIONS OF A

NEW SOCIAL ORDER, 1954–1961

The rapidity and relative ease with which the District of Columbia accepted the outlawing of racial segregation astonished outsiders. Yet in the summer of 1954 all Washington, like Caesar's Gaul, was divided into three parts. One segment was made up of people confident that civil rights and race relations were now incontrovertibly and, on the whole, satisfactorily settled. The second consisted of the irreconcilables who, because of their unshaken belief in Negroes' innate inferiority, looked upon the Supreme Court's decisions as a tragic mistake that sooner or later would have to be corrected. The third group hailed the decrees as a major triumph but a victory that was still incomplete: desegregation, by no means all-encompassing as yet, was in itself only a first step toward the ultimate goal of building a solidly based biracial community free of color bias. The realists saw that in a number of areas the removal of legal obstacles had merely cleared the terrain and, that until racial discrimination in all its subtle forms was checked or eradicated, a new structure of community life would rest on shaky foundations. Victims of decades of bigotry, moreover, would need help in making a fresh start. Even then the scars left by the past would take years to fade.

Of the tasks confronting the architects of a new social order, none was more important or more difficult than broadening Negroes' economic opportunities. For as long as thwarted ambition and bitter poverty bestrode entire

313

sections of the city, neither mixed schooling, nor "open occupancy" housing, nor nondiscriminatory treatment in public and quasi-public accommodations could bridge the gap between white and colored citizens. The problem was of course two-pronged: first, to discover or create the openings and, second, to find Negroes with the qualifications to fit or to whom employers would give adequate on-the-job training.

Legislation giving Korean War veterans preferential civil service ratings and chances at further schooling was some help, and a presidential order of September 1954 further brightened the picture by strengthening the standard non-discrimination clause written into all government contracts with private firms. But except in the construction industry and in Greater Washington's mushrooming "r & d" companies that were engaged in designing and fabricating automated mechanisms and electronic devices, openings for skilled workmen looking for jobs were few. Negro membership was still nominal in most of the building trades unions, and the requirements for jobs in research and development plants were so exacting as to exclude most colored men. In November 1955 the U.S. Employment Service reported 30 percent more job openings in the area than the year before, but virtually all of them calling for more specialized training than ghetto-bred Negroes educated in segregated schools could offer. Furthermore, "a whole gamut of jobs in industries which require little training," according to NAACP investigators, were still closed to Negroes. For all practical purposes "occupations such as laundry truck drivers, ticket sellers in bus and railroad stations, desk clerks in hotels, and distributors of bakery and milk products" were as completely barred to Negro workers in 1957 as in 1946. And except for the Negro-owned Industrial Bank of Washington, no finance company or bank in the city employed a colored teller, clerk, or secretary.

By conferences, persuasion, and prodding, however, the President's Committee on Government Contracts, the

Urban League, the NAACP, and other volunteer organizations made some headway in opening to Negroes jobs formerly reserved for whites and in inducing employers to provide on-the-job training. By April 1956 the Chesapeake and Potomac Telephone Company had integrated twenty-one categories of jobs and placed Negro clerks in its central office. A few months later tactful but insistent negotiations with the new owners of the transit system convinced that powerful corporation that without risking a union walkout it could hire and train a few Negro platform workers. General Services, Inc., operator of cafeterias and snack bars in government buildings, began to promote Negroes to positions as cashiers and managers. In nearby Maryland a large electronics firm which had never employed a colored person in any capacity until the President's Committee jogged the management responded by putting Negroes into a number of skilled jobs. In 1957 three airlines engaged some Negro clerical help. The department stores came next. Subjected to a one-day boycott organized by a volunteer Committee for Equal Employment Opportunities, the largest downtown stores undertook token hiring of Negroes. Overall progress was nevertheless disappointing to facile optimists in Washington, who, as the *U.S. News and World Report* noted in late 1957, had until then taken it for granted that "the problem of race relations had been solved."[1]

It was charges brought by the NAACP in the autumn of 1957 against the Metropolitan Police that awakened much of the white community to the extent of discrimination still extant in the employment and utilization of the city's Negro manpower. After public hearings the District commissioners exonerated the police, but charts prepared from statistics supplied by the department itself presented figures

[1] NAIRO *Rpt*, 1959, pp. 19, 27, 30; *Post*, 17 Feb 1957; *Afro-American*, 31 Aug 1957; Washington Urban League newsletter, Jan-Feb 1956 (mimeo), and other papers in clipping file on Racial Discrimination, 1946-1960, Washingtoniana Room, D.C. Lib.

, the public could not dismiss: of the 2,243 men on the ce in October 1957, only 250 were Negroes, none above .e rank of corporal; and of the 1,300 privates who had .pplied for promotion, only 4 of the 56 Negroes allowed to compete in the written examination qualified, in contrast to 74 of the 510 white men. Yet most of the Negro candidates who failed had had some college training. By 1959, in a city whose population was 53 percent Negro, a single colored man had risen to a police lieutenancy. Comparisons with the criteria for promotion in eight other cities suggested possible reasons for this curious record. Whereas other cities gave the written examination a weight of from 50 to 90 percent, Washington alone allotted only 40 percent, nothing at all to seniority; 60 percent of the candidate's final score depended upon the subjective efficiency ratings of his superior officers. If conscious prejudice did not affect the results, many people believed that old habits of thought were still influencing judgments.[2]

As street crime, housebreaking, and juvenile delinquency were mounting year by year along with the number of unskilled Negroes migrating to the District, the question arose as to whether a larger proportion of Negroes on the force would not only multiply jobs for colored men but provide more effective policing of potential Negro misdemeanants than a nine-tenths white force could. Conversely, some people wondered whether the colored officer did not engender greater hostility among his own people than did the white. Certainly the consensus among law-abiding citizens ran that the efficiency of the police must not be impaired.

In the fire department colorphobia was an admitted fact. Twenty-two companies—twenty-one white and one colored—out of thirty-three were completely segregated in 1957, six years after the collapse of Chief Mayhew's attempt at integration. The anger expressed by Local 36 of the AFL Fire Fighters Association at Mayhew's plan had

[2] NAIRO *Rpt*, 1959, 20-24.

sprung partly from the necessity of having on-duty firemen share eating and sleeping quarters in the engine houses. Powerful members of the House District Committee objected to such an arrangement as fiercely as did union leaders. Resistance to it had run so strong that when the District commissioners issued their desegregation order of November 1953, they expressly made an exception of the fire department. Nine months later, after Mayhew's successor had admitted to failure in trying to convert the union to cooperation, a delegation representing several citizens' organizations persuaded Commissioner Samuel Spencer to rewrite the order so as to include the fire department. Token integration ensued, and, because vacancies in the upper ranks of the service occurred mostly in the all-white companies, Negro promotions continued to be a rarity. One of the department's three Negro lieutenants with twenty-three years of service behind him sued when he was passed over for a captaincy, and still in June 1958 out of 45 captains in the fire fighting division only one was a colored man.

In striving to combat the segregationist sentiment governing Local 36, sponsors of the interracial workshops that had won converts to school integration discovered that only the union president and ten to twelve members felt strongly on the subject, but that minority dominated the rest. Unless Chief Sutton were to dismiss the recalcitrants, defy the union, and, by incurring the wrath of congressmen intent on restoring segregation, disrupt his department completely, he had to have some more powerful leverage than verbal pleas. The weapon given him in 1958 came to hand upon the appointment of the Commissioners' Council on Human Relations and the launching of an intensive official drive against discrimination. Even then effective action took several years. By 1960 twenty-four companies were integrated, and in May 1961 a new District commissioner and the department chief hit upon a magic formula: the inauguration of a 56-hour week, provided all fire fighters could be rotated from one engine house to another. The scheme proved irresistible. The union opened membership to all firemen the next year.[3]

The new Council on Human Relations was the District's counterpart of the President's Committee on Government Contracts and faced similar problems. Appointed to investigate complaints, to advise the commissioners on "means of assuring and maintaining equality of opportunity for employment and advancement in the District Government," and to recommend procedures to ensure "compliance with the nondiscrimination-in-employment clause" written into District contracts, the new body had no independent authority. But the caliber of the seven men selected, the dedication of the full-time salaried executive director, and the fact that their contacts constantly widened combined to give their recommendations weight. Equally important, at the end of the 1950's they had the backing of a majority of Washingtonians, individually inarticulate and politically inexperienced though many of them were. Yet like the President's Committee, the council in dealing with employers frequently found itself caught up in struggles with the unions, particularly in the building trades. In every major negotiation, the executive director observed, the unions blamed employers for perpetuating discrimination, while employers blamed the unions. At the commencement exercises of a predominantly Negro high school in 1958 the announcement that three graduates had been accepted for apprenticeship training evoked "an outburst of joyful exclamations . . . from the audience of some six hundred parents." In January 1960 the *Courier* estimated that 2,000 Negroes aged sixteen to eighteen were out of school and out of work because they could not find jobs in which to use the vocational skills they had acquired in high school.

Some unions were less exclusive than others. The Operating Engineers local had 120 Negro members, the Plasterers Local 96 about 40. The Brickmakers Local 4 was 90 percent colored, but assignments to the big jobs usually went to members of Local 1, which, like the locals of several other craft unions in Washington, was lily-white. Local 26 of the Brotherhood of Electrical Workers was the toughest to crack. As big building contractors engaged the men union bosses referred to them and the bosses naturally sent union members, the Negro electrician had to turn for a job to one of the small nonunion firms where work was usually less steady and pay rates were generally lower. Union leaders' contention that Negroes preferred to work for nonunion contractors manifestly smacked of excuse-making. When the President's Committee talked of asking the General Services Administration to cancel the government's contract with a local electrical company that was installing the wiring in a new government building, the contractor pointed out that he had to have the skilled men only the electrical workers' local could supply in sufficient numbers. Local 26 remained unmoved, while George Meany, president of the AFL-CIO, accused the committee of being soft on guilty employers. During this impasse the Urban League proposed that governmental authorities instruct all companies to train apprentices for heavy construction work, instead of letting Local 26 take sole responsibility; the District Apprenticeship Council and the city's vocational schools were working on the problem. Whether the suggestion put the fear of God and government into the BEW, or whether the unfavorable publicity enveloping union dealings with federal and local officials induced a slight change, is a matter of conjecture. In October the *Afro-American* announced a "break-through"; one Negro electrician employed on the government building project.[4]

[4] NAIRO *Rpt*, 1959, pp. 34-38; Charles A. Miller, *Citizens Advisory Groups in the District of Columbia Government*, pp. 14-15 (Sep 1961); *Post*, 17, 28 Feb 1960; Pittsburgh *Courier*, 2 Jan 1960; *Afro-American*, 12 Mar, 22 Oct 1860; *Star*, 20 Mar 1960; David A. Sawyer, "Fair Em-

Although a job of any kind was presumably better than one, the low earnings of most Negroes caused as much anxiety to Washingtonians concerned about race relations as did unemployment itself. When the figures for 1956 came to light, every Pollyanna about Negro progress suffered a shock, for the differential between the median white family income and the median nonwhite was greater than in 1950. In midcentury median white income was $3,425, Negro $2,190, six years later $6,643 and $3,918 respectively, a drop of 6 percent in Negroes' relative position. In federal employment itself, 85 percent of the city's 25,840 Negroes in white-collar jobs were in grades 1 through 4, with base pay ranging from $2,690 to $3,415 a year. The proportion of Negroes in Washington in the interval had risen from 35.5 to 44 percent of the population, an increase of which an estimated 45 percent was due to in-migration. If, as appeared to be the case, most of the in-migrants came from the bottom socio-economic layers of the Southeastern black belt, the lack of skills of the newcomers partly accounted for the sorry record, but manifestly Washington's past efforts, so far from netting gains, had merely slowed the grim advance of poverty.

The disturbing facts, however, served as a challenge. As the easy optimism of mid-1954 vanished, the number of persons actively working for equal opportunity swelled. While a half dozen church and civic organizations set themselves to devising neighborhood projects to help Negro youths, and the Urban League's Vocational Training Clinic opened "TST," training for "Tomorrow's Scientists and Technicians," the District commissioners, the Council on Human Relations, school officials, and administrators of the recently established Eugene and Agnes Meyer Foundation examined the situation carefully. Anxious not to act on faulty assumptions of cause and effect, the commissioners authorized a whole sheaf of professional studies of various

ployment in the Nation's Capital, A Study of Progress and Dilemma," *Journal of Intergroup Relations,* IV, No. 1, pp. 37-41.

over, also

aspects of the overall problem. And the press kept the public informed.

Fresh disappointment was in store, for the 1960 census showed a slight further decline in Negro income compared to white—a median of $4,800 a year over against $7,692. By the end of 1960, on the other hand, Washington contained 22,000 nonwhite families with an income of above $8,000 and 10,800 with more than $10,000 a year. Again the increase in the colored population to 54 percent of the whole, chiefly by in-migration of impoverished Negroes and a continuing white exodus to the suburbs, partly explained without redeeming the situation. Job bias, averred the president of the Board of District Commissioners, was the main cause of school dropouts and poverty, but he was apparently startled to learn from Sterling Tucker of the Urban League that 63.9 percent of the District's 10,843 Negro employees were in the four bottom civil service grades and only 1.3 percent in the brackets above grade eleven. The major item of cheer lay in the number of Negroes promoted during the preceding four years from minor to responsible federal positions; since 1956 colored people in the upper grades of government service in Washington had risen from 4,215 to 7,414.

The occupational distribution of the nonwhite labor force in 1960 in contrast to 1950 also looked somewhat encouraging:

TABLE VII

	1950	Percent	1960	Percent
Total nonwhite labor force	149,726	100	209,258	100
Professional, technical	6,753	5	14,668	7
Clerical	24,163	16	35,259	17
Sales	2,131	1	3,099	1
Craftsmen, foremen	9,003	6	12,065	6
Operatives	22,691	15	24,626	12
Service, except private house	36,081	24	41,473	20
Laborers, except farm and mine	22,485	15	19,329	9
Others	26,419	18	58,719	28

321

But while the numbers of colored professional people more than doubled, and the colored clerical and sales force increased 50 percent during the decade, the 10 percent rise in the confusing category "Others" diminished confidence. If, as most thoughtful people agreed, improved economic status was the key to Negro advancement, the local community must do more to achieve it and, in the interim, must explore the weak spots in related areas.[5]

Housing was one weak spot, weaker and sorer in fact in 1957 and 1958 than earlier. Not only did voluntary restrictive covenants still keep well-to-do Negroes out of a number of agreeable neighborhoods within the District, but the accelerated pace of block-busting and the mounting volume of Negroes displaced by urban renewal gave new dimensions to the problem. The former procedure generally involved potential Negro homeowners, the latter, people whose earnings precluded purchasing homes and who had to find low-cost accommodation. The plight of each group exacerbated that of the other.

As the city's colored population exceeded the white and the sheer pressure of numbers intensified the thrust of Negroes into formerly all-white areas, speculators and "panic peddlers" exploited their opportunities to the full. Playing upon the fears of white householders that property values would drop precipitately if a single Negro family settled nearby, speculators bought up whole residential blocks cheap, sold the houses to Negroes at inflated prices, and then repeated the process in another block. Once started, the scheme worked more and more automatically, fanning racial animosities as it spread from one area to the next.

[5] NAIRO *Rpt*, 1959, pp. 31-33; Eunice S. Grier, *Understanding Washington's Changing Population*, pp. 9-31; *Post*, 5 Apr, 22, 23 May, 3 Aug, 3 Oct 1960; *Anl Rpt Wshg Urban League*, 1959; Duncan Howlett, Foreword to Dagmar Perman, *The Girard Street Project; 18th U.S. Census, Population of Standard Metropolitan Statistical Areas: 1960 and 1950;* George B. Nesbitt and Marian P. Yankauer, "The Potentiality of Equalizing Housing Opportunity in the Nation's Capital," *Journ Interg Relns*, IV, No. 1, pp. 80-81.

And since the cost to Negro purchasers was generally exorbitant, some of them had to let out rooms, overcrowd their dwellings, and, by thus changing the character of the neighborhood for the worse, feed the anti-Negro propaganda mills.

Morton Kaplan, a newspaperman who had watched panic spread in his own neighborhood, hit upon the best method of combatting it. In 1958, with a group of friends, he organized Neighbors, Inc., to persuade white property owners in Manor Park that they were hurting themselves as well as the community as a whole by succumbing to the specious arguments of real estate manipulators. Manor Park at the time was nearly equally divided between white and colored. By personal visits, by letters to the newspapers, and by holding meetings to expound the economics of the vicious system, the volunteers of Neighbors halted the white exodus first from Manor Park and then from two adjoining areas. By 1960 they had induced eight formerly lily-white citizens' associations to join with thirty-odd other organizations in a campaign to get the city's leading newspapers to drop racial designations in advertisements of property for sale or rent. When Shepherd Park, an affluent neighborhood of $30,000 to $40,000 mansions built in the 1920's along upper 16th Street east of Rock Creek Park, dropped the color bars, the major fight against block-busting was won. Within five years Shepherd Park would become the Negro "Gold Coast" where colored and white families lived amicably side by side.

For the uprooted slumdwellers of Southwest Washington and Foggy Bottom the story was different. Rebuilding in Southwest included a few, but very few, low-cost housing units; the rest of the reclaimed land not reserved for public buildings and new highways was filling up with town houses and apartments far too expensive for the impecunious. Redevelopment in Foggy Bottom and private piece-meal restoration of houses on Capitol Hill were having similar consequences. Dollars rather than racial discrimination as such accounted for most of the problem. The National Capital Housing Authority, headed by a Negro, maintained an open occupancy policy, but the price of real estate even in the trans-Anacostia section had reached a level to make new public housing developments within the District of Columbia an expensive proposition.

While the very word "redevelopment" had a connotation of displacement for Negro families, they could welcome rehabilitation of deteriorating neighborhoods if homeowners, landlords, and tenants living there had a voice in the planning. In 1959 "citizen-government teamwork," as participants called it, evolved that kind of program for a section of Northwest Washington above Florida Avenue composed of a congerie of small neighborhoods, some white, some Negro, and some mixed. As early as 1952, under the leadership of the PTA president and the principal of the white Adams School, teachers and parents of children there and at the nearby colored Morgan School had begun to discuss how to revitalize the area without dislocating its residents. When a federal grant to the District government enabled the commissioners seven years later to engage a group at American University to study the possibilities, the Adams-Morgan Project came into being. By organizing block units, each with representatives on a planning committee, and by establishing a community council, people of widely different social and economic status achieved a sufficient sense of community to reach a consensus on wanted changes and to set the machinery of rehabilitation in motion. Governmental red tape, accompanied by delays and rising costs, later strangled the project before it had made more than a start, but the principle of drawing into a new scheme the people who would be most affected by it would be put to use in planning in the mid-1960's.

President Eisenhower had stated in the summer of 1954 that he had tried as hard as he knew how to have the idea accepted that where federal funds and federal authority were involved, there should be no discrimination based upon any reason that was not recognized by the Constitution. Maryland and Virginia suburbanites appeared to prefer their prejudices to federal funds. In actuality they did not have to choose, for federally guaranteed bank loans to homeowners and housing development companies were still available with all the recial strings of the 1930's attached. So the central city of 1960 contained nearly 84 percent of all the Negroes in Greater Washington. And thousands of the city's 411,000 colored inhabitants lived in quarters as overcrowded and fetid as the shanties of Murder Bay ninety-five years before.[6]

Yet every medical man, every social worker, and most laymen in the District knew that wretched housing contributed to serious health problems, to crime and juvenile delinquency, and to a paralyzing of occupants' will to help themselves. Yearly the District Tuberculosis Association called attention to the fact that TB, popularly supposed to be a virtually extinct disease, was taking its toll in the city. The incidence of venereal infections, health officers reported, was "alarmingly high." Their data came "from a clinic located in a belt of low economic and slum housing," and, as was to be expected, most of the cases recorded occurred among Negroes, the principal slumdwellers in the city. While health authorities and school officials were at pains to explain that multiple social factors entered into the venereal disease record, they were sharply critical of the inadequate facilities for treatment and were appalled at the conditions that helped spread infection. The public services that might have palliated some of the evils of slum living were understaffed and ill-equipped. In short, while

[6] Grier, *Understanding Wshg's Changing Pop,* pp. 28-29; NAIRO *Rpt,* 1959, pp. 41-43; interview Margery Ware, formerly executive director Neighbors, Inc., 7 Dec 1965; *Experiment in Planning, Citizen-Government Teamwork in Planning for the Renewal of Adams-Morgan,* April 1963; G. Franklin Edwards, "The Changing Status and Self Image of Negroes in the District of Columbia," and Nesbitt and Yankauer, "Potentiality of Equalizing Housing," *Journ Interg Relns,* IV, No. 1, pp. 13, 90-97.

poverty, racial prejudice, and lack of decent housing for the victims of both were basic sources of troubles, meager budgets for public health and welfare had only slightly less disastrous immediate consequences.

Racism was not a discernible factor in the performance of the District health department. By 1958 some 2,000 of its 3,000 employees, including a considerable part of the professional staff, were Negroes, and, of the 360,000 patients treated, 310,000 were colored. Integration, begun at Gallinger Hospital in 1948, went into effect at Glendale, the municipal tuberculosis center, in the early 1950's; it had become a matter of course when the new District General Hospital replaced Gallinger a few years later. More remarkable from several standpoints, Freedmen's Hospital, for eighty-four years after its founding in 1864 the only federally supported hospital in which Negro doctors could serve, not only accepted white patients but some white interns and white nurses. The District Medical Association voted in 1952 to accept Negro members, and one private hospital after another thereafter gave a few Negro doctors staff privileges; Group Health and Group Hospitalization, Inc., followed that example within two or three years. Hospital doors were not yet open wide, but they were open more than a crack. Indeed, the changes in attitude of the local medical profession were one of the most extraordinary features of the shifting patterns of the community in the 1950's. And integration of public health services offset many of the worst handicaps of severely limited congressional appropriations.[7]

Like the health service, the District welfare department was constantly pinched for money, but criticisms of the public assistance program occasionally implied that racial discrimination as well as meager funds affected it. Welfare officials indignantly denied the charges. The principal sore

[7] Knox, *Democracy and the D.C. Schools*, pp. 22-25; NAIRO *Rpt*, 1959, pp. 62-64; *Afro-American*, 6 Aug 1960.

point was the workings of the "man-in-the-house" rule. The regulation had originated in the mid-1930's when the welfare department had felt obliged to stretch its skimpy appropriations by refusing relief payments to any family with an employable man in the house. The directors of the Community Chest had protested at the time, since a jobless man without savings could not support a family, and the wife and children of a man with only part-time work were in an only less precarious position. Then, as later, the penalty of male unemployment fell most heavily upon the Negro family. The consequences of the rule came into sharpened focus in 1959 after publication of statistics from a survey undertaken by the District health department. Although based not on an actual citywide count but on a sampling in sections of the community likely to draw heavily upon public health services, the tabulation revealed that 6.5 percent of the city's Negro families with five or more members had no breadwinner; for white families of similar size, those with no earner constituted only .8 percent. What happened, people asked, to the household in which an able-bodied man had failed to get or keep a job or had not really tried to find work? The answer of welfare officials was as disturbing as the data prompting the question: the father either deserted his family or "hid out" in the house, where he lived on the payments intended to enable the woman to rear her fatherless children.

The effect upon children in such circumstances was clear. They either grew up in a broken home, were sent to Junior Village, the public institution for the District's neglected children, or, if their father succeeded in avoiding discovery by the welfare inspector and remained at home, they learned to accept fraud and lying as the normal way to survive. Detailed sociological analyses had not yet proved to the public the far-reaching character of the traumatic experiences to which Negro children of broken homes were ordinarily subjected, but common sense pointed to many ills. The undesirability of placing a child in a public institu-

327

tion if any other arrangement were possible had long been a basic tenet of the social work profession. Yet to blink at dishonesty and fraud on the part of recipients of public assistance seemed to moralists an unthinkable alternative. Just how much cheating was going on was not a matter of public information, but insofar as Washingtonians believed it not uncommon among indigent Negroes, it tended to lower white respect for all Negroes. No one in 1960 had a satisfactory solution to offer.[8]

Education, the traditional American panacea for social ills, in turn faced troubles in the capital.[9] "Blind optimism that the legal fact [of desegregation] automatically will give birth to the spiritual fusion implied in physical unity" prevailed in much of Washington in the summer of 1954. Eight years later, three of the District's leading school officials in summarizing the difficulties attendant upon the transition to integrated schools in any community observed that, after "the terrific push" to win the court order, too many people lost sight of the necessity of planning "beyond the stage of the 'opened school door.'" In Washington as elsewhere, "'Open' hearts on the part of all the pupils, parents, teachers, officers, citizens and politicians concerned" were an essential but seldom recognized basis for integration. Furthermore, the experts noted, "Hearts may be open but minds may not be informed about differences in background, achievement, cultural mores and conditioned attitudes." Hence well-intentioned teachers and staff, readily accepting integration in theory, often turned out to have no true conception of the adjustments inherent in so sweeping a

[8] NAIRO *Rpt*, 1959, pp. 56-58; Biostatistics and Health Education Div, D.C. Dept of Public Health, *Family Composition in Washington, D.C. and Related Data, 1957* (Dec 1958), Table 4. See also U.S. Dept of Labor, Office of Policy Planning and Research, *The Negro Family, The Case for National Action, 1965.*

[9] In the discussion of the schools in the paragraphs that follow, the data, unless otherwise noted, come from Francis A. Gregory, Carl F. Hansen, and Irene C. Hypps, "From Desegregation to Integration in Education," *Journ Interg Relns,* IV, No. 1, pp. 55-70.

social change. Because of that misconception, the most open-hearted frequently tended to become the least open-minded, and disillusionment followed. So, although Washington had made more advanced preparation than most cities, the assumptions of a good many people that the community would easily make all the necessary adaptations proved faulty.

In early September 1954 demonstrations had occurred at the Baltimore and Wilmington, Delaware, schools when they opened on an integrated basis. If the agitators stirring up hostility there were to arrive in the District, would the calm which Washington integrationists had been prophesying hold? During the summer the board of education itself had been divided about how to proceed. The final decision to allow children under special circumstances to remain for a year or more in the schools they had attended during 1953-1954 instead of transferring to those within the newly established geographical zones meant a compromise with full-scale integration. When the day for Washington's school opening arrived, white pupils at the McKinley, Eastern, and Anacostia high schools began milling about at the entrances. A delegation of adults dispatched by the Urban League to fortify the school authorities quickly persuaded the students at the first two to behave suitably. At the Anacostia High School some 2,500 boys, girls, and onhangers were less tractable, but they too eventually dispersed without anything more ominous than some grumbling. A walkout of white students from several schools occurred a day or two later, but, as the press summarized the episodes, they were more "larks" than expressions of deep-seated protest. Within the first week classes were meeting peaceably in all the partially integrated schools.

Some teacher transfers took place at once; at the supervisor and principal level, shifts were far fewer. But by June 1955 Superintendent Corning reported that 75 percent of all schools, from kindergarten through the teachers colleges, contained pupils of both races, and one school in five had racially mixed faculties. By September 1955, he added, integration should be complete "except for the options." That autumn the teachers colleges would become one institution. Yet as late as 1959 no colored principal had been put in charge of a predominantly white school. Negroes believed their chances for promotion into the administrative hierarchy dim.

Interestingly enough, white parents rarely complained at having their children in classes taught by Negro teachers. Indeed, measured by standards of formal education, the colored teachers were generally better qualified than the white. Objections, however, soon arose from white parents upon finding their children in schools where enrollments were largely Negro. And inasmuch as the board of education sanctioned transfers of children who suffered "psychological hardship" from being part of a small racial minority, several hundred white children shifted to predominantly white schools, thereby increasing the disproportion. Supposedly, school psychologists were to examine the evidence of psychic damage to every applicant for a transfer, but no case, the head psychologist averred, was ever referred to her or her staff; parental pressure sufficed to effect the move. Although the requests for transfers dropped from 1,000 the first year to 500 in 1955-1956, six years after integration began the process was still incomplete. Yet on the whole the physical placement of pupils and teaching staff proceeded more rapidly and with less friction than knowledgeable officials had expected.

Educational troubles, on the contrary, quickly took on larger proportions than anticipated. The workshops conducted during late 1953 and 1954 had in fact reached only a minority of teachers and had only partly prepared even those attending for what lay ahead. Within the first few months of the 1954-1955 school year, teachers in charge of racially mixed classes found that Negro pupils generally lagged behind their white classmates. Not invariably, to be sure: bright Negro children sometimes outstripped gifted white, just as some white children, particularly in schools in the poorer sections of the city, had achievement records as far below the national norm for a given age as those of the slowest learners among their Negro contemporaries. But the overall performance of colored pupils in 1955 and 1956 was dismaying to environmentalists who had assumed that in an identical school setting the average Negro child's intellectual capacity would blossom as early and as fully as the white child's. If Negroes were to need several generations to slough off the social inheritance of three centuries of oppression, how were integrated schools to function in the interim? School administrators concluded that the only feasible procedure was to start the "track" system in the third grade. On the basis of achievement tests to be given in the third and sixth grades, pupils in the elementary schools were to be assigned either to a "basic" or to a "general" track; a few with exceptionally high scores might land in classes for gifted children. At the junior high school level, the two tracks became three to allow for a college preparatory group, and in the senior high schools a fourth, an "honor" track, was added.

During most of 1955-1956, the first year, Negro parents were more interested in the new system than critical of it. They listened attentively to the school psychologists' explanations of its purposes and workings. But with the later discovery that colored children constituted a great majority of those assigned to the basic track and that the initial placement tended to become permanent, resentment at the scheme flared up. Negroes saw it as a device to perpetuate segregation under another name. And the fact that lack of staff prevented giving each child a new test and a new rating more than once in three years meant that he would have to spend three years of his school life in a group which he might outgrow in a few months. More disastrous was the likelihood that the very label "basic tracker" would stifle his ambition and, because lessons were adapted to children with below-normal intelligence quotients, he would

331

miss exposure to the kind of knowledge and training needed to prepare him for the general, college preparatory, or honor track. Carl Hansen, who became superintendent of schools in 1957, always insisted that good instruction, irrespective of the track, would overcome every child's learning problems. The system consequently remained unmodified.[10]

Meanwhile, much publicized data about what I.Q. and achievement tests appeared to show supplied Southern congressmen on a subcommittee of the House District Committee with ammunition for an attack on school integration. Hearings held in late September 1956 produced a published report of selected testimony calculated to convince the country that desegregation in Washington was a catastrophic failure, a dreadful warning to other communities attempting to obey the Supreme Court order. Since 1954 at every stage the national spotlight had been turned on the District's school administration. Its accomplishments had received favorable notice in some newspapers, but even the most sympathetic segment of the press had called attention to every weakness; events in the capital were always news. It was in that setting that the community had to face the interrogation of hostile men on the Hill. Their central thesis was that standards of education had fallen because of integration and that intolerable social conditions had developed under the new system. The subcommittee heard much of the testimony in executive sessions and released in its published report chiefly the derogatory comments.

In order to put the whole story before the public and correct the false implications of the congressional report, a Citizens Committee against Defamation published in 1957

[10] Margery T. Ware, "Some Aspects of the Student Strikes in Public School Integration," in rpt to Urban League, 14, 25 Oct 1954; Paul V. Cooke, "Racial Integration in Education in the District of Columbia," *Journ Negro Ed*, xxv, No. 3, pp. 237-45; interview Dr. Irene Hypps, 14 Dec 1965; NAIRO *Rpt*, 1959, pp. 70-71; Edwards, "Changing Status," *Journ Interg Relns*, iv, No. 1, pp. 22-28.

an exhaustive rebuttal entitled *Democracy and the District of Columbia Schools*. Prepared by Ellis O. Knox, a former member of the Strayer team, the study explored all aspects of the situation. The text explained, as had witnesses at the hearings, that integration had not caused a lowering of educational standards but merely brought to light shortcomings that had existed for years. Since the 1920's, if not before, practically all Negro schools had been overcrowded, understaffed, without special service facilities, and with a smaller per-pupil expenditure rate than the white schools. The entire city was now learning the extent and the costliness of that cumulative neglect. A great many people and the press, moreover, misinterpreted the recent statistics on Negro and white pupils' records. The achievement medians of Negro pupils reflected not innate racial differences in intelligence but rather the impact of socio-economic factors upon school performance. Because the children who at-tended schools in lower-middle-class or substandard neighborhoods where achievement averaged below the national norm were preponderantly Negroes, people mistakenly attributed the results to race. Negro pupils in wealthier neighborhoods generally did well.

In refuting piece by piece the charges that school integration had multiplied disciplinary problems, increased juvenile delinquency, spread venereal disease, and added to the number of illegitimate births in the city, Knox pointed out that desegregated schooling was not responsible for the city's too often deplorable social conditions. Figures, in fact, revealed a slight decline in juvenile delinquency since desegregation began. Due to their culturally deprived background, the 8,000 school enrollees of 1955-1956 whose parents had newly come from the Southern states complicated Washington's school problems, but a study of Philadelphia's Negro in-migrants showed that five or six years in a more favorable educational environment largely offset the initial handicap. Distressing inadequacies did exist in the District's school program; realization of their seriousness was a first step toward remedies.[11]

By 1960 the community had reached a fairly clear understanding of what the schools had accomplished and what remained to be done. People who considered Superintendent Hansen's pamphlet of 1957, *Miracle of Social Adjustment,* an overstatement of past achievement were nonetheless gratified as his reporting citywide averages on achievement tests "markedly improved" in 1960. Colored enrollments by then had risen to 79.7 percent, while 1,465 white teachers and 4,117 Negro brought the latter to 68 percent of the total faculty. People in a position to know agreed that the schools had better facilities than in 1953, made better use of space, had more special services, better morale, and more harmony within the system. Victor Daly of the U.S. Employment Service, on the other hand, pointed to the 2,000 to 3,000 school dropouts every year, a commentary on the deficiencies in the city's educational program which required no elaboration. *De facto* segregation, moreover, was a constant irritant to Negroes. Closely related to housing patterns, it was only partly a matter of overcoming white parents' prejudices. It was a problem shared by virtually all big cities that were conscientiously seeking to establish racially mixed schools. When a recently arrived gadfly on the staff of the *Afro-American* declared that the slow progress of Negroes in Washington was due to their own indifference to their opportunities, he startled his readers. But white Washington's growing awareness of the psychic drag imposed upon Negroes by the past curbed white impatience and encouraged "the spiritual fusion" necessary for true integration.[12]

In no realm of life in the capital during the late 1950's was the equal opportunity doctrine accepted without occa-

---

[11] Subcomee, H Dis Comee, 84C, 2S, Hrgs, "Investigation Public School Conditions," pp. 470-500; Knox, *Democracy,* pp. 4-32.

[12] *Afro-American,* 20 Mar 1960, 13 May 1961; *Star,* 4 Apr 1960; *Post,* 10 Apr 1960.

sional quibbling. Even biracial use of public and quasi-public accommodations, taken for granted though it generally was after the Thompson Restaurant decision, met with some opposition. In 1955 and 1956 bowling alley proprietors refused to admit Negro patrons until a law suit, brought under the provisions of the municipal antidiscrimination ordinances of 1869 and 1870, forced open the doors of establishments within the old city limits; when company contentions that those ancient laws did not run outside the Washington bounds of 1870 kept the racial bars in alleys in the rest of the District, a fiat from the commissioners quickly settled the matter. The Metropolitan Police Boys' Club defied public policy more successfully, for although much of the money to support the five white and four Negro clubhouses and the summer camps came from uniformed policemen's door-to-door solicitation and from free use of tax-supported facilities, the self-perpetuating board of directors, consisting of some 125 white professional and businessmen and 50 high-ranking police officers, insisted that here was a private organization outside public control. When the trustees of the racially integrated All Souls Unitarian Church requested the directors to take Negro boys into the club which for years had used the church premises, the directors disbanded the unit. The Unitarian Service Committee thereupon organized the Columbia Heights Boys' Club, serving hundreds of boys of both races. Two other Metropolitan Police Boys' Clubs closed down before mid-1956 in order to avoid any form of integration. A combination of factors finally brought about change: new members on the board of directors who disliked segregation, the loss of funds when in 1959 Commissioner McLaughlin forbade uniformed policemen to solicit subscriptions, and, amid multiplying complaints about police brutality, the department's wish to conciliate public opinion. Opposition to club integration collapsed in 1962.[13]

[13] NAIRO *Rpt*, 1959, pp. 52-54; Phineas Indritz, Opinion of American Veterans Committee, Analysis of Laws in Force in the District of

Other pockets of resistance would endure even longer, but in 1960 any Washingtonian whose memory reached back to 1947 could only marvel that they were but pockets, not solidly entrenched battle lines. The loss of 172,000 white residents between 1950 and 1960 was a blow to the community, if only because a sizable proportion of the new Negro majority consisted of economically dependent families. Washington, in short, had indeed become the poorhouse for the Maryland and Virginia suburbs. At the opening of the new decade the Secret City still existed. The walls were down, but outside them stretched a no man's land that few people of either race knew how to cross. Yet by the end of the year, with a new administration about to take over, a give-and-take was beginning to develop between whites and Negroes in the upper ranks of society.

On the numerous advisory committees set up in the District government white and Negro members worked together harmoniously, if not always effectively.[14] Although exchanges of hospitality were infrequent, self-consciousness in social intercourse was thinning perceptibly, a process hastened by the opening of embassies of new African states. If a native Washington Negro sometimes resented the privileges accorded African dignitaries, he knew that officialdom had always commanded prestige in the American capital. The American Negro social hierarchy based upon degree of color had disappeared before 1950. Upper-class Negroes took pride in being Negro, in some cases with a truculence disconcerting to whites, more often displaying a pleased amusement at white acquaintances' interest in their ideas. National politics, international affairs, and civil rights largely preoccupied the capital. And in the realm of race relations most Washingtonians proudly felt they were setting an example to the rest of the country.

Columbia Prohibiting Racial Discrimination, 22 Sep 1953 (mimeo); Ex Dir AVC to Comr Robert McLaughlin, 9 Jul 1956; Indritz, "Segregated Youth in Our National Capital," *Crisis,* LXIII, 581-85; *Post,* 18 Mar 1957.
[14] Miller, *Citizens Advisory Groups.*

To some of the generation born in the early 1940's the achievements of their elders looked insignificant. Young members of the "Movement" believed it solely their own creation. In the District of Columbia, as elsewhere, they were increasingly impatient at any delay in effecting a full-scale social revolution, but a good many of them vaguely knew that Washington had made extraordinary adjustments without recourse to violence. Measured by the distance still to be traversed to reach the goal of a truly interracial society, the advances of the past were small. Gauged by the obstacles overcome, they were tremendous. The next five years would enormously quicken the pace of change in the city, but the new social order in the making rested on foundations laid by earnest citizens over the preceding decades.

BIBLIOGRAPHICAL NOTE

Materials on Negro life in antebellum Washington are at best fragmentary. For the 1790's I found no primary data whatsoever other than a list of local planters' bondsmen and one or two allusions to slave gangs working on contruction of the Capitol. Even about Benjamin Banneker, "sable son of Africa," to whom some Negroes today mistakenly attribute a major role in planning the capital city, facts are few, and a number of those were first put on paper more than forty years after his death. For the period from 1800 to 1862 personal papers of Negro families are extremely rare. The best clue to how free Negroes supported themselves lies in the *Washington City Directory* compiled by local printers in 1822 and 1830, for they give residents' occupations as well as names and addresses. Hence official records form the backbone of the sources.

Congressional reports and the debates as set forth in the *Annals of Congress,* the *Register of Debates,* and the *Congressional Globe* deal almost exclusively with the domestic slave trade and occasional, quickly dismissed proposals for emancipation. Citizens' petitions to the House and Senate, located in the National Archives, in turn concentrate on the slave trade and abolitionism. Nor do court records contain more than five or six entries about freedmen. More rewarding for the historian are the census enumerators' returns on Free Inhabitants of the District of Columbia for 1850 and 1860, to be found in the National Archives, and the folios in the office of the Recorder of Deeds which identify the real estate holdings of every local property owner. *The Acts of the Corporation of the City of Washington,* 1805-1816, and the *Laws of the Corporation of the*

City of Washington, 1817-1862, contain the text of the black codes adopted between 1808 and 1850 and here and there brief summaries of city councilmen's ideas of the freedman's place in the scheme of things. The black codes appear also in James W. Sheahan, *Corporation Laws of the City of Washington,* 1853. Georgetown's city records are incomplete and comparatively uninforming. The one document that gives any attention to Negro aspirations and accomplishments in the pre-Civil-War District cities is a historical sketch of Negro schools and churches incorporated in the *Special Report of the Commissioner of Education* prepared at the end of the 1860's and published in 1870 as House Executive Document 315. If uncritical in its judgments, it includes more specifics about the free colored community before 1861 than does any earlier material.

To this meager array may be added Ellen M. O'Connor's *Myrtilla Miner, A Memoir,* William B. Simmons' *Men of Mark,* published in 1887, a few items in the *National Intelligencer,* and, from 1848 to 1859, five or six editorials in the *National Era.* The *Intelligencer* usually confined its comments to the peculiar institution and white attitudes toward it.

Books on the slave trade, slavery, and abolitionists' activities in Washington eke out official and newspaper accounts. Basil Hall's *Travels in North America during the Years 1827 and 1828* first carried the text of the initial appeal of the Washington Society for the Abolition of Slavery in the District of Columbia, although the memorial and the names of its signatories appeared six years later in a House report. Walter C. Clephane, "Local Aspects of Slavery in the District of Columbia," in the Columbia Historical Society *Records* gives a helpful analysis of the legal problem. Frederic Bancroft's *Slave Trading in the Old South,* based on sources no longer available, has four or five pages on the slave trade in Washington which supplement Jesse Torrey's *A Portraiture of Domestic Slavery in the United States* of 1817. Three or four paragraphs of

Frederick Law Olmsted's *Journey in the Seaboard Slave States in the Years 1853-1854* give a first-hand version of the situation at a later date. Although conditions in the District cities differed in many particulars from those in other Southern cities, the parallels were close enough to make Richard Wade's *Slavery in the Cities* a useful secondary source.

Primary sources for the history of Negroes in the District of Columbia during the Civil War and the early years of Reconstruction are relatively abundant. Congressional documents and debates, petitions, the District of Columbia files of the Freedmen's Bureau papers, 1865-1872, in Record Group 105 of the National Archives, the *Annual Reports of the National Freedmen's Relief Association,* and the reports of the trustees of the colored schools in the annual reports of the Secretary of the Interior, 1864-1870, all contain a wealth of information. Furthermore, the *Journals* of the Washington city councils become all-important, inasmuch as they outline clearly the differences of local public opinion on Negro voting, mixed schooling, and civil rights.

After the demise of the District municipalities in 1871, official records bearing upon Negroes shrink in value. As Congress left the running of the District to the new territorial government, congressional materials diminish in bulk. Two investigations into "The Affairs of the District of Columbia," one in 1872, the second in 1874, are largely concerned with the financial maladministration of the presidentially appointed board of public works. The attempts of Senator Sumner of Massachusetts, begun in 1870 and continued into 1872, to forbid racially segregated schools in the District get short shrift. The *Journals* of the territorial Governor's Council and the House of Delegates, 1871-1874, are diffuse, badly indexed, and generally confusing. In order to follow court action on civil rights suits, recourse to the newspapers is a necessity, for the police blotters listing day-by-day arrests and complaints are voluminous and unindexed, the municipal court was never a court of

341

record, and, as the District Supreme Court dockets preserved in the National Archives are unindexed, appeals are virtually untraceable unless the press reported the original cases and the names of the defendants.

Fortunately, nonofficial sources multiply in the early 1870's. The first local Negro newspaper, the *New Era*, renamed the *New National Era*, 1871-1874, John Mercer Langston's *From the Virginia Plantation to the National Capitol*, and some passages in Frederick Douglass' autobiography, *Narrative of the Life and Times of Frederick Douglass*, and Booker T. Washington's *Up from Slavery* provide substantial data from Negro experience. Unhappily the extant files of the *New National Era* are incomplete after early 1874. The *Evening Star*, the *Sentinel*, and John Forney's *Chronicle* and *Sunday Chronicle*, on the other hand, reflect the attitudes of white people toward colored Washington. Scrapbooks treasured by descendants of Negro families of the 1870's sometimes contain a few sidelights on individuals. Furthermore, white scholars' recently awakened interest in Negro history and Negro-white relations has produced several valuable studies. Of these the most directly relevant to the local story are two articles by Phineas Indritz, "Post Civil War Ordinances Prohibiting Racial Discrimination in the District of Columbia" and "Racial Ramparts in the Nation's Capital" in the *Georgetown Law Journal*, XLII and XLI. Of wider geographical coverage but also useful for my purposes is James McPherson's *The Struggle for Equality*.

With the substitution of presidentially appointed commissioners for locally elected representatives in 1874, a new dearth of official information about Negroes begins. Indeed this type of material dwindles for the next sixty years to some six categories, none of them rich in detail. The most valuable on the whole are the reports of the Superintendent of the Colored Schools incorporated in the *Annual Report of the Board of Trustees of Public Schools in the District of Columbia*, 1875-1901, and the comparable data included thereafter in the *Annual Report of the Board of Education*. A second category consists of court decisions, particularly Supreme Court decrees that gradually pared Negro civil rights down to the vanishing point. Third are congressional hearings on District charities and, between 1910 and 1927, on bills designed further to restrict Negro liberties. Fourth, in addition to census tabulations and two or three Labor Department studies of wages and child welfare, are reports on slum housing, such as the report of President Theodore Roosevelt's Homes Commission, the data presented to Congress preliminary to passage of the Alley Dwelling Act of 1914, and the later amendments thereto; fifth, edicts of the War and Navy departments in 1917 and 1918; and sixth, the perennial passages on Negro crime in Metropolitan Police reports. Negro petitions to Congress come to an end in the late 1880's, local civil rights suits at the turn of the century.

White newspaper accounts of colored Washington and individual Negroes also decrease steadily in number and quality from the mid-1870's until the 1930's. Records of charity societies—notably the Associated Charities, the Monday Evening Club, and, in the 1920's, the Council of Social Agencies—and articles in social work journals carry some precise information about Negro indigents, but, as is true also of the governmental reports on poverty and housing, analyses of cause and effect and of differences in racial impact are rare. Although a spate of articles appeared in white periodicals when the Wilson administration endorsed segregation of government employees in 1913 and 1914 and again after the race riot of 1919, magazines, like newspapers, largely ignored the city's Negro population. I. A. Newby's *Jim Crow's Defense: Anti-Negro Thought in America, 1900-1930*, to be sure, points to books, articles, sermons, and political speeches harping upon the inferiority of the Negro race, but needless to say, the materials quoted merely spell out white bigotry.

Doctor Daniel Lamb, a white physician who taught for

thirty-five years at the Howard University Medical School, compiled in 1901 a history of the Medical Department which fills some gaps, for his pages cover far more than medical education in the community. Two books written by "outsiders" also throw light on the local scene of the 1880's and after: a Johns Hopkins study, published in 1891, by Edward Ingle, *The Negro in the District of Columbia*, and August Meier, *Negro Thought in America, 1880-1915*. The former, though not profound, supplies some factual data but, more important, depicts white Washington's points of view before white citizens had completely washed their hands of their colored neighbors. Meier's book, published in 1963, deals with Negro intellectuals throughout the country, but, as a considerable number of the men whose ideas he examines spent at least part of their lives in the capital, his text reveals a good deal about the thinking of local Negro leaders.

Negro writers themselves furnish the bulk of evidence about how two generations of colored Washingtonians fared vis-à-vis whites and each other. The local Negro press is indispensable. The *People's Advocate*, 1878-1884, published by the talented and temperate John Cromwell, the stinging Washington *Bee*, 1882-1922, edited by the emotionally erratic Calvin Chase, and the *Tribune*, 1921-1946, are the most rewarding, although after 1938 the *Tribune* becomes so skimpy that the Washington editions of the Baltimore *Afro-American* and, in 1944, of the Pittsburgh *Courier* supersede it as a vehicle of news. *New Negro Opinion*, mouthpiece of the New Negro Alliance from 1933 to 1938, interprets effectively the economic struggle of most of the New Deal era. Two slim books illuminate the picture of the last two decades of the nineteenth century: John Cromwell's *History of the Bethel Literary and Historical Association* and Andrew Hilyer's *The Union League Directory*. At the end of the 1890's come the series of reports edited by W. E. B. DuBois on the conferences held yearly at Atlanta University to which data on Washington add a good deal. An occasional piece in liberal journals such as the *Independent* and the *Survey* contribute a little in the first decade of the twentieth century. And after 1910 periodical literature, beginning with *Crisis*, organ of the NAACP, and the *Journal of Negro History*, opens up a broad range, most of it countrywide but some of it clearly showing colored Washington's role in the national battle. At the end of the 1920's several books supply further insights. William H. Jones, *Recreation and Amusement among Negroes in Washington, D.C.*, and *The Housing of Negroes in Washington, D.C.*, furnish sociological data, while V. F. Calverston's *Anthology of American Negro Literature*, Jean Toomer's poems, and Rudolph Fisher's novels reveal the literary talents within the colored community.

The decade from 1935 to the end of World War II produces less written evidence than the scholar would expect to find for a period of such social and economic ferment. Until the Fair Employment Practices Committee came into being in 1941, governmental reports on Negro living conditions and opportunities are astonishingly meager. Malcolm Ross's description of FEPC functioning in *All Manner of Men* and Lewis Ruchames' *Race, Jobs and Politics* are helpful but, except for the accounts of the Capital Transit Company fight and congressional opposition to the committee, are applicable to Washington in only general terms. Census tabulations are fuller in 1940 than ever before, and reports of the Alley Dwelling Authority and its successor, the National Capital Housing Authority, convey an idea of local housing problems, but otherwise neither federal nor District records are of much help in clarifying the Negro story. Dr. Howard A. Long's study of achievements of colored school children from 1935 to 1943 was never publicly released, and the statistics published in the annual reports of the board of education appear to gloss over conditions in the Negro schools. Again the student must rely chiefly upon privately assembled data—upon autobiographies such as Mary Church Terrell's *A Colored Woman in a White*

World, Walter F. White's *A Man Called White,* and W. E. B. DuBois' *Dusk of Dawn,* upon the reports of private social agencies such as the *Council Bulletin* and *Community Service* put out between 1936 and 1938, upon magazine articles, newspapers, and, after 1943, the correspondence and newsletters of local organizations springing up to oppose racism. Many of the papers in the last category are still in private hands, although the clipping files started by the staff of the Washingtoniana Room of the District Public Library contain copies of some of the duplicated materials. Interviews plug many of the holes, for a great many participants in the events of the past forty years are still living. To save some of my informants embarrassment and to avoid the lengthy explanations necessary to justify my reliance upon them I have ordinarily not identified them. Nevertheless they represent, I believe, if not a wide sampling of local opinion, a selective guide to leaders' ideas and a trustworthy version of the hows and whys of what occurred.

Interviews are equally essential for rounding out the story of the fifteen postwar years. While court records are vitally important, accounts of the efforts that went into preparation of law suits and into effecting social change without legal action constitute a still more significant element; the former present the outcome, the latter the means employed, in the sociologist's phrase, "the dynamics of change." The material private organizations assembled is voluminous and scattered. Of the unpublished papers, I have drawn chiefly upon four collections: the working papers of National Committee on Segregation in the Nation's Capital, 1947-1948; the files of a group that started as the Minorities Workshop, became in 1946 the Committee for Racial Democracy and in 1948 the Council for Civil Rights; the files of the American Veterans Committee's national counsel; and the duplicated releases of such organizations as the American Friends Service Committee, the Interracial Workshops, and the Urban League.

346

Published pieces in turn mount in number and value, particularly after 1948 when the civil rights battle was joined in earnest and commanded nationwide attention. Executive orders, congressional hearings on District home rule and on the public schools, the Strayer Report of 1949, District health and welfare statistics, board of education, recreation board, and housing authority reports, and statements of the National Capital Park and Planning Commission, all are informing. Articles in the *Afro-American*, the Washington edition of the Pittsburgh *Courier*, and the *Journal of Negro Education* portray the situation as colored citizens saw it, while the Washington *Post* and the *Evening Star* carry an ever-rising volume of news items, editorials, and letters to the editors about race relations. The publication that had the most immediate effect before 1954 was the Report of the National Committee on Segregation in the Nation's Capital, which appeared in December 1948. Three books pull together the multiple strands of three issues: Clement Voss traces in *Caucasians Only* the course of the long fight against legally enforceable housing covenants; Wilson Record's *The Negro and the Communist Party* straightens out the tangled web of communists' unsuccessful overtures to Negroes; and Ellis O. Knox's *Democracy and the District of Columbia Schools* presents in 1957 the evidence to counter a congressional committee's attack on school integration in Washington.

Despite the numberless commentaries on various aspects of race relations in the capital at the end of the 1950's, only two overall summaries cover the many-faceted developments. The first is a booklet entitled *Decade of Progress*, a report of the National Association of Intergroup Relations Officials, popularly reduced to NAIRO. Put out in 1959, the text points to the changes in the ten years since the National Committee on Segregation released its scathing findings; each topic is handled by an expert who shared in the ten-year struggle in his or her own field. The second summary benefits from the perspective of three additional years. The winter issue, 1962-1963, of the *Journal of Inter-group Relations Officials* is given over to five articles on Washington's progress and unresolved problems of racial adjustments. Together the two offer a temperate and inform-ing evaluation of the recent past.

All told, the variations in the nature, quantity, and quality of sources about Negro life in Washington over 170 years are striking. In themselves they are an index of the changes in status of colored people in the capital. As long as most of America equated the Negro with the slave, official records supply more information than any private papers or artifacts. For a period of a dozen years after emancipation, official materials expand to deal at length with the freedman's problems and his relations with whites, while the spread of Negro literacy and the interest freedmen awakened in white Americans multiply nonofficial sources. Thereafter until the mid-1930's, federal and municipal data, except for census figures, all but evaporate, leaving personal correspondence, Negro newspapers, and periodicals to tell the story. From about 1935 to 1945 the federal government again displays an awareness of the Negro but without accumulating much information on his mode of life. By 1943, however, the papers of private organizations deter-mined to give colored people a recognized place in American society begin to increase and by 1948 overshadow in im-portance every governmental source. Thenceforward court records, executive orders, newspaper pieces, and, above all, materials published by civic, religious, charitable, and labor organizations constitute a volume of specifics that nearly overpowers the historian. Simultaneously it proclaims in unmistakable language the new stature the Negro has at-tained in Washington and in the United States.

Category by category, the materials that I have used are listed in the Bibliography.

BIBLIOGRAPHY

I. UNPUBLISHED SOURCES

OFFICIAL PAPERS

Enumerator's returns for the District of Columbia, schedules of Free Inhabitants, for the Seventh and Eighth United States Censuses, and Schedules of Population for the Ninth and Tenth Censuses, National Archives

Letters Sent by the Board of Commissioners for the District of Columbia, 6 vols., 1791-1802, Record Group 42, National Archives

Dockets of the Court of Appeals for the District of Columbia, 1870-1874, National Archives

Library of Congress Manuscript Division, Woodrow Wilson Papers

Petitions to the House of Representatives, 1800-1915, Record Group 233, National Archives

Petitions to the Senate, 1816- , Record Group 46, National Archives

Records of the Bureau of Refugees, Freedmen and Abandoned Lands, 1865-1872, District of Columbia file, Record Group 105, National Archives

RECORDS OF PRIVATE ORGANIZATIONS, MONOGRAPHS, AND THESES

American Friends Service Committee, Community Relations Programs, I-XXIII, 1949-1953 (duplicated)

American Veterans Committee, Greater Washington Area, briefs, attorney's opinions, and correspondence on civil rights cases, 1947-1961, copies in possession of Phineas Indritz, national counsel for AVC

Bulletins of Summer Interracial Workshops, 1949-1953 (duplicated)

Carter, Wade H., ed., "Anacostia," typescript notes compiled after meetings of the surviving first settlers on the Barry Farm, September 1921

Citizens Committee against Segregation in Recreation, 1945-1948 (duplicated)

Committee for Racial Democracy in the Nation's Capital 1946-

1948, continued as Council for Civil Rights in the Nation's Capital, correspondence, newsletters, and releases, 1948-1950, in possession of Ida Fox, executive secretary, 1946-1948

Family and Child Services of Washington, D.C., Minutes of the Board of Managers of the Associated Charities of the District of Columbia, 1921-1934, continued as Family Service Association, 1934-

Health and Welfare Council of the National Capital Area, Minutes of the Board of Managers of the Washington Council of Social Agencies, 1921-1941

Lindsay, Inabel, "Participation of Negroes in the Establishment of Welfare Services, 1865-1900, with special reference to the District of Columbia, Maryland and Virginia," Ph.D. dissertation, University of Pittsburgh, 1959

Lofton, Williston, "The Development of Public Education for Negroes in Washington, D.C., A Study of Separate but Equal Accommodations," Ph.D. dissertation, American University, 1944

Long, Howard A., "Intelligence and Achievement of Colored Pupils in the Public Schools of the District of Columbia," Parts II and III, 1948 (mimeograph)

Long, Kathleen Dudley, "Woodrow Wilson and the Negro, 1912-1916," M.A. thesis, Bryn Mawr College, 1956.

Minorities Workshop Papers and Correspondence, 1943-1945, in possession of Miss Ida Fox of Washington

National Committee on Segregation in the Nation's Capital, Working Papers, 1947-1948

Piper, Ada, "Activities of Negroes in the Territorial Government of the District of Columbia, 1871-1874," M.A. thesis, Howard University, 1943

Records of the Proceedings of the Presbyterian Churches in the District of Columbia, October 5, 1841–May 2, 1842, relating to the Founding of the Fifteenth Street Presbyterian Church for Negroes, Carter Woodson Papers

Robinson, Henry S., "Some Aspects of the Free Colored Population of Washington, D.C., 1800-1862"

Washington Urban League, "The Founding of the Washington Urban League," statement of Garnet Wilkinson at the Twenty-first Annual Meeting, April 1959

————, Newsletters, 1950-1959 (duplicated)

PERSONAL PAPERS

Sayles J. Bowen Papers, 1846-1892, in possession of Professor Charles A. Barker of The Johns Hopkins University

Howard University Library, Moorland Room
  John F. Cook's Diary, 1850-1851
  Papers relating to Aletha Tanner
Library of Congress Manuscript Division
  Christian A. Fleetwood Papers, 1863-1912
  Benjamin Baker French Papers, 1835-1870
  William Owner Diary, 1860-1867
  Michael Shiner Diary, 1813-1863
  Mary Church Terrell Papers, 1890-1940
  Booker T. Washington Papers, 1870-1915
  Carter Woodson Papers
University of North Carolina Library, Southern Historical Collection
  William Curry Harrllee Papers, 1860
  Leonidas Polk Papers, 1828-1830

II. PUBLISHED SOURCES

OFFICIAL RECORDS

Annals of the Congress of the United States, 1789-1824, 42 vols,
  Washington, 1834-1856
Annual Reports
  Alley Dwelling Authority for the District of Columbia, 1935
  Board of Charities of the District of Columbia, 1901-1925
  Board of Health of the District of Calumbia, 1872-1878
  Board of Trustees of Public Schools of the District of Columbia,
    1845-1900, continued as *Board of Education of the District
    of Columbia,* 1901-
  Commissioners of the District of Columbia, 1874-1935, continued as *Government of the District of Columbia,* 1936-1960
  Home for Destitute Colored Women and Children, 1879-1892
  National Capital Park and Planning Commission, 1927-1932
  Public Assistance Division, Board of Public Welfare, 1934-1936
  Trustees of the Industrial Home School, 1879-1925
  United States Commissioner of Education, 1870-1953
Congressional Record, Washington, 1873-
Congressional Serials, Bills, and Hearings, 1817-
  House of Representatives
    Bills
    Documents, especially:
      Document 215, 20C, 1S, "Memorial from citizens of Washington and Alexandria Counties praying for the abolition

351

of the slave trade and gradual emancipation of slaves,"
Serial 173

Document 140, 23C, 2S, "Memorial of inhabitants of the
District of Columbia, praying for the gradual abolition of
slavery in the District of Columbia," Serial 274

Executive Documents, especially:

"Final Report of the Provost Marshal General," 1865, Serial
1251, and Executive Document 315, 41C, 2S, "Special
Report of the Commissioner of Education on the Condition and Improvement of Public Schools in the District
of Columbia, Serial 1427

Hearings, especially Committee on the District of Columbia,
and on Reform in the Civil Service

Joint Hearings with Senate, especially House and Senate Committees on the District of Columbia, 80C, 1S and 2S, "Home
Rule and Reorganization of the Government of the District
of Columbia"

Miscellaneous Documents

Reports

Senate

Bills

Documents, especially Document 185, 55C, 1S, "Investigation
of Charities and Reformatory Institutions in the District of
Columbia," Serial 3565

Executive Documents, especially:

Executive Documents 53, 38C, 1S, 27, 34C, 1S, and 6, 39C,
2S, "Report of the Assistant Commissioner of the Freedman's Bureau," Serials 1176, 1238, 1276

Executive Document 56, 40C, 3S, 20, 41C, 3S, "Report of
the Trustees of Colored Schools," Serials 1360 and 1440

Hearings of committees and select joint committees, especially: Subcommittee of the Senate Judiciary Committee,
77C, 1S, on Senate Joint Resolution 35, and Committee on
the District of Columbia, 78C, 1S, on S 1420, "Reorganization of the Government of the District of Columbia"

Index to Hearings in the Senate Library, 2 vols., 1907-1934,
and 1935-1958

*Index to Laws, Senate Reports, Documents and Committee
Prints Relating to the District of Columbia,* 1887-1963

Miscellaneous Documents

Reports, especially Report 453, 43C, 1S, "Report of the Joint
Select Committee of Congress appointed to Inquire into the
Affairs of the District of Columbia," Serials 1590, 1591, 1592

Federal Housing Authority, *Underwriters Manual,* Washington, 1938

Federal Register
Journals of the Council of the City of Washington (61st through 67th Council), Washington, 1864-1871
Journals of the Council of the District of Columbia, 5 vols., Washington, 1872-1874
Journal of the House of Delegates of the District of Columbia, 5 vols., Washington, 1872-1874
Judicial, Legal, and Related Materials
  Acts of the Corporation of the City of Washington, 11 vols., Washington, 1805-1816, continued as *Laws of the Corporation of the City of Washington,* 45 vols., Washington, 1817-1862
  Atlantic Reporter, Second Series
  Burch, Samuel, *A Digest of the Laws of the City of Washington to June 1823*
  Code of Laws of the District of Columbia, 1929, 1940, 1951
  Corporation Laws of the City of Washington, 1853, comp. James W. Sheahan
  Federal Cases, Comprising Cases Argued and Delivered in Circuit and District Courts of the United States, 1789-1880
  Federal Reporter, Second Series
  United States Reports, Cases Adjudged in the Supreme Court
  United States Supreme Court, *Records and Briefs*
  United States Statutes at Large
  Washington Law Reporter
National Capital Planning Commission, *Washington Past and Future,* 1950
Official Register of the United States, 1863- , originally entitled *Register of Officers and Agents, Civil, Military, and Naval, in the Service of the United States,* 1817-1859
President's Committee on Civil Rights, *To Secure These Rights,* Washington, 1947
Register of Debates in Congress, 14 vols., Washington, 1824-1837
Report of the Comptroller of the Currency, 1933
Report of the Division of Emergency Relief, Board of Public Welfare of the District of Columbia, Washington, 1934
Report of the President's Homes Commission, Washington, 1908
Reports and Addresses, Documents Relating to Freedmen, Howard University Library
Strayer, George D., *Report of a Survey of the Public Schools of the District of Columbia, conducted under the auspices of the chairmen of the subcommittees on District of Columbia appropriations of the respective appropriations committees of the Senate and House,* Washington, 1949
United States Census, Second through Eighteenth, 1800-1960

353

United States Department of Commerce and Labor, *Conditions of Living Among the Poor*, Bureau of Labor Bulletin 64, 1906

United States Labor Department, Office of Policy Planning and Research, *The Negro Family, The Case for National Action*, Washington, 1965

REPORTS OF CIVIC, EDUCATIONAL, AND SOCIAL AGENCIES
AND ORGANIZATIONS

Adams-Morgan Project, *Experiment in Planning, Citizen-Government Teamwork in Planning for the Renewal of Adams-Morgan*, April 1963

Associated Charities of Washington, *Annual Reports*, 1897-1920

Citizens' Committee on Race Relations, First Annual Report, 1944, and *Second Annual Report*, 1945

Community Advisers on Equal Employment, *Equal Employment in the Nation's Capital, Progress and Prognosis*, Washington, 1966

Community Chest and Council of Social Agencies, *Council Bulletin*, 1936-1937, continued as *Community Service*, 1937-1938

DuBois, William Edward Burghardt, ed., *Mortality among Negroes in Cities, together with proceedings of the 1st conference for the study of Negro problems, Atlanta University, 1896*, Atlanta, 1896

———, ed., *Some Efforts of Negroes for Their Own Social Betterment, together with proceedings of the 3rd conference for the study of Negro problems, Atlanta University, 1898*, Atlanta, 1898

———, ed., *The Negro in Business, together with proceedings of the 4th conference for the study of Negro problems, Atlanta University, 1899*, Atlanta, 1899

———, ed., *The College-Bred Negro, together with proceedings of the 5th conference for the study of Negro problems, Atlanta University, 1900*, Atlanta, 1900

Medical Society of the District of Columbia, *Report on the Sanitary Conditions of the Cities of Washington and Georgetown, Presented to the Society, March, 1864*. Washington, 1864

Monday Evening Club *Yearbook, 1930*, Washington, 1930

National Association for the Advancement of Colored People, *Annual Reports*, 1911-

National Association of Intergroup Relations Officials, *Civil Rights in the Nation's Capital, A Report on a Decade of Progress*, Washington, 1959

Negro Status and Race Relations in the United States, 1911-1946, The Thirty-Five Year Report of the Phelps-Stokes Fund, New York, 1946

National Association of Social Workers and Washington Center for Metropolitan Studies, *The Public Welfare Crisis in the Nation's Capital, a Call to the Conscience of the Community,* Washington, 1963

National Committee on Segregation in the Nation's Capital, *Segregation in Washington,* Washington, 1948

National Freedmen's Relief Association, *Annual Reports,* 1863-1867

Perman, Dagmar, *The Girard Street Project,* Washington, 1964

Washington Board of Trade, *Annual Reports,* 1890-1929, 1936-1938

Washington Federation of Churches, *Yearbook,* 1936

Washington Urban League, *Annual Reports,* 1948-1959

AUTOBIOGRAPHIES AND MEMOIRS

Brownlow, Louis, *A Passion for Anonymity,* Chicago, 1958

Davidson, Eugene, *Black Boy on a Raft,* Washington, 1958

Douglass, Frederick, *Narrative of the Life and Times of Frederick Douglass,* New York, 1893

DuBois, William Edward Burghardt, *Dusk of Dawn: An Essay toward an Autobiography of a Race Concept,* New York, 1940

Fremont, Jessie Benton, *Souvenir of My Time,* New York, 1887

Keckley, Elizabeth, *Behind the Scenes, Life of a Colored Woman Thirty Years a Slave, Four Years at the White House,* Buffalo, 1868

Langston, John Mercer, *From the Virginia Plantation to the National Capitol, or the First and Only Negro Representative in Congress from the Old Dominion,* Hartford, 1894

Lundy, Benjamin, *The Life, Travels and Opinions of Benjamin Lundy,* Philadelphia, 1847

Smith, Margaret Bayard, *The First Forty Years of Washington Society, portrayed by the family letters of Mrs. Samuel Harrison Smith,* ed. Gaillard Hunt, New York, 1906

Taft, Mrs. William Howard, *Recollections of Full Years,* New York, 1914

Terrell, Mary Church, *A Colored Woman in a White World,* Washington, 1940

Washington, Booker T., *Up from Slavery,* New York, 1909

White, Walter Francis, *A Man Called White, The Autobiography of Walter White,* New York, 1948

OTHER PUBLISHED PRIMARY SOURCES

Adams, Francis A., *Our Little Monarchy; Who Runs It and What It Costs,* Washington, 1873

355

Andrews, Ethan Allen, *Slavery and the Domestic Slave Trade in the United States*, Boston, 1836

Cromwell, John, *History of the Bethel Literary and Historical Association*, Washington, 1898

Goodell, William, *Slavery and Anti-Slavery, A History of the Great Struggle in Both Hemispheres, With a View of the Slavery Question in the United States*, 3rd ed., New York, 1855

Hall, Basil, *Travels in North America in the Years 1827-1828*, 3 vols., 3rd ed., Edinburgh, 1830

Hilyer, Andrew F., *The Twentieth Century Union League Directory, A Historical, Geographical and Statistical Study of Colored Washington*, Washington, 1901

[Ingeroll, Charles Jared,] *Inchiquin, The Jesuit's Letters during a Late Residence in the United States*, New York, 1810

Latham, Henry, *Black and White, A Journal of a Three-Months' Tour in the United States*, London, 1867

A Memorial Discourse; by Rev. Henry Highland Garnet, delivered in the hall of the House of Representatives, Washington city, D.C., on Sabbath, February 12, 1865, Philadelphia, 1865

New Negro Alliance Yearbook, Washington, 1939

Olmsted, Frederick Law, *A Journey in the Seaboard Slave States in the Years 1853-1854*, 2 vols., 2nd ed., New York, 1904

Paynter, John H., *A Souvenir of the Anniversary and Banquet of Oldest Inhabitants Association (Colored) of the District of Columbia, April 14, 1914*, Washington, 1914

Report of the Proceedings at the Formation of the African Education Society: Instituted at Washington, December 28, 1829, with an Address to the Public by the Board of Managers, Miscellaneous Pamphlets 411:20, Rare Book Division, Library of Congress

Republican National Committee, *Republican Campaign Textbook, 1912*

Sherman, *Directory and Ready Reference of the Colored Population of the District of Columbia*, 1913

Torrey, Jesse, *A Portraiture of Domestic Slavery in the United States*, Philadelphia, 1817

Warden, David B., *A Chorographical and Statistical Description of the District of Columbia, the Seat of the General Government to the United States*, Paris, 1816

The Washington Directory, 1822, comp. Judah Delano

The Washington Directory, 1830, comp. S. A. Elliot

Washington and Georgetown Directory, 1855, 1858, 1860, 1862, 1863, 1867-

III. SECONDARY SOURCES

Allen, Robert S. and Drew Pearson, *Washington Merry-Go-Round*, New York, 1931

Bemis, Samuel Flagg, *John Quincy Adams and the Union*, New York, 1956

Benjamin Banneker, The Afro-American Astronomer from Data Collected by Will W. Allen assisted by Daniel Murray, Washington, 1915

Bryan, Wilhelmus Bogart, *A History of the National Capital*, 2 vols. New York, 1914-1916

Calverston, V. F., *Anthology of American Negro Literature*, New York, 1929

Coulson, Thomas, *Joseph Henry, His Life and Work*, Princeton, 1950

Chapin, Elizabeth M., *American Court Gossip, or Life in the Nation's Capital*, Marshalltown, Iowa, 1887

Church of God, A Pictorial Review, Washington, 1944

Cox, Lawanda and John H. Cox, *Politics, Principle and Prejudice, 1865-1866: Dilemma of Reconstruction America*, New York, 1963

Daly, Victor, *Not Only War, A Story of Two Great Conflicts*, Boston, 1932

Davis, Allison, Burleigh B. Gardner, and Mary B. Gardner, directed by W. Lloyd Warner, *Deep South, A Social and Anthropological Study of Class and Caste*, Chicago, 1941

Dollard, John, *Caste and Class in a Southern Town*, 2nd ed., New York, 1949

Dulles, Foster Rhea, *The American Red Cross, A History*, New York, 1950

Dupree, A. Hunter, *Science in the Federal Government, A History of Policies and Activities to 1940*, Cambridge, 1957

Dyer, Frederick H., *A Compendium of the War of Rebellion*, Des Moines, Iowa, 1908

Fleming, Walter Lynwood, *The Freedman's Savings Bank, A Chapter in the Economic History of the Negro Race*, Chapel Hill, 1937

Frazier, Edward Franklin, *Black Bourgeoisie*, Glencoe, Ill., 1957

Gray, Edgar M., *The Washington Race Riot, Its Cause and Effect*, New York, 1919 (Arthur M. Schomburg Negro Collection, New York Public Library)

Grier, Eunice S., *Understanding Washington's Changing Population*, Washington Center for Metropolitan Studies, Washington, 1961

Hansen, Carl F., *Miracle of Social Adjustment*, New York, 1957

Harmon, John H., Jr., Arnett G. Lindsay, and Carter G. Woodson, *The Negro As a Businessman*, Washington, 1929

Hayes, Laurence J. W., *The Negro Federal Government Worker: A Study of His Classification Status in the District of Columbia, 1883-1938*, Washington, 1941

Hughes, Langston, *Fine Clothes for the Jew*, New York, 1927

Hundley, Mary G., *The Dunbar Story*, Washington, 1955

Ingle, Edward, *The Negro in the District of Columbia*, in *The Johns Hopkins University Studies in History and Political Science*, 11th Series, Nos. III and IV, 1891

Jackson, Richard P., *The Chronicles of Georgetown, D.C. from 1751 to 1878*, Washington, 1878

Jones, William Henry, *Recreation and Amusement Among Negroes in Washington D.C.: A Sociological Analysis of the Negro in An Urban Environment*, Washington, 1927

———, *The Housing of Negroes in Washington, D.C.: A Study in Human Ecology*, Washington, 1929

Kennedy, Louise Venable, *The Negro Peasant Turns Cityward*, New York, 1950

Kleinberg, Otto, *Negro Intelligence and Selective Migration*, New York, 1935

Knox, Ellis O., *Democracy and the District of Columbia Schools: A Study of Recently Integrated Schools*, Washington, 1957

Lamb, Daniel, *The Howard University Medical Department, A Historical, Biographical and Statistical Survey*, Washington, 1901

Lee, William I., *Nineteenth Street Baptist Church, One Hundredth Anniversary, 1839-1939*, Washington, 1939

Lewison, Paul, *Race, Class and Party: A History of Negro Suffrage and White Politics in the South*, Universal Library ed., New York, 1965

Link, Arthur S., *The New Freedom*, Princeton, 1947

Lofton, John, *Insurrection in South Carolina, The Turbulent World of Denmark Vesey*, Yellow Springs, Ohio, 1964

McPherson, James M., *The Struggle for Equality; Abolitionists and the Negro in the Civil War and Reconstruction*, Princeton, 1964

Meier, August, *Negro Thought in America, 1880-1915*, Ann Arbor, 1963

Meneely, Alexander Howard, *The War Department, 1861, A Study in Mobilization and Administration*, New York, 1928

Miller, Charles A., *Citizens Advisory Groups in the District of Columbia Government*, Washington Center for Metropolitan Studies, Washington, 1961

358

Moore, Joseph West, *Picturesque Washington,* Providence, 1884

Murray, Pauli, *Proud Shoes, The Story of an American Family,* New York, 1956

Murray, Robert K., *Red Scare: A Study in National Hysteria, 1919-20,* Minneapolis, 1955

Nelson, Bernard H., *The Fourteenth Amendment and the Negro since 1920,* Washington, 1946

Newby, I. A., *Jim Crow's Defense, Anti-Negro Thought in America 1900-1930,* Baton Rouge, 1965

Nowlin, William F., *The Negro in American National Politics,* Boston, 1931

O'Connor, Ellen M., *Myrtilla Miner. A Memoir,* New York, 1885

Osofsky, Gilbert, *Harlem, The Making of a Ghetto, Negro New York, 1890-1930,* New York, 1965

Pauli, Hertha E., *Her Name Was Sojourner Truth,* New York, 1962

Record, Wilson, *The Negro and the Communist Party,* Chapel Hill, N.C., 1951

Reitzes, Dietrich C., *Negroes and Medicine,* Cambridge, 1958

Rose, Arnold M., *The Negro's Morale: Group Identification and Protest,* Minneapolis, 1949

Ross, Malcolm H., *All Manner of Men,* New York, 1948

Ruchames, Louis, *Race, Jobs and Politics,* New York, 1953

Schlesinger, Arthur M., Jr., *The Coming of the New Deal,* Cambridge, 1959

Seaton, Josephine, *William Winston Seaton of the "National Intelligencer,"* Boston, 1871

Simmons, William J., *Men of Mark: Eminent, Progressive and Rising,* Cleveland, 1887

Stampp, Kenneth M., *The Peculiar Institution: Slavery in the Antebellum South,* New York, 1956

Stern, Helen B. and Philip M. Stern, *"O, Say Can You See?" A Bifocal Tour of Washington,* Washington, 1965

Taft, Mrs. William Howard, *Recollections of Full Years,* New York, 1914

Toomer, Jean, *Cane,* New York, 1923

Vose, Clement E., *Caucasians Only, The Supreme Court, the NAACP and the Restrictive Government Cases,* Berkeley and Los Angeles, 1950

Wade, Richard C., *Slavery in the Cities, The South, 1820-1860,* New York, 1964

Washington League of Women Voters, *Washington, D.C.: A Tale of Two Cities,* Washington, 1962

Waters, Walter T., as told to William C. White, *B.E.F.: The Whole Story of the Bonus Army*, New York, 1933
Wecter, Dixon, *The Saga of American Society; A Record of Social Aspiration, 1607-1937*, New York, 1937
Woodson, Carter G., *A Century of Negro Migration*, Washington, 1918
———, *The History of the Negro Church*, Washington, 1945
Woodward, C. Vann, *The Strange Career of Jim Crow*, New York, 1955
Work, Monroe N., ed., *Negro Year Book, An Annual Encyclopedia of the Negro*, Tuskegee, Ala., 1912

NEWSPAPERS

Afro-American, 1936-
Alexandria *Daily Advertiser*, 1801-1807
Baltimore *Sun*, 1837-
Chronicle, 1861-1911
Cleveland *Leader*, 1865-1901
Colored American, 1898-1904
Columbia Gazette, 1829-1833
Daily News, 1921-
The Express, 1867-1869
Evening Star, 1853-
Georgetown *Advocate*, 1839-1842
Georgetown *Courier*, 1865-1876
Herald, 1906-1939
The National Era, 1847-1860
The National Freedman, 1865
National Intelligencer, 1800-1867
National Republican, 1860-1888
New Era, renamed *New National Era*, 1870-1875

New Negro Opinion, 1934-1937
News, 1847-1858
New York *Times*, 1851-
Patriot, 1870-1872
People's Advocate, 1878-1884
Pittsburgh *Courier*, 1941-
Richmond *Times-Dispatch*, 1903-
Sentinel, 1873-1901
Sunday Morning Chronicle, under slightly varying titles, 1861-1881
Times, 1895-1939
Times Herald, 1939-1951
Washington *Bee*, 1882-1922
Washington *Daily American*, 1924-1925
Washingtonian, 1834
Washington *Post*, 1877-
Washington *Sun*, 1914-1915

PERIODICALS AND OTHER SERIALS

American Historical Review
American Journal of Sociology
Atlantic Monthly
Century Magazine
Charities

Christian Century
Columbia Historical Society, *Records*
Crisis
Current History

BIBLIOGRAPHY

Georgetown Law Journal
Harper's Magazine
Independent
Jet
Journal of American History
Journal of Intergroup Relations
*Journal of the National Medical
    Association*
Journal of Negro Education
Journal of Negro History
Literary Digest

Maryland Historical Magazine
Monthly Labor Review
Municipal Affairs
Nation
National Business
North American Review
Outlook
School Life
Survey
Virginia Quarterly Review
The World Today

INDEX